Language, Culture, and Community
in Teacher Education

Language, Culture, and Community in Teacher Education

Edited by
María Estela Brisk

Published by
Lawrence Erlbaum Associates/Taylor & Francis Group
for the American Association of Colleges
for Teacher Education

 Lawrence Erlbaum Associates
Taylor & Francis Group

New York   London

Serving Learners

Lawrence Erlbaum Associates
Taylor & Francis Group
270 Madison Avenue
New York, NY 10016

Lawrence Erlbaum Associates
Taylor & Francis Group
2 Park Square
Milton Park, Abingdon
Oxon OX14 4RN

American Association of Colleges for
Teacher Education
1307 New York Avenue., N.W.,
Suite 300
Washington, DC 20005-4701

© 2008 by Taylor & Francis Group, LLC
Lawrence Erlbaum Associates is an imprint of Taylor & Francis Group, an Informa business

Printed in the United States of America on acid-free paper
10 9 8 7 6 5 4 3 2 1

International Standard Book Number-13: 978-0-8058-5698-9 (Softcover) 978-0-8058-5697-2 (Hardcover)

Library of Congress Cataloging-in-Publication Data

Language, culture, and community in teacher education / editor, Maria Estela Brisk.
        p. cm.
    Includes bibliographical references and index.
    ISBN 978-0-8058-5698-9 (alk. paper)
    1. Linguistic minorities--Education--United States. 2. Teachers--Training
of--United States. 3. Language and education--United States. 4. Language and
culture--United States. I. Brisk, Maria. II. Title.

    LC3728.L36 2007
    370.71'1--dc22
                                2007014915

Visit the Taylor & Francis Web site at
http://www.taylorandfrancis.com

and the LEA and Routledge Web site at
http://www.routledge.com

Visit the American Association of Colleges
for Teacher Education Web site at
http://www.aacte.org

Serving Learners

Contents

Part III   Policy

AACTE Statement

This book is sponsored by the American Association of Colleges for Teacher Education (AACTE), a national, voluntary association of higher education institutions and related organizations. Our mission is to promote the learning of all PK–12 students through high-quality, evidence-based preparation and continuing education for all school personnel.

The approximately 800 AACTE member institutions prepare more than two-thirds of the new teachers entering schools each year in the United States.

AACTE operates under the guiding principle of Serving Learners—learners who include the children in classrooms, the teachers who instruct them, and the faculty who prepare the teachers. Four strategic goals drive our work:

1. Build consensus on professional issues.
2. Advocate in state and federal policy arenas.
3. Strengthen programs and enhance their capacity.
4. Improve all educators' ability to serve diverse learners.

AACTE is publishing this document to stimulate discussion, study, and experimentation among educators. The findings, interpretations, and conclusions presented herein are entirely those of the author(s) and do not necessarily reflect the official position or policies of AACTE, nor does sponsorship of this publication imply endorsement by AACTE. Although AACTE and the author(s) have used their best efforts in preparing this document, they make no representations or warranties with respect to the accuracy or completeness of its contents and specifically disclaim any implied warranties of merchantability or fitness for a particular purpose. Neither AACTE, its Board of Directors or officers, nor the author(s) of this document shall be liable for any loss of profit or any other commercial

Note from Dr. Sharon P. Robinson

*President and CEO, American Association of
Colleges for Teacher Education (AACTE)*

I write this introductory note with a great sense of pride in AACTE's
role as a sponsor of this fine volume—the culmination of a 3-year
effort on the part of some of today's outstanding thinkers and doers
in the education of culturally and linguistically diverse students.
This work is being published at a most critical, and thus opportune,
time when the nation, more than ever, is watching and waiting for
answers about how best to prepare teachers of the children of our
"new demography." It is past time, but the challenge now looms so
large, it can no longer be ignored.

K–12 students with a foreign-born parent tripled from 1970
to 2000, from 6% to 19%. Today, nearly half of all children in the
United States under the age of 5 are members of minority groups.
Those of Hispanic origin comprise both the largest and fastest-grow-
ing group. By 2010, children of immigrants will represent over one-
quarter of U.S. students. These are the students our teachers must be
prepared to teach.

It has always been the job of teachers to teach every child and the
job of teacher educators to prepare teachers of all children, including
those of differing cultures and languages. It has always been incum-
bent upon teacher preparers to inculcate the knowledge, skills, and
abilities in teacher candidates to ensure that diverse children have
equitable opportunities to succeed. But even our efforts to create
specialized programs have been insufficient; and those to prepare
mainstream teachers to engage these students in meaningful learning have been unconscionably meager.

This book is intended to provoke a significant and essential change
in teacher education: the infusion of a language and cultural diversity subtext throughout every aspect of preparation. Bringing on
change requires confronting uncomfortable realities. The book will

immediately offer such an opportunity. Macedo's essay will doubt-lessly challenge many readers' paradigms of what multicultural education and research should look like. The ensuing chapters of the book serve as a response to this provocation by presenting models of research and practice in teacher preparation that effectively address the needs of the ever more diverse student population in our schools. The voices in these chapters are those of diverse scholars and teachers working with and for real children in real classrooms. These are important voices that can inform real change.

We expect that the volume will serve as a launching pad for a policy agenda for culturally relevant pedagogy on the part of the teacher education and multicultural communities. We now have a clearer view of where to promote rigorous policy provisions concerning language and culture in law, regulation, and general practice.

Acknowledgments

This volume concludes the last 3 years of work of the American Association of Colleges for Teacher Education (AACTE) Committee on Multicultural Education. The Committee has constituted the main channel through which the AACTE's commitment to diversity has been manifested since the publication in 1973 of the landmark "No One Model American" statement. Since then, the Committee has taken on the analysis and discussion of the most urgent issues related to multicultural education, diversity, and equity in teacher preparation. A significant number of books, policy documents, research studies, and conferences have been produced as result of the work of the Committee throughout the years. The impact of this work has had important repercussions on the national education arena.

In 2003, the Committee turned the focus of its work to the preparation of teachers for culturally and linguistically diverse children. After a successful 2003 conference at the Wingspread Center, the Committee decided to prepare a volume that compiles current work on the understudied practice of preparing teachers for English language learners. María Brisk, then chair of the Committee, undertook the task of organizing and editing this volume. Her nationally recognized knowledge and expertise on issues of linguistic diversity and language acquisition opened the doors at Lawrence Erlbaum Associates, where the idea of the book was immediately accepted. She was able to bring together an outstanding group of researchers and practitioners to contribute chapters for this volume.

Brisk's commitment was echoed by all of the 2004–2006 Committee members—Leslie Agard-Jones, Ray Barnhart, David Beaulieu, Gloria Swindler Boutté, Socorro Herrera, Gerardo Lopez, P. Rudy Mattai, Yoon Pak, Ronald Rochon, and Jeanette Haynes Writer—who contributed their valuable input by reviewing, presenting, or moderating sessions on the book at various conferences and/or by authoring several of the volume's chapters.

The Johnson Foundation, and particularly Carole Johnson, its program officer for education, provided a forum to initiate this work by funding two conferences at the Wingspread Center and encouraging AACTE to further the effort. The National Education Association (NEA) provided additional funding for both conferences.

The 35 participants at the 2005 Wingspread conference, "Culture, Language, and Community in Teacher Preparation," discussed the draft chapters of this book and provided valuable feedback to authors. This very diverse group, representing an array of national organizations and institutions, also developed the policy recommendations for the preparation of highly qualified teachers that have been included at the end of this volume. Their names and affiliations are listed in the appendix. Alicia Ardila-Rey, associate director for research at AACTE, coordinated the work on the preparation of this volume and served as the liaison between AACTE and the editor, authors, reviewers, and publisher.

This work would not have been possible without the momentum and vision provided by Mary Dilworth, former AACTE senior vice president, who for many years wisely guided the work of the Committee and encouraged the group to take on the task of preparing this book.

In 2006, the Committee was sunseted after the reorganization of AACTE's governance structure. AACTE maintains its commitment to diversity, equity, and multiculturalism, and this commitment is now part of the Association's strategic goals. The new Committee on Global Diversity has taken the torch handed by the Multicultural Education Committee and is carrying on this important work with the added dimensions of gender equity and internationalism.

Foreword

1957

When I was in the first grade, we started every day by pledging allegiance to the flag, listening to a passage from the King James Bible, and saying the Lord's Prayer. Then, the day's academic work began with in-unison phonics recitation and reading groups. This was not a Catholic school, as some might guess, or a religious school of some other kind. This was a public 1–8 grammar school in working class Washington, Pennsylvania—30 miles west of Pittsburgh and 30 miles east of Wheeling, West Virginia. The school was named simply—perhaps for expediency, perhaps due to a failure of imagination—the First Ward School, in keeping with the voting ward in which it was located. To the best of my recollection, none of my classmates was an English language learner (ELL) or an African American, although Washington, which was the county seat, had a visible African American population. *Brown v. Board of Education's* 1954 Supreme Court decision notwithstanding, the African American children in Washington were educated across town at the Fifth Ward School. For me, at the age of 6, none of this was remarkable or disturbing. It was only years later that the religious, cultural, racial, and language aspects of this situation even entered my consciousness as something to notice, contemplate, and question.

2006

As is widely known, teacher education programs seeking National Council for Accreditation of Teacher Education (NCATE) accreditation must meet standards regarding teacher candidate performance and institutional capacity and resources. According to Standard #1, all candidates must demonstrate the content, pedagogical, and professional knowledge, skills, and dispositions necessary to help all students learn. NCATE defines dispositions as "the values, commitments, and ethics that influence behaviors and affect learning, motivation, and development"(NCATE, 2000).[1] Until recently, NCATE stated that dispositions were "guided by beliefs and attitudes related to values such as caring, fairness, honesty, responsibility, and social justice." In November of 2005, however, the conservative National Association of Scholars (NAS) requested that the U.S. Department of Education formally investigate

propriety of the reference in NCATE's standards to social justice, a term
the NAS argued was fraught with contested ideological significance.
The NAS position was that teacher education programs should be based
on objective standards and core knowledge rather than ideology. At a
Washington, DC, meeting in June of 2006, in the face of intense pressure, NCATE President Art Wise announced that NCATE had decided
to withdraw from its standards all language related to social justice on
the grounds that the term was susceptible to multiple definitions.

The two incidents described above were separated by 50 years in
time, by dissimilar geographic locations, and by decidedly different social and political contexts. My rendering of these incidents
adds more differences. The first, written as a brief memoir, relies on
impressions and childhood memories, which inevitably suffer from
the imperfections and vagaries of selective attention. The second
recounts the outcome of a recent and highly visible professional con-
troversy, which, although a matter of public record, is also subject to
multiple interpretations and selective emphases. Despite their differences, both of these incidents are related in certain ways to the central topic of this book—language, culture, and community in teacher
preparation, and in particular, the inclusion of language diversity in
the teacher education curriculum.

I use these two incidents as a kind of epigraph to this foreword
to remind us how far we have come in teaching and teacher education—from a time when a first-grade teacher (along with the principal and the other teachers in the school) thought nothing whatsoever
about the language, cultural, religious, and political values that were
implicit in the act of reading the Bible to a racially segregated class
of very young children in a public elementary school, to a time when
the purposes of education and the role of ideology and values in
shaping the knowledge base for teacher preparation are highly publi-
cized, politicized, and contested. This is progress of a sort. We live in
an era when the values of the dominant group are no longer simply
taken for granted by everyone and when there is much public debate
about whose voices and perspectives are included and omitted from
curricula and whose interests are served and not served.

But I also use these two incidents to remind us how far we still
have to go. The recent NCATE brouhaha reveals that although many
issues related to diversity in teacher preparation are now publicly
acknowledged, we are still operating in a context where some quite
vocal (and powerful) segments of the population assert, on the one
hand, that knowledge and schooling are meant to be neutral and

value-free and, on the other hand (and often without a trace of irony), that schools ought to promote traditional "American" melting pot values. From this perspective, one can strongly argue that issues related to the inclusion of language and other kinds of diversity are "too ideological" and "too political" and are, thus, outside the proper purview of the schools and the teacher education curriculum. This book thoroughly challenges these assumptions and, in fact, begins with a set of dramatically different set of assumptions about the purposes of schooling, the nature of knowledge, and the inevitably political aspects of teaching and schooling.

María Brisk has skillfully organized and edited this collection of chapters related to *Language, Culture, and Community in Teacher Preparation*, which is the culmination of the work of an American Association of Colleges for Teacher Education (AACTE) committee charged with making policy-related recommendations related to the inclusion of language diversity in teacher preparation. It is important to point out that although the individual terms that are part of the title and the description of this volume—culture, teacher preparation, diversity, language, community—have been widely used in the field for more than three decades, the particular and much-needed focus of this volume is *language* diversity, which until very recently had been the forgotten—and ignored—piece of the diversity puzzle in teacher education.

More than three decades ago, in 1972, the first of several Commissions on Multicultural Education sponsored by the AACTE made three key assertions: (1) cultural diversity is a valuable resource; (2) multicultural education preserves and extends the resource of culture diversity rather than merely tolerating it or making it "melt away"; and (3) a commitment to cultural pluralism ought to permeate all aspects of teacher preparation programs (Baptiste & Baptiste, 1980).[2] In 1976, NCATE added multicultural education to its standards, requiring that institutions seeking accreditation show evidence that multicultural education was planned for (by 1979) and then provided (by 1981) in all programs of teacher preparation (Gollnick, 1992).[3] These were groundbreaking steps in teacher education, and much as been accomplished since then. But there was little emphasis on linguistic diversity in these early efforts, and not much attention was paid to preparing teachers to work successfully with ELLs.

Rather, over the last several decades, when teacher education research and practice focused on diversity, the emphasis was primarily on culture and race, including what prospective teachers needed to know about how identity influences both teaching and learning. But there was very little on language diversity per se and even less on how to prepare teachers—not to mention teacher educators—to teach an increasingly linguistically diverse school population. The paucity of research in this area was starkly revealed at the time when the American Educational Research Association Panel on Research and Teacher Education, which I cochaired with Ken Zeichner, was conducting its reviews of teacher education research published prior to 2004; the group synthesizing research on preparing teachers for populations traditionally not well served by the system found very few empirical studies designed to investigate the outcomes and effects of teacher preparation for work with linguistically diverse populations.[4] In the few years since that time, the situation has improved slightly, so that the third *Handbook of Research on Teacher Education,* which is currently in the final stages of preparation, has a chapter devoted entirely to empirical research on preparing teachers to teach ELLs.[5] Despite some strides, however, much more needs to be done, and this volume makes a significant contribution.

Under the editorship of María Brisk and with the consultation of the AACTE committee, the current volume takes on a previously unemphasized and unstudied problem in teacher education, raising thoughtful questions and offering trenchant analyses. The volume is provocative and inclusive in that it takes a broad and rich view of language diversity in the first place. That is, it constructs language diversity to include issues related to teaching children who are deaf and also pays special attention to research and practice related to preparing teachers to work successfully with native American Indian students and with immigrant students from a variety of cultural and linguistic groups. The volume also takes up questions related to what it means to prepare teachers to work with students who speak Black English. There is little previous work in teacher education that links together concerns about preparing teachers for diversity with issues related to bilingual education and teaching ELLs. In fact, as noted above, in most discussions about preparing teachers to work with culturally diverse populations, considerations about language have either gotten short shrift or have not been included at all.

This volume is organized in three parts. The knowledge section takes on a number of the most complex questions about what teachers need to know in order to teach well, especially what they need to know about bilingualism, culture, and identity. The practice section, which comprises most of the volume, focuses on practices in teacher education and in K–12 schools, including not only discussions of broad issues related to teacher preparation but also specific cases such as preparation of teachers to work with Native Hawaiian children and working with Hmong educators in specific areas of the country. Importantly, this section also focuses on the education of teacher educators themselves and what it means to provide transformative experiences for teacher educators who are interested in integrating issues related to bilingual education in their own courses and programs. The volume concludes with a short section on policy. The two chapters in this section provide much-needed analyses of the language diversity–specific aspects of certification requirements across the 50 states and accreditation standards for teacher education programs. Again, the sharp focus on language diversity is much needed in the field.

The generally conservative political climate, coupled with policymakers' preoccupation with testing accountability, make the task of including language diversity in the teacher preparation curriculum an extremely daunting one at this point in time. The early part of the 21st century is dominated by a relentless focus on high-stakes testing, a growing underclass that many fear will be permanent, and a convergence of factors that places the least well-qualified teachers in schools with students in the greatest peril. In addition, in many areas of the country, there is a significant backlash against affirmative action, bilingual and other language education programs, and race-based admissions and scholarship policies in higher education. Now more than ever, those who are committed to teacher education practice, research, and policy that includes language diversity need to understand and be strategic about the complex political circumstances that threaten these agendas. This volume is big step in the right direction.

Marilyn Cochran-Smith
John E. Cawthorne Millennium Professor
of Teacher Education for Urban Schools

Lynch School of Education
Boston College
October, 2006

Endnotes

1. NCATE. (2000). *Professional Standards for the Accreditation of Schools, Colleges, and Departments of Education*. Retrieved November 5, 2006, from http://www.ncate.org.
2. Baptiste, H. & Baptiste, M. (1980). Competencies toward multiculturalism. In H. Baptiste, M. Baptiste & D. Gollnick (Eds.), *Multicultural teacher education: Preparing teacher educators to provide educational equity* (Vol. 1) Washington, DC: American Association of College for Teacher Education.
3. Gollnick, D. (1992). Multicultural education: Policies and practices in teacher education. In C. Grant (Ed), Research and multicultural education: From the margins to the mainstream (pp. 218–239). Bristol, PA: Falmer Press.
4. Hollins, E. & Torres Guzman, M. (2005). Research on preparing teachers for diverse populations. In M. Cochran-Smith & K. Zeichner (Eds.), Studying teacher education: The report of the AERA panel on research and teacher education (pp. 477–548). Washington, DC: American Educational Research Association and Mahwah, NJ: Lawrence Erlbaum Associates.
5. Lucas, T., & Grinberg, J. (Forthcoming 2007). Responding to the Linguistic Reality of Mainstream Classrooms: Preparing all teachers to teach English language learners. In M. Cochran-Smith, S. Feiman-Nemser, & J. McIntyre (Eds.), *Handbook of Research on Teacher Education: Enduring Issues in Changing Contexts*. Mahwah, NJ: Lawrence Erlbaum.

Preface

The purpose of this volume is to address the preparation of teachers and teacher educators to serve culturally and linguistically diverse (CLD) students with particular focus on language. The literature on multicultural education has widely impacted the field as to the cultural knowledge needed by teachers of CLD students (Cochran-Smith, Davis, & Fries, 2004)[1]. Language has begun to draw attention only recently (Fillmore & Snow, 2002[2]; Valdés, 2004[3]). Language is necessary for students to understand instruction, instructional materials, and assessment instruments. Students need language to participate in classroom discourse and express their knowledge and ideas in writing. Teachers need knowledge of students, teaching practices, and language itself to be able to support students in acquiring English as their second language.

Overview

The book opens with Donaldo Macedo's chapter, "The Poisoning of Racial and Ethnic Identities: An Educational Challenge," a provocative piece explaining tensions in educational efforts to address multiculturalism in the context of strong values toward Western heritage. Macedo proposes that genuine multicultural education is essential for a democratic society. The chapters that follow are organized in three sections. Part I, *Knowledge*, explores existing knowledge about the populations addressed in this volume. Chapter 2, "Language, Culture, and Identity," by Courtney Clayton, Ray Barnhardt, and María Estela Brisk, introduces the concepts of bilingualism, culture, and identity. This chapter lays the foundation for the perspective toward CLD students taken in this volume. Language, culture, and identity are examined in their relation to CLD students' needs. Chapter 3, "Teaching Students Who Speak African American Language (AAL): Expanding Educators' and Students' Linguistic Repertoires," by Gloria Swindler Boutte, explains the language background of many African American students and explains why these students need to be viewed and educated as individuals who come to school speaking a language other than English. This chapter includes specific information about features of African American language. Similarly, chapter 4, "Language and the Deaf World: Difference not Disability," by Robert Hoffmeister, addresses language issues in the deaf world and what it means to be deaf and bilingual or bicultural. The chapter presents the deaf as a cultural and linguistic minority and not as people with physical problems. It also advocates for the importance of keeping the language and culture of the deaf community strong and proposes implications for education. Chapter 5, "Rethinking the Case for Culture-Based Curriculum: Conditions that Support Improved Mathematics Performance in Diverse Classrooms," by Sharon Nelson-Barber and Jerry Lipka, examines the impact of culture on learning. It also introduces indigenous populations that speak a language other than English. This chapter describes research on the impact on urban students' learning of mathematics. Mathematics instruction was based on a newly developed culture-based curriculum resulting from long-term collaborative work among Yup'ik elders, teachers, university researchers, and Alaskan schools.

Part II, *Practice*, documents various efforts in teacher education to work with teacher candidates and with teacher education faculty. In chapter 6, "ESL Is Good Teaching 'Plus': Preparing Standard Curriculum Teachers for All Learners," Ester de Jong and Candace A. Harper argue that "just good teaching" is not enough to educate CLD students with limited English proficiency. Such students have specific linguistic and cultural needs that need to be addressed. Chapter 7, "Classic: Transforming Hearts and Minds," by Socorro G. Herrera, Kevin G. Murry, and Della Pérez, illustrates a program for professional development that focuses on more than instructional practices. Through activities, discussions, and reflection, teachers go through six stages of readiness, from critical reflection on practice, to learning about their students and families, to working on curriculum and instruction, to finally reaching the ability to advocate for their students. The authors consider the early readiness stages essential foundation for modifying instructional practices to serve

CLD learners. In chapter 8, "Highly Qualified Teachers for Our Schools: Developing Knowledge, Skills, and Dispositions to Teach Culturally and Linguistically Diverse Students," Jorgelina Abbate-Vaughn reports on a model of preservice teacher development that provides urban field experiences with two coursework strategies: process writing and reading ethnic autobiographical literature. This approach brings preservice teachers close to CLD urban children and their families while they process their prior knowledge and understandings through reading, writing, and reflection. Chapters 9 and 10 address preparation of CLD teacher candidates. Chapter 9, "Teacher Education to Serve a Native Hawaiian Community: Lessons Learned," by Kathryn H. Au, Yvonne Kaulukane Lefcourt, and Alice J. Kawakami, documents the 10-year development of a program to prepare teachers serving Native Hawaiian children. The program is community based and strives to attract members of the community to the teaching profession. The chapter proposes lessons learned to be considered by other teacher preparation programs working with CLD teacher candidates and their communities. In chapter 10, "'Does She Speak English?': Hmong Educators in Western Wisconsin," Ronald S. Rochon, Clifton S. Tanabe, and Tamara H. Horstman-Riphahn outline research that is relevant to increasing the number of certified teachers of Hmong descent in Western Wisconsin. This chapter sketches a set of key observations and experiences of Hmong educators who have graduated from a teacher education program, as well as observations and experiences of non-Hmong administrators who have worked with these teachers.

Chapters 11 and 12 address the preparation of faculty in teacher education programs. In order to educate preservice teachers to work with CLD students, the faculty who educate them also need knowledge. Traditionally, such preparation has been relegated to specialized courses taught by faculty knowledgeable about the education of CLD students. In chapter 11, "Program and Faculty Transformation: Enhancing Teacher Preparation," María Estela Brisk describes the activities of one such effort to prepare all faculty in a teacher education program. It also outlines the elements that made faculty and program transformation possible. Chapter 12, "Faculty Perspectives on Integrating Linguistic Diversity Issues into an Urban Teacher Education Program," by Aida A. Nevárez-La Torre, Jayminn S. Sanford-DeShields, Catherine Soundy, Jaqueline Leonard, and Christine Woyshner, presents detailed experiences and reflections of faculty engaged in transforming themselves and their courses. It also illustrates at length the impact that those efforts had on students.

In Part III, *Policy*, chapters 13 and 14 describe efforts of state and federal policies as well as professional organizations to address language and culture needs in their recommendations for teacher preparation. In chapter 13, "Educational Policy and Linguistic Diversity: A Critical Analysis of Teacher Certification Requirements," Lisa Patel Stevens includes a complete survey of all U.S. state policies on including language requirements as part of teacher preparation, particularly with respect to secondary content instruction teachers. Patel considers that not only research but also policies influence teaching practices.

Given the complex and interrelated nature of these influences, a comprehensive consideration of culturally responsive teaching must address not just existing research and practices but also policy sources as a potential constraint or support of pedagogy that affirms students' diverse backgrounds. In chapter 14, "Language, Culture, Policy, and Standards in Teacher Preparation: Lessons from Research and Model Practices Addressing the Needs of CLD Children and Their Teachers," Alicia Ardila-Rey explores policies at the federal level and within professional organizations as well as accrediting organizations. Ardila-Rey relates policies and recommendations with the contents of the book.

In an effort to address implications on policy, the AACTE convened a group of language scholars in September 2005, including the authors of this book's chapters, and various representatives from national education organizations at Wingspread. The group discussed the issues presented in this book and developed a series of policy recommendations that address the inclusion of language diversity in teacher preparation. They also developed a definition of "Highly Qualified Teacher" that includes the ability to work with CLD populations (see Appendix).

Truly serving *all* children is a complex endeavor requiring knowledge that most teachers and teacher educators are not presently receiving. This book suggests what some of this knowledge includes and provides a variety of examples being carried out around the country. These examples illustrate that it is possible to acquire this knowledge and to carry out practices that eventually will benefit CLD students, an important percentage of the "all."

Endnotes

1. Cochran-Smith, M. Davis, D., & Fries, K. (2004). Multicultural teacher education: Research, practice, and policy. In J. A. Banks & C. A. M. Banks (Eds.), *Handbook of research on multicultural education. Second Edition* (pp. 931–975). San Francisco: Jossey-Bass.
2. Fillmore, L. W. & Snow, C. E. (2005) What teachers need to know about language. In C. t. Adger, C.E. Snow & D. Christian (Eds.), *What teachers need to know about language* (pp. 7–54). Washington, DC: Center for Applied Linguistics.
3. Valdes, G. (2004). The teaching of academic language to minority second language learners. In A. Ball & S. W. Freedman (Eds.), *Bakhtinian perspectives on language, literacy and learning* (pp. 66-98). New York: Cambridge University Press.

1

Poisoning Racial and Cultural Identities
An Educational Challenge

Donaldo Macedo
University of Massachusetts, Boston

Rare is the university or college that has escaped the debate over multiculturalism and diversity. In some schools, the issue has given rise to extraordinarily volatile contexts where racism, anti-Semitism, antifeminism, and ethnic xenophobia characterized campus life. In some instances, the high level of xenophobia has so much poisoned the campus environment leading to drastic measures such as the evacuation of "scores of minority students from [the Trinity College] campus [in Chicago] after menacing letters, including one in which a threat to shoot a Black student was made, were received by at least three minority students" (Ferkenhoff, 2005, p. A3). This current incident is the continuation of the racial violence that characterized, for example, "At the University of Massachusetts at Amherst – scene of some of the worst outbreaks of racial violence on campus in recent years – an African-American residential adviser was beaten up by a White visitor and feces were smeared on the door of his room. Enraged, scores of black students rampaged through a 22-story dormitory. Police had to warn residents not to leave their rooms" (Elfin & Burke, 1993, p. 52).

In this chapter, I want to argue that, as we enter the 21st century, one of the most pressing challenges facing educators in the United States is the specter of an "ethnic and cultural war," which constitutes, in my view, a code phrase that engenders our society's licentiousness toward racism. Central to the current cultural war is the facile call for a common culture and the overcelebration of myths that attempt to inculcate us with beliefs about the supremacy of Western heritage at the same time as the dominant ideology creates other instruments

1

that degrade and devalue other cultural narratives along the lines of race, ethnicity, language, and gender.

In the past two decades or so a large body of literature has amply demonstrated the advantages of multiculturalism, which range from greater cultural democracy to more harmonious intercultural relations. Ironically, although these studies unequivocally point to the underlining value of multiculturalism, Western hegemonic forces are imposing themselves with arrogance and disrespect toward the dignity and integrity of subordinated cultures that are still struggling to sever the yoke of cultural imperialism. Against a backdrop of Western cultural hegemony, conservative educators continue to demonize any and all forms of multiculturalism while many liberal educators have selectively embraced a sloganized form of multicultural and diversity education as a means to address the current dance of bigotry that characterizes education in most countries, particularly in developed nations. In this chapter, I want to also argue that before we can announce the existence of multicultural programs based on a truly cultural democracy, we need to denounce the false assumptions and naïveté that inform the present development of multicultural education and often lead to a form of "charitable paternalism." For example, instead of developing a cogent multicultural education that could teach us about the arduous and complex process of coming to cultural voice, a process that invariably involves tensions, contradictions, fears, doubts, hopes, and dreams, many educators (including many liberals) usually reduce the process of coming to cultural voice to a facile proposition such as "we need to empower minorities" (a euphemism for the oppressed) or "we need to give them voice." What these seemingly progressive educators fail to realize is that emergence of submerged voices almost always involves political clarity, pain, and hope. In other words, voice is not something to be given through an added-on multicultural curriculum by those in power; for if one has the power to give voice, one must also retain the same power to take it away. What is important to understand is that cultural voice requires struggle and the understanding of both possibilities and limitations. For most subordinate cultural groups, coming to voice represents a process through which they come to know what it means to be at the periphery of the intimate and yet fragile relationship between the colonizer and the colonized. It also means that the colonized becomes fully aware that cultural voice is not something to be given by the colonizer. The very discourse of giving voice points to the inherent power and cultural arrogance that are usually inculcated in the psyche of the colonizers as well as the colonized, particularly in those individuals who remain unable to decolonize the mind. Thus, during the struggle to end apartheid in South Africa, one may have heard, for instance, "the White South African minority government has decided to give the Black majority the right to vote" where "to give the right to vote" is linguistically and psychologically structured as a gift package. The true reality is that racial democracy in South Africa and elsewhere came about due to the persistent struggles of citizens who courageously resisted the oppressive yoke of White supremacy rule. We need to understand and courageously announce that cultural voice cannot be prepackaged as a gift. Cultural voice is a human right. Cultural voice is a democratic right. Against a landscape of charitable multicultural education, I want to propose that the failure of most multicultural education programs and curricula to achieve cultural democracy is primarily due to two fundamental factors: (1) the teaching of cultural tolerance as an end in itself and (2) the lack of political clarity in the multicultural education movement which, in turn, prevents even the most committed educators from understanding how the school of positivism that many of them embrace informs and shapes multicultural program and curriculum developments, often neutralizing the possibility for the creation of pedagogical structures that could lead to an authentic cultural democracy.

The Paternalism of Cultural Tolerance

A simple analysis would readily show preponderance in the field of multicultural education to teach tolerance. This posture is not only paternalistic but it also fails to critique its underlying assumptions so as to understand the power asymmetry that characterizes the constellation of cultures within which we live, particularly in the age of globalization. The emphasis on the teaching of cultural tolerance often fails to denude the privilege inherent in such posture. In other words, promising the "other" a dose of tolerance so we can get along not only eclipses real opportunities for the development of mutual respect and cultural solidarity but also hides the privilege and paternalism inscribed in the proposition: "I will tolerate you even though your culture is repugnant." The teaching of tolerance that is ushering multicultural education into the 21st century has brought with it highly complex and challenging realities that are still ill understood but have enormous ramifications for a more human-ized world. Not only has the teaching of cultural tolerance not dealt with the great economic disparity created by the widening gap between the so-called "first" and "third worlds," the resulting gulf between the rich and poor countries has manifested itself in unpre-dictable immigration patterns that have exacerbated our already rac-ist societies. For example, in the last few years, for the first time in human history, over 100 million people immigrated from one part of the globe to another. This exponential increase in immigration has given rise to a dramatic increase of racism and xenophobia. In France, the ultra-right National Front Party, headed by Jean-Marie LePen, has mounted an incessant attack on immigrants, particu-larly the Muslims from former French colonies. In Germany, there has been a significant increase in the number of neo-Nazi groups who have been responsible for a number of house bombings against Greeks and Turks. The Turks, in turn, have remained no less violent against the Kurds as they arbitrarily wiped out hundreds of Kurd villages, killing more than 30 thousand people and sentencing the remaining Kurds to a life of half-citizenry in the margins of ghetto existence. In Austria, Russia, and some Scandinavian countries, the level of anti-Semitism is also on the rise. Israel, in turn, fueled by uncontained racism, has elevated racist violence against the Pales-tinians to unacceptable levels. In Portugal, the discrimination and segregation of Africans from the former colonies are attested by the inhumane ghetto reality that characterizes shantytowns that dot some peripheries around Lisbon. Similar levels of xenophobia are also found in Spain, where Gypsies and North African immigrants are a constant target. The violent eruption against North Africans in the town of El Ejido, where 22 people were injured, point to the outbreak of racism in a country that always claimed to be nonracist. Even in Greece, where many people would deny that racism exists, we would have to acknowledge the discriminatory practices leveled against Albanians and other recent immigrants. Against a backdrop of increased globalized racism and xenophobia, I doubt very much that the teaching of tolerance alone will enable us to critically under-stand how capitalist forces construct, shape, and maintain the cruel reality of racism. I also doubt that the teaching of tolerance could equip educators with the necessary critical tools to understand how language is often used to ideologically construct realities that veil the raw racism that devalues, disconfirms, and poisons other cultural identities. Even within the multicultural education movement, most educators fail to understand the neocolonialist ideology that informs the multicultural debate to the extent that they almost always structure their arguments within a reductionistic view of culture that has its roots in a colonialist legacy.

If we closely analyze the ideology that informs and shapes the present debate over multicultural education and the present polemic over the primacy of Western heritage, we can begin to see and understand that the ideological principles that sustain those debates are consonant with the structures and mechanisms of a colonial ideology designed to devalue the cultural capital and values of the colonized.

Only through a full understanding of our colonial legacy can we begin to comprehend the complexity of our multiculturalism in the Western countries. For example, for most cultural subordinate individuals in the United States, their multiculturalism is not characterized by the ability to have two cultures. There is a radical difference between a dominant person adopting a second culture and a cultural subordinate individual struggling to acquire and be accepted by the dominant culture. Whereas the former involves the addition of a second culture to one's cultural repertoire (for example, a middle-class White American student who goes to Paris to learn French and enjoy the French culture), the latter usually provides the subordinate person with the experience of subordination in his or her native culture, which is devalued by the dominant values and the dominant culture that he or she is attempting to acquire, often under coercive conditions. This is the case for most lower-class immigrants in the United States, particularly those from Third World countries. Both the colonized context and the asymmetrical power relations with respect to cultural identity in the United States (and other Western countries as well) create, on the one hand, a form of forced multiculturalism and, on the other, what could be called a "cultural drama." That is, the reality of being forced to live in a borrowed cultural existence. This is an existence that is almost culturally schizophrenic—that is, being present and yet not visible, being visible and yet not present. It is a condition that invariably presents itself to the reality of cultures that have been subordinated—the constant juggling of two worlds, two asymmetrical cultures, and two languages of which the subordinate language is usually devalued and demonized. An example par excellence concerning how our society treats different forms of multiculturalism is reflected in our tolerance toward certain types of biculturalism and lack of tolerance toward other bicultural realities. Most of us have tolerated various degrees of biculturalism on the part of cultural anthropologists and language teachers that range from a simplistic form of anthropolizing the so-called primitive cultures to serious deficiency in the mastery of the foreign language on the part of many foreign language teachers. Nevertheless, these cultural anthropologists and foreign language teachers, with rare exceptions, have been granted tenure, have been promoted within the institutions they teach and, in some cases, and have become "experts" and "spokespersons" for various cultural and linguistic groups in our communities. On the other hand, for example, if a teacher is a speaker of a subordinated language who speaks English as a second language with an accent, the same level of tolerance is not accorded to him or her. Take the case of Westfield, Massachusetts, when "about 400 people there signed a petition asking state and local officials to ban the hiring of any elementary teacher who speaks English with an accent" (Lupo, 1992, p. 19), because according to them, "accents are catching" (*The Boston Globe,* 1992, p. 16). The petition was in response to the hiring of a Puerto Rican teacher assigned to teach in the system. As one can readily see, any form of multicultural education that neglects to fully investigate this cultural drama and treat multiculturalism as having mere competencies in two cultures invariably ends up reproducing those ideological elements characteristic of the relationship between colonizer and colonized through which the colonized is always and falsely discriminated, devalued, and demonized.

Fracturing Cultural Identities through Scientism

Throughout history, oppressive dominant ideologies have resorted to science as a mechanism to rationalize crimes against humanity that range from slavery to genocide by targeting race and other ethnic and cultural traits as markers that license all forms of dehumanization. If we did not suffer from historical amnesia, we would easily understand the ideology that informed Hans Eysenck's psychological proposal that suggested "there might be a partly genetic reason for the differences in IQ between black and white people" (Eysenck,

1971). The same historical amnesia veils dangerous memories that keep us disconnected from Arthur Jensen's racist proposals published decades ago by the Harvard Educational Review.

One could argue that the above-cited incidents belong to the dusty archives of earlier generations, but I do not believe we have learned a great deal from historically dangerous memories, considering our society's almost total embrace of scientism as characterized by the success of *The Bell Curve,* by Charles Murray and former Harvard professor Richard J. Hernstein. It is the same blind acceptance of "naïve" empiricism that continues to fuel and shape both educational research and curriculum development, including multicultural programs with a misguided focus on testing and objectivity.

By and large, the present debate over bilingual and bicultural education in the United States is informed by the positivistic and management models that hide their ideologies in the false call for objectivity, hard data, and scientific rigor. This can be seen, for example, in the comments of Pepi Leistyna's term paper on the political nature of bilingual and bicultural education: "These are unsupported politically motivated claims! [the Harvard professor called for] a more linguistic analysis" (Leistyna, 1998). As Leistyna recounts, this same professor told him: "I hope you have been reading some hard science." The false call for hard science in the social sciences represents a process through which "naïve" empiricists hide their anti-intellectual posture, a posture that is manifested either through censorship of certain bodies of knowledge or through the disarticulation between theories of the discipline and the empirically driven and self-contained studies that enable the pseudoscientists to:

> not challenge the territorialization of university intellectual activity or in any way risk undermining the status and core beliefs of their fields. The difference, [for scientists] is that this blindness or reluctance often contradicts the intellectual imperatives of the very theories they espouse. Indeed, only a theorized discipline can be an effective site for general social critique—that is, a discipline actively engaged in self-criticism, a discipline that is a locus for struggle, a discipline that renews and revises its awareness of its history, a discipline that inquires into its differential relations with other academic fields, and a discipline that examines its place in the social formation and is willing to adapt its writing practices to suit different social functions. (Nelson, 1997, p. 19)

As these theoretical requirements make abundantly clear, Pepi Leistyna's professor's arrogant dismissal of Freire's social critical theories unveils the ideology behind the prescription that Leistyna should have been "reading some hard science." The censorship of political analysis in the current debate over bilingual and bicultural education exposes the almost illusory and schizophrenic educational practice in which "the object of interpretation and the content of the interpretive discourse are considered appropriate subjects for discussion and scrutiny, but the interests of the interpreter and the discipline and society he or she serves are not" (Nelson, 1997, p. 19).

The disarticulation between the interpretive discourse and the interests of the interpreter is often hidden in the false call for an objectivity that denies the dialectal relationship between subjectivity and objectivity. The false call for objectivity is deeply ingrained in a positivistic method of inquiry. In effect, this has resulted in an epistemological stance in which scientism and methodological refinement are celebrated while "theory and knowledge are subordinated to the imperatives of efficiency and technical mastery, and history is reduced to a minor footnote in the priorities of 'empirical' scientific inquiry" (Giroux, 1983, p. 87).

The blind celebration of empiricism has created a culture in which pseudoscientists, particularly in schools of education, who engage in a form of "naïve empiricism," believe "that facts are not human statements about the world but aspects of the world itself" (Schudson, 1978, p. 6). According to Michael Schudson (1978):

> This view was insensitive to the ways in which the "world" is something people construct by the active play of their minds and by their acceptance of conventional—not necessarily 'true'—ways of seeing and talking. Philosophy, the history of science, psycho-analysis, and the social science have taken great pains to demonstrate that human beings are cultural animals who know and see and hear the world through socially constructed filters. (p. 6)

The socially constructed filters were evident when Massachusetts, Arizona, and California voters passed referenda banning bilingual education. Although the school administrators and politicians were gearing up to disband bilingual programs, data from both San Francisco and San Jose school systems showed that bilingual graduates were outperforming their English-speaking counterparts ("Bilingual grads," 1998, p. 143). This revelation was met by total silence from the media, the proponents of English-only and political pundits. This is where the call for objectivity and scientific rigor is subverted by the weight of its own ideology.

What these educators do not realize is that there is a large body of critical literature that interrogates the very nature of what they consider research. Critical writers such as Donna Haraway (for a comprehensive and critical discussion of scientific objectivity, see Haraway, 1988), Linda Brodkey, Roger Fowler, and Greg Myers, among others, have painstakingly demonstrated the erroneous claim of "scientific" objectivity that permeates all forms of empirical work in social sciences. According to Linda Brodkey (1966), "scientific objectivity has too often and for too long been used as an excuse to ignore a social and hence, political practice in which women and people of color, among others, are dismissed as legitimate subjects of research" (p. 10). The blind belief in objectivity not only provides pseudoscientists with a safe haven from which they can attempt to prevent the emergence of counterdiscourses that interrogate "the hegemony of positivism and empiricism," but it also generates a form of folk theory concerning objectivity believed only by nonscientists. In other words, as Linda Brodkey (1966) would so eloquently put it, "that any and all knowledge, including that arrived at empirically, is necessarily partial, that is, both an incomplete and an interested account of whatever is envisioned" (p. 8). In fact, what these pseudoscientists consider research—that is, work based on quantitative evaluation results—can never escape the social construction that generated these models of analysis. Theoretical concepts are always shaped by the pragmatics of the society that devise such evaluation models in the first place (Fowler et al., 1979, p. 192). That is, if the results are presented as facts that were originally determined by a particular ideology, "these facts cannot in themselves illuminate issues that lie outside of the ideological construction of these facts to begin with" (Myers, 1986).

I would warn educators that these evaluation models can provide answers that are correct and nevertheless without truth. A study that concludes that African American students perform way below White mainstream students in reading is correct, but such a conclusion tells us very little about the material conditions with which African American students work in the struggle against racism, educational tracking, and the systematic negation and devaluation of their cultural histories. I would propose that the correct conclusion rests in a full understanding of the ideological elements that generate and sustain the cruel reality of racism and economic oppression. Thus, an empirical study produces conclusions without truth if it is disarticulated from the sociocultural reality within which the subjects of the study are situated. For example, an empirical study designed to assess reading achievement of children who live in squalid conditions must factor in the reality faced by these children as accurately described by "a boy named Daniel in the fourth grade of an elementary school (1,500 children in attendance, 99% minority) in the large and sprawling district of Los Angeles" (Kozol, 2005, p. 172):

> The room smelled very bad and it made me sick to my stomach. There was blood all over the place...
> "I saw a rat," another child in the class named Ashley whose friends reported seeing one of the live rats climbing on her hair. "It was hard for me to breathe. I asked the teacher to send me to the nurse."
> "Ashley got sick because of dead rats," wrote another child. (Kozol, 2005, p. 172)

An empirical study that neglects to incorporate in its design the cruel reality just described (and this is often the case in our supposedly colorblind and classless society) will never be able to fully explain the reasons behind the poor performance of these children. Although pseudoscientists will go to great lengths to prevent their research methodologies from being contaminated by the social ugliness described by Kozol so that they can safeguard their "objectivity" in, say, their study of underachievement of children who live in ghettos, the residents of these ghettos have little difficulty identifying and understanding the root causes of their misery described by children in one of these ghetto schools:

> I see lots of thinings in this room. I see new teachers omots every day.... I see pictures in my school.... I see rithmetic paper a spellings paper. I see a chart. I see the flag of our Amerrica. The room is dirty.... The auditotium dirty the seats are dusty. The light in the auditorium brok. The curtains in the auditorium are ragged they took the curtains down because they was so ragged. The bathroom is dirty sometime the toilet is very hard. The cellar is dirty the hold school is dirty sometime. (Kozol, 2005, p. 172)

What these children would probably say to researchers is that they do not need another doctoral dissertation to state what is so obvious to the people sentenced to live in this form of human misery. In other words, by locking children in material conditions that are oppressive and dehumanizing, we are invariably guaranteeing that they will be academic underachievers. Once the underachievement is guaranteed by these oppressive conditions, it is then very easy for research studies, such as those described in the *Bell Curve* by Richard J. Hernstein and Charles Murray which, in the name of objectivity, are disarticulated from the political, cultural, and social reality that shaped and maintain these oppressive conditions, to conclude that Blacks are genetically wired to be intellectually inferior to Whites. Along the same lines, an empirical study that concludes that children who engage in dinner conversation with their parents and siblings achieve higher rates of success in reading is not only academically dishonest but also misleading to the degree that it ignores the class and economic assumptions that all children are guaranteed daily dinners in the company of their parents and other siblings. What generalizations can such a study make about the 12 million children who go hungry every day in the United States? What can a study of this type say to the thousands and thousands of children who are homeless, who do not have a table and who sometimes do not have food to put on the table that they do not have? A study that makes such sweeping and distorted generalizations about the role of dinner conversations in reading achievement says little about children whose houses are without heat in the winter, houses that reach dangerously cold conditions that led a father of four children to remark: "You just cover up ... and hope you wake up the next morning" (Kozol, 2005, p. 39). If the father really believes the study results, he will suggest to his children, after they've all made it through another freezing night alive, that they should have a conversation during dinner the next night since it will be helpful in their reading development should they be lucky enough to make it through another night alive. What dinner conversation would the Haitian immigrant, Abner Louima, have with his children after being brutally sodomized with a toilet plunger by two White policemen in a New York police precinct? Would his children's reading teacher include as part of his or her literacy development the savage acts committed by the White New York police against their father?

These questions make it clear how distorted empirical study results can be when they are disconnected from the sociocultural reality that informs the study to begin with. In addition, such distortion feeds into the development of cultural stereotypes that, on the one hand, blame the victims for their own social misery and, on the other hand, rationalize the genetic inferiority hypotheses that are advanced by such pseudoscholars as Charles Murray and former

Harvard professor Richard J. Hernstein. What empirical studies often neglect to point out is how easily statistics can be manipulated to take away the human faces of the subjects of study through a process that not only dehumanizes but also distorts and falsifies the reality.

What needs to be fully understood is that educators cannot isolate their so-called scientific objectivity from social class and from cultural identity factors that ultimately shape such objectivity. That is, an honest academic analysis must always include all pertinent factors (and their interaction with one another) that produce, shape, and guide multiple cultural realities—realities that usually exist in asymmetrical power relationships.

Conclusion

As I have attempted to demonstrate, before we can announce a more democratic pedagogy around multiculturalism based on a truly cultural democracy (this obviously would involve languages as factors of culture), we need to denounce the false assumptions and distortions that often lead to a form of entrapment pedagogy whereby dominant values are usually reproduced under the rubric of progressive approaches. However, to denounce invariably involves courage that, unfortunately, is in short supply. During a conference in which I attempted to unmask the dominant ideology mechanisms involved in the present assault on bilingual and bicultural education, a woman approached me and said: "Thank you very much for your courage to say things that many of us are too afraid to say." Since I was taken by surprise, I did not know how to respond but managed to make a point with the following question: Isn't it ironic that in a democracy to speak the truth, at least one's truth, one must have courage to do so? She squeezed my hand and politely said goodbye. After she left, I began to think that what I should have told her is that to advocate for the democratic rights of subordinate students and to denounce the inequities that shape their (mis)education, "it is not necessary to be courageous; it is enough to be honest" (Cabral, 1974, p. 16). And to be honest would require that we denounce those conservative educators who believe that bilingual education [which is also a form of multicultural education] "is highly contentious and politicized ... and there is a lack of clear consensus about the advantages and disadvantages of academic instruction in the primary language in contrast to early and intensive exposure to English" (Snow, Burns, & Griffin, 1998, p. 29).

To be honest would also require that we denounce the research industry that makes a living by pointing out the "lack of clear consensus" in the multicultural debate without providing alternative pedagogies that would effectively address the specificities of needs among subordinate students while the same research industry remains complicit with the very oppressive structures responsible for the poverty and human misery that characterize the lives of a large segment of subordinate students who go to inner-city public schools. Let's take the Head Start research. Many White Head Start researchers are rewarded by the dominant ideology for their complicity with the doctrinal system. They are again rewarded through large grant awards to study the early exposure to literacy as a compensation for the poverty and "savage inequalities" (Kozol, 1992) with which many of these White researchers remain in total complicity. Often, these studies end up stating the obvious, pointing to the proverbial "lack of clear consensus" which, in turn, calls for more research. Although the call for more research ultimately benefits the researchers themselves, it invariably takes away precious resources that could be spent to diminish the adverse consequences of the savage inequalities that inform the lives of most minority children. To be honest would require that conservative educators acknowledge the existence of the intimate interrelationship between society's discriminatory practices and the savage inequalities that shape the (mis)education of most subordinate students. This would, invariably, point to the political nature of education that conservative educators call "politicizing" education.

Politicizing education becomes a negative "shock word" to muffle rigorous academic debate concerning both the grievances and the educational needs of subordinate students. Only through a thorough deconstruction of the ideology that prevents subordinate students' sociocultural reality from becoming an area of serious inquiry can educators who want to falsely take politics out of education learn that it is erroneous to think that "[s]peaking a nonstandard variety of English can impede the easy acquisition of English literacy by introducing greater deviations in the representation of sounds, making it hard to develop sound-symbol links." (Snow et al., 1998, pp. 27–28). This position makes the assumption that standard dialects are monolithic and show no phonological variations which, in turn, restricts the "deviations in the representation of sounds, making [it easier] to develop sound-symbol links" (Snow et al., 1998, pp. 27–28). Such posture is sustained only by a folk theory believed only by nonlinguists. Anyone who has been exposed to the Boston dialect notices that its speakers almost always drop the phoneme /r/ in the final position, as in "car," yet middle-class speakers of such dialect have little difficulty linking the dropped phoneme /r/ and its respective graphemic representation. This form of folk theory is possible due to the present excess in positivism whereby numbers are elevated to an almost mythical status which, in turn, dismisses other fundamental factors that have important pedagogical implications that remain largely ignored. For example, as Celia T. Leyva (1998) recounts:

> Growing up, I was often reprimanded for speaking Spanish in class and even in the lunch room, and also discriminated against because I spoke English with a Cuban accent. I was ridiculed not only by classmates, but also by my teachers who insisted that I had to speak English like Americans do. Because of the humiliation I went through growing up, I felt the need to prevent my own children from similar situations, and robbed them the opportunity to learn my native language and, at the same time denied them their own culture.... I hated English and I hated learning it. (p. 7)

Perhaps more than the mere ability to link sound and symbol in English, factors such as linguistic and cultural resistance play a greater role in the acquisition of the dominant Standard English. Bell Hooks painfully acknowledges for most African Americans, the dominant Standard English, far from being a neutral tool of communication, is viewed as the "oppressor's language [which] has the potential to disempower those of us who are just learning to speak, who are just learning to claim language as a place where we make ourselves subject" (Hooks, 1996, p. 168). In learning the "oppressor's language," we are often forced to experience subordination in speaking it. Upon reflection, Hooks states that "it is not the English language that hurt me, but what the oppressors do with it, how they shape it to become a territory that limits and defines, how they make it a weapon that can shame, humiliate, colonize" (Hooks, 1996, p. 168). I would argue that the shaming, humiliation, and colonization nonspeakers of the dominant standard English feel in their relationship with English have a great deal more to do with the lack of reading success in the standard English than the mechanical struggles these students face in making sense of sound-symbol link due to unavoidable phonological variations found in all dialects, including the dominant Standard English. The nature of the nonstandard variety does not determine the subordinate students' inability to learn the ABCs which, in turn, warrants that they be taught "how to learn." These students have little difficulty learning what the chief of psychiatry at San Diego's Children Hospital rightly describes as the "more relevant skills of the DBSs (drive-by-shootings)" (Levine, 1993, p. 11) and other survival skills, which are vividly and painfully mastered by any student whose reality is characterized by violence, human misery, and despair.

To be honest would require that we reconnect with history so as to learn from the thousands of Chicano high-school students who, in 1968, walked out of their respective high schools as a protest against their miseducation. They walked out to demand quality education, cultural dignity, and an end to cultural violence. The passion, courage, and determination those Chicano students demonstrated will serve us well again as we attempt to refigure how to best educate subordinate students. Their courage, passion, and determination energized educators, political leaders, and community activists to coalesce so to address the urgent needs that Chicanos, as well as other subordinate students, were then facing. The needs of most subordinate students are, in a sense, greater today given the added vicious assault on civil rights and bicultural education. For this reason, teachers, parents, researchers, and community members need to again coalesce with the same determination to not only provide quality education to all subordinate students but also to work aggressively to dismantle the social and cultural fabric that informs, shapes, and reproduces the despair of poverty, fatalism, and hopelessness. To be honest would require that White liberals as well as conservative educators understand the underlying ideology in their assumption that what multicultural education needs is basic research. I would counter this argument by saying that what most subordinate students need is social justice and cultural and economic equity.

By incorporating subordinate students' cultural and linguistic forms of textual, social, and political analysis, educators will not only develop means to counter the dominant attempt to impose English and the dominant cultural values but will also need to equip themselves with the necessary tools to embrace a pedagogy of hope based on cultural production where specific groups of people produce, mediate, and confirm the mutual ideological elements that emerge from and affirm their cultural experiences. These include, obviously, the languages through which these experiences are reflected and refracted. Only through experiences that are rooted in the interests of individual and collective self-determination can we create democratic education. Cultural production, not reproduction by imposing dominant values, is the only means through which we can achieve a true cultural democracy. In this sense, multicultural education not only offers us a great opportunity to democratize our schools but "is itself a utopian pedagogy" (Freire, 1985, p. 57). By the very fact that it is a utopian pedagogy, according to Paulo Freire (1985)

> It is full of hope, for to be utopian is not to be merely idealistic or impractical but rather to engage in denunciation and annunciation. Our pedagogy cannot do without a vision of man [and woman] of the world. It formulates a scientific humanist conception that finds its expression in a dialogical praxis in which the teachers and learners together, in the act of analyzing a dehumanizing reality, denounce it while announcing its transformation in the name of the liberation of man [and woman]. (p. 57)

References

Bilingual grads outperform others in 2 districts. (1998, July 8). *San Diego Union Tribune*, 143.

Brodkey, L. (1966). *Writing permitted in designated areas only*. Minnesota: Minnesota University Press.

Cabral, A. (1974). *Return to the source*. New York: Monthly Review Press.

Elfin, M. & Burke, S. (1993, April 9) Race on campus. *U.S. News and World Report, 114*(15), 52.

Eysenck, H. J. (1971). *The IQ argument: Race, intelligence, and education*. New York: Library Press.

Ferkenhoff, E. (2005). College in Ill. Evacuates minorities after threats. *The Boston Globe*. Retrieved April 23, 2005, from http://www.bostoncom/news/nation/articles/2005/04/23/college_in_ill_evacuates_minorities_after_threats/.

Fowler, R., et al. (1979), *Language and control*. London: Routledge & Kegan Paul.

Freire, P. (1985). *The politics of education: Culture, power, and liberation*. New York: Bergin & Garvey Publishers.

Giroux, H. A. (1983). *Theory and resistance: A pedagogy for the opposition*. South Hadley, MA: J.F. Bergin.

Haraway, D. (1988). Situated knowledges: The science question in feminism and the privilege of partial perspectives. *Feminist Studies, 14*, 575–599.

Hooks, B. (1996). *Teaching to transgress: Education as the practice of freedom.* New York: Routledge.

Humanities 101. (1992, March 3). Westfield style. *The Boston Globe,* 16.

Kozol, J. (1992). *Savage inequalities: Children in America's schools.* New York: Harper Perennial.

Kozol, J. (2005). *The shame of the nation: The restoration of apartheid schooling in America.* New York: Crown Publishers.

Leistyna, P. (1998). *Presence of mind: Education and politics of deception.* Boulder, CO: Westview Press.

Levine, S. (1993, August 12). On guns and health care. The U.S. caves in to force. *San Diego Union Tribune,* 11.

Leyva, C. T. (1998, Fall). *Language philosophy research.* Paper presented to graduate class at University of Massachusetts, Boston.

Lupo, A. (1992, March 4). Accentuating the negative. *The Boston Globe,* 19.

Myers, G. (1986, February). Reality, consensus, and reform in the rhetoric of composition teaching. *College English, 48*(2), 154–174.

Nelson, C. (1997). *Manifesto of a tenured radical.* New York: New York University Press.

Schudson, M. (1978). *Discovering the news: A social history of American newspapers.* New York: Basic Books.

Snow, C. E., Burns, S., & Griffin P. (Eds.). (1998). *Preventing Reading Difficulties in Young Children.* Washington, DC: National Academy Press.

Part I

Knowledge

2

Language, Culture, and Identity

Courtney Clayton
Boston College

Ray Barnhardt
University of Alaska, Fairbanks

María Estela Brisk
Boston College

Language, culture, and identity are closely related factors that impact the academic achievement and personal development of culturally and linguistically diverse (CLD) students. Students who function in more than one language present educators with complex needs that can be understood through the lenses of students' cultures and their sense of self. In this chapter, language, culture, and identity are examined in their relation to CLD students' needs. The first section provides demographic information on CLD students in the United States and stresses the need for all teachers to be well prepared to meet these students' needs. The second section, an analysis of language, includes a discussion of bilingualism and second-language acquisition, with particular emphasis on knowing CLD students' oral, reading, and writing language proficiency in their languages even when students are fluent in English. The next section, an examination of culture, stresses cultural responsiveness as an effective approach to developing educational programs and school systems for CLD students. The final section on identity underscores how CLD students' languages and cultural experiences are critical elements in students' identity development, with particular focus on implications for educators in the classroom.

Context

It was not until the end of the 19th century that the United States adopted English as the national language and the language for education. Therefore, native speakers of other languages were relegated to language minority status regardless of whether they were indigenous, descendants of colonizers, immigrants, descendents of Africans, colonized populations, refugees, sojourners, or Deaf. Presently, descendents of these populations or new arrivals have to contend with a second language, English, and a different culture when they enter schools.

Nearly two million American Indian and Alaskan natives live throughout the country and speak about 175 languages (McCarty & Watahomigie, 1998). Europeans of many different language backgrounds established colonies in the United States. In addition to English, Spanish, French, Dutch, Swedish, German, and Russian were used in communities, churches, and schools (Brisk, 1981). In the 19th and 20th centuries, millions of immigrants from different parts of the world entered the United States. The trend continues into the 21st century. Peak periods occurred in the first two decades of the 20th century and from 1985 to the present. Another source of linguistic variety resulted from the incorporation of new lands, including Alaska, Puerto Rico, and several Pacific Islands. International business and the popularity of U.S. higher education attract nearly 6 million sojourners and their families.

More than 37 million people in the United States claim a Spanish-speaking background; more than 60% of them are of Mexican origin. Asians constitute 4% of the population of the United States. Of those 4%, 24% are Chinese, 18% Filipino, 18% Asian Indian, 10% Vietnamese, 10% Korean, 7% Japanese, and 12% other Asian (U.S. Census Bureau, 2002). About one in five students throughout the nation comes from a home in which a language other than English is spoken (Crawford, 2001). These students present challenges to a mostly monolingual English-speaking teaching staff in American public schools (see de Jong, chapter 6). These students tend to concentrate in poor urban areas (see Abbate-Vaughn, chapter 8), although the numbers are increasing in rural and suburban areas.

During the 17th and 18th centuries, large numbers of African people were forcibly transported to the United States to work on farms and in households. Their descendants speak language varieties presently included under the label of African American Vernacular English or African American Language (AAL) (see Boutte, chapter 3). Rickford (1999) maintains that although it is often said that 80% of African Americans speak a variety of AAL, this is an estimate. He also notes that it is often a matter of degree. Age, gender, and social class are important factors determining the degree to which speakers use features of AAL in their speech. The major impact on the education of these children is the negative attitude toward their language. "Such negative attitudes may lead [teachers] to have low expectations of such students, to assign them inappropriately to learning disabled or special education classes" (Rickford, 1999, p. 283). Instead, approaching these children as CLD has lead to more successful teaching and learning.

The Deaf in the United States have their own culture and language, American Sign Language (ASL). Approximately 1.8% of the school-age population, or 2,309,000 children ages 3 to 17, have some degree of hearing difficulty. A much smaller proportion of these children are deaf. Full data on children who cannot hear in either ear is not available. However, children who, at best, can hear and understand words shouted in their better ear constitute 52,000, or 0.10% of the population that age (Holt, Hotto, & Cole, 1994). The greatest challenge for these students is the fact that 95% of them are born to hearing parents who do not know ASL and thus cannot provide language input from birth (see Hoffmeister, chapter 4).

In discussing the persistent academic achievement gap of great numbers of deaf students, Marschark, Convertino, and Larock (2006) conclude that "the mainstream classroom does not provide deaf students with a 'level playing field' in their pursuit of academic achievement" (p. 184). They believe that "the problem is that deaf students often receive instruction that is inconsistent with their prior knowledge, learning strategies, and language comprehension skills" (p. 184).

CLD students enter schools in the United States at different ages and with different educational and linguistic backgrounds. They live in urban, rural, and suburban areas in all 50 states of the country. The three types of students included in our definition of CLD—speakers of languages other than English, speakers of AAL, and the Deaf—have similar and distinct strengths and difficulties. However, they all have in common a native language other than the Standard English used in schools and a cultural background that differs from most of the school personnel and values espoused by schools. The lines between these three groups are not clearly defined. Among the Deaf are students of families that speak a language other than English at home. Some of these students know more than one sign language. Speakers of varieties of English are often immigrants from the Caribbean. These students experience similar negative attitudes toward their language as AAL speakers.

All these children can equally benefit from an approach to their education that is additive—in other words, one in which knowledge of Standard English is added to their linguistic repertoire. Thus the acquisition of Standard English does not come as a replacement of the language they already know. And although knowledge of Standard English is clearly useful in the United States' context, it is not necessarily a "better" language.

The education of speakers of languages other than English, the Deaf, and in a few cases AAL speakers, has been viewed as the prerogative of special programs charged with preparing children to function in mainstream classes by mastering Standard English. Teachers in these programs acquired expertise in bilingualism, second-language acquisition, the use of varieties of English for instruction, role of culture, and other knowledge and skills that prepared them to successfully educate these children. No effort was made on preparing classroom teachers in general. However, more CLD students are served in mainstream classrooms than in specialized programs. Most AAL speakers, an increasing number of speakers of languages other than English, and 83% of deaf or hard-of-hearing students are served in mainstream classes (Lucas & Grinberg, in press; Luckner & Howell, 2002).

The majority of mainstream classroom teachers are monolingual English speakers who have received little preparation to work with CLD students and, for the most part, come from different cultural and ethnic backgrounds than their students (Kindler, 2002; Lucas & Grinberg, in press). More important, few of these teachers have had experiences comparable to that of CLD students in their own schooling. Therefore, providing the knowledge, attitude, and tools for these teachers to work with CLD populations is especially important because drawing on their own backgrounds is of limited assistance (Ball & Lardner, 2005; Lucas & Grinberg, in press).

Efforts have been made to increase the number of teachers that come from backgrounds comparable to those of their students (Torres,

Santos, Peck, & Cortes, 2004). This type of solution is limited, however, because not enough people go into the teaching profession .

Preparation of teachers is in the hands of teacher education programs and faculty. Within teacher education programs are specialized programs to train bilingual, second language, and teachers of the Deaf. Candidates preparing to be classroom teachers do not participate in these programs or, at most, take a course in multicultural education. Any effort to prepare mainstream teachers to work with CLD students has to start with teacher preparation programs (see Brisk, chapter 11; Nevárez-La Torre, Sanford-DeShields, Soundy, Leonard, & Woyshner, chapter 12).

Language

Children develop the languages and dialects that are used in the environments in which they grow up. This rich knowledge they bring to their schooling experience is the basis for further language development, the medium for acquiring concepts, and an important aspect of their identity. Finding out what these languages and dialects are is an important aspect of getting to know students. Because many students speak other languages and dialects, often in addition to Standard English, teachers need to understand bilingualism and second language-acquisition.

Bilinguals know more than one language to different degrees and use these languages for a variety of purposes (Mackey, 1968). Proficiency and use change over the course of the life of a bilingual individual. Students are defined as bilingual if they know and use at least two languages, even if their fluency and use of the languages vary. Some are fluent in both languages, others are stronger in one language, and yet others are literate in only one of their languages. Bilinguals use both languages to different degrees. Some converse, read, and write in both languages daily, whereas others find occasional use for one of their languages. These patterns also may change over time. For example, in her short 9 years of life, Alejandra has experienced four different languages. Fluency and use in particular languages, except for English, changed over time. She heard and used English and Spanish since she was born. At age 3, she entered an English-medium preschool. Her English flourished, but she seldom used Spanish any more. At age 5, she entered a two-way bilingual school, where she was instructed in Spanish and English on alternate weeks. A new babysitter spoke only Portuguese to her. Alejandra became increasingly fluent in all three languages and biliterate in English and Spanish. Her Brazilian babysitter ceased to care for her when she entered third grade, which affected her development of Portuguese. At the same time, she started taking Mandarin as a foreign language in school.

Every bilingual presents a different pattern of proficiency and use over his or her lifetime (Grosjean, 1989; Mackey, 1968; Romaine, 1995). In addition, personal and social variables, independent of instruction, influence language development and language loss of bilinguals. Therefore, bilingual students present a variety of profiles, depending on the level of development of each language, whether they are literate in either or both, to what extent they use each language, and for what purpose.

Bilinguals have a unique ability to shift languages. While communicating with monolinguals, they partially deactivate their other language. To communicate with similar bilinguals, they make use of both languages, alternating and even mixing the languages. This process, called *codeswitching*, is a natural phenomenon and is not evidence of poor language skills or confusion. On the contrary, bilingual children develop the ability to codeswitch and use it to enrich communication (Genishi, 1981). Bilinguals alternate languages for many reasons. Often, a word in the other language comes to mind first or more accurately expresses the meaning. Topic, addressee, environment, and the need to call attention to, give emphasis to, or express solidarity with an ethnic group are among the many reasons why bilinguals codeswitch (see Boutte, (chapter 3; Mackey, 1968; Romaine, 1995).

Bilingualism is an advantage to societies and individuals. Knowledge of languages helps nations in international commerce and business and gives an advantage in political negotiation and conflict. Individuals who are bilingual benefit from opportunities offered to those who know other languages. Children's development benefits from bilingualism. Bilingual and biliterate students have the greatest advantage because proficiency in two languages enhances academic achievement and language proficiency. It also benefits possible long-term needs of learning additional languages. High levels of bilingualism are correlated with higher achievement in a variety of areas, including educational expectations, reading, vocabulary, and math

(Fernandez & Nielsen, 1986); ability to formulate scientific hypotheses (Valdesolo, 1983); cognitive flexibility (Cummins, 1979; Peal & Lambert, 1962); deductive reasoning skills in mathematics (Dawe, 1983); metalinguistic awareness, or ability to think about language and analyze linguistic input (Ben-Zeev, 1977; García, Jiménez, & Pearson, 1998; Hakuta & Diaz, 1985; Ianco-Worrall, 1972); and better scores on reading tests (Fernandez & Nielsen, 1986; Lindholm, 1991). Bilingualism in childhood positively affects the ability to learn additional languages later in life (Penfield & Roberts, 1959).

Besides the benefits of bilingualism, home language proficiency is important because strong home language proficiency (including ability to read and write) positively affects second-language acquisition and academic achievement (Cummins, 1984). "The strongest predictor of L2 student achievement is the amount of formal L1 schooling. The more L1 grade-level schooling, the higher L2 achievement" (Thomas & Collier, 2002, p. 9), even with a language like Chinese that has a very different writing system from English (Townsend & Fu, 1998). In addition, home language proficiency assists sociocultural integration. Students' ties with family and community depend on home language fluency; without it, family relations are often conflicted and may even collapse (Fillmore, 1991; Portes & Rumbaut, 2001).

With specific regard to second-language acquisition, some bilingual children develop two languages from infancy. The progress in the two languages depends on exposure and schooling. Others are introduced to their second language later when they first encounter schooling (see Hoffmeister, chapter 4). Yet others may start schooling in their home language in their native countries and are exposed to English when they move to the United States. The experience of learning a second language varies depending on age and level of literacy when English is introduced as a second language.

The acquisition of a second language takes time and effort. A number of personal and external factors affect the speed and level of proficiency. Fluency in conversational English may be accomplished within a few months of exposure to the language. However, acquisition of English to function in academic settings takes several years (Collier, 1989; Hakuta, Butler, & Witt, 2000).

As children encounter school in English, their second language, they go through four broad stages of second language acquisition: L1 use, silent period, telegraphic and formulaic use, and productive language use (Tabors, 1997; Genesee, Paradis, & Crago, 2004). L1 use can be a very short period, even a few days, especially in a school environment that does not foster languages other than English. The realization that people do not understand the L1 often results in children refusing to speak. Despite these generalizations, there is great variation among children. Some skip the silent period altogether, whereas others remain there for a long time. Once students start using the second language, it takes time to develop. They need to develop oral discourse and text structure patterns, vocabulary, grammar, pronunciation, and spelling rules. Younger learners may have more difficulty with vocabulary because they need to learn concepts as well as language, whereas older learners have more difficulty with pronunciation and grammatical structures.

Contextual and personal variables affect the process of second-language development (oral and written) and the level of achievement of bilingual students. Linguistic, economic, social, cultural, and political factors influence the environment and families and peers of second-language learners, facilitating or challenging the acquisition of English. Yuri, the son of a Russian scientist whose family settled in a suburban community with an excellent school system, quickly acquired proficiency in English and the ability to function in school. Personal characteristics such as age, motivation to learn the second language, attitudes toward first and second language, level of schooling, and personality also influenced the process. Yuri had a gregarious personality. Having arrived at 11 years old with a strong development of Russian and an academic background, he quickly adjusted to school. His motivation to develop English and his attitude toward his own language and culture supported this development. In contrast, for example, Mexican American students who believed that losing Spanish was a precondition to learning English averaged poorly in English proficiency tests (Hakuta & D'Andrea, 1992).

Understanding bilingualism, second-language acquisition, and the particular characteristics of their students allow teachers to structure instruction using what students already bring and providing for their needs. Paramount is not to stereotype, to hold high expectations of bilingual learners, and to understand that bilingual learners have particular needs (see de Jong & Harper, chapter 6). Mrs. Montes knew better when she first met Pedro, a fifth grader who had recently arrived from the Dominican Republic. Although most people think that such a child's destiny is either the major leagues or a life of crime, Mrs. Montes immediately spotted this child's potential. Through encouragement and rigorous teaching in Spanish and English, she set the ground for a successful academic career. Pedro graduated from an Ivy League medical school and now works at a prestigious hospital.

Culture

Having examined aspects of bilingualism and second-language acquisition for CLD students, the focus now turns to culture and its influence on CLD students' needs. A cultural system is more than the surface or visible attributes of the language, arts and crafts, eating habits, or subsistence practices of the people who sustain it. Being Hispanic, or Amish, or Navajo, or Black, or Deaf (see Hoffmeister, chapter 4) also means a way of thinking, a way of seeing, a way of behaving, a way of doing things, and a way of relating to the world around you. Education must take all of these aspects of CLD students' cultural existence into account if it is to be truly "multicultural."

One of the biggest challenges that schools serving CLD populations face is bringing the educational experiences provided by the school in line with the social, cultural, and economic aspirations of the community it serves (see Abbate-Vaughn, chapter 8). To the extent that the cultural fabric of the minority community being served is different from that of the school, some kind of accommodation is necessary if the two are to come together in a mutually productive manner. Most often it has been the CLD community and the CLD student that have been called upon to make the adjustment, but increasingly, more culturally responsive approaches have sought to meet the students and communities halfway (Richards, Brown, & Forde, 2004). These efforts have been particularly evident in communities where a language other than English is spoken and schools have attempted to incorporate the local language and culture in the curriculum, such as the Ka Lama Teacher Education Initiative in Hawaii (see Au et al., chapter 9).

Although it is not easy, it is possible for a school to provide an integrated educational program that builds on the local cultural environment and knowledge base (including language) as a foundation for learning about the larger world beyond, such as the Yup'ik curriculum described by Nelson-Barber and Lipka (chapter 5). Learning about one's own cultural heritage and community need not be viewed as supplanting opportunities to learn about others, but rather as providing an essential infrastructure through which all other learning is constructed. It is often a reality of today's existence that CLD students have a foot in more than one world, so their education should reflect the symbiotic and synergistic potential of that existence.

There are many layers of shared understandings in any cultural community, and for anyone from outside that community (e.g., a teacher) to even begin to recognize that the deeper layers exist requires a considerable openness of mind and a great deal of time and effort. Our first impressions of a new culture are usually formed in response to the more obvious surface aspects that we can see, hear, and relate to our own prior experience, and once we formulate an opinion (often in the form of a stereotype), we begin to rely on that explanation for guiding our subsequent behavior and hesitate to assimilate new information that may lead to a deeper understanding. The resulting myopia can contribute to numerous problems, including inappropriately low expectations regarding student abilities (see Rochon et al.'s discussion of Hmong students, chapter 10).

Because learning a culture is a lifetime undertaking, where do we start and what are the most important aspects to be considered? One of the first things to recognize is that the more we learn about another culture, the more we find out about ourselves, which can be done through the use of critical reflection, for example, as described by Herrera, Murry, and Pérez (chapter 7). We all carry around our own subconscious, culturally conditioned filters for making sense out of the world around us, and it is not until we encounter people with a substantially different set of filters that we have to confront the assumptions, predispositions, and beliefs that we take for granted and that make us who we are. It is not necessary (nor is it possible) for an outsider to fully comprehend all the subtleties and inner workings of another cultural system to be able to perform a useful role in that cultural community. What is necessary, however, is a recognition that significant differences do exist, an understanding of how these potentially conflicting cultural forces can impact people's lives, and a willingness to set aside one's own cultural predispositions long enough to convey respect for the validity of others. In doing so, we must be willing to question all aspects of our approach to education, including the very purposes to which it is directed (for a further discussion, see Abbate-Vaughn, chapter 8).

Cultural Factors Impacting the Role of the School

In most instances, the goals of schools are bound to universalistic intellectual or social functions associated with the dominant society. The most explicit function to which schools are directed is to the inculcation of the broadly shared knowledge and skills deemed necessary for individual participation in the larger society. This is sometimes refined to place a more specific emphasis on the development of academic capabilities, with a primary concern for factual knowledge and intellectual skills. In other situations, the emphasis is placed exclusively on the development of particular occupational or practical skills aimed at the workplace. Either approach is obviously narrowly selective from the totality of human experience and is inevitably bound to a specific cultural definition of appropriate knowledge and skills. A less-direct, but often explicit function attributed to the school is that of developing "citizenship" and the appropriate attitudes and understandings necessary for participation in a democratic society. Again, the emphasis is on preparation for the roles and expectations associated with membership in the larger society.

Some of the least-direct and least-explicit functions of the school become apparent when they are viewed in the context of educating CLD students. The traditional intellectual social and economic functions indicated above are then confounded by the additional and seemingly invidious factors associated with cultural differences, such as conflicting values, varied learning styles, diverse behavior patterns, nonconforming social allegiances, and alternative perceptions of reality. These factors, when thrust into the amalgam of traditional school policies and practices, reveal the extent to which the school serves a concomitant function of inducing acculturative influences in the domains of values, attitudes, beliefs, and social behavior. In an effort to more directly accommodate these additional cultural factors, schools involved with CLD education have been called upon to adopt some variant of the goals of cultural assimilation or cultural pluralism (see Au et al., chapter 9).

Cultural Assimilation   Though it is rarely made explicit, and is often unintended, one of the most common distinguishing features of schools in CLD settings is their overwhelming press toward assimilation of students into mainstream cultural patterns. Whether intentional or not, the basic thrust of schooling is toward the breaking down of particularistic orientations and developing in their place a more universalistic outlook. Even where accommodations are made to include ethnic studies or bilingual education in the curriculum content, the structure, method, context, and processes through which the content is organized and transmitted are usually reflective of mainstream patterns and exert a dominant influence on the student. Schools are agents of the dominant society and, as such, they reflect the underlying cultural patterns of that society. As long as they reflect the structure and cultural fabric of the dominant society, they can be expected to perpetuate its values, attitudes, and behavior patterns within an implicit framework of assimilation.

What then, does an educational goal of assimilation have to offer the CLD student, and what are some of its limitations? On the surface, a cultural assimilation orientation would seem to offer the CLD student an opportunity to gain access to the skills and resources necessary to participate in the larger society on equal terms with others. This expectation often goes unfulfilled, however, because of the school's inability to adequately respond to the differences in learning dispositions associated with differences in ways of thinking, seeing, behaving, doing things, and ways of relating to the world on the part of the CLD student. Consequently, the requisite academic skills are not learned, status differentials are reinforced, and access to societal resources is further impeded, thus thwarting the CLD student's aspirations. The school cannot contribute effectively to the assimilation process without careful attention to the unique cultural conditions out of which the CLD student emerges.

If assimilation is desired and is to be achieved in full by members of a cultural minority population, social, political, and economic forces beyond those available through the school must support it. Though the school may serve a useful and even necessary function in the assimilation process, it cannot accomplish the task alone. If cultural assimilation is not desired, alternative goals must be adequately articulated and the extent to which schools may or may not be able to contribute to their attainment must be assessed. One such alternative goal that has received widespread attention is that of cultural pluralism.

Cultural Pluralism   Whereas assimilation stresses the ways of the dominant society, cultural pluralism is intended to stress the ways of CLD societies. Cultural pluralism is advocated as an educational goal by those who seek a pluralistic, multicultural society in which each ethnic, racial, or religious group contributes to the larger society within the context of its own unique cultural frame of reference. The school's task, therefore, is to recognize the minority culture and to assist the student to function more effectively within that culture. Heavy emphasis is placed on ethnic studies and minority language programs, but these programs are usually offered within the traditional structural framework of the school and have only tangential effect in terms of CLD development goals. The primary beneficial effects are in the symbolic implications of the formal recognition of the CLD group's existence by the school.

As typically espoused, however, with an emphasis on cultural autonomy and homogeneity, cultural pluralism in its isolationist form falls short of being a realistic goal toward which schools may direct their efforts. In addition to participating in various ways in the cultural traditions of their own society, most (if not all) minority group members also participate to varying degrees in the cultural traditions of the larger society (the Amish arguably may be an exception). To maintain true cultural pluralism, a structural separation of cultural groups must exist, which is rarely the case in American society, with the school being but one example of structural interaction. Members of diverse cultural groups interact with each other in various ways for various purposes, resulting in diffuse acculturative influences and constant adaptation. Under such conditions, the goals of education must necessarily extend beyond CLD group boundaries if students are to be prepared for the larger social reality they will face as adults.

Even if cultural pluralism were to be viewed as a realistic goal, we would still have the problem of using an institutional artifact of one society (i.e., the school) to promote the cultural traditions of another. To change the subject matter (content) without a concomitant change in the structure, method, context, and processes through which that content is conveyed, may in the end only strengthen rather than weaken the influences of the larger society on the CLD student. Achieving educational independence does not necessarily lead to cultural independence, especially if the educational experiences remain within the structural framework of the dominant culture.

It would appear then that neither extreme of complete cultural assimilation or ethnic separation is appropriate or adequate as an educational goal, and neither are realistically attainable through the traditional framework of the school. How then might schools be situated to provide a middle ground between cultural assimilation and cultural pluralism that can fulfill the aspirations of CLD communities while at the same time preparing students to function in the wider world?

Cultural Responsiveness   Because there are multiple considerations that come into play and varied consequences with both the assimilationist and pluralist approaches to developing educational programs for CLD students, it is no longer an either/or proposition and thus becomes a political question of who controls the educational system and determines the uses to which it will be put. The challenge has become one of providing a means for local selection of curricula and adaptation of those features of schooling that are deemed most suitable by members of the community being served. The goal of such an approach is to draw upon the local cultural context to enliven the curriculum and tailor schooling to the world in which students live, what Herrera et al. (chapter 7) refer to as "mutual accommodation." This term is not meant to imply that schools are to present a hodge-podge of cultural practices from which students choose at whim, but rather that the schools will assist students with understanding the nature of the diverse experiences that are a natural part of their existence and thus contribute to the development of an integrated cultural perspective suitable to students' needs and circumstances. In chapter 5, Nelson-Barber and Lipka describe such a program that builds on indigenous community experiences and epistemologies.

In developing such an eclectic approach, it is assumed that each CLD community has unique characteristics that distinguish it from other communities and that all groups share characteristics common to the larger society. It is also assumed that variations exist within and between groups in orientation toward minority versus dominant cultural characteristics. Some individuals and some groups may wish to stress the minority culture, whereas others are oriented toward the dominant culture, with still others desiring the "best of both worlds." The concern then is with the development of an educational approach that respects this vast diversity while introducing everyone to the range of options available so they themselves are able to exercise a degree of choice in their individual or group lifestyle and goals. Such an approach must recognize the multifaceted and dynamic nature of a large, complex, open, continually evolving society and must allow for the varied cultural expressions of ethnic, linguistic, religious, and political beliefs and practices within the broader framework of that society. It is through such variation and diversity that the vitality of the society at large is maintained and our understanding of the range of human potential and capabilities is deepened.

Thus, the goal of "cultural responsiveness" for CLD education incorporates features of both the assimilationist and pluralist ideologies, with emphasis on an evolutionary form of cultural diversity to be attained through the informed choices and actions of individuals who are well grounded in the dynamics of human and cultural interaction processes. Cultural responsiveness implies an open-ended process (rather than a dead-ended condition) whereby individuals or groups can adapt and define the functions of the school in response to their changing needs, assuming that they understand those functions and are in a position to influence school programs sufficiently to make them fully compatible with their needs.

In seeking to develop an approach to education that has the potential for application to varied cultural and situational conditions, we must go beyond the simple revision of curriculum content or classroom teaching practices. We must take into account the educational setting itself and find ways to restructure the social organization of that setting to allow the participants to pattern their interaction to fit the goals they are attempting to achieve. As with the content, we need a structure that is flexible and adaptable enough to accommodate a wide range of cognitive, communicative, and interactional patterns, while maintaining some degree of order and continuity in terms of overall direction and effort.

The values and skills to be taught in school should mirror those encouraged in the home and the cultural community (assuming they are still intact). Education is a community responsibility, with the school serving as one player, albeit a key one, in the process. That which is expected of students in the school should be reinforced in explicit ways by the parents and the community, and that which is expected by the parents and community should be reinforced in the school. Parents should be active participants and contribute their own knowledge and expertise to the school.

Identity

In order to understand the totality of cultural responsiveness and CLD needs, an exploration of CLD student identity is needed. A person's identity is more than the attributes ascribed to him or her by the outside world, such as "White female." These attributes do not define the complexity of a person's being because identity is multi-dimensional. Though at one point in time identity was considered a lucid and lasting concept, new work on identity attempts to understand how identities are crafted and recrafted over time. Identity is being considered now in the work of researchers as multifaceted, coconstructed, and dynamic through time (Day, 2002; Kanno, 2003; Norton, 1997; Suarez-Orozco & Suarez-Orozco, 2001).

The idea of identity being multifaceted is grounded in the notion that multiple factors influence who we are. These include historical, social, cultural, and political factors. One's history is defined not only by where one was born and where one grew up but also by the history of one's ancestors and one's current cultural group, including the status they held and hold coming to the United States. That is, if a person is White, he is generally more well-received in this country and thus has greater access to opportunity. The opposite is true for people who come to the United States and are not able to access opportunity in the same way, such as Cape Verdeans who are imposed with racial issues simply by being Black in this country—something that was not an issue in their own country. In other words, they are imposed with an American Black identity to which they cannot relate because this is completely unfamiliar to them. Furthermore, in relation to identity, being White in this country holds more value in the sense that White people can, in general, more easily access power. Feelings of being powerful can create a positive sense of self reflected by the larger society. Feelings of powerlessness can have the opposite effect—a more-negative sense of self.

The idea of how a sense of self is positively or negatively affected by outside factors has been defined as "social mirroring" (Suarez-Orozco & Suarez-Orozco, 2001). Society and significant others reflect back to us images of ourselves that can be both positive and negative. When the reflection is positive, we generally feel that we are worthwhile and competent. When the reflection is negative, feelings of self-doubt can pervade our sense of who we are.

The idea of mirroring relates also to the notion of identity being coconstructed. Our identity is something we can construct, but it is also constructed by others—more of an imposed identity, as mentioned earlier. Certainly, we can adjust the way we act in particular situations, taking on the role in the moment, such as daughter, teacher, student, or professional, and shifting identities in this sense under our own control; but our identities can also be shaped by others and larger society in both positive and negative ways. We cannot shift the color of our skin and, although our socioeconomic status can change, we are defined by the outside world in terms of where we are now. We often cannot shape how others view us or construct ideas of us in their own minds—this is more of a reflection of society that connects certain attributes, such as skin color, to ideas of who we are and what we can become in the world (for a further discussion of issues related to perception of outside attributes, see Rochon et al., chapter 10).

Language can be of particular importance in the area of society imposing certain identity values upon us and how we view ourselves in the world. One's language is intimately linked to how we define ourselves and how we have been defined over the course of our lives. As Blot (2003) states, "Language is inescapably a badge of identity" (p. 3). In this country, if English has been our first language and we have had access to being well schooled in that language, we hold a certain type of identity—one that is quite powerful and privileged. On the other hand, people who were born in the United States who do not speak Standard English as their first language or who have immigrated to this country without speaking English tend to be positioned by society in a less positive light (see Boutte, chapter 3). As Bourdieu (1977) states: "A language is worth what those who speak it are worth, so too, at the level of interactions between individuals, speech always owes a major part of its value of the person who utters it" (p. 652). In this sense, we hold specific "language identities"—what the language is "worth" in relation to larger society and what we feel we are worth because of our language.

The idea of identity being dynamic across time means that one's identity is not static but rather is ever-shifting, depending on such factors as mirroring, age, membership (the groups to which we belong and want to belong), and our relations with others. For example, a CLD student wants to become a part of the "popular group" in high school. She may adjust the way she dresses, try to go to the parties where the "popular" people are, and begin dating someone in this group. By virtue of association (with her boyfriend), she is able to access this group and take on a new identity of "popular." Her identity shifts within the space of the possibilities of group membership.

What do these identity issues and definitions mean for CLD students? How do CLD students come to construct their identities and what kinds of identity shifts occur according to their relation to various groups and to the larger society? In order to answer these questions, two major areas will be examined: ethnic identity formation and social mirroring. Tse (1999) argues that the process of ethnic identity development follows a common pattern of four stages for most ethnic minorities (EMs). The first stage is ethnic unawareness, in which EMs are unaware of their minority status. This is typically a relatively short period before EMs enter school. As they come into contact with other ethnic groups and become aware of their minority status, they move to the second stage, ethnic ambivalence or evasion. This usually occurs in childhood and adolescence, when EMs begin to distance themselves from their own ethnic groups and adopt the norms and behaviors of the dominant group. The third stage is ethnic emergence, beginning in adolescence or early adulthood, in which EMs awake to their minority status and recognize that joining the dominant group is not wholly possible. In this stage, they begin to look toward alternate group associations, and many look to their ethnic homeland for acceptance. The fourth and final stage, according to Tse, is ethnic identity incorporation, in which EMs join the ethnic minority group and resolve many of their ethnic identity conflicts (pp. 122–124).

In theory, all EMs, including CLD students, should eventually move through these stages. However, multiple factors can interfere with this movement, the most powerful of which appears to be social mirroring. As indicated earlier, social mirroring can be both positive and negative and can heavily influence how people feel about themselves and identify with the larger world. Suarez-Orozco and Suarez-Orozco (2001) describe three specific styles of adaptation to social mirroring for CLD children: ethnic flight, adversarial identities, and transcultural identities. Children who structure their identities around the ethnic flight style most strongly identify with the dominant mainstream culture. These youth "hang out" with peers from the mainstream culture, rather than with peers from their own cultural groups. They also generally want to learn to speak Standard English as a way of not only communicating but also identifying with the dominant culture and see school as a way to "symbolically and psychologically move away from the world of the family and ethnic group" (Suarez-Orozco & Suarez-Orozco, 2001, p. 104). However, this type of ethnic flight can come with major consequences. In many cases, identification with the mainstream group weakens important ties to members of their own ethnic group, most importantly family members. Furthermore, these children can experience shame, doubt, and self-hatred for turning their backs on their roots. As the authors state: "We contend that while ethnic flight is a form of adaptation that can help a person 'make it' by the mainstream society's standards, it frequently comes at a significant social and emotional cost" (p. 104).

At the opposite end of the continuum for ethnic adaptation are CLD children who adapt "adversarial identities." These children "construct identities around rejecting—after having been rejected by—the institutions of the dominant culture.... Children who find themselves structurally marginalized and culturally disparaged are more likely to respond to these challenges to their identities by developing an adversarial style of adaptation" (Suarez-Orozco & Suarez-Orozco, 2001, p. 107). CLD children who react in this way tend to have problems in school, are more likely to drop out, and consequently face multiple challenges in the future, including unemployment, gangs, and jail. With regard to language, children who react with an adversarial style of adaptation tend to see learning Standard English as "acting White" and reject it, thus limiting their potential access to greater power in society. Generally, however, CLD children who adopt this style of adaptation and identity are ostracized by mainstream society, have parents who are not able to help guide them through the period of adolescence; live in poor, unsafe neighborhoods; and come to feel "powerless and hopeless" (Suarez-Orozco & Suarez-Orozco, 2001, p. 107). It is no wonder, then, that many CLD students go down this road and do not achieve ethnic emergence, let alone ethnic identity incorporation.

Having said this, however, some CLD children develop positive identities through developing "transcultural identities." For most CLD children, the work of childhood and adolescence is crafting these bicultural identities that become an integral part of self for them. Most children fall between the extremes of ethnic flight and adversarial styles and successfully navigate their two (or three or four) identities into hybrid ones. Suarez-Orozco and Suarez-Orozco

(2001) view developing transcultural identities as the "most adaptive of the three styles. It preserves the affective ties of the home culture while enabling the child to acquire the skills required to cope successfully in the mainstream culture. This identity style not only serves the individual well, but also benefits society at large" (p. 113). Kanno (2003) describes the stories of four Japanese sojourners who learned to successfully develop hybrid, transcultural identities as both Japanese and Canadian. Though they experienced the second stage of ethnic identity development, ethnic ambivalence, they were all successful in moving toward ethnic emergence and eventual ethnic identity incorporation due to multiple factors, such as strong family ties and family commitment to home culture and home language maintenance.

Educators of CLD students must realize the impact that both negative and positive social mirroring can have on their students. Negative mirroring can lead to rejection of a critical element in CLD students' identity formation—their own ethnic identity. Negative mirroring can occur in such acts as denying students the right to use their own language to communicate and learn in class and placing values on students' identities (i.e., second language speaker deficit models, which means viewing a student speaking a language other than English as a problem to be overcome). Negative mirroring can also be seen in not making space for children's multiple cultural identities in the classroom and in providing low expectations for CLD students, leading to students' sense of helplessness and feeling a lack of prospects for the future.

Furthermore, educators need to be aware of warning signs that indicate children are experiencing a great deal of trouble in navigating their bicultural identities, such as depression, major feelings of stress, and low morale. Educators also need to be aware of children experiencing role reversals, particularly immigrant students, where students need to take on the parental identity at times to help their families adapt to the new cultural environment. In some cases, the students may be the only family members who can speak English and thus must navigate a new role in their family, which is not the way it was for them in their home countries. As Suarez-Orozco and Suarez-Orozco (2001) point out, "roles are often reversed, turning culturally scripted dynamics of parental authority upside down" (p. 75).

On the opposite side of negative mirroring is the great impact that positive social mirroring can have on students' sense of self and their ability to develop transcultural identities. The school itself can create an environment that recognizes and affirms cultural diversity and the use of multiple languages. "Schools provide critical contexts where [CLD students] must find a voice, through which new identities may be negotiated or indeed resisted" (Miller, 2004, p. 294). Within a positive school context, CLD students can learn to feel like full-fledged members of the community and can learn to negotiate their transcultural identities.

Teachers can also not underestimate the potential power they have over helping their CLD students create positive senses of themselves and their ethnic identities. For example, Day (2002) described one teacher's positive interactions with a boy from the Punjab who entered her class as a new student. She said, "The teacher gave the child a place in the interactions [with herself and with other students] and held it for him; she gave him a voice that could speak from a desirable and powerful identity. The child gained social capital in the classroom" due to the teacher's positive mirroring (Day, 2002, p. 112). In this sense, teachers need to reflect on their own power and how they project images of children to the children with whom they work.

Educators need to understand that identities are complex and multifaceted and that they are influenced by multiple factors. Although we may be able to speak of attributes about people, outside factors, we often do not know about the whole of the person, inside factors. As educators of CLD students, it is particularly critical that we be aware of inside factors and encourage and reflect positive images to children. In this way, we can help students move through the stages of ethnic identity to becoming transcultural and holding greater self esteem, particularly around issues of culture and language.

Conclusion

Language, culture, and identity intertwine in the lives of CLD students. In order to have a complete picture of CLD students and their needs, teachers must understand the development of bilingualism and the process of second language acquisition. Schools striving for cultural responsiveness also aid in the success of CLD students under their care and reflect a commitment to the various cultures existing inside and outside of the school walls. Supporting this success are schools and teachers who understand CLD students' identity development and help to promote positive images of students' cultures and languages. Teacher education programs need to incorporate the notions developed in this chapter so that teachers entering the profession can make informed decisions when working with CLD students.

References

Ball, A. & Lardner, T. (2005). *African American literacies unleashed: Vernacular English and composition classroom*. Carbondale, IL: Southern Illinois University.

Ben-Zeev, S. (1977). The influence of bilingualism on cognitive strategy and cognitive development. *Child Development, 48,* 1009–1018.

Blot, R. K. (2003). Introduction. In R. K. Blot (Ed.), *Language and social identity* (pp. 1–9). Westport, CT: Praeger.

Bourdieu, P. (1977). The economics of linguistic exchanges. Social Science Information, 16, 645–668.

Brisk, M. E. (1981). Language policies in American education. *Journal of Education, 163*(1), 3–15.

Cochran-Smith, M., Davis, D., & Fries, K. (2004). Multicultural teacher education: Research, practice, and policy. In J. A. Banks & C. A. M. Banks (Eds.), *Handbook of research on multicultural education* (2nd ed., pp. 931–975).

Collier, V. P. (1989). How long? A synthesis of research on academic achievement in a second language. *TESOL Quarterly, 23,* 509–531.

Crawford, J. (2001). Census 2000: A guide for the perplexed. Retrieved 1/16/02, 2002, from http://ourworld.compuserve.com/homepages/JWCRAWFORD/census02.htm

Cummins, J. (1979). Linguistic interdependence and the educational development of bilingual children. *Review of Educational Research, 40,* 222–251.

Cummins, J. (1984) Bilingualism and special education: Issues in assessment and pedagogy. Clevedon, UK: Multilingual Matters.

Dawe, L. C. (1983). Bilingualism and mathematical reasoning in English as a second language. *Educational Studies in Mathematics, 14,* 325–353.

Day, E. M. (2002). Identity and the young English language learner. Clevedon, UK: Multilingual Matters.

Fernandez, R. M., & Nielsen, F. (1986). Bilingualism and Hispanic scholastic achievement: Some baseline results. *Social Science Research, 15,* 43–70.

Fillmore, L. W. (1991). When learning a second language means losing the first. *Early Childhood Research Quarterly, 6,* 323–346.

García, G. E., Jiménez, R. T., & Pearson, P. D. (1998). Metacognition, childhood bilingualism, and reading. In D. J. Hacher, J. Dunlosky, & A. C. Graesser (Eds.), *Metacognition in educational theory and practice* (pp. 193–219). Mahwah, NJ: Lawrence Erlbaum Associates.

Genesee, F., Paradis, J., & Crago, M. B. (2004). *Dual language development and disorders: A handbook on bilingualism & second language learning*. Baltimore: Paul Brooks.

Genishi, C. (1981). Codeswitching in Chicano six-year-olds. In R. P. Duran (Ed.), *Latino language and communicative behavior* (pp. 133–152). Norwood, NJ: Ablex.

Grosjean, F. (1989). Neurolinguists, beware! The bilingual is not two monolinguals in one person. *Brain and Language, 36*, 3–15.

Hakuta, K., Butler, Y. G., & Witt, D. (2000). *How long does it take English learners to attain proficiency?* Santa Barbara, CA: Linguistic Minority Research Institute, University of California, Santa Barbara.

Hakuta, K., & D'Andrea, D. (1992). Some properties of bilingual maintenance and loss in Mexican background high-school students. *Applied Linguistics, 13*, 72–99.

Hakuta, K., & Diaz, R.M. (1985). The relationship between degree of bilingualism and cognitive ability: A critical discussion and some new longitudinal data. In K. E. Nelson (Ed.), *Children's language* (Vol. 5, pp. 319–344). Hillsdale, NJ: Lawrence Erlbaum.

Holt, J., Hotto, S., & Cole, K. (1994). *Demographic aspects of hearing impairment: Questions and answers.* (3rd ed.). Washington, DC: Center for Assessment and Demographic Studies, Gallaudet University. Retrieved May 18, 2006, from http://gri.gallaudet.edu/Demographics/factsheet.html

Ianco-Worrall, A. D. (1972). Bilingualism and cognitive development. *Child Development, 43*, 1390–1400.

Kanno, Y. (2003). *Negotiating bilingual and bicultural identities.* Mahwah, NJ: Lawrence Erlbaum.

Kindler, A. L. (2002). *Survey of the states' limited English proficient students and available educational programs and services 2000–2001 summary report.* Washington, DC: National Clearinghouse for English Language Acquisition & Language Instruction Educational Programs.

Lindholm, K. J. (1991). Theoretical assumptions and empirical evidence for academic achievement in two languages. *Hispanic Journal of Behavioral Sciences, 13*(1), 3–17.

Lucas, T., & Grinberg, J. (in press). Responding to the linguistic reality of mainstream classrooms: Preparing all teachers to teach English language learners. In M. Cochran-Smith, S. Feiman-Nemser, & J. McIntyre (Eds.), *Handbook of research on teacher education: Enduring issues in changing contexts.* Mahwah, NJ: Lawrence Erlbaum.

Luckner, J. L., & Howell, J. (2002). Suggestions for preparing itinerant teachers: A qualitative analysis. *American Annals of the Deaf, 147*(3), 54–61.

Mackey, W. (1968). The description of bilingualism. In J. A. Fishman (Ed.), *Readings in the sociology of language* (pp. 554–584). The Hague: Mouton.

Marschark, M., Convertino, C., & Larock, D. (2006). Optimizing academic performance of deaf students: Access, opportunities, and outcomes. In D. F. Moores & D. S. Martin (Eds.), *Deaf learners: Developments in curriculum and instruction* (pp. 179–200). Washington, DC: Gallaudet University.

McCarty, T. L., & Watahomigie, L. J. (1998). Language and literacy in American Indian and Alaska native communities. In B. Perez (Ed.), *Sociocultural contexts of language and literacy* (pp. 69–98). Mahwah, NJ: Lawrence Erlbaum Associates.

Miller, J. (2004). Identity and language use: The politics of speaking ESL in schools. In A. Pavlenko & A. Blackledge (Eds.), *Negotiation of identities in multilingual contexts* (pp. 290–315). Clevedon, UK: Multilingual Matters.

Moores, D. F. (1992). An historical perspective on school placement. In T. N. Kluwin, D.F. Moores, & M. G. Gaustad (Eds.), *Toward effective public school programs for Deaf students: Context, process, and outcomes* (pp. 7–29). New York: Teachers College Press.

Norton, B. (1997). Language, identity, and the ownership of English. *TESOL Quarterly, 31*(3), 409–429.

Peal, E., & Lambert, W. E. (1962). The relationship of bilingualism to intelligence. *Psychological Monographs, 76*(27), 1–23.

Penfield, W., & Roberts, L. (1959). *Speech and brain-mechanisms.* Princeton, NJ: Princeton University Press.

Portes, A., & Rumbaut, R. G. (2001). *Legacies: The story of the immigrant second generation.* Berkeley: University of California Press.

Richards, H. V., Brown, A. F., & Forde, T. B. (2004). *Addressing diversity in schools: Culturally responsive pedagogy.* Denver, CO: National Center for Culturally Responsive Educational Systems.

Rickford, J. R. (1999). *African American vernacular English.* Oxford: Blackwell.

Romaine, S. (1995). *Bilingualism.* New York: Basil Blackwell.

Suarez-Orozco, C., & Suarez-Orozco, M. M. (2001). *Children of immigration.* Cambridge: Harvard University Press.

Tabors, P. O. (1997). *One child, two languages: A guide for preschool educators of children learning English as a second language.* Baltimore, MD: Paul H. Brooks.

Thomas, W. P., & Collier, V. P. (2002). *A national study of school effectiveness for language minority students' long-term academic achievement.* Santa Cruz: Center for Research on Education, Diversity & Excellence, University of California, Santa Cruz.

Torres, J., Santos, J., Peck, N. L., & Cortes, L. (2004). *Minority teacher recruitment, development, and retention.* Providence, RI: The Education Alliance at Brown University.

Townsend, J. S., & Fu, D. (1998). A Chinese boy's joyful initiation into American literacy. *Language Arts,* 75, 193–201.

Tse, L. (1999). Finding a place to be: Ethnic identity exploration of Asian Americans. *Adolescence, 34*(133), 121–139.

U.S. Census Bureau. (2000). *QT-P13: Ancestry: 2000, 2004.* Retrieved from http://www.census.gov/main/www/cen2000.html

Valdesolo, E. T. (1983). *The effect of bilingualism on the ability to formulate scientific hypothesis.* Unpublished doctoral dissertation, Boston University, Boston.

3

Teaching Students Who Speak African American Language
Expanding Educators' and Students' Linguistic Repertoires

Gloria Swindler Boutte
Benedict College

> (I)f school considers someone's language inadequate, they'll probably fail.
>
> Stubbs, as cited in Delpit & Dowdy, 2002, p. xvii)

Despite decades of literature on African American language (AAL)—both classic and contemporary—little information has filtered into the instructional practices in schools and universities (Hollie, 2001). Indeed, many AAL speakers and their teachers do not recognize that it has a distinctively different set of rules than Standard English (SE). This chapter provides definitions of AAL derived from more than four decades of linguistic, educational, and anthropological literature. This knowledge base on AAL, which is typically not addressed in teacher preparation programs and professional development efforts, will be presented.

Using Paulo Freire's "Dimensions of Oppression" as a conceptual framework, this chapter relates cultural invasion (one dimension of oppression) to commonly perceived notions about AAL. These perceptions are commonly inaccurate, negative, uninformed, and incomplete. A brief summary of some of the features of AAL from sociolinguistic literature is also provided. A preliminary caveat is offered because the body of literature on AAL is quite complex, extensive, and sometimes contradictory (Baugh, 1999). Therefore, this chapter provides only a cursory overview of the literature on AAL. Educators desiring additional information should consult works of interest cited in the reference list.

In this chapter, consideration is given to the pervasive misunderstandings about AAL. Finally, this chapter includes educational implications for teacher educators, prospective and in-service teachers, speakers of AAL, and speakers of SE. An overview of recommended strategies that have been shown to be particularly successful for developing SE proficiency (without denigrating or eradicating AAL) is presented. The importance of viewing SE and AAL as coequal language systems is a key premise of this chapter.

African American Language

Also referred to as "Black English," "African American English," "Black English vernacular," "African American vernacular English," "Ebonics," and a host of other names (Baugh, 1999; Lindfors, 1987; Nieto, 1996; Perry & Delpit, 1998; Smitherman, 1985, 1997; Wolfram, 1969, 1991; Wolfram & Christian, 1989), AAL refers to "the language system characteristically spoken in the African American community" (Nieto, 1996, p. 389). The term "African American Language" acknowledges the relationship to West African languages (Nieto, 1996; Smith, 1998) and is used to emphasize that it is a complete language system and to counter notions that AAL is substandard and nonsubstantive. While "dialect" is perfectly respectable among linguists, it is almost always used in a pejorative sense (Smitherman, 2001). As noted by Rickford (1998), the decision to classify a variety as a dialect versus a language is typically made more on social and political grounds than on linguistic grounds. Rickford notes that many subjective factors inform the terminology decision. Although we recognize AAL as a variety of English, we use the term AAL to emphasize that it is the most distinct "dialect" in the United States (Rickford, 1998; Smitherman, 2001).

The Linguistic Society of America (1997), the largest linguistic society in the world, affirmed and substantiated that AAL is *legitimate, rule-based, and systematic*. Additionally, it is the primary language of most (approximately 80% of) African American students (Linguistic Society of America, 1997; Perry & Delpit, 1998). The Linguistic Society of America resolved that speakers of AAL and other language varieties "can be aided in learning the standard (English) variety by pedagogical approaches which recognize the legitimacy of the other varieties of a language" (no pagination).

Features of AAL should not be confused with slang or writing errors stemming from insufficient experience with literacy, grammar, and spelling. Instead, AAL is derived from historical phonological, syntactic, semantic, and pragmatic rules that have been and are currently reinforced in African American communities (Smitherman, 1985). Preservice and in-service teachers (regardless of ethnicity, variations in language, and the like) should understand the historical origins and linguistic validity of AAL.

Sociohistorical and Sociopolitical Issues

"In the study of language in school, pupils were made to scoff at the Negro dialect as some peculiar possession of the Negro which they should despise, rather than directed to study the background of this language as a broken-down African tongue—in short to understand their own linguistic history."

Carter Godwin Woodson (1990, p. 19)
The Miseducation of the Negro

Perceptions of AAL or any other language often have more to do with larger sociopolitical beliefs about the group speaking the language than with the actual language itself. As a group, African Americans continue to be marginalized in the United States. In order to fully comprehend why AAL is often viewed negatively requires at least a rudimentary understanding of how oppression occurs and maintains itself. Viewing AAL from a larger framework of oppression helps demonstrate how and why African Americans also may not understand their own linguistic history, as the quote by Carter G. Woodson aptly notes. Learning to respect AAL and other aspects of Black culture in general requires the deconstruction of the dominant ideology about Black intellectual inferiority (Hale, 2001; Perry, Steele, & Hilliard, 2003).

One framework for understanding how AAL came to be regarded as inferior is Paulo Freire's "Dimensions of Oppression." For decades, Freire's work emphasized methods for teaching students from oppressed groups (Freire, 1999, 1973/1998, 1985). According to Freire, oppression of all types (e.g., gender, class, religion) have four dimensions that remain constant: 1) conquest, 2) divide and conquer, 3) manipulation, and 4) cultural invasion. Because oppressive structures exist in schools (e.g., instructional methods, curricula), even well-intentioned educators can unknowingly contribute to oppression.

Conquest　In order to conquer a group of people, conquerors present themselves as "authorities" and "prototypes." In this process, the oppressed must be silenced and controlled in as many arenas as possible (e.g., economically, culturally, educationally). For example, historically, when the Europeans "colonized" parts of Africa, schooling and religion fell under the jurisdiction of the Europeans and information was presented from a European, rather than African, perspective.

Relating the concept of conquest to contemporary education, methods that silence the worldviews of certain groups are oppressive and part of the colonization process. The role of language is central to teaching and learning. Each individual has the right to, as Freire (1999) puts it, "say his or her own words, to name the world" (p. 15). "In a democracy, people should be educated to tell their stories, to make their own voices heard, and to act together to defend and expand their rights" (Featherstone, 1995, p. 14). In order to become liberated and to participate in the transformation of society toward new possibilities, people must have a voice in the process (Freire, 1999; Greene, 1995).

Some students come to school with worldviews that are more synchronized with what is valued and considered appropriate in American society. Hence, their cultural tools are more closely represented in textbooks and assessments and they tend to fare well (Boutte, 1999; Gallard, 1993). On the other hand, students whose cultural orientations are not synchronized with schools may not fare well or may have to disassociate themselves from their cultural identities in order to succeed (Boutte, 2002; Fordham, 1988, 1996).

In the case of AAL, little attempt is made to understand the histories or associated sociopolitical issues (Perry & Delpit, 1998; Walsh, as cited in Tobin, 1993). Myths about the intellectual capabilities of African Americans are still prevalent (Perry et al., 2003). Hence, many educators do not consult the voluminous knowledge base on AAL because AAL is viewed as an aberration of SE that must be eradicated.

The evolutionary ranking of one language system as superior or inferior to another causes divisions. Hence, the language deemed at the top—preferential forms of English—reigns as the only one that is legitimate. Such inaccurate distinctions not only separate speakers of AAL from SE speakers (or English speakers from speakers of other languages) but also create divisions between the homes, families, and communities of many AAL speakers from schools.

Divide and Conquer   When oppressed groups are divided by ethnicities, language, religion, skin color, or socioeconomic status, disharmony exists within and between groups. Hence, focus is centered on intercultural and intracultural disagreements and the reigning power structure is not challenged.

Manipulation   Central to Freire's pedagogy of the oppressed is the vision of liberated humans who are capable of questioning and critically thinking about information (Freire, 1985). Historically, Eurocentric information has been presented as official stories to impose the will of the dominant culture (Morrison, 1997). Information has also been intentionally manipulated and presented inaccurately.

A recent but classic case of manipulation occurred during the 1997 Oakland Ebonics debate. The media and powers that be totally misconstrued the intent of the Oakland School Board and put forth erroneous information indicating that the Oakland Schools were planning to *teach* "Ebonics." Actually, the Oakland schools were simply using children's home language, AAL (i.e., Ebonics) as a bridge to teach SE. (Obviously, no one would have to teach AAL speakers "Ebonics" because they were already proficient in it.) Nevertheless, the negative publicity successfully undermined their efforts, which included directing resources to support programs.

Intentionally or not, schools have done an excellent job of teaching Americans not to critically question authority (a key part of manipulation). Hence, the media's perspective was rarely questioned and was accepted as legitimate and official knowledge. Thereby, the integrity and reputation of the Oakland programs were severely undermined. As long as information in schools is presented from a primarily Eurocentric perspective and not questioned, other worldviews will be considered illegitimate (Boutte, 1999). Likewise, acknowledgement of AAL and use of strategies to teach AAL speakers will continue to be on the periphery—if at all.

Cultural Invasion

"They saw themselves as others had seen them. They had been formed by the images made of them by those who had the deepest necessity to despise them."

James Baldwin (1983)

Cultural invasion occurs when marginalized groups internalize the negative messages that their oppressors have about them. For cultural invasion to succeed, those who are invaded must become convinced of their intrinsic inferiority (Freire, 1999). Historically and currently, this influence has been done overtly and covertly via books, curricula, media, legal decisions, and the like. In the early 1900s, studies on language and culture routinely classified non-European cultures as "under-developed," "primitive," or inherently inferior in comparison to Western civilizations (Wolfram & Fasold, 1974). In the United States, this ideology has been reinforced legally through laws designating African Americans as inferior and denying them the same rights as Whites. Vestiges of the inferiority ideology are factors in the present disproportionate placement of African Americans in special education classes, invisibility of Africans and African Americans in curricula and the media, and a host of other examples that contribute to the belief that African Americans are inferior (Hale, 2001; Perry et al., 2003).

Although prevailing beliefs about the inferiority of Blacks historically and presently are incorrect, many people (African Americans and others) have internalized these pervasive messages. In other words, the inherent strengths of Black culture (such as AAL, with its rich historical legacy) have come to be viewed as liabilities by many people, including African Americans.

Knowledge Base on AAL

Dillard (1972) estimated that 80% of African Americans spoke only African American English, another 10% to 14% were bidialectal, and the remainder spoke only SE. Recent estimates show that these percentages have changed little since then. AAL is the primary language used by 80% to 90% of African American children in their homes and communities (Banks & Banks, 1997; Baugh, 1999; Hoover, 1998b; LeMoine, 1999; Smitherman, 1997).

Despite the presence of AAL throughout the United States, many Americans have a highly distorted perception of the language system (Banks & Banks, 1997). Much of what the nation understands as AAL (Ebonics) is a result of distorted and stereotypic characteristics displayed on television and in movies. These stereotypes converge with listeners' attitudes about the social class and educational levels of communities with heavy AAL use and obscure the true task before educators of AAL speakers.

Although AAL is a logically structured, rule-based system (comparable linguistically to other language systems), educators frequently mistakenly attribute discrepancies between AAL and SE, coupled with educators' limited linguistic and historical knowledge about AAL, to poor school performance and lack of success for African American students in the United States (Hoover, 1985, 1998a, 1998b; Labov, 1972, 1999; Perry & Delpit, 1998; Smitherman, 1985, 1997). These misconceptions emerge from a lack of understanding that AAL is a logically structured, rule-based linguistic system comparable to any other language.

A fundamental role of American schools is to teach the reading and writing of SE. Although students are required to complete 12 years of language arts and English to ensure SE proficiency, schools have generally been unsuccessful with African American students in this important endeavor (Baugh, 1999; Delpit, 1995). Much of the literature reveals that African American students are *capable* of becoming proficient in SE and being successful in school and society; however, conventional instructional methods have been ineffective for a significant number of African Americans (Rickford, 1999). The need for alternative instructional methods and changes in attitudes about AAL is evident.

As Hollie (2001) aptly notes

> One would really think that after the Oakland Ebonics controversy of 1997 and beyond, the literacy community would be seriously interested in, or at least curious about, the possibility of an alternative to traditional English/language arts teaching that inherently attempts to eradicate the African American Language that most African American students across the nation bring to class every day. *Still many African American students will ... be discreetly taught in most cases, and explicitly told in others, that the language of their forefathers, their families, and their communities is bad language, street language, the speech of the ignorant and/ or undereducated* {emphasis added}. (p. 54)

The educational statistics of limited SE-proficient African American students are extremely disconsolate (LeMoine, 1999). African American

students who are not proficient in SE are disproportionately overrepresented in special education classes, on the caseloads of language-speech
pathologists, and in the ever-enlarging pool of middle-school dropouts
(Baugh, 1999; Boutte, 1999; Delpit, 1995; LeMoine, 1999).

A dominant view among educators is that differences between AAL
and SE are major obstacles to educational achievement of Black students
(Baugh, 1999). However, it should be noted that these results are not due
to linguistic inadequacies in AAL and are commonly influenced by economic and motivational factors among students, instructional methods,
and teacher attitudes. Indeed, some African American students view
the adoption of SE as an abandonment of Black culture and, thus, are
not motivated to learn SE (Baugh, 1999; Ogbu, 1994).

Patterns of Language Spoken By African Americans and Corresponding Perceptions

Like those of other cultural and racial groups, the speech patterns of
African Americans are not monolithic. All normally developing children acquire language that is spoken in their home environment without
the aid of formal instruction (Baugh, 1999; Chomsky, 1965). Therefore,
most African Americans speak AAL, SE, or a combination of both,
depending on the dominant style used in the home. Literature on African American students typically reveals three language patterns.

The first pattern is evidenced by speakers who resist (consciously
or unconsciously) acculturation attempts by schools and continue to
operate in the African American style regardless of the school setting. Phillips (1994) noted that these children often experience difficulty in the classroom because they may be regarded as "uneducable"
since their language is in direct contrast to "school language."

A second pattern occurs when children capitulate to the school
demands and completely abandon the African American communication style in all settings. Schools typically regard these
students as "successful" because they use SE. However, they may
encounter anxiety in their communities because of discrepancies
between their home and school language (Fordham, 1996; Phillips, 1994; Tatum, 1997).

A third pattern is seen in bidialectal children, who operate in both
styles, each in the appropriate setting. Although these styles are over-
simplified and generalized in their description here, Phillips (1994)

concluded that the third pattern appears to be adaptive within the socio-political context in this society. This pattern permits children to move through the two contexts of school and family-community. Phillips suggests that educators support this pattern because it empowers children by helping them become proficient in both communication styles. Solomon and Winsboro's (1993) and Heath's (1992) work echo Phillips' analysis regarding the importance of knowing when to use each language system (code-switch). Code-switching is defined as "the use of two or more linguistic varieties" (Scotton & Ury, 1977, p. 7). Solomon and Winsboro noted that some African American children code-switch more than others. Specifically, children from middle- and upper-income homes tend to code-switch more than children from low-income homes. Apparently, exposure to SE also affects the frequency. Additionally, age seems to play a role in code-switching. Older children are more likely to code-switch than younger ones are. Code-switching is also more likely to occur in the presence of White audiences.

Generally, SE speakers are viewed as more likeable and more competent than their AAL-speaking counterparts. Doss and Gross' (1994) study found that even African American college students perceived SE speakers to be more likeable than those who either spoke AAL or those who routinely code-switched and used both SE and AAL. Koch, Gross, and Kolts (2001) confirmed that African American college students view SE more favorably than AAL. Students rated SE speakers higher on sociointellectual status and quality of voice. Lovett and Joneka's (1997) study concurred with others and found that AAL speakers were viewed as less competent than those who speak SE. In general, the literature convincingly shows that AAL is often considered substandard and is not viewed as a language system that is equal to SE. Overcoming negative perceptions of AAL is a major challenge for teacher educators and teachers. Both students and educators need to familiarize themselves with key features of AAL in order to counter the culturally invasive messages.

Features of African American Language

Although different variations of AAL exist (i.e., Creole, Gullah), the language has common underlying rules and patterns across geographic regions in the United States. Additionally, linguistic patterns among some people in the African diaspora who speak English are similar to those of AAL speakers in the United States (Bailey, 1965; Baugh, 1980; Holm, 1984; Smitherman, 1985, 2001; Turner, 1949). In the mid-90s, when a delegation from Sierra Leone visited St. Helena, South Carolina, where Gullah (an AAL variety) is spoken, speech patterns were indistinguishable between the two groups (Riggs, 1995). The existence of common patterns among AAL speakers in various regions of the United States and in the African diaspora counters assertions that features of AAL are simple SE errors. A parallel can be made to Jean Piaget's theory of cognitive development. Piaget's theory was developed based on his observations that children at various stages made the same type of "errors" (e.g., four-year-olds consistently made errors in conservation tasks). Piaget concluded that the "errors" were indeed developmental *patterns* governed by underlying cognitive structures. Likewise, AAL is a well-ordered, complete system with rules for forming sounds, words, sentences, and nonverbal elements. Common examples of phonology, syntax, semantics, and pragmatics are presented in the subsequent section. The samples are not intended to be exhaustive. Additionally, readers should consult referenced literature in order to understand the complexity and scope of AAL.

Phonology

Phonology refers to the sound system of a language. Like other languages, AAL has common sound patterns. Many of the phonological rules are derived from West African languages (LeMoine, 1999; Smitherman, 1985, 2001). A few sample features are listed in Table 3.1. AAL examples are presented first and then contrasted with SE.

TABLE 3.1 Phonological Features of AAL and SE

Features/Rules	AAL	SE
Substitution of the "th" phoneme	demwif, wit, wid	themwith
Different stress patterns	po'lice	po lice'
No distinction between words that sound alike	finecoalmass	fine/findcold/coalmask/mass
Consonant blends are often substituted or deleted	axe	ask

Sources: Smitherman, 1985; Wolfram & Fasold, 1974.

Syntax

Syntax refers to the rules for combining words into acceptable phrases, clauses, and sentences. Examples contrasting syntactic structures in AAL and SE are shown in Table 3.2.

Semantics

Semantics refers to the meaning of words and word relationships in messages. Because of the rules guiding the semantic feature of AAL, new words are continuously generated (Smitherman, 1994). The regenerative semantic feature of AAL is probably the source of the misconception that AAL is slang. While slang exists in *any* language system, underlying rules for AAL include continuous suspension of literal definitions and use of cultural inversion. Historically, African Americans needed to speak in codes that others could not understand. For example, many spirituals, folktales, and quilts contained symbolism and messages that were purposely disguised so that White slave owners could not detect them. Bell Hooks (1994) comments on this "protective" semantic phenomenon (linguistic guerrilla warfare):

> To heal the splitting of mind and body, we marginalized and oppressed people attempt to recover ourselves and our experiences in language. We seek to make a place for intimacy. Unable to find such place in standard English.... When I need to say words that do more than simply mirror or address the dominant reality, I speak black vernacular. There, in that location, we make English do what we want it to do. We take the oppressor's language and turn it against itself. We make our words a counter hegemonic speech, liberating ourselves in language. (p. 175)

Because of the constant generation of new words, there are generational differences in the use of new terminology in AAL, and older generations are unable to decipher the meanings used by youth. Hence, the intent to cloak the meaning of the word is achieved. Again, this serves a purpose. Some semantic examples are presented here (Smitherman, 1985, 1994, 1998; Wolfram & Fasold, 1974):

- Frequent use of metaphors—lyrics, poems, folktales, ministers, orators. Consider Martin Luther King's "I have a dream" speech or Maya Angelou's poem "Still I Rise."

TABLE 3.2 Examples of AAL Syntax

Features/Rules	AAL	SE
Make it simple (e.g., delete linking verbs)	You a pretty girl.	You are a pretty girl.
Two or more negatives are allowed	You don't have no shoes.	You don't have any shoes.
Use of the habitual "be" to connote perpetual emphases	He be hittin/me.	He is always hitting me. Note: There is no direct literal SE interpretation for the habitual be.
Regularize when possible and maintain same form	I is We is You is You is He, She, or It is They is. Note the verb remains the same throughout (regularization)	I am We are You are You are He, She, or It is They are. Note the verb changes—is irregular
	I swim We swim You swim You swim He, She, or It swim They swim	I swim We swim You swim You swim He, She, or It swims They swim. Note the verb change in 3rd person singular
	His/Hisself Their/Theirselves	His/Himself Their/Themselves
	five cent Note the plural marker is the number itself (more than one = plural)	five cents Note there are two plural markers: the number "five" and the "s" on "cents"
	John chair. Note that the possessor (John) serves to indicate possession	John's chair. Note two possessive markers (name of possessor— John and apostrophe "s")
	I look out the window. Note: typically will not hear or see the "ed" in writing or orally. However, sometimes the "ed" is overemphasized (hypercorrection) and the oral pronunciation becomes "look-D" (Smitherman, 1985)	I looked out the window
Topicalization	That teacher she mean.	The teacher is mean.

Sources: Smitherman, 1985, 1998; Wolfram & Fasold, 1974.

- Cultural invasion—the meaning of words that may have been intended to be inflammatory are reversed to remove the impact (e.g., dog/dawg; nigger/nigger). While the word "nigga" is used as a term of endearment among some (e.g., contemporary song lyrics) and viewed as obscene and offensive to others, it illustrates the concept of cultural inversion.
- Tonal semantics—changing the meaning of a word by varying the tone (adding more or less emphasis), rhythm, and vocal inflection. For example, "Girl, you *wearing* that hat" means that the hat looks extremely good on her.

Pragmatics

AAL has two dimensions: language and style (Smitherman, 1985, 1998). *Pragmatics* refers to the rules for using the language in social contexts. Many describe it as the style or spirit of the language (Rickford & Rickford, 2000). Anyone who has communicated cross-culturally understands that *how* something is said is as important as *what* is being said. The stylistic beauty of AAL is best appreciated by those who are linguistically informed (Smitherman, 1985). In general, the rules reflect characteristics of Black culture (Hale-Benson, 1986; Hilliard, 1992)—involve the audience or listener, be engaging and animated, and use nonverbals. As with other cultural communication styles, certain ways of communicating are discourteous. For example, in the case of AAL, it is discourteous for the listener not to give a response or feedback to the speaker (Smitherman, 1985). Here are a few pragmatic examples:

- Signification/Joanin'/The Dozens refers to the verbal art of insult in which a speaker humorously puts down and talks about the listener. The ultimate insult is to talk about the listener's "mama." To be proficient, quick-wittedness is required.
- Conarration and overlapping is allowed in conversations. That is, more than one speaker can speak at a time. (In schools, AAL speakers are often disciplined for this stylistic form of discourse.)
- Different ways of questioning and telling a story are used. Stories tend to be episodic (focusing on episodes) rather than topic-centered (Delpit, 1998). Heath (1992) reports that AAL speakers ask more open-ended versus closed-ended, school type questions (e.g., "What is that like?" versus "What color is the sky?").

- Direct prevail over indirect commands (e.g., "Sit down now!" versus "Can you sit down now?") (Delpit, 1995)
- Circular is more common than linear conversation interrelating several points
- Nonverbals (e.g., giving "five," sucking teeth, rolling eyes, hands on hips, stomping)
- Call and response—involving the audience in an African tradition
- Dramatic repetition
- Frequent use of metaphors and proverbs
- Cultural familiarity (e.g., "dawg," "brotha," "sista")
- Tonal semantics to engage the listener.

Linguistic Parallels Between AAL and Other Languages

Examining parallels between AAL and other languages further illustrates the point that AAL is based on a linguistic rule system (see Table 3.3). Curiously, AAL tends to be regarded as substandard, whereas other languages applying the same linguistic rules are not. In sum, in order to effectively teach speakers of AAL, both educators and speakers first need to understand the legitimacy and history of AAL. The next section addresses educational implications.

Educational Implications

While recognizing that a standard (mainstream) form of English (SE) exists and that students need to become proficient in SE for success in school and society (Delpit, 1995; Delpit & Dowdy, 2002), the world is richer with the presence of a variety of languages. The goal of school, then, should not be to eradicate a child's first language but to add other language systems to his or her repertoires.

Viewing SE as the prototype and AAL on the opposite end of the continuum is culturally invasive. AAL is a coequal language system, albeit not the language of mainstream society (Delpit & Dowdy, 2002; Perry & Delpit, 1998). Teachers and students from all ethnic groups would benefit from ongoing counter-narratives that reject dominant notions about AAL as inferior and ahistorical (Perry & Delpit, 1998; Perry et al., 2003; Smitherman, 1985). In sum, AAL must be recognized as a legitimate, rule-governed system; embraced in classrooms; and used as a bridge for SE proficiency.

TABLE 3.3   Linguistic Parallels of AAL and Other Languages

Linguistic Feature	Standard English Example	AAL Example	Other Languages
Syntax—double negation	"I don't have a hat." Two negatives are not permitted.	"I **don't** have **no** hat." Two or more negatives are permitted (negatives are bolded).	French "Je **n'**ai **pas** un chapeau." Two negatives are required. (negatives are bolded).
Syntax—using an "s" to designate plural nouns	"That costs five dollars." Two plural markers	**"That costs five dollar."[1] One plural marker. The number serves to indicate plurality.**	Chinese (speaking English) "That costs five dollar." One plural marker. The number serves to indicate plurality.
Phonology	This is my hat.	Dis is my hat. I am going wif you. Substitution of "th" phoneme with "d."	French-speaking Zis is my hat. I am going wiz you. Substitution of "th" phoneme with "z." Another common substitution can be seen in many East Indian speakers who substitute the "w" sound with "v." Example: "Vife" for "Wife."

[1] Another variation that would typically be noted in AAL would be subject-verb disagreement (regularization). For the purpose of example, only one feature is highlighted.

A common belief is that many speakers of AAL could speak "properly" if only they put forth sufficient effort (Baugh, 1999). Because teaching practices are not always linguistically informed, language can become a primary source of inequality surrounding the lives of students who come to school labeled with a speech variety that is stigmatized in society (Banks & Banks, 1997). The goal of education, however, should be to *add to* what is already present in the lives of students. Since cognitive repertoires are built on prior knowledge, educators must validate and affirm the students' home language if proficiency in SE is to be obtained (Genishi, Dyson, & Fassler, 1994; LeMoine, 1999). John Rickford, professor of linguistics at Stanford

University, and his son emphasized the importance of validating AAL. Quoting Nobel and Pulitzer Prize winner Toni Morrison, Rickford and Rickford (2000) assert that, "The worst of all possible thing that could happen would be [for Blacks] to lose that [their] language" (p. 4). Indeed, educators should help AAL speakers learn to negotiate both AAL and SE, thus gaining access to wider opportunities while honoring the history and traditions of their families and communities.

Educators wishing to help AAL speakers develop SE proficiency need to enhance their linguistic knowledge and understanding of AAL. In addition to reading selections from the reference list, the video "American Tongues," which examines American language varieties and their social implications, is recommended (Alvarez & Kolker, 1987). Educators should also inquire into their own language histories to illuminate their beliefs about different language varieties. Additionally, the affective aspect of language must be acknowledged. Like any new concept, students will not likely learn SE if they are not motivated or if they feel anxious (LeMoine, 1999).

Strategies for teaching AAL speakers SE proficiency should focus on both oral and written language. Young children may spend more time with oral activities (such as role-playing different scenarios). A large collection of literature written in AAL and SE is important to share with students. Appropriate lyrics from songs can also be used to translate AAL to SE or vice versa.

Although not promoting a specific program, *English for Your Success* (LeMoine, 1999) is a straightforward guide and resource with strategies and activities that can be used in prekindergarten through eighth grade classes. It contains curriculum guides for each grade level and videos of actual classrooms. It is not a tightly scripted program and is more of a philosophy that can be adapted for a variety of settings. In order to help AAL speakers learn to translate SE, numerous and ongoing written and oral activities are used (see Table 3.4).

Presenting SE and AAL as coequal language systems requires relevant student engagement with both AAL and SE. Reframing AAL as a legitimate language system implies that the goal is not to *correct* AAL speakers because they are following the *correct* rules for *AAL*. Rather than correcting AAL, it is actually being *translated* and students' linguistic repertoires are being expanded so that they have more than one way to communicate and so that they can learn the "language of power," SE (Delpit, 1995). Activities

TABLE 3.4   "English For Your Success" Activities

Written	Oral	Oral/Written
Report writing	Class discussions	Story/event retell
Logs	Formal speeches	Audiovisual presentations
Journal writing	Dramatizing	Class and individual projects
Creative writing	Oral reports	
Personal biographies	Role playing	
Letter writing	Interviewing	
Research reports	Musical interpretation	
	Dialogue	
	Oral reading	
	Debating	
	Sharing opinions	

Source: Lemoine (1999).

should be bidirectional (translation of AAL to SE and SE to AAL). Students should be led to understand that there are appropriate times for each language system.

A key strategy recommended is *contrastive analysis.* Contrastive analysis involves comparing and contrasting of the linguistic structures of two languages or language systems (see Tables 3.5 to 3.7). It allows AAL speakers to engage in metalinguistic analysis of their own language and can be done orally and in writing. Research has demonstrated that contrastive analysis resulted in 59.3% fewer AAL features in writing, as opposed to 8.5% fewer AAL features when traditional methods were used (Lindblom, 2005). Other benefits of contrastive analysis include:

- increased ability to recognize differences between AAL and SE
- more-proficient student editing of their own work for differences, vocabulary, and syntax
- greater facility in the use of SE structure in both oral and written forms
- enhanced appreciation and acceptance of their home language (Academic English Mastery Instructional Support Reference Binder, n.d.)

AAL has primarily operated as an oral language. Readers who are unfamiliar with AAL may initially find some words difficult to pronounce and written words may not be readily recognizable. Many books, songs, and other information are currently written in AAL as well as audio recordings of books.

TABLE 3.5   Sample Oral Contrastive Analyses

The following activities are small-group oral activities. Students should spend time examining prerecorded television and radio clips of the desired SE format. Additionally, students must be familiar with features of AAL and SE.

Students are divided into small groups to plan a 3- to 5-minute presentation illustrating scenarios like the ones below (only one at a time is recommended). In order to help students view SE and AAL as coequal language systems, each scenario must be done in both AAL and SE. Activities should be regarded as a regular assignment instead of as extra or "fun" activities. Videotaping student presentations and allowing them to identify the feature of AAL and SE is recommended.

It is important for students to compare and contrast the AAL and SE. Care should be taken to present AAL in a respectful manner versus comical or stereotypical. The scenarios can be related to topics covered in the curriculum and integrated in as needed. Additionally, the scenarios require attention to other presentation skills in addition to speaking (e.g., eye contact, posture).

1. Present a commercial selling a product. Demonstrate how the commercial might be presented on a Black radio station aimed at getting the attention of African American youth who are part of Hip Hop culture. Demonstrate how the commercial might look if it were to air on the national news on a major network.

2. Report a sports event in AAL and again in SE.

3. Serve as a witness to an accident using AAL and again using SE.

4. Give a speech intended to persuade a group of African American youths from an urban area to vote for a political candidate. Then give a speech convincing a group of African American professionals to vote for a political candidate.

Conclusion

Ideally, the discussion of AAL should fall under the broader framework of respect for differences and cultural diversity and teaching for liberation. Although this chapter provides an overview of AAL, readers who seriously want to address instructional issues surrounding AAL need to engage in further study. Collaboration with other interested colleagues will provide support for educators attempting to address the issue. In pre-K–12 schools, administrative and parental support and orientations will also facilitate the goal of validating AAL. Using AAL as a basis for developing SE proficiency will require ongoing and systematic instructional and curricular changes.

Since many aspects of African American culture are currently and have historically been viewed in a marginalized fashion, it is difficult for many educators to recognize the validity of AAL as a distinct, rule-governed language system. Because of emotionally

TABLE 3.6 Example of Linguistic Contrastive Analysis Using Language Samples from Elementary Students[1]

Students' Language Sample	Standard English Translation	Rules
Dey friends.	They are friends.	Substitution of "th" phoneme with "d." Deletion of linking verb ("are")
How you know?	How do you know?	Deletion of linking verb
'Cause dey always …	Because they always …	"th" phoneme substitution
What month come after December?	What month comes after December?	Verb agreement
August got three and July has three.	August has three and July has three. or August has three and so does July.	(This is not necessarily AAL, but it is not Standard English). Colloquial replacement of "got" with "has"
She don't look mean. (referring to Bertha character in the book that you read).	She does not (doesn't) look mean.	Verb agreement (Note: I discourage contractions in formal speech although it is not incorrect grammatically.)
Where she at?	Where is she?	Deletion of linking verb. Syntax—word order for question
Dat dog big now.	That dog is big now.	Use of "th" phoneme. Deletion of linking verb

[1]Translations are noted for the purpose of illustration only. The second and third columns would be left blank so that students can complete them.

intense, often negative, reactions to AAL, educators sometimes have difficulty engaging in academic discussions about the language system. Finding strategies for effectively teaching African American English speakers remains a challenge for many educators.

Educators will have to acknowledge that students bring their own language varieties into classrooms. Typically, people favor those that are similar to their own. Therefore, the challenge for educators is to find ways to broaden the repertoires of not only their students but also themselves. Since literacy issues are important in all content

TABLE 3.7[1]   Example of Written Contrastive Analysis Translating Both AAL and SE

Sentence	Translation	AAL/SE Rules
The candy cost 25 cent.		
When the boy doesn't get it right, he tries again.		
Look at her. She beautiful.		
My sister's bicycle is yellow.		
Bobby run everyday wit his two friends.		
She did not want the dentist to pull her tooth.		
Dat zoo has a elephant and more.		
She be grubbing.		

[1]Sentences taken from Academic English Mastery Program Grade Level Collaboratives, Los Angeles Unified School District, Los Angeles Unified School District, 333 South Beaudry Avenue, 25th Floor, Los Angeles, California 90012, (213) 241-3340.

areas, the information presented in this chapter should not be considered to only be relevant for language arts courses.

Finding ways to effectively teach African American English speakers in contexts that discourage nonconventional approaches remains a challenge. Yet, as pervasive evidence indicates, conventional methods are generally ineffective. Because of intense, often negative, reactions to AAL, it is sometimes difficult to engage in academic discussions about the language system. Since many aspects of African American culture are currently viewed and have historically been viewed in a marginalized fashion, it is difficult for many educators to recognize the validity of AAL as a distinct, rule-governed, language system.

Although this chapter provides an overview, readers who seriously want to address instructional issues surrounding AAL and literacy need to gain a thorough understanding. Additionally, adequate knowledge of AAL is needed in order for students to take it seriously and handle it with respect. Collaboration with other like-minded colleagues will provide support for educators attempting to address the issue. Administrative and parental support and orientations will also facilitate the goal of validating AAL. It is suggested that teachers start by focusing on the broader framework of respect for differences and cultural diversity. SE is only one part of what students should learn; however, it is central to all learning.

References

Academic English mastery instructional support reference binder. (n.d.) Available from Los Angeles Unified School District, 333 South Beaudry Avenue, 25th floor, Los Angeles CA 90012.

Alvarez, L., & Kolker, A. (Producers/Directors). (1989). *American tongues* [Motion picture]. Available from http://www.cnam.com/flash/index. html or The Center for New American Media (CNAM) Film Library, 22-D, Hollywood Avenue, Hohokus, NJ 07423.

Bailey, B. (1965). Toward a new perspective in Negro English dialectology. *American Speech, 40,* 171–177.

Baldwin, J. (1983). *Notes of a native son.* Boston: Beacon Press.

Banks, J. A., & Banks, C. A. M. (1997). *Multicultural education: Issues and perspectives* (3rd ed.). Boston: Allyn and Bacon.

Baugh, J. (1980). A reexamination of the Black English copula. In W. Labov (Ed.), *Locating language in space and time* (pp. 83–106). Orlando, FL: Academic Press.

Baugh, J. (1999). *Out of the mouths of slaves: African American language and educational malpractice.* Austin, TX: University of Texas Press.

Boutte, G. (1999). *Multicultural education: Raising consciousness.* Atlanta: Wadsworth.

Boutte, G. S. (2002). *Resounding voices: School experiences of people from diverse ethnic backgrounds.* Needham Heights: Allyn & Bacon.

Chomsky, N. (1965). *Aspects of a theory of syntax.* Cambridge, MA: MIT Press.

Delpit, L. (1995). *Other people's children: Cultural conflicts in the classroom.* New York: The New Press.

Delpit, L. (1998). What should teachers do? Ebonics and culturally responsive instruction. In T. Perry & L. Delpit (Eds.), *The Real Ebonics debate: Power, language, and the education of African-American children* (pp. 17–26). Boston: Beacon Press.

Delpit, L., & Dowdy, J. K. (2002). *The skin that we speak: Thoughts on language and culture in the classroom.* New York: The New Press.

Dillard, J. L. (1972). *Black English: Its history and usage in the United States.* New York: Random House.

Doss, R. C., & Gross, A. M. (1994). The effects of Black English and Standard English in the African American linguistic repertoire. *Journal of Multilingual and Multicultural Development, 13*(1/2), 157–167.

Featherstone, J. (1995). Letter to young teacher. In W. Ayers (Ed.), *To become a teacher: Making a difference in children's lives* (pp. 11–22). New York: Teachers College.

Fordham, S. (1988). Racelessness as a factor in Black students' school success: Pragmatic strategy or Pyrrhic victory? *Harvard Educational Review, 58*(1), 54–84.

Fordham, S. (1996). *Blacked out: Dilemmas of race, identity, and success at Capital High.* Chicago: The University of Chicago Press.

Freire, P. (1999). *Pedagogy of the oppressed.* New York: Continuum Publishing Group.

Freire, P. (1998). *Education for critical consciousness.* New York: Continum.

Freire, P. (1985). *The politics of education: Culture, power, and liberation.* Westport, CT: Bergin & Garvey.

Gallard, A. J. (1993). Learning science in multicultural environments. In K. Tobin (Ed.), *The practice of constructivism in science education* (pp. 171–180). Hillsdale, NJ: Lawrence Erlbaum.

Genishi, C., Dyson, A. H., & Fassler, R. (1994). Language and diversity in early childhood: Whose voices are appropriate? In B. L. Mallory & R. S. New (Eds.), *Diversity and developmentally appropriate practices: Challenges for early childhood education* (pp. 250–268). New York: Teachers College Press.

Greene, M. (1995). *Releasing the imagination: Essays and education, the arts, and social change.* San Francisco: Jossey-Bass.

Hale, J. (2001). *Learning while black: Creating educational excellence for African American children.* Baltimore: John Hopkins University Press.

Hale-Benson, J. E. (1986). *Black children: Their roots, culture, and learning styles* (Rev. ed.). Baltimore: Johns Hopkins University Press.

Heath, S. B. (1992). *Ways with words: Language, life, and work in communities and classrooms.* New York: Cambridge University Press.

Hilliard, A. G. (1992). Behavioral style, culture, and teaching, and learning. *Journal of Negro Education, 61*(3), 370 –377.

Hollie, S. (2001). Acknowledging the language of African American Students. *English Journal, 90*(4), 54–59.

Holm, J. (1984). Variability of the copula in Black English and its Creole kin. *American Speech, 59,* 291–209.

hooks, b. (1994). *Teaching to transgress: Education as the practice of freedom.* New York: Routledge.

Hoover, M. R. (1985). Ethnology of Black communications. *Journal of Black Reading/Language Education, 2,* 2–4.

Hoover, M. R. (1998a). Ebonics speakers and cultural, linguistic, and political test bias. In T. Perry & L. Delpit (Eds.), *The real Ebonics debate: Power, language, and the education of African-American children* (pp. 126–133). New York: Teachers College Press.

Hoover, M. R. (1998b). Ebonics: Myths and realities. In T. Perry & L. Delpit (Eds.), *The real Ebonics debate: Power, language, and the education of African-American children* (pp. 71–76). New York: Teachers College Press.

Koch, L. M., Gross, A. M., & Kolts, R. (2001). Attitudes toward Black English and code-switching. *Journal of Black Psychology, 27*(1), 29–43.

Labov, W. (1972). The logic of nonStandard English. In R. D. Abraham & R. C. Troike (Eds.), *Language and cultural diversity in American education*. New Jersey: Prentice Hall.

Labov, W. (1999). Foreword. Out of the mouths of slaves/African American language and educational malpractice. Austin, TX: University of Texas Press.

LeMoine, N. (1999). *English for your success*. Maywood, NJ: Peoples Publishing.

Lindblom, K. (2005). Teaching English in the world. *English Journal, 94*(3), 81.

Lindfors, J. (1987). *Children's language and learning* (2nd ed.). Englewood Cliffs, NJ: Prentice-Hall.

Linguistic Society of America. (1997). LSA resolution on the Oakland "Ebonics" issue. Retrieved February 28, 2005, from www.lsadc.org

Lovett, M., & Joneka, N. (1997). On becoming bilingual. *Journal of Black Psychology, 23*(3), 242–245.

Morrison, T. (1997). The official story. Dead man golfing. In T. Morrison & C. Brodsky Lacour (Eds.), *Birth of a Nation'hood: Gaze, script, and spectacle in the O. J. Simpson case*. New York: Pantheon.

Nieto, S. (1996). *Affirming diversity: The sociopolitical context of multicultural education* (2nd ed.). White Plains, NY: Longman.

Ogbu, J. U. (1994). Overcoming racial barriers to equal access. In J. I. Goodlad and P. Keating (Eds.), *Access to knowledge: An agenda for our nation's schools* (pp. 58–89). New York: College Entrance Examination Board.

Perry, T., & Delpit, L. (1998). *The real Ebonics debate: Power, language, and the education of African-American children*. Boston: Beacon Press.

Perry, T., Steele, C., and Hilliard, A., III. (2003). *Young, gifted, and Black: Promoting high achievement among African-American students*. Boston: Beacon Press.

Phillips, C. B. (1994). The movement of African American children through sociocultural contexts: A case of conflict resolution. In B. L. Mallory & R. S. New (Eds.), *Diversity and developmentally appropriate practices. Challenges for early childhood education* (pp. 197–204). New York: Teachers College Press.

Rickford, J. (1998). Holding on to a language of our own: An interview with linguist John Rickford. In T. Perry & L. Delpit (Eds.), *The Real Ebonics debate: Power, language, and the education of African-American children* (pp. 59–66). Boston: Beacon Press.

Rickford, J. R. (1999). Using the vernacular to teach the standard. In D. Ramirez, T. Wiley, G. deKerk, & E. Lee (Eds.), *Ebonics in the urban education debate* (pp. 1–15). Long Beach: Center for Language Minority Education and Research, California State University, Long Beach.

Rickford, J. R., & Rickford, R. J. (2000). *Spoken soul: The story of Black English*. New York: John Wiley and Sons, Inc.

Riggs, M. (Producer/Director). (1995). *Black is … Black ain't* [Motion picture]. (Available from California Newsreel, www.newsreel.org).

Scotton, C., & Ury, W. (1977). Bilingual strategies: The social functions of code-switching. *International Journal of the Sociology of Language, 13,* 5–20.

Smith, B. J. (1998). Black English: Steppin up? Look back. In T. Perry & L. Delpit (Eds.), *The Real Ebonics debate: Power, language, and the education of African-American children* (pp. 71–76). Boston: Beacon Press.

Smitherman, G. (1985). *Talkin' and testifyin: The language of Black America.* Boston: Houghton Mifflin.

Smitherman, G. (1994). *Black talk: Words and phrases from the hood to the amen corner.* Boston: Houghton Mifflin.

Smitherman, G. (1997). Black language and the education of black children: One mo once. *Black Scholar, 27*(1), 28–36.

Smitherman, G. (1998). Black English/Ebonics: What it be like? In T. Perry & L. Delpit (Eds.), *The Real Ebonics debate: Power, language, and the education of African-American children* (pp. 29–37). Boston: Beacon Press.

Smitherman, G. (2001). *Talkin that talk. Language, culture, and education in African America.* London: Routledge.

Solomon, I. D., & Winsboro, B. L. (1993). Black English in the classroom: The implication of rhetoric vs. reality. *The Negro Educational Review, XLIV (1–2),* 12–22.

Tatum, B. D. (1997). *Why are all the Black kids sitting together in the cafeteria?* New York: Basic Books.

Tobin, K. (1993). *The practice of constructivism in science education.* Hillsdale, NJ: Lawrence Erlbaum.

Turner, L. D. (1949). *Africanisms in the Gullah dialect.* Chicago: University of Chicago Press.

Wolfram, W. (1969). *A sociolinguistic description of Detroit Negro speech.* Washington, DC: Center for Applied Linguistics.

Wolfram, W. (1991). Dialects and American English. Englewood Cliffs, NJ: Prentice Hall and Center for Applied Linguistics.

Wolfram, W., & Fasold, F. (1974). *The study of social dialects in American English.* Englewood Cliffs, NJ: Prentice-Hall.

Wolfram, W. A., & Christian, D. (1989). *Dialects and education: Issues and answers.* Englewood Cliffs, NJ: Prentice Hall.

Woodson, C. G. (1990). *The miseducation of the Negro.* Trenton, NJ: Africa World Press.

4

Language and the Deaf World
Difference not Disability

Robert J. Hoffmeister
Boston University[1]

In considering the needs of culturally and linguistically diverse populations, schools must include the Deaf. In this chapter, I will present
the Deaf World as a linguistic and cultural minority that thrives as
a bilingual/bicultural group in our society (Hoffmeister, 1996a). The
focus will be on language issues in the Deaf World, the importance
of keeping the language and culture of the Deaf Community strong,
educational issues and implications for change, and finally what it
means to be Deaf and bilingual/bicultural. The information in this
chapter differs greatly from the traditional pathological view commonly presented in the literature and looks at Deaf people as they see
themselves: as a cultural and linguistic minority.

In order to see Deaf children and adults as competent bilinguals
in society, we need to redefine "success" for a linguistic and cultural
minority. It is critical to see success as more than competence in English and to explore new definitions of success for Deaf children and
adults. Traditionally Deaf education has focused on a monolingual
approach, using English (spoken, written, or signed) as *the* measure
of success. During the last several years, we have begun to see several
shifts in both thinking and programming for Deaf students. We have
started to redefine "success" for Deaf high-school graduates to include
full linguistic competence in both American Sign Language (ASL)
and English, academic abilities on grade level, social and emotional
well-being, high aspirations for one's life, pride, and general satisfac-
tion and happiness with who we are (Czubek & Greenwald, 2001).

Deaf People as a Cultural Group: A Deaf Framework

There appears to be a natural tendency in our society to compare and contrast what we know versus what we don't know, what we have versus what we don't have, what we can do versus what we cannot do, and so on. This tendency, or orientation, when applied to the Deaf World promotes a narrow and exclusive view of Deaf people and can be characterized as looking through an "ethnocentric lens" (Bahan, in press; Bahan & Hoffmeister, 1991). When viewing Deaf people through this ethnocentric lens, we are only able to see them in contrast to hearing people and thus they become characterized as "disabled." Deafness, through this lens, becomes a negative and disabling condition, a view that is in direct opposition to how Deaf people view themselves.

The Hearing Framework: Difference as Negative[2]

Often, the ethnocentric lens is applied to the Deaf World and creates a cultural view that sees difference as a negative. The term *different* has come to mean "not good" and to be different is based on a standard from the majority point of view. Therefore, any comparison to the majority standard is either positive (as good as or better than) or negative (does not have X or cannot do Y). Comparing and contrasting people in this way creates a distorted and more divisive ethnocentric lens and continues to categorize Deaf people as "disabled." Deaf people are seen as people who cannot hear (do not have X) and therefore cannot learn a spoken language, English (cannot do Y). In contrast, Deaf people see themselves as belonging to a linguistic and cultural group who identify themselves as Deaf, have a culture and rich language, and live in the world much like anyone else.

As in any culture, the majority culture provides the definitions and rules by which all people are expected to abide. In the case of Deaf people, they reside in the Hearing culture. This distinction has two meanings, depending on which side of the cultural border one lives (Hoffmeister, 2001). Much like the borders of two countries where people use two different languages and translations of linguistic terms are necessary, the translations do not always carry the same meaning. In this case, the idea of what it means to be Deaf is very different depending on which side of the Deaf-Hearing border we are on. It is interesting to note that the term "Hearing people" is difficult for hearing people to understand. In the Deaf World, the meaning is clear and universally understood to mean those who are not Deaf (Lane, Hoffmeister, & Bahan, 1996). However, in the Hearing culture, there is no definition or use of this term among the general population. In the general Hearing population, terms have been created to distinguish specific groups such as Hispanic, Asian, Caucasian, African Americans, and so on. However, those to whom the labels apply may not use these terms. For example, Alire Saenz (1997) mentions that "El Paso is 70 percent 'Hispanic' (*I hate that word*)" and explains that "It is nice knowing that 'Chicano' was the name Mexican Americans chose for themselves" (p. 69). White people tend not to use the term Chicano and may or may not know to whom it refers. In the East, there are not many Mexican Americans and most white people may not be able to differentiate between the various Spanish-speaking groups. Similarly, a number of labels have been developed on the Hearing side of the border to refer to Deaf people, "hearing impaired" being the most common and most disliked by Deaf people (Lane, 1992). Just as Alire Saenz is proud that "Chicano" is a term chosen by Mexican Americans, Deaf people are proud to be called "Deaf." To be "Deaf" is to use ASL and identify oneself as Deaf. In most countries of the world, one is considered to be a member of the Deaf World if he or she uses the natural signed language of his or her country and identifies himself or herself as Deaf.

Deaf Framework: Difference as Positive

If we are to truly understand the Deaf World, we need to look at it from the Deaf perspective, including how Deaf adults live, how they cherish their community and bilingual abilities, and the best ways to educate Deaf children. When we examine issues of culture, we need to look at the values of each community. If we look at Deaf people from their perspective, we find that Deaf Culture is based on a Seeing Culture (Hoffmeister & Bahan, 1991). This view helps us see things quite differently. Understanding the term "Seeing Culture" helps us look at Deaf Culture in a positive way. Seeing is a positive attribute, a position of strength from which to build a theory or cultural description.

Padden and Humphries (1988) have defined "culture" as a set of learned behaviors of a group of people who have: 1) their own language, 2) their own values, and 3) their own rules for behavior and traditions. It is clear that ASL or any of the other signed languages of the world, as visual languages, have been used by Deaf people since the beginning of time and have evolved based on visual processing principles similar to auditory processing principles for language. Veditz (1910), at the time president of the National Association of the Deaf (NAD)[3], called Deaf people "The people of the eye." Sign language is a natural language adapted and evolved for use by the eye.

Bahan (in press) aptly sums up why ASL is the language of seeing people:

> The essence of what may appear as simple eye gazing behavior may in fact be part of a complex multi-layered linguistic system in ASL. That is, the signer's eyes are always moving in a saccadic manner to signal various linguistic information in different layers from a single word to interactions with a large group. (p. 9)

Deaf people have developed their own rules of behavior that are different from Hearing people. Cultural norms, attitudes, and perspectives are based on a world that is visual as opposed to auditory. Deaf and hearing differences in cultural norms, attitudes, perspectives, and ways of analyzing the world are numerous. To maximize learning opportunities, teachers must acknowledge, respect, and celebrate these differences when educating Deaf children. Using a Deaf studies template or Deaf lens enables Deaf students to look at literature through their own eyes, capitalizing on their own experiences and perspectives (Czubek & Greenwald, 2005).

An intriguing and complex issue in the Deaf World involves who is and who is not considered "Deaf." This status is not attributed to those with hearing loss or audiological information per se. Instead, persons with any hearing loss who learn a signed language and identify with the Deaf World are considered "Deaf." In fact, in Deaf culture, the idea of someone becoming Deaf means not to lose one's hearing but rather to learn and use ASL (Lane et al., 1996). In other words, according to the Deaf perspective, what defines someone as being Deaf is not connected to the level of one's hearing loss. The Deaf perspective is based on the concept of *sameness.* A person who is Deaf and a member of the culture depends on the *seeing* way of life.

Values and traditions develop over time as the culture ages and grows. The native language, ASL, developed and transformed into a linguistic system and is acquired using the same mental device that allowed the development and acquisition of spoken Navajo, French, English, and Chinese Sign Language as well as all the other signed languages of the world. Once a language is acquired, the person becomes a social being in the culture that uses the language.

A seeing way of life requires face-to-face communication. This fact, in combination with technological advances, have both hindered and supported the Deaf community and affected cultural changes. On the one hand, the TTY[4], which supports the use of a telephone, and captions[5], which increase access to television or movies, may have contributed to the demise of the Deaf club (a cultural keystone of the Deaf Community). The Deaf club of the past was a central place to meet where the lack of long distance interaction was compensated for by the fact that you could always find companionship and interaction at the club. Technological advances have increased communication and interaction with the Hearing world. Access to televisions, computers, and other technologies has increased the details in the quality of life but may be restricting individual Deaf persons social interactions with other Deaf people. Deaf people no longer have to congregate in specific areas (Deaf clubs) for socialization. They can stay home and chat with friends on the computer or rent captioned movies. One of the new and most positive technological advancements is the video relay service that uses a videophone to provide "face to face" communication access for the Deaf community. The videophone will probably expand interaction among Deaf people as well as interaction between the Hearing and Deaf communities due to communication accessibility via ASL. Using videophones or video relay services[6] allows Deaf to use ASL and hearing to use voice, skipping the need to type the message in English when communicating on the phone. Many Deaf people were uncomfortable using their rudimentary knowledge of a second language to conduct business with Hearing persons via TTY and can now communicate more freely through video relay systems. The members of the Deaf World have adapted to these technological changes and continue to maintain a strong sense of community.

The Natural Language of Deaf People

There are many confusing beliefs and statements about ASL in the Hearing World and in Deaf education. Among Deaf people of the world, a signed language is their natural language because it is based on vision (a seeing language). It is the most accessible language to people with hearing loss. ASL (or any natural signed language) is *the* language that all Deaf children (regardless of the amount of hearing loss) can access through their eyes. Often in Deaf education, people believe that for those children who can access some spoken English through a hearing aid or cochlear implant, ASL is "not necessary." However, this does not make sense because it denies children a language that they have total access to in favor of a language that they cannot access 100% of the time easily, comfortably, and naturally. When we think about bilingual education and the benefits for students, this thinking becomes even more ludicrous. Why would we deny children the opportunity to be bilingual in favor of "forcing" them to be monolingual in a language to which they have limited access? The opportunity to be bilingual should be capitalized on for *every* Deaf and hard of hearing child. Acquiring a strong first language (e.g., ASL) for both social and academic purposes and learning a second language (e.g., English) for both social and academic purposes can only enhance one's cognitive, linguistic, social, emotional, and creative abilities. This is not to say that some Deaf people cannot learn a spoken language, but natural signed languages provide the greatest accessibility for everyone in terms of ease of learning, acquisition, use, comfort, and success. To reiterate, ASL has evolved like all natural languages of the world. ASL meets the requirements of efficiency and speed of production based on its seeing/visual principles, use of space, use of hands as articulators, movement, and the combination of these to form meaningful linguistic units (Lane et al., 1996).

What Is the Issue Surrounding Language and the Deaf?

People are either born or enculturated into a culture. How does being Deaf impact this process? The issue that makes Deaf children unique is that the process of language acquisition and socialization into the Deaf World is horizontal and not vertical for more than 95%

of Deaf children. Because 95% of Deaf children are born to hearing parents (DCHP) (Mitchell & Karchmer, 2004), the traditional vertical socialization process by which culture and language are passed from adults (parents) to children does not occur. Instead, Deaf children typically learn ASL and cultural norms from their Deaf peers, Deaf teachers, and dorm counselors at school. In many cases, Deaf children are not able to communicate fluently and effectively with their hearing parents or many of the hearing people in their environment and depend on peers and the Deaf community for information. In many cases, hearing parents are not provided comprehensive information on bilingual education for Deaf children, the critical emphasis on ASL as the most accessible language for their child, and the importance of early comprehensible input and consistent language and communication access in the family. Parents are often led to believe that spoken English will be acquired "some day" with a lot of hard work and practice. Unfortunately, while they are struggling to achieve this goal, the precious language acquisition clock is ticking and Deaf children are losing valuable learning opportunities. The situation with Deaf children from hearing families is unique to the Deaf World. We cannot think of any other linguistic minority in which the children do not share the language and culture of their parents. Many hearing parents *do* learn to sign and are able to effectively communicate with their Deaf children. Parent involvement is often a critical factor in a child's success and DCHP are no exception (Czubek & Greenwald, 2001, 2005).

A model for ensuring early acquisition of ASL for Deaf children of Hearing parents is critical. Including Deaf adults in the professional referral process (Hoffmeister & Shettle, 1984) and early intervention programs can result in parents and children becoming more fluent in ASL. Providing native language models in the home and at school also enhances language development. Incorporating trained Deaf adults as ASL models into the classroom ensures access to native language models, academic information, background knowledge, and incidental learning (Greenwald, Hoffmeister & Czubek, 2003; Hoffmeister, Greenwald, & Koubetis, 1987; Hoffmeister, Greenwald, Czubek, & DiPerri, 2003a, 2003b; Hoffmeister, Greenwald, Czubek, DiPerri, Cole, & Bambach, 2002).

It is imperative that medical persons, audiologists, and educators include professional Deaf adults at the policy-making tables to represent the Deaf community and needs of Deaf students in their educational environments. Collaboration between those hearing professionals who traditionally make decisions, Deaf professionals, and the Deaf Community needs to become the norm in order to provide fully accessible language models for Hearing parents and Deaf children and to establish comprehensive bilingual programming at all levels of education (from early intervention through high school).

Acquisition of a Natural Language

All children are born with the propensity to acquire language. Deaf children have the same language acquisition device (LAD) that hearing children have except that the LAD of Deaf children works on visual input rather than auditory input. All Deaf children have the capacity to learn a language naturally if they are exposed to language models that are accessible (Hoffmeister et al., 2003a). As with any child who is learning a language, a Deaf child needs interaction with competent users (Jackendof, 1994; Pinker, 1994). If Deaf children depend on seeing or vision to fully access a language, then Deaf children need to interact with a language that is based on seeing or visual principles. Deaf children of Deaf parents (DCDP) are born into families that reflect the typical nature of how language acquisition works. In most instances, DCDP are exposed to the signed language of their Deaf parents, ASL, and acquire this language following the same path as hearing children acquiring a spoken language (Newport & Meier, 1985).

In the past four decades, a tremendous amount of research has been conducted on the acquisition of ASL in DCDP (see for example, Chamberlain, Morford, & Mayberry, 2000; Hoffmeister, 1978; Hoffmeister & Wilbur, 1980; Klima & Bellugi, 1979; Newport & Meier, 1985). This research has demonstrated that a language transmission process occurs from parent to child that is natural and effortless. In addition, this process imputes the traditional passage of cultural information from parent to child. DCDP learn both the language and culture in a natural setting. DCHP are also able to learn a complete natural language, such as ASL, but require exposure to it very early from competent users.

ASL has evolved into a linguistic system that is acquired using the same mental device that supports the acquisition of Navajo, French, and English. The following properties of a signed language are necessary for a Deaf child to acquire a visual language:

1. The visual language must have recognizable units at different levels of the language:
   - phonological—the smallest unit level
   - morphological—the word level
   - syntactic—the sentence level
   - semantic—the meaning level
   - discourse—the interaction level.
2. The visual language must contain a cohesive set of rules that can be acquired.
3. The visual language must contain rules that are predictable and learnable.
4. The visual language must be used consistently and with increasing complexity by those who interact with Deaf children.

If these principles are met, Deaf children will be able to make sense out of visual input and acquire a natural language. DCDP appear to acquire ASL efficiently and effortlessly and follow a path similar to Hearing children acquiring a spoken language. DCDP arrive at school with a fully developed language, much the same as hearing children who enter school at age 5. In contrast, DCHP come to school with varying degrees of language development. Many are significantly delayed in both ASL and English (Lane et al., 1996; Moores, 2001). Schools are thus charged with a tremendous task: teach academic information while providing language instruction and support in two languages (both social and academic forms) (Hoffmeister, 2005a, 2005b).

Philosophical differences, ethnocentric lenses, and ignorance have resulted in what some people refer to as the "language war in Deaf education." Educators and many people in the medical profession have created a system in which ethnocentric transmission of information is conveyed to Hearing parents of newly identified Deaf babies. Hearing parents are often not exposed to Deaf adults and do not receive information on the impact of all the options for their Deaf child and family. They are typically not told about the natural process of linguistic and cultural transmission that can happen in families with Deaf children. Language opportunities are limited to spoken English and lipreading, which are often inaccessible to Deaf children.[7] Conflicts continue, circling back to the differences in perspective between Deaf adults (many of whom are parents themselves) and Hearing professionals within the medical, educational, and rehabilitation systems.

When Deaf Children Enter School

When Deaf children enter school, three concerns are of major import:

1. Learning a signed language (ASL)
2. Learning English as a language
3. Learning how to read English.

For the most part schooling for Deaf students has concentrated on learning how to read and write English. To date, the educational process has focused solely on the teaching of English, which is only one of the two languages Deaf children need to be successful. Again, we need to look at what it means to be successful in our society today. The view that success involves more than knowing English in written and spoken forms is critical in supporting bilingual education for Deaf students. Success involves knowing and using two languages (ASL and English); learning and developing academically, socially, and linguistically; and becoming social beings (Czubek & Greenwald, 2001)

DCHP do not have the same exposure to ASL from birth as DCDP do. This fact causes several major learning issues: First, how does a child gain fluency in ASL? Second, how do we promote social and academic competence in both ASL and English. Third, how do we educate Deaf children to ensure academic, social, and linguistic success? Again, it appears that the most significant issue for Deaf children is complete access to a natural language. Once DCHP learn ASL, they have access to information, more complex language use, and more world knowledge. A strong foundation in ASL as the L1 (first language) also provides the foundation for learning English as a second language (L2). Research has shown that significant delays in learning ASL create delays in learning English. If the delays extend to the end of or beyond the critical period, Deaf children have difficulty learning both ASL *and* English. These language delays in either ASL or English have ramifications well into adulthood (Mayberry, 1993; Mayberry & Lock, 2003; Mayberry, Lock, & Kazmi, 2002).

The language-learning process in Deaf children suggests that the natural learning of ASL functions as a first language and English is learned as a second language. This view of Deaf children as bilinguals recognizes that they must have a first language in order to fully access the second language. This means that, for the Deaf child, learning ASL is a critical variable for learning in school. Unfortunately, the current system of educating Deaf children is not structured to enhance the earliest possible learning of ASL. Instead, educators have chosen to modify the signing aspect of ASL and remove much of its structure and predictability (Hoffmeister, 1996a; Kuntze, 1998; Supalla & McKee, 2002). This process has been implemented because ASL has word order and grammatical processes that differ from those in English. This inability on behalf of hearing educators and speech and hearing professionals to see ASL as a viable language for Deaf children is summed up in the following:

> The lack of success of the purely oral method in the United States has been documented thoroughly and is supported by statistics.... Less obvious is the method of bimodalism, which changed surface behavior without changing the underlying conceptions of deaf education. By bimodalism, I mean the now widespread belief that spoken languages such as English may be signed, and that, in the signing of English, spoken English is being represented. Much of the world still accepts the notion that if hearing teachers speak a spoken language and represent that language simultaneously with some kind of signs, that it will provide a child with a natural language learning environment for that spoken language. Many current approaches depend heavily on the employment of "systems" for the signing of the spoken language. We now see signed English, signed Spanish, signed Thai, and possibly signed Swahili, built on these principles. They are used in school systems throughout the world. (Johnson, 1998, p. 10)

As previously mentioned, however, some researchers and educators do not believe that ASL can be an effective first language to support the learning of English as a second language through print (Mayer & Wells, 1996; Paul, 1998).

As a result of the misguided understanding of the impact of ASL, educational systems often use a form of signing called *signed English* (SE)[8]. This is a combination of signs (lexical items) taken from ASL, adding newly created signs for those English words that do not have a one-to-one sign (lexical) correspondence in ASL. This newly created reorganization of signed lexical items is produced in English word order, and teachers are supposed to simultaneously sign and speak to create a one-to-one sign and spoken word correspondence. This process is believed to provide a way to represent spoken English on the hands. The problem is that the signing portion is visual-spatial and the ordering of the signs is auditory-linear (following spoken English). The combination of the auditory-linear and visual-spatial works against the ability to learn a natural language for Deaf children. The visual nature of SE is seen by the Deaf child, but the spoken portion has little relevance as input to support the spoken language acquisition processes. Some educators believe that Deaf children are able to "fill in" the gaps by using either the signed or the spoken (lipreading or sound for some Deaf children) portion when errors in delivery occur (Bernstein & Finnegan, 1983).

ASL is a natural language that is learnable and has predictable linguistic properties. SE is an engineered language that has been created, making it an artificial code. This process creates conflicts in the natural acquisition of a signed language. A major issue is what happens when a Deaf child is exposed to the reorganization of ASL signs into the SE format. SE is focused on the morphemic level of English, where new signed forms are created to represent morphemes that occur in English and do not have separate signs in ASL. The past-tense marker –ed, the plural marker –s, and the determiners "the" and "a" are examples of morphemes for which signs have been created in SE. These new forms then combine with the borrowed ASL forms that are presented in linear order to create the idea of visually representing an "English sentence."

ASL sentences are presented to a child taking advantage of the visual nature of the language. That is, ASL incorporates the use of space by using parameters such as the position of the hands to each other, the orientation of the palm, the movement of the hands through space, and the location of the hands in space to represent meaning. In addition, handshapes alone or in combination with movement can be used to modify meanings depending on how they are moved in space. Unlike English, in which morphemes tend to be presented linearly and sequentially, ASL presents many morphemes simultaneously. ASL also has a great deal of sequentiality; the key linguistic point is that all linguistic levels of language cohere: morphological inflections are made via phonological ones and vice versa and syntactic relations involve morphological and phonological changes. This is the linguistic property that makes languages learnable; an artificial language is not a language and thus children cannot make linguistic predictions for learning based on what they know because the linguistic rules are not internal to the language but have been cut and pasted from another language (Mayberry, September, 28, 2005, personal communication).

When children are exposed to SE, they continue to make "errors," leaning to the more natural tendencies of a signed language. For example, when Deaf children use SE, they use ASL properties, such as the relationship between hands, directionality, and the like, to indicate grammatical function (subject, object, theme, etc.). The Deaf child, as a *seeing* child, focuses on the visual input and operates on the visual components, making visual language predictions that do not match the predictions one would expect from a spoken language like English. When the linear aspect of English is presented to the Deaf child, the predictability of the system breaks down further. The errors Deaf children make when learning SE may reflect an active attempt to infer linguistic regularities or generalizations (Hoffmeister, 1996b; Supalla & McKee, 2002). An illustration of a visual generalization, made by children acquiring both SE and ASL, is the hand shape used in the signs "park" and "garage" (see Figure 4.1). Both of these signs make use of a vertically oriented primary hand shape with two fingers and the thumb extended and a secondary flat handshape with fingers in contact and extended (Bornstein, Hamilton & Saulnier, 1981). Like many SE signs, these signs were adapted from the ASL lexicon, creating further confusion.

The similarity in form in the signs "park" (verb) and "garage" (noun) is highly relevant in ASL because the primary or moving handshape represents the "vehicle" classifier. In the ASL sign for "park," one hand forms the handshape for vehicle and locates it on top of a surface formed by the other hand, palm up. In the sign for "garage," the hand shape for vehicle is located under the surface formed by the other hand, flat palm down, effectively signaling storage of the car in an interior space.

park (verb)
LH open B palm up, tips out.
Three shape RH palm left, tips
out. Drop base of right 3 in left
palm.

garage
LH open B palm down, tips out.
Slide right 3 (palm) under left
hand.

Figure 4.1

Children exposed to SE appear to extract the visual generalization, correct for ASL but not for SE, that one of the hand shapes in
the signs "park" and "garage" refer to a vehicle. A frequent error for
Deaf SE users is to use this hand shape to refer to a car instead of
employing the SE sign, which is two hands moving together as if
steering the drivers wheel (Hoffmeister, 1996b; Allen, Greenwald, &
Hoffmeister, 2000).

SE learners tended to modify the visual parameters of the input
to make it more regular, as in the "park"/"garage" example described
above. DCHP who are not exposed to adult ASL nevertheless are able
to intuitively understand ASL components, such as classifiers, direc-
tional and locational verbs, spatial verb agreement, and gestural
indicators of complex sentence constructions (Allen et al., 2000;
Hoffmeister, Philip, Costello, & Grass, 1997a, 1997b, 1997c; Supalla
& McKee, 2002). We have also found that deaf children learning
SE intuitively categorize SE signs according to their sign parameters (handshape, movement, location), not their similarity in print
(DiPerri, 2004). That is, for SE Hearing teachers, the handshape for
the English letter "B" brings to mind signs such as "boy" and "ball."
For deaf learners of SE, the handshape for English letter "B" brings
to mind a sign such as "school," which contain the handshape B but
not the English letter B as a component (DiPerri, 2004).

Many of these studies demonstrate that the nature of language
acquisition is one of interaction and mental processing of the input.
Singleton's (1989) study of Simon confirms that Deaf children have
the language processing capability to operate on the input and make it
more efficient. However, with respect to visual modality, Deaf children
do not appear to be able to transfer generalizations available in a spoken language to identical generalizations when Deaf children try to
map the spoken language using components of the visual language.

Deaf children who are enrolled in SE programs have an additional
problem besides trying to figure out the visual nature of SE. They
are also trying to learn English as part of the reading process. Both
DCDP and DCHP are faced with this complicated learning process.
For Deaf children, English in print is also visual and the task is to
figure out how to abstract meaning from the printed text. They must
do this without initially knowing English. Hence, both groups are
learning English while learning how to read. Most English-speaking Hearing children arrive at school already knowing English.
Their job is to learn how to map English to the printed symbols on

the page. DCHP are often two language levels behind because they do not even have a primary language (ASL) and they do not know English. Typically, DCDP are only one language level behind; they have yet to learn English. However, DCDP have an advantage, similar to bilingual hearing children, in that they bring a fully formed and usable language to school. This advantage is seen in the many research studies that demonstrate that DCDP are significantly more advanced in reading and academic achievement than their DCHP peers (see Ewoldt, Israelite, & Hoffmeister [1992] for a comprehensive review).

Many Deaf children are unaware that the signed language they are using does not follow the same rules as English. They are not taught about ASL, its rules, or its grammatical structures, and therefore do not have opportunities to develop metalinguistic skills in their first language.

Language of Schooling   Finally, schools use two types of language registers: conversational/social language and academic language. For some time, we have known that children who are able to crack the code and understand the differences in both of these registers are successful in school. Those who are unable to fully comprehend and master the academic language struggle throughout their school years (Cummins, 1994; Pattison, 1982).

The school-aged Deaf child is now faced with the need to become proficient in both the conversational language and the academic language in both ASL and English. In spoken language, this principle division has been clearly discussed by numerous authors. Pattison (1982) relates this issue to literacy development in all children. To be successful, all children, regardless of hearing status, must learn the language of the street, home, or community *and* the language of school. Cummins (1991, 1994, 2003) has defined the relationship between conversational/social language and school language in his concepts of basic interpersonal communication skills (BICS) and cognitive academic language proficiency (CALP). School, or academic, language is the language we use to talk about the language or the language processes we use in school. For example, in the United States, when we talk about learning English in school, we are mainly referring to learning about categorizing nouns, verbs, and adjectives and what their "correct" usage is. In addition, we learn how to represent and map English to print. Through this process, we learn about the principles of English in writing. This involves learning how to structure and represent complex sentences, how to structure text, and so forth. In math, we learn about addition, subtraction, multiplication, and division. We learn to map names to printed symbols, similar to print but with a different layout (i.e., numerator, denominator, etc.). Then we move to word problems and learn specific sentence structures and vocabulary that relate back to math functions. The aim of school is to learn how to manipulate this school language (academic English) for the purpose of learning. Learning the academic language of school allows the child to access information about the world and to be successful in school.

Consider a DCHP who enters school with a rudimentary knowledge of SE. This Deaf child must figure out that the conversational language he or she is acquiring (with all the visual processing issues described above) needs to be linked to the language of schooling: the academic language. This must be accomplished without the teacher providing strategies linked to a spatial visual processing process but to strategies that modify a natural signed language (the changes required to use SE). These unnatural SE strategies must be linked to strategies to understand how print is organized and used to extract meaning. In reality, the Deaf child is processing the signed input (ASL lexical items) one way and the print input (English) another way. Print is also a visual process and, to date, we do not have a clear understanding of how Deaf children make sense of print in an organized strategic manner. Almost every study of print commonly referred to under the term "language" for Deaf children has been focused on the mapping of sound or spoken language principles to print (see Easterbrooks [2005] for reviews).

Complicating the issue even further, DCHP attempt to learn their first language, English, via reading. For the past 100 years, this educational process has resulted in the average DCHP learning how to read at the 3rd to 4th grade level. This means that the average Deaf child is only able to function in English at approximately the 4th grade. Since averages are reported, it has been observed that there are a great many Deaf children functioning well below average (Moores, 1990), and some estimate that 30% of Deaf high-school graduates are functionally illiterate (Vernon & Andrews, 1990).

Academic Language: Academic ASL and Academic English   The issue of conversational language involves issues of acquisition: Can we test the relationship between learning English through print and the level of knowledge of ASL? This is a clear examination of the relationship between knowledge of a first language and its influence on knowledge of a second language for Deaf children. A number of studies have demonstrated that there is a significant relationship between knowledge of ASL as a first language and the learning of English as a second language in Deaf children (Hoffmeister, 1994, 2000; Kuntze, 2004; Strong & Prinz, 1997, 2000). If this relationship is significant, we must examine the factors that affect the learning of ASL as a first language, such as the critical period in language acquisition.

The impact of the critical period in the learning of ASL has tremendous implications for schooling. The age at which a Deaf child has learned ASL significantly effects both ability in ASL and fluency level in English reading tasks when the child reaches adulthood. The earlier ASL is learned by Deaf children, the more fluent and knowledgeable about the language those children will be as adults (Boudreault & Mayberry, 2006; Mayberry & Eichen, 1991). It appears that Deaf children who are not exposed to an adult model of ASL as children suffer academic delays that last throughout life. The critical period thus impacts two significant areas of learning: the level of conversational fluency and the knowledge of English structures (Mayberry & Lock, 2003; Mayberry et al., 2002).

Another critical problem is the fluency and knowledge of ASL as a language in Hearing teachers (or any professional working with Deaf children). It is important to recognize that almost all Hearing teachers of Deaf children (except for Hearing children of Deaf adults, who are called *Codas*) are second language learners of signed languages, such as ASL. Many Hearing teachers are the only language models that a large number of Deaf children encounter. Typically, Hearing teachers are not only unaware of the structure and rules of ASL, but they are also not conversationally fluent in ASL. The issue of impoverished input from classroom language models (teachers) presents a tremendous challenge to Deaf students. Imagine a Hearing child sitting in a classroom with a teacher who does not effectively speak English. A large percentage of the student's time will be spent trying to decode the words while figuring out the message. This tedious task does not leave much time for the learning of academic information. How then do we expect Deaf students to learn ASL, English, *and* academics when the input is incomprehensible? Even though DCHP are not formally exposed to ASL, a number of studies demonstrate that Deaf children operate on the input and produce ASL-like features in their interactions (Hoffmeister, 1994, 1996b; Hoffmeister, Philip, Costello, & Grass, 1997a,b,c; Strong & Prinz, 1997; Supalla & McKee, 2002). This suggests that Deaf children reanalyze input and internalize rules based on that input. If these children's language models are inadequate, what kind of rules can these young Deaf children be producing? This question is only in the initial stages of investigation.

If Deaf children internalize and reformulate input into ASL-like features, it is important to know how this reformulation process might support the learning of a complete language. A recent series of research studies has begun to examine the impact of level of fluency in ASL and the resulting level of knowledge about English. A number of research studies have investigated the structures of ASL that have particular impact on the learning of English in Deaf children (Brendel, Hoffmeister, & Fish, 2005; Fish, Hoffmeister, & Thrasher, 2005; Hoffmeister, 2000; Kuntze, 2004; Padden & Ramsey, 2000; Mayberry, 1993; Mayberry & Lock, 2003; Mayberry et al., 2002).This research focused on the academic language knowledge in Deaf children and suggests that there are some critical variables, including extent of vocabulary knowledge, ability to fluently use fingerspelling processes, and the extent of knowledge about the sentence structures of ASL.

The level and extent of vocabulary knowledge in ASL has a direct relationship to the level and extent of vocabulary in English (Fish, Hoffmeister, & Thrasher, 2005). Deaf children who are capable of higher-level synonym and antonym knowledge have better skills in reading (Hoffmeister, 1994, 2000). Deaf adults who had better knowledge of sentence structure in ASL were also more knowledgeable about sentence structure in English (Mayberry et al., 2002) In addition, the receptive and expressive ability to fingerspell, not necessarily in the sense of recognizing every letter but in the understanding of fingerspelling's overall structure, is related to scores on English tasks. The recognition of fingerspelled lexical items following the rules of ASL was found to be particularly important when related to academic success in Deaf children (Padden & Ramsey, 1998). Essentially, the better academic knowledge a Deaf child has of ASL, the better the Deaf child is able to handle higher levels of English (Chamberlain & Mayberry, 2000; Hoffmeister, 1994, 1996b; Hoffmeister, deVilliers, Engen, & Topol, 1997; Hoffmeister, Philip, Costello, & Grass, 1997a,b,c; Strong & Prinz, 1997, 2000; Singleton & Supalla, 1998).

Conclusion

Historically, a number of studies support the premise that Deaf children who are exposed to ASL adult models in their everyday lives acquire conversational skills in this language naturally and easily. The critical period research underlies the need to have the exposure occur very early in the Deaf child's life. The earlier the exposure to ASL, the better the child is able to acquire the language in all its varying levels of complexity. This in turn supports the learning of English as a second language for Deaf children. The research in this area is just beginning to provide the evidence for the early exposure to ASL and the need for Deaf children to be taught about ASL as an academic subject, much the way we teach about English in Hearing schools.

Provided with this new research, the future for the Deaf child is filled with promise and greater expectations. We all know that the average Deaf person grows up into a solid citizen; we now know that with the approach of ASL as a first language and English as a second language, the average Deaf person will have the tools to succeed at even higher levels.

Successful education mandates the teaching of ASL to all Deaf students regardless of specific hearing loss and use of hearing aids and cochlear implants. In many cases, professionals ignore or oppose the use of ASL for students who have some residual hearing and opt for English-only classrooms. This view not only perpetuates the ethnocentric lens, it ignores the positive outcomes of bilingual/bicultural education for children. The current rage of teaching Hearing babies ASL to encourage early language acquisition, cognitive development, and enhancement and socialization is ironic when educators deny this same visual language to Deaf babies. Research on bilingual hearing children has shown us repeatedly that learning two (or more) languages has positive outcomes and does not hinder the learning of a second (or third or fourth) language (Greenwald & Czubek, 2004; Hoffmeister, 2000; Kuntze, 1998; Lane et al., 1996).

The proposition for Deaf children to grow up bilingually/biculturally and be educated throughout their school years in both ASL and English is paramount. The goal is to provide language instruction in ASL and English on a daily basis to ensure proficiency in both languages. A strong L1 foundation is crucial for both social and academic language purposes. It is not enough for children to converse socially in ASL; they must also learn and use academic ASL.

The same is true for the development of both social and academic English (Greenwald & Czubek, 2004; Hoffmeister, 2000).

Finally, teacher preparation programs need to incorporate the information that has been generated in the last couple of decades regarding ASL, including how it is used by Deaf adults and what impact this would have on classroom instruction. Clearly, teacher preparation programs need to clarify the distinction between ASL and the SE systems, including the advantages and disadvantages of each. ASL as a second language needs to be learned by all teachers of Deaf children so that they can obtain a much more foundational understanding of ASL and its relationship to SE. Teachers need to become proficient in ASL, hence standards need to be developed and levels of language proficiency need to be determined prior to teachers entering classrooms with Deaf children. Teacher preparation programs need to provide more information regarding the structure of ASL and the assessment of what Deaf children know in ASL. This information is needed for two reasons: First, we need to be clear as to how proficient a child is in their visual language (ASL) and, second, we need to know what is important in the first language to assist the Deaf child in learning a second language (English) from print. Teacher preparation programs need to incorporate research and instructional processes from the bilingual literature. Teachers need to understand the relationship between what a Deaf child knows in ASL and what they know in English. Techniques and strategies used in teaching bilingual children can be adapted and used for instructing Deaf children. For too long, educators of the Deaf have modeled their teaching after monolingual instruction and have not taken advantage of the bilingual nature of the Deaf child. It is critical that we recognize the positive differences between DCDP and DCHP. DCDP arrive at school with an intact language, whereas most, if not all, DCHP arrive at school with at the minimum a language delay. This does not have to be the case with what we know today. Changes in attitudes toward ASL and its benefits to support learning in Deaf children, no matter what the degree of hearing loss, is a necessary step to improve the education of the Deaf. All children are capable of learning a visual language. All children are capable of learning via a visual language. All Deaf children (and hard of hearing children) are capable of learning and using ASL. It is the responsibility of teacher preparation programs to ensure that our future teachers have the skills to create the best possible learning environment for all Deaf children.

References

Alire Saenz, B. (1997). In the borderlands of Chicano identity, there are only fragments. In S. Michaelson & D. Johnson (Eds.), *Border theory: The limits of cultural politics*. Minneapolis, MN: University of Minnesota Press.

Allen, S., Greenwald, J., & Hoffmeister, R. (2000, Spring). *Temporal simultaneity in ASL: Deaf children's use of complex sentences* (Working Paper No. 35 Center for the Study of Communication and the Deaf, Boston University, Boston, MA.

Bahan, B. (in press). Memoir upon the formation of a visual variety of the human race. In D. Bauman & B. Bahan, Eds., *Sightings: Reading in deaf studies*. Minneapolis, MN: University of Minnesota Press.

Bahan, B., & Hoffmeister, R. (1991, February). *Transferring literacy skills in ASL to English: A comparison of narratives produced by Deaf children using ASL and writing English*. Paper presented at the American College Educators of the Deaf and Hard of Hearing, Jekyll Island, GA.

Baynton, D. (1996). *Forbidden signs*. Chicago, IL: University of Chicago Press.

Bernstein, M. E., & Finnegan, M. H. (1983). Internal speech and deaf children. *American Annals of the Deaf, 128*(4), 483–489.

Bornstein, H., Hamilton, J., & Saulnier, K. (1981). *Signed English: A basic guide*. Washington, DC: Gallaudet University Press.

Boudreault, P., & Mayberry, R. I. (2006). Grammatical processing in American Sign Language: Age of first-language acquisition effects in relation to syntactic structure. *Language and Cognitive Processes, 21*(5), 608–635.

Brendel, S., Hoffmeister, R., & Fish, S. (2005, July). Deaf children acquiring ASL classifiers: Errors and pattern of development in a signed language. 10th International Congress for the Study of Child Language, Berlin, Germany.

Chamberlain, C., & Mayberry, R. (2000). Theorizing about the relations between ASL and reading. In C. Chamberlain, J. P. Morford, R. I. Mayberry (Eds.), *Language acquisition by eye* (pp. 221–260). Mahwah, NJ: Lawrence Erlbaum.

Chamberlain, C., Morford, J. P., and Mayberry, R. I. (Eds.). (2000). *Language acquisition by eye*. Mahwah, NJ: Lawrence Erlbaum.

Cummins. J. (1991). The development of bilingual proficiency from home to school: A longitudinal study of Portuguese-speaking children. *Journal of Education, 173*, 85–98.

Cummins, J. (1994). Primary language instruction and the education of language minority students. In C. Lebya (Ed.), *Schooling and language minority students: A theoretical framework* (pp. 3–46). Los Angeles, CA: Evaluaton, Dissemination and Assessment Center, UCLA.

Cummins, J. (2003). Reading and the bilingual student: Fact and fiction. In
G. G. Garcia (Ed.), *English learners: Reaching the highest level of English
literacy* (pp. 2–33). Newark, DE: International Reading Association.

Czubek, T., & Greenwald, J. (2001). *Redefining success for Deaf students:
A look at American Sign Language, English, academic performance,
social/emotional development, and pride.* Presentation at the Gover-
nor Baxter School for the Deaf, Portland, ME.

Czubek, T., & Greenwald, J. (2005, September). Understanding Harry Potter: Parallels to the deaf world. *Journal of Deaf Studies and Deaf Education, 10*(4), 442–450.

DiPerri, K. (2004). *ASL phonemic awareness in Deaf children: Implications
for instruction.* Unpublished doctoral dissertation, Boston University, Boston.

DiPerri, K., Hoffmeister, R., Greenwald, J., & Czubek, T. (2003, October). *Literacy support for Deaf children: Teaching Deaf children English using ASL.*
Paper presented at the Annual Symposium on Language & Education of
the Deaf, Sioux Falls, SD: Communication Services for the Deaf.

Easterbrooks, S. (2005). *Review of the literature in literacy development and
instruction in students who are deaf and hard of hearing.* Unpublished
master's thesis, Georgia State University, Atlanta.

Ewoldt, C., Israelite, N., & Hoffmeister, R. (1992). *A review of the literature on the effective use of native sign language on the acquisition of
a majority language by hearing impaired students.* A Final Report to
Minister of Education, Ontario. Faculty of Education, York University, and Center for the Study of Communication and Deafness, Boston University.

Fish, S., Hoffmeister, R., & Thrasher, M. (2005, July). Knowledge of rate
vocabulary in ASL(L1) and its relationship to vocabulary knowledge
in English (L2) in Deaf children. 10th International Congress for the
Study of Child Language, Berlin, Germany.

Gabrielson, E., Hoffmeister, R., & Fish, S. (2005, January). *Acquisition of verb
agreement in American Sign Language: A special focus on non-native
signing children.* Paper presented at the Third Annual Hawaii International Conference on Arts and Humanities, Honolulu, Hawaii.

Greenwald, J., & Czubek, T. (2004, June). *Deaf literature & the Deaf World.*
Presentation at Boston University, Boston.

Greenwald, J., Hoffmeister, R., & Czubek, T. (2003, October). *The ASL models program.* Paper presented at the National Symposium on Childhood Deafness, LOCATION.

Hoffmeister, R. (1978). *The development of demonstrative pronouns, loc-
atives, and personal pronouns in the acquisition of American Sign
Language.* Unpublished doctoral dissertation, University of Minnesota, Minneapolis.

Hoffmeister, R. (1980). *The Influential POINT.* Proceedings of the National Symposium on Sign Language and Sign Language Teaching, National Association of the Deaf, Chicago, IL.

Hoffmeister, R. (1994). Metalinguistic skills in Deaf children: Knowledge of synonyms and antonyms in ASL. In B. Snider (Ed.), *Proceedings of the Post Milan: ASL and English Literacy Conference,* Gallaudet University Press, Washington, DC.

Hoffmeister, R. (1996a). Cross cultural misinformation: What does special education say about the Deaf? *Journal of Disability & Society, 11*(2), 171–189.

Hoffmeister, R. (1996b). *What do Deaf kids know about ASL even though they see MCE!* In proceedings of Deaf Studies IV (pp. 273–308), Gallaudet University Press, Washington, DC.

Hoffmeister, R. J. (2000). A piece of the puzzle: ASL and reading comprehension in Deaf children. In C. Chamberlain, J. Morford, & R. Mayberry (Eds.), *Language acquisition by eye.* Mahwah, NJ: Lawrence Erlbaum.

Hoffmeister, R. (2001). *Border crossings by hearing children of Deaf parents: The lost history of Codas!* Paper presented at Deaf Studies Think Tank, Washington, DC: Gallaudet University.

Hoffmeister, R. (2005a, July). *Sign language in Deaf children: Development and education.* Keynote lecture, 20th International Conference on the Education of the Deaf, Maastricht, The Netherlands.

Hoffmeister, R. (2005b, July). The American Sign Language Assessment Instrument (ASLAI). Paper presented at the 20th International Conference on the Education of the Deaf, Maastricht, The Netherlands.

Hoffmeister, R., & Bahan, B. (1991, February). *The relationship between American Sign Language, signed English and Sim-Com in the language development of deaf children.* Paper presented at the American College Educators of the Deaf and Hard of Hearing's Annual Conference, Jekyll Island, GA.

Hoffmeister, R., Costello, P., & Grass, W. (1997a, April). *Evaluating American Sign Language in Deaf children: ASL influences on reading.* Paper presented at Deaf Studies V, Gallaudet University.

Hoffmeister, R., Costello, P., & Grass, W. (1997b, June). *Charting the future: Paradigm shifts in education of the Deaf.* Paper presented at the Bi-Annual Conference of American Instructors of the Deaf, Hartford, CT.

Hoffmeister, R., Philip, M., Costello, P., & Grass, W. (1997c). *Evaluating American Sign Language in Deaf children: ASL influences on reading.* Proceedings of Deaf Studies V, Washington, DC: Gallaudet University Press.

Hoffmeister, R., deVilliers, P., Engen, E., & Topol, D. (1997). English reading achievement in ASL skills in Deaf students. In E. Hughes, M. Hughes, & A. Greenhill (Eds.), *Proceedings of the 21st Annual Boston University Conference on Language Development,* Cascadilla Press, Somerville, MA.

Hoffmeister, R., Greenwald, J., Czubek, T., & DiPerri, K. (2003a, October). *Establishing a dual language program for Deaf children: What is needed?* Paper presented at the Annual Symposium on Language & Education of the Deaf, Sioux Falls, SD: Communication Services for the Deaf.

Hoffmeister, R., Greenwald, J., Czubek, T., & DiPerri, K. (2003b, October). *Dual language assessment.* Paper presented at the Annual Symposium on Language & Education of the Deaf, Sioux Falls, SD: Communication Services for the Deaf.

Hoffmeister, R., Greenwald, J., Czubek, T., DiPerri, K., Cole, J., & Bambach, D. (2002, July). *Model of dual language programming for deaf children.* Paper presented at DeafWay II, Washington, DC.

Hoffmeister, R., Greenwald, J., & Kourbetis, V. (1987). *A model for assessing communicative competence in Deaf students: A team approach.* Paper presented at the International Congress on Education of the Deaf, Manchester, England, August 7, 1985

Hoffmeister, R., & Harris, C. (2005). *Proposal to develop an American Sign Language assessment.* Unpublished manuscript. Center for the Study of Communication and the Deaf, Boston University, Boston, MA.

Hoffmeister, R., Philip, M. J., Costello, P., & Grass, W. (1997a, June). *American Sign Language assessment instruments (ASLAI): The impact of ASL on reading in Deaf children.* Paper presented at the Bi-Annual Conference of American Instructors of the Deaf, Hartford, CT.

Hoffmeister, R., Philip, M., Costello, P., & Grass, W. (1997b, April). *Evaluating American Sign Language in Deaf children: ASL influences on reading.* Papers at Deaf Studies V, Washington, DC: Gallaudet University..

Hoffmeister, R., Philip, M., Costello, P., & Grass, W. (1997c, June). Charting the future: Paradigm shifts in education of the Deaf. Paper presented at the Bi-Annual Conference of American Instructors of the Deaf, Hartford, CT.

Hoffmeister, R., & Shettle, C. (1984). Adaptations in communication made by deaf signers to different audiences. In R. Hoffmeister & J. Gee (Eds.), *Special edition on American Sign Language discourse, discourse processes: A multidisciplinary journal.*

Hoffmeister, R., & Wilbur, R. (1980). The acquisition of American Sign Language: A review. In H. Lane & F. Grosjean (Eds.), *Current perspectives on sign language* (pp. 61–78). Mahwah, NJ: Lawrence Erlbaum.

Jackendof, R. (1994). *Patterns in the mind: Language and Human Nature.* New York: Basic Books.

Johnson, R. E. (1998). Beliefs and practices in Deaf education: Magical and logical. *El Bilingismo de los Sordos, 1*(3), 13–20.

Klima, E., & Bellugi, U. (1979). *The signs of language.* Cambridge, MA: Harvard University Press.

Kuntze, M. (1998). Literacy and Deaf children: The language question. *Topics in Language Disorders, 18*(4), 1–15.

Kuntze, M. (2004). Literacy Acquisition and Deaf Children: Study of the Interaction between ASL and written English. Unpublished doctoral dissertation, Stanford University Palo Alto, CA.

Lane, H. (1992). *The mask of benevolence.* San Diego, CA: Dawn Sign Press.

Lane, H., Hoffmeister, R., & Bahan, B. (1996). *A journey into the deaf-world.* San Diego, CA: Dawn Sign Press.

Mayberry, R. I. (1993). First-language acquisition after childhood differs from second-language acquisition: The case of American Sign Language. *Journal of Speech and Hearing Research, 36,* 1258–1270.

Mayberry, R., & Eichen, E. (1991). The long-lasting advantage of learning sign language in childhood: Another look at the critical period for language acquisition. *Journal of Memory and Language, 30,* 486–512.

Mayberry, R. I., & Lock, E. (2003). Age constraints on first versus second language acquisition: Evidence for linguistic plasticity and epigenesis. *Brain and Language, 87,* 369–383.

Mayberry, R. I., Lock, E., & Kazmi, H. (2002). Linguistic ability and early language exposure. *Nature, 417,* 38.

Mayer, C., & Wells, G. (1996). Can linguistic interdependence theory support a bilingual-bicultural model of literacy education for deaf students? *Journal of Deaf Studies and Deaf Education, 1*(2), 93–106.

Mitchell, R., & Karchmer, M. (2004). Changing the mythical ten percent: Parental hearing status of deaf and hard of hearing student in the United States. *Sign Language Studies, 4*(2), 138–163.

Moores, D. (1990). *Old w(h)ine in new bottles.* Unpublished manuscript, Washington, DC: Gallaudet University.

Moores, D. (2001). *Educating the deaf: Principles and practices.* Boston, MA: Houghton-Mifflin.

Moores, D., & Sweet, C. (1990). Factors predictive of school achievement. In D. Moores & K. Meadow-Orlans (Eds.), *Educational and Developmental Aspects of Deafness* (pp. 154–201). Gallaudet University Press, Washington, DC.

Newport, E. L., & Meier, R. P. (1985). The acquisition of American sign language. In D. I. Slobin (Ed.), *The crosslinguistic study of language acquisition* (Vol. 1, pp. 881–938). Hillsdale, NJ: Erlbaum.

Padden, C., & Humphries, T. (1988). *Voices from another culture*. Cambridge, MA: Harvard University Press.

Padden, C., & Ramsey, C. (1998). Reading ability in signing deaf children. *Topics in Language Disorders, 18*, 30–46.

Padden, C., & Ramsey, C. (2000). American Sign Language and reading ability in deaf children in C. Chamberlain, J. P. Morford, & R. I. Mayberry, (Eds.) Language Acquisition by Eye (p. 221–260). Mahwah, NJ: Lawrence Erlbaum Associates.

Pattison, R. (1982). *On literacy*. New York: Oxford University Press.

Paul, P. (1998). *Literacy and deafness*, Boston, MA: Allyn & Bacon.

Pinker, S. (1994). *The language instinct*. New York: Harper-Collins.

Reagan, T. (in press). Language rights and the deaf: Compensatory and empowerment approaches in language policy. In P. Benson, P. Grundy, H. Itakura, & T. Skutnabb-Kangas (Eds.), *Access to language rights*. Amsterdam: John Benjamins.

Singleton, J. (1989). *Restructuring of language from impoverished input: Evidence for linguistic compensation*. Unpublished doctoral dissertation, University of Illinois, Urbana-Champaign.

Singleton, J., & Newport, E. (2004). When learners surpass their models: The acquisition of American Sign Language from impoverished input. *Cognitive Psychology, 49*, 370–407.

Singleton, J., & Supalla, S. (1998). *The effects of ASL fluency upon deaf children's cognitive, linguistic, and social development*. Final report to the U.S. Department of Education: OSERS. University of Illinois, Urbana-Champaign.

Strong, M., & Prinz, P. (1997). A study of the relationship between American Sign Language and English literacy. *Journal of Deaf Studies and Deaf Education, 2*(1), 37–46.

Strong, M., & Prinz, P. (2000). Is American Sign Language skill related to English literacy? In C. Chamberlain, J. P. Morford, & R. I. Mayberry (Eds.), *Language acquisition by eye* (pp. 132–142). Mahwah, NJ: Lawrence Erlbaum.

Supalla, S. (1986). *Manually coded English: The modality question in signed language development*. Unpublished master's thesis, University of Illinois, Urbana-Champaign.

Supalla, S. (1991). Manually coded English: The modalitiy question in signed language development. In P. Siple & S. Fisher (Eds.), *Theoretical issues in sign language research, Volume 2: Psychology* (pp. 85–109). Silver Spring, MD: TJ Publishers.

Supalla, S., & McKee, C. (2002). The role of manually coded English in the language development of deaf children. In R. Meier, P. Cormier, A. Kearsy, & D. Quinto (Eds.), *Modality and structure in signed and spoken languages* (pp. 143–165.). Cambridge; Cambridge University Press.

Supalla, T. (1982). *Structure and acquisition of verbs of motion and location in American Sign Language.* Unpublished doctoral dissertation, University of California, San Diego.

Supalla, T. (1986). The classifier system in American Sign Language. In C. Craig (Ed.), *Noun classes and categorization* (pp. 181–214). Philadelphia: John Benjamins.

Veditz, G. W. (1910). *The preservation of sign language* [Videotape]. Silver Springs, MD: Sign Media, Inc.

Vernon, M., & Andrews, J. (1990). *The Psychology of Deafness*, New York: Longman.

Endnotes

1. This paper would not have been possible without the help of the following people: Ben Bahan, Janey Greenwald-Czubek, Todd Czubek, Kristin DiPerri, Sarah Fish, and Melissa Thrasher. I would like to especially thank Janey Greenwald-Czubek for her feedback on previous drafts. All of the ideas presented in the paper are my own, and I take full responsibility for them.

   I would like to dedicate this paper to the memory of Marie Jean Phillip, who as a Deaf leader fought tirelessly for the recognition of the Deaf World as a bilingual community.

2. An interesting conflict arises when cultures clash, such as when Deaf people are placed by hearing people. The passage of the Americans with Disabilities Act and other laws (IDEA in education, Section 504 of the Rehab Act, etc.) have expanded the rights of disabled people in the United States. It is under these laws that Deaf people must seek protections because the U.S. government does not recognize that Deaf people who use a signed language are members of a minority group. Deaf people may not consider themselves disabled, but the protections of the government require that they identify themselves as such to gain access to the rights afforded by the United States Constitution. In some other countries (in the Scandinavian countries, for example), the Deaf notably receive government protections as both a disabled group and as a linguistic minority.

3. The NAD is an advocacy organization and its mission is as follows: "The mission of the NAD shall be to promote, protect, and preserve the rights and quality of life of deaf and hard of hearing individuals in the United States of America" (from current bylaws).

4. The TTY is a teletypewriter device that connects with another TTY, allowing people to type messages back and forth. It is based on the transmission of data that is converted to print, much like the email systems of today.

5. Captions are subtitles that reflect what is being said in a movie or television program.

6. Current technology now allows video interaction between two linked computers. The use of special modems and cameras allows Deaf people to communicate with other persons using ASL by contacting a central site (relay center) via a video connection that is similar to the video link between two computers. The U.S. government funds these relay centers by hiring people who translate and interpret what a Deaf person signs into voice for a hearing person who is called via the telephone.

7. Currently, with the medical focus of cochlear implantation, there is an underlying bias that if one uses a signed language with a child with this implant, it will somehow delay or negatively affect the ability of the child to acquire a spoken language. There is very little discussion on how language acquisition is measured and the impact of the cochlear implant when it is not working to its optimum. This is an area of discussion not faced by those in the bilingual world. Although there is a negative attitude toward the use of two languages in the United States, the medical profession is not searching for ways to alter one's body to prevent a biological process from happening.

8. Signed English systems are also referred to as manually coded English (MCE). MCE as a term covers the wide variations of the signed English systems that are available.

5

Rethinking the Case for Culture-Based Curriculum

Conditions that Support Improved Mathematics Performance in Diverse Classrooms[1]

Sharon Nelson-Barber
WestEd

Jerry Lipka
University of Alaska Fairbanks[2]

With today's emphasis on addressing the needs of students from all backgrounds and contexts, there is a push to better understand not only appropriate curricular and pedagogical strategies for success but also the conditions that support success given the wide-ranging diversity in our nation's schools. A growing body of literature speaks to a style and flavor in U.S. indigenous classrooms that is believed to be conducive to academic excellence. These include linguistic and cultural congruence between home and school (cf., Au & Kawakami, 1994; Lipka, Mohatt, & the Ciulist Group, 1998; Philips, 1983; Trumbull, Rothstein-Fisch, Greenfield, & Quiroz, 2001), education of students in their heritage languages within their associated cultural contexts (cf., Ovando, 1994; Smith, 1998; Watson-Gegeo, 1989), and use of local knowledge and culture in the curriculum (cf., Alaska Native Knowledge Network, 1998; Barnhardt, 1999; Lipka, Parker Webster, & Yanez, 2005; Nelson-Barber, 2001; Swisher & Deyhle, 1987; Watahomigie & McCarty, 1994). Not only are these elements believed to be key means to improving the academic performance of indigenous students, but they are also believed to lower dropout rates (Eberhard, 1989), enhance literacy skills (Demmert, 2001; George & Just, 1992) and interpersonal development (Smith, Leake,

99

& Kamekona, 1998), and increase enrollment in college-level mathematics, science, and engineering courses (Alaska Native Knowledge Network, 1998).

Despite the reasonableness of these claims, Demmert and Towner (2003) note the paucity of culture-based research that supports positive outcomes for indigenous students. In their extensive review of the literature, these authors found only a few studies that met their criteria for rigorous research. Within this body of work, one research group in Alaska is producing a series of compelling investigations around the implementation of a newly developed culture-based mathematics curriculum.

Cultural Context and Curriculum

Math in a Cultural Context (MCC) is a series of supplemental, elementary-level mathematics modules that are the result of long-term collaborative work among Yup'ik elders, teachers, university researchers, and Alaskan schools. Originally devised to address outcome differences between Alaska Native students (rural students in particular) and their mainstream counterparts, the MCC research team set out to understand and explicitly connect pedagogy to Yup'ik elder knowledge, the practice of expert Yup'ik teachers, and local Yup'ik culture. During collaborative development sessions, elders discussed and demonstrated a range of Yup'ik cultural experiences (such as navigating the tundra using celestial navigation, designing and building fish racks for drying fish, crafting geometric designs to decorate clothing, and so forth) and, together with expert Yup'ik teachers, math educators, and cultural specialists, explored the mathematical concepts and reasoning associated with this everyday knowledge and activities.

As the effort unfolded, it became evident that elder ways of communicating, teaching, and valuing were as much a part of the process as depicting subject matter knowledge. Thus, as the elders collaborated with curriculum developers and educators to transform their understandings into schooling practices, they essentially created a "third space" where their wisdom, school-based mathematics, and reform-oriented math coalesced. The resulting unique instructional approaches, rooted as they are in Yup'ik learning and systems of problem solving, have provided a rich context for exploring the use of cultural and community-based knowledge and led to a character-ization of the approach as "culture-based."

During *MCC*'s early implementation, Lipka and Adams (2004) describe promising effects derived from a quasi-experimental study of the performances of students who experienced the curriculum. These authors discovered that *MCC* produced statistically signifi-cant results for all students who received this instruction versus instruction based on a regular mathematics curriculum. A series of subsequent studies found this to be true for rural Alaska Native stu-dents specifically (Lipka, Parker Webster, et al., 2005), and a rigorous experimental design (preliminary data from *MCC*'s interim report, 2006) involving 67 teachers, 50 schools, and more than 800 students showed that Athabaskan, Caucasian, Inupiaq, Yup'ik, and Tlinglit students all outperformed their control group counterparts at statis-tically significant levels in both rural and urban settings.

A series of recent ethnographically oriented case studies span-ning a spectrum of Alaskan contexts—rural novice teachers (Lipka, Hogan, Parker Webster, 2005), an experienced teacher of Athabas-kan and Caucasian students (Adams, Adam, and Opbroek, 2005), an experienced Yup'ik teacher teaching Yup'ik students (Lipka, Sharp, Brenner, Yanez, & Sharp, 2005), and an experienced urban teacher teaching mostly Caucasian and some Alaska Native students (Rick-ard, 2005)—offer deep descriptions that capture the impacts of *MCC* and its pedagogical approaches. Each case illustrates how teachers organize their classes, involve students, and keep the math challeng-ing—processes that are invaluable for helping other teachers optimize student experiences with *MCC* and also helpful for understanding the gains experienced by students in all of these classrooms. In fact, student gains extend from better than average all the way to outperforming all others. The fact that positive results have occurred in experimental and quasi-experimental studies with repeated outcomes strongly sug-gests that *MCC* and other materials of this nature have great potential for use with all students. But herein lies the conundrum.

How is it that a so-called "culture-based" curriculum ostensibly shaped to mirror the knowledge and experiences of rural Yup'ik students turns out to be effective for diverse groups of students who experience it? If culture-based implies making learning more accessible to a specific cultural group and context, then what is actu-ally happening in *MCC* classrooms given the range of teachers, stu-dents, and settings in which MCC is having a positive effect? Or is there something about the curriculum objects, tools, and interactional patterns as designed and implemented that are responsible for the found effects? What *are* the conditions that support the improved mathematics performances evident in such different classrooms?

The emerging findings, together with group reflections on the origins and intents that have shaped *MCC,* now compel the team to rethink early conceptions and to consider a *re*characterization of the processes taking place. In so doing, it becomes important not only to examine curricular effectiveness beyond contexts that are relatively homogeneous and connected to Native traditions, such as urban districts, but also to begin to understand students' experiences as they interact with *MCC* and similar curricula to begin to learn how what was thought to be a curriculum organized for a particular group generalizes to other groups. The increased number of indigenous families and other diverse groups relocating to urban areas suggests that this is an essential research focus (cf., Goldsmith, Howe, & Leask, 2005).

MCC in an Urban Context

Exploratory qualitative research begun by Nelson-Barber, Villegas, and Lipka (2004) in Fairbanks, AK, provides initial descriptions of ways in which urban sixth-grade students from a range of backgrounds viewed *MCC* as they experienced the *Drying Salmon* module. These authors argue for the inclusion of pedagogical conceptions and approaches like those used by *MCC* to support improved student performance.

The present paper returns to the same data set in order to examine more closely the nature of these *MCC* teacher-orchestrated classroom contexts that capitalize on community and cultural experience and that challenge students to solve problems practically and to assess their solutions mathematically. Analyses will center on ways in which *MCC*'s culture-based mathematics activities, concepts, and processes connect with diverse urban students' intuitive and community-based knowledge, their understandings of the cognitive demands of everyday life in Yup'ik communities, local practices and people in the community, demonstration as a teaching method, peer-assisted instruction, connecting the lesson to a community purpose, and use of local examples. Ultimately, these findings will be considered along with analyses of other data collected throughout the primary study (e.g., module pretest and posttest data) as a means to better understand classroom and cultural factors that contribute to improving student performance in mathematics.

Methods

Participants   Students and their teachers in four urban Alaskan sixth-grade classrooms in the Fairbanks North Star Borough School District participated in the study. Teachers were all experienced and nonindigenous, with English as their language of instruction. Each was also a seasoned user of the MCC series but not necessarily the *Drying Salmon* module. Classes were composed of diverse students, with military families and indigenous students rather than immigration accounting for most of the diversity. For example, of the approximately 30,000 people who live in Fairbanks proper, about 10,000 are active military and their dependents. Though some of the indigenous students have relocated from rural villages in the state, a number have grown up in Fairbanks with limited exposure to village life. As Table 5.1 indicates, the majority of students interviewed in each treatment class [TC] were non-

TABLE 5.1

	Native Interviews	Total Interviews	Total Students
TC 1	4	14	20
TC 2	3	14	22
TC 3	3	14	21
TC 4	3	12	20

Native, making them key figures in daily interactions with both their Native classmates and their teachers. The analysis considers the performances of all students as they experience one *MCC* module in each of the four classrooms.

The Treatment Module: Drying Salmon   As described earlier, the *MCC* curricular modules derive from real world Yup'ik activities and introduce students to Yup'ik elder knowledge, specific problems that elders encounter and need to solve, and mathematical tools that elders draw on to solve them. The *Drying Salmon* module draws on the knowledge of the late Mrs. Mary George of Akiachak, AK—a long-term teacher aide and bilingual instructor and an accomplished and knowledgeable subsistence provider. In fact, the theme and foundation for this module came alive as Mrs. George demonstrated her specialized experience with estimation as she reviewed processes of drying and smoking salmon. Key features included assigning equivalent body measures to the widths of different salmon species (red, silver, king, chum); taking into account the disposition of the fish (uncut, cut, fresh, and dried); and establishing relationships between different species types (king and red salmon) as each represented distinct body measures (see Table 5.1).

In her review of common practices for drying salmon, she regularly and accurately approximated how many of each combination type (king uncut, king cut, etc.) would fill her drying rack. She also introduced the practice of making special cuts in the fish to speed the drying process—a strategy that increases the surface area of the fish, allowing it to dry more quickly. The breadth of knowledge conveyed by Mrs. George allowed developers to extend the content of the module to include topics such as surface area and volume and also to make connections to science.

In its final form, *Drying Salmon* focuses on measuring, estimating, proportional thinking, and algebraic reasoning more generally. Students formulate questions, engage in hands-on learning, and present their solutions verbally, numerically, graphically, geometrically, and symbolically. The approach makes use of strategies that are: 1) *thematic*, using culture-based storylines (such as drying the salmon catch); 2) *cognitive*, connecting elder knowledge and everyday tasks related to spatial abilities; 3) *sociocultural*, entailing expert and apprentice modeling, peer collaboration, and a hands-on inquiry approach to learning, and 4) *self-determined*, orchestrating problem-solving skills so that students can solve problems independently in their peer groups. Thus, the module aligns with National Council of Teachers of Mathematics [NCTM] standards that call for more focus on geometry and spatial reasoning (NCTM, 2000) and that also incorporates relevant cultural and community knowledge (including cooperative learning, local knowledge and discourse structures, and classroom organization that supports Yup'ik values of group harmony and student autonomy).

Treatment teachers implemented the *Drying Salmon* module for up to 5 weeks in lieu of the standard sixth-grade mathematics curriculum they would have used otherwise. Per NCTM standards, the module addressed the same grade level content as the standard curriculum, particularly patterns, relationships, and functions and use of mathematical models to understand and represent quantitative relationships. The primary difference was the context of the lessons—Yup'ik subsistence activities. In this case, teachers connected activities around the summer salmon run—particularly the drying of fish on racks—to develop physical models related to linear measures and, later in the module, a more abstracted way of representing quantitative data. The module progressed from physical and body measures to algebraic expressions and equations showing proportions.

Data Sources   Teacher and student interview data, videotape recordings of treatment classes (students experiencing *Drying Salmon)*, and regular classroom observations were sources of data for analysis. The research team was familiar with the setting, having observed each classroom, taken notes, collected videotaped data, and conducted interviews with teachers and treatment students at regular intervals earlier in the year. Researchers spent an intensive week observing, gathering a videotaped record of each mathematics class, and conducting follow-up interviews with the four teachers and their students (Appendix 5.A). Further, this work was part of a larger ongoing research project with the Alaska/MCC group. Thus, most of the teachers in this study were observed and videotaped over a number of semesters.

Teacher and Student Interviews   To better understand teachers' pedagogical content knowledge and ways of connecting to students, teacher interviews elicited foundational information about mathematics classroom organization, student interactive styles, teaching strategies, and ways of assessing classroom performance. Documentation included how teachers organized their classrooms for mathematics content, structured social interaction to support math learning, and facilitated and mediated student knowledge building and levels of cognitive demand. Hard and anecdotal evidence that culture-based curricula had an affect on urban Native students' math performance were considered.   Students were asked to reflect on other mathematics curricula in their experience and to compare those experiences to the *MCC* module. Researchers noted whether students found the module to be more interesting and connected with daily life and whether it promoted a sense of inclusion. Students also offered some ideas on problem solving, their understanding of mathematics, and their ability to think mathematically.

Classroom Observations   Observers focused on teacher use of *Drying Salmon* and how choices and changes were made, as well as how teachers supported student ability to communicate mathematically. How did students explain the processes for determining answers? Did they raise questions or engage in peer-peer teaching? How did teachers demonstrate mathematical knowledge? Teachers' understanding of student use of math content/procedures as well as students' ability to collaborate and problem solve were also important. How did students handle cognitive demands, and how well could they explain the processes they used/followed? Would students connect their out-of-classroom experiences to classroom experiences while they were engaged in the culture-based math curriculum?

Videotape Recordings   Videography captured the classroom both in broad stroke and in selected small groups. Teacher-student and student-student interactions were documented and cross-referenced with other collected data. Special attention was paid to the nature of mathematical discourse, demonstrations of depth of mathematical understanding, and particular cognitive strategies that were in use.

Analysis and Findings

For the present purpose, researchers spent an intensive week observing, gathering a videotaped record of each mathematics class, and conducting follow-up interviews with the four treatment teachers and selected students. However, as is often the case in schools, changes in schedules, absences, and unforeseen teacher commitments prevented collection of consistent records across all four classes. In addition, the small number of urban Native students (whose perceptions of mathematics were of particular interest), together with the fact that some of them were less forthcoming during interviews, precluded our ability to collect lengthy Native student narratives for comparative purposes. Still, despite this disparity, all students offered insightful commentary about the curriculum. The findings are thus a compilation of source information explaining how *Drying Salmon* supported urban Native and non-Native student learning. We describe how the curriculum generated classroom organization, teacher strategies, and student interactions structured to meet students' learning needs, with culture an important consideration.

Classroom Organization   Student interview data suggest that, while using the *Drying Salmon* curriculum, treatment teachers employ various classroom organization models that impact student engagement and student mathematics learning. Organization models include individual hands-on, group hands-on, teacher lecture, small-group discussion, and teacher-led whole class discussion. According to students, these models differ from the approaches commonly used in their traditional mathematics classes: teacher-led individual work from the math book or at the board. Almost all of the students stated that they preferred learning math using the Yup'ik curriculum. Typical responses included mention of practicality and utility. For example:

> It's kind of fun because the math book is boring. There's nothing to talk about. You can't have discussions. [With the *Drying Salmon* curriculum] you can disagree with people. And in the math book you get homework.

What surfaces in this student's comments is the view that math is open—that you can explore ideas and disagree with the ideas of others. Such an approach, which is built into the *MCC* curriculum, presumes a high level of engagement, as suggested by other students who noted that the curriculum required them to think about their learning. One student stated:

> I like the curriculum more than what we normally do. Normally we just do things with the chalkboard; it takes forever. But with this, it's quicker and it's more efficient because it teaches you to think a lot more than you usually do in the classroom.

According to another student:

> In the math book it only gives examples and you can't do as much, just read about it. And then you have to do the work. With this you can read about it and find out what it's more about.

From another:

> [For] some kids that really need help I'd say it's a lot better because they actually have objects around them that they can work with and real life situations and all this other stuff—like with the drawing out with the poles and the drying out with the fish. In the math book it can get confusing because they just give you formulas and all this other stuff and tell you what to do, rather than saying figure it out on your own.

Here students indicate that the curriculum gives them more opportunities to figure out the mathematics on their own, rather than being given answers. They understand that students learn at different rates and, if given the chance to grapple with math concepts, they can become more engaged and reach better understanding.

Yet another student concurs, remarking that having to do the work on his own makes it more challenging, making him "think harder." In other words, the curriculum is not only hands-on, it propels students toward more complex conceptual thinking. According to this student:

> It's a lot different from the math book. I was sort of comfortable with the math book because it was less challenging. Like usually the way I do math, I go for the pattern first, then I slide right through. But this makes me think a lot more harder in the ways I do it. I have to make up everything on my own…. Usually the way teachers teach it is they just tell you what to do, they don't really ask you why it happens, why you think it works that way. That's been the hardest challenge.

As all of these comments indicate, *MCC* incorporates a variety of activities that encourage teachers to use individual, small group, and whole class organization. As a result, students exercise more control over the pace of their own learning and have multiple opportunities and contexts in which to display their skills. One student explains:

> [W]hat I really did like was that, um, when we did do our activities, or our work, or whatever, we did it with our group, and then we did it with the whole class, as a whole class and got the whole class ideas and that kind

of stuff. And we'd work it out together, and I know that was a lot more productive than-than just-just saying, "Okay, this is what happens, what are you going to do?" You know you kind of let other things flow with your own, and we did it as class and, um, we worked together on the problem.

We didn't just think of our answer and say, "Okay that's right." We said, "Oh, maybe there's other ways to do this even if the book doesn't say it."

This group dynamic yields much more productive responses from students. As they work on problems together, they see multiple possibilities, multiple ways of approaching math problems. By both arguing about understandings and coming to agreements, they come to understand that mathematics subject matter is open and spirited. As another student attests:

> We use our hands a lot more and we usually get into groups. And we can have conversations about agreements, disagreements we have. And that way we're not shouting across the whole classroom arguing with each other.

Having opportunities to discuss a problem with peers in small groups to identify different solution strategies before the teacher asks the whole class to respond permits students to use these occasions to "test" or develop their unique approaches with less risk for individual students who might be intimidated by the whole class structure. It also allows more time for all students to think about the problem and to develop a solution in comparison to the more "rapid-fire" question-and-answer exchange that can occur when teachers use the whole-class approach without initial small-group work.

Organizing the class to allow students more time for contemplation, to deliberate with peers, and essentially to practice privately before displaying knowledge publicly is a well documented way to create positive classroom experiences for Native students (cf., Philips, 1983, Swisher & Deyhle, 1987). In fact, one of the Native students specifically commented on how much she appreciated the pace of *Drying Salmon*. She stated:

> It's much better because the math book is kinda direct.... The book rushes you. The one we're doing now, it's calm and you understand it.

During in-class observations, teachers used individual hands-on, group hands-on, small-group discussion, and teacher-led whole-class discussion. The teacher lecture model was not used, and according to student interviews, this approach was reserved for the lessons at the beginning of the module, when teachers introduced stories or provided background for the work students would do in math.

Teaching Strategies   As any teacher will attest, classrooms are electric places where teacher versatility and flexibility go a long way. Though *Drying Salmon* follows a progression of strategies and activities that build one on one another, the nonprescriptive nature of these elements allows teachers a great deal of latitude to make adaptations and adjustments when needed. Novice teachers may be more likely to rely on the routines delineated in each module; however, more-experienced teachers come up with their own innovations and approaches. Teachers who have a great deal of experience with *MCC* (like the treatment teachers in this paper, who have used the curriculum with multiple classes) understand the modules less as culture-based and more as avenues for manipulating the multiple modalities built into the curriculum. By so doing, teachers make it their own and create experiences for students that are at once, cultural, constructivist, and reform-oriented, as illustrated below.

In TC 1, the teacher maintained a student-centered classroom in which student math dialogue and student participation were emphasized. Small-group work was used to monitor individual and group progress, but students were also required to report back to the whole class and discuss their strategies. Direct teaching at the front of the class modeled the task for students and facilitated class discussion about the task through open-ended questions, such as: "What do you notice about this chart [fish to body measures chart]?" or "Which cutouts should we use [oversized or regular king salmon]?" Some student groups were called to the front of the class to explain their approaches and solutions, while other groups were asked to compare their responses and offer comments.

During a lesson on proportions, ratios, and pre-algebraic thinking, manipulatives required for the hands-on activity posed particular challenges. Students were given two sheets of paper with drawings of a fish rack pole, rows of fish in three different sizes (chum, red, king), and the Yup'ik body measurements associated with each of the three different-sized fish. Students were asked to cut out the fish and, by first placing them on the fish rack pole in various combinations, predict additional combinations that could fit on the pole. Developers had not anticipated the length of time students actually needed to cut out the materials in preparation for the lesson. Also, instructions to the teacher to Xerox the three sizes and shapes did not take into account the degree of variation introduced by the enlarge and reduce functions on the school copy machine. Because students were not necessarily working with like materials, there was a huge variance in their calculations and they understandably could not come up with consistent equations. Still the students came to understand the meaning of using standard measures and the kinds of issues that can arise in more real-world situations requiring estimation.

On the following day, the teacher made necessary adjustments—including providing the students with like-sized manipulatives for each fish size as well as a chart to ensure equivalent comparisons. This strategy not only resulted in increased time on the task, students now used more math-related language to pose questions about the task, such as how to measure the fish (by length or by "thickness"); why the king salmon cutout had various widths but the chum and red salmon cutouts had only one; and whether they had to use the fish cutouts as opposed to the Yup'ik body measurement cutouts for purposes of estimation.

In TC 2, the teacher effectively posed complex problems to evoke the use of particular approaches, to guide learning, and to encourage the students' use of various resources. This teacher frequently used open-ended questions that encouraged student discussion and conjecture. During the in-class observation, the teacher mentioned that a substitute teacher had filled in the previous two days, and she now wanted to know what the students had learned about circumference and the formula for *pi* during that time. The teacher posed questions such as, "You figured out the average [of the circumference to diameter relationship], but what did that mean?" "It meant *pi*, but what is that?" Observing students closely, the teacher noticed that students had been responding by supplying the value for *pi* (3.14) without understanding where it came from. The teacher commanded, "Open your books and put your calculators away. We're just talking about why the formula works." The teacher built on what they knew about parallelograms, radius, circumference, and diameter to guide students' inquiry into the meaning of *pi*. Students were investigating, responding to the teacher's questions, and posing their own questions about aspects of the problem that were unclear.

Student Interactions   In many math classrooms, students focus on being the first to get the right answer and lose sight of the process they use to get to the solution. Competition among students can often undercut cooperative learning and understanding about critical math procedures. In the classrooms observed, students worked collaboratively, recognizing the value of multiple perspectives and approaches to thinking about math problems. Peer teaching was also frequently used in small groups and in whole-class activities to facilitate learning.

When one group of students in TC 1 came forward to present their findings about how many different fish cuts could be hung on the same length of pole, other students found that they had very different answers. When several alternative totals emerged, even given the significant adaptations to the materials, the teacher established that there were inconsistencies in how students had cut or arranged the fish cuts on the diagram. This led to boisterous discussion. A group of students in the back of the class recognized that they had different combinations because they had allowed for more space between their fish cuts. But one student noted that placing the cuts closer together would "give you a small hanging area [and allow] less air for drying." Students were engaged and, as is common in sixth grade, determined to compete or even argue to justify the correctness of their own answers. So one might wonder whether they were losing sight of the purpose of the lesson. However, in their interviews, students did remark that it was important to hear the "different perspectives" of their classmates and, as noted earlier, that they believe they learn more when they "have conversations about agreements [and] disagreements."

These students were willing to hold their ground and explain how they approached the problem, something that greatly assisted the teacher in understanding why their answers differed, and providing more context to establish why consensus was important. After the teacher explained that they needed to come to an agreement for the second part of the exercise (developing equations), students understood what was expected of them.

In TC 1, peer teaching was also a key feature. On one occasion when a student had worked ahead independently to determine equations for the combinations of fish cuts, the teacher asked him to explain his method to the class and offer guidance as other students tried to analyze their results. This student reviewed the other students' work and asked questions that directed them to errors and succeeded in getting them to think about the relationships between measurements and equations. He established, for example, that he could fit either 5 king salmon or 20 red salmon on one pole. By looking at these measures, he determined that one king was equivalent to 4 reds. Whenever another student would report his equation, he would check it using this relationship. If there was an error, he would ask, "How can that be correct?" In explaining his approach to the other students, he asked them to reflect on their measures and substitute different fish cuts into their equations to determine whether it worked. This process was instructive for the teacher as well, having noticed that students were struggling to make equivalencies because they only had one pole to work with.

In TC 2, students interacted more with the teacher than with other students in their small groups. Here it was apparent that different student ideas and approaches to problem solving were valued in the classroom. As students explained how they had worked through a word problem, one student remarked, "I did it differently. I didn't use a chart; I made a number line." During this lesson, there seemed to be no perceptible competition between students. In fact, student comments were paced together such that they built from one another's ideas as they tried to work through the math problems with their teacher. For example, the teacher asked if anyone else had a different approach to a word problem they were working through (a woman had to purchase several items at the store; students are given the amounts she spends and must determine how much money she had originally). Students shared their strategies:

S1:   I did guess and check. I went from 30 to 50 and back and forth until I could figure it out.
S2:   I didn't times it; I added.
S3:   There's another way; you could add all the money she had.

Students used a great deal of math language and engaged with each other and the teacher about the math content.

In TC 3, the teacher introduced the day's lesson on calculating surface area and volume by first reviewing earlier learnings about drying and preserving salmon for later consumption. Students received worksheets and manipulatives as the teacher described their task and posed questions to the entire class. Students then worked individually and in groups to note their observations about the surface area and volume of their manipulatives. One student who quickly completed the worksheet compared her observations to those of her neighbors. When she found a discrepancy, she asked, "How did you get this?" The teacher came over and the second student said, "I put 88; she put 66." The teacher asked the first student to explain how she arrived at 66. She picked up the manipulative and counted all of the sides of one block, then linked that block with another to show how two sides were lost when two blocks were joined. The other student immediately picked up her blocks and started subtracting from her original result. The teacher asked the first student to continue to explain her approach to other groups of students who were struggling.

Student Learning The *MCC* facilitates classroom organization, teaching strategies, and student interactions that work to support Native and all-student learning. It has four essential components. It allows students to 1) learn at their own pace, 2) display learning when they are ready, 3) work with peers instead of responding to direct questions from teachers, and 4) connect a task's everyday relevance and use to its application in the classroom.

Interviews with students from all classrooms revealed that the instruction about body measurement in the curriculum expanded their use of measurement and estimation outside of the classroom. Students described how they used what they learned to build a fort or lean-to at camp and to measure the size of a floor to know what size rug to purchase. In TC 1, a student asked if everyone had to use the fish cuts to measure, as he held up the Yup'ik body measure cutouts that were also provided.

As in the previous example, in TC 2, as students worked on a word problem, one student noted, "I was working backwards and I wasn't focusing; I was looking at it, 'she spent half of her dollars;' I wondered how you could take half of something that wasn't there yet." The teacher enlisted the feedback of other students to help address this concern. By the end of the exchange, the student who posed the question had begun to work the problem again by using one of the approaches offered by a peer.

In TC 3, students worked individually and in groups to solve a question about the relationship between surface area and volume. The teacher initially asked students to think about what happens to the volume of an object when it is sliced into multiple pieces. Students quickly established that the volume of the total would be the same, but less for the individual slices. The teacher then asked why fish is cut before it is hung on the fish rack. Students explained, "A smaller piece of fish dries faster;" "The more you cut up, the faster it dries;" and "The big piece only dries up on the outside." Students were able to connect what they knew about fish and food preparation from outside of the classroom to the task at hand. The teacher then asked why the observation was true. Students conjectured, "with smaller pieces, you can stack them on each other" and "with smaller pieces, air can get inside on all sides."

Many of the non-Native students stated that their Native classmates were instrumental in helping them with these kinds of understandings. Many said that they knew very little about Yup'ik culture beforehand and enjoyed learning about Native culture in their math classes. One non-Native student explained, "I sit by one of my friends who's Native and he tells me what the meaning is." Another non-Native student concurred, "One of the girls in my class who knew more helped me out." Others observed, "The Native kids help get a picture in your head about how it's done" and "Some of the Native students knew more about it already and they got to share with us how it worked. We found out more about it [Native life]." The process seemed matter of fact for one Native student, "We have partners and if someone doesn't understand we help them."

On the other hand, some non-Native students characterized the Native students as "quieter" or "really shy" and observed that they "just sorta listen." In one class a number of students identified a particular Native student as "very helpful," remarking that she always assisted fellow classmates when they moved into small groups. However, when that student was asked to comment, she replied that she didn't really know more than any other student and didn't offer any special help.

Never spotlighting one's special knowledge or expertise can be typical of students raised never to boast or set oneself apart from others in a peer group, a common cultural norm in Native communities. In this case, fellow students attested that this particular student was knowledgeable and helpful, but others, including teachers and others in authority roles, who are accustomed to assertive, even competitive classroom interaction, might see only "quiet" or "shy" behavior.

Summary and Conclusions

These preliminary results strongly support the notion that culture-based experiences and ways of learning are rich resources for designing daily instruction that can provide students with tools to address their own needs and solve their own problems. Interview and observational data illustrating ways in which the curriculum is structured to meet student needs are very much in keeping with the traditional Native approaches to teaching and learning defined by research (Trumbull, Nelson-Barber, & Mitchell, 2002) (i.e., allowing students to learn at their own pace, to display learning when they are ready, to work with peers instead of responding to direct questions from teachers, to connect a task's everyday relevance and use to its application in the classroom, and so forth). Students engaged in *Drying Salmon* simulated everyday, practical activities, often working in groups with the expectation that different students, who likely had different skill sets, would take on different leadership roles (expert-apprentice model). Solutions and procedures learned by one group were shared with other groups (community-based discourse). As students completed the instructional activities, teachers carefully and regularly observed, listened, and challenged their students' thinking in order to assess learning (authentic assessment). Evidence in the data essentially highlights ways in which organization, strategies, and interaction were structured during the math lessons and assists in tying the data to the lessons and back to student learning. As it turns out, with respect to improved academic performance, module pretest and posttest data compiled at the end of the year show student gains in mathematics in each of the classrooms observed (see Table 5.2).

Although this preliminary evidence suggests that *MCC* leads to urban students' improved performance (this includes the Native students), due to the small numbers of Native students in each classroom, a larger, more-controlled study that looks into the specific performances of Native students in mathematics is needed. Still, these findings make a strong case for thematic culture-based instruction as a means of improving the mathematics performances of all students. The success of the non-Native teachers in this study support the notion that teachers need not share culture with students to be effective. Rather, teachers who are insiders to such knowledge can inform instruction and assist other teachers in learning how

TABLE 5.2

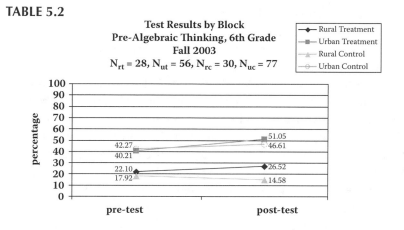

particular students learn best, how to organize schooling, how to discipline children, and so forth. Both teachers who come from the communities of their students and teachers who have gained valuable knowledge through working in students' communities can be effective because, in addition to understanding content and ways to teach content, they develop high-quality relationships with their students, extending their knowledge of the learners and helping them better understand who it is they are teaching.

Still, in addition to these relationships, we need to take into account why this math curriculum based on Yup'ik elders resonates across cultural and geographical boundaries. The results from this exploratory study provide clues about the efficacy of the curriculum across contexts. *MCC* seems to provide students with a more highly contextualized approach to math learning, which students report to be more interesting than their regular math textbooks. Students stress that *MCC* teaches them or forces them to think more and that it is more challenging. From social organizational and pedagogical perspectives, students appear to enjoy working in collaborative groups. It gives them the opportunity to explore math by disagreeing with one another and to prove their points mathematically.

The results suggest that mathematics taught and learned in a defined cultural context (drawing upon student experiences that have elements of mathematics in them and linking classroom learning to community-based practices) increases opportunities for students to relate to it and find it meaningful. Of course, this is nothing new. Decades of research focused on disparities in educational achievement across racial groups argues that any content area taught in the defined cultural context that has socialized its students will advantage those students and can explain higher achievement scores (cf., Delpit, 1995; Gutiérrez & Rogoff, 2003; Secada, 1992; Solano-Flores & Nelson-Barber, 2001; Steele, 1991). Those socialized in what is deemed a mainstream "normal" or "neutral" schooling context are seen as "intelligent" and others are seen as "deficient." The fact that cultural context or "rules" are not shared across communities becomes the "fault" of the student. In this case, the Native cultural context is named and many of the rules are shared—the mainstream cultural context is almost never named and rules are not shared.

The three main ideas that emerge from the present analysis resonate with findings in many of the other analyses documented around this work. *MCC* frames mathematics problems in a contextual way, as if mathematics is a larger scene—a huge tapestry that interweaves student experiences, engaging them, permitting them to make use of their own interests and purpose, such that they want to solve the given mathematical problems. It is also clear that *MCC* presumes joint engagement between teacher and students. Teachers often engage in the same activity as their students and do so in an atmosphere of collaboration that allows coconstruction of problem responses. The teacher takes on dual roles—one of expert and one of member—as they work together to solve mathematical problems. There are shifts in power and authority, especially when the teacher joins in with students trying their own solutions to the problems posed. Because *MCC* is not prescriptive and the teacher has latitude to draw from multiple strategies and approaches, multiple pathways are created for student engagement, which increases the potential for students to take on leadership roles. This stance suggests the two are engaged in a cognitive apprenticeship in which both join in a common purpose.

It is these "culture-based" elements that must be built into the preparation and on-going professional development of teachers to support improved student performance. As Trumbull, Nelson-Barber, and Mitchell (2002) attest, we know from social action research that students of all ages and backgrounds become highly motivated to learn complex concepts and skills when what they are learning about is supporting the well-being of their own communities. With *MCC* curriculum objects contextualized in local Yup'ik culture, the numerous students we have encountered from all backgrounds find points of connection with their own backgrounds and understandings, no matter the teacher and no matter where *MCC* is taught. We believe this is exactly what expands the effectiveness and thus the scope of culture-based curriculum beyond a single culture-specific group to many groups.

One student interviewee captured it well when asked to summarize the main lessons he takes away from *MCC*:

> I think the math that we did was one huge big story and we were trying to learn it—like a math equation. I think it was a good thing. What you really have to think about when you're in school, when you do Yup'ik and all the different tribes, they had to use math to figure out how much food they could eat, how much they had to save, how much they had to get. You have to do that at the store, too—everyday life. You gotta figure out how much you want, how much you want to save, how much you want to eat, how much you have to get—all types of different things—the power of life—math.

References

Adams, B., Adam, A., & Opbroek, M. (2005). Reversing the academic trend for rural students: The case of Michelle Opbroek. *Journal of American Indian Education*, 44(3), 55–79.

Alaska Native Knowledge Network. (1998). *Alaska rural systemic initiative: Year three annual progress report. December 1, 1997–November 30, 1998*. Fairbanks: University of Alaska.

Au, K., & Kawakami, A. (1994). Cultural congruence in instruction. In E. Hollins, J. King, & W. Hayman (Eds.), *Teaching diverse populations* (pp. 5–23). Albany, New York: State University of New York Press.

Barnhardt, C. (1999). *Kuinerrarmiut Elitnaurviat: The school of the people of Quinhagak. Case Study*. Portland, OR: Northwest Regional Educational Laboratory, and Fairbanks, AK: University of Alaska.

Demmert, W. (2001). Improving academic performance among Native American students: A review of the research literature. Charleston, WV: ERIC Clearinghouse on Rural Education and Small Schools.

Demmert, W., & Towner, J. (2003). *A review of the research literature on the influences of culturally based education on the academic performance of Native American students*. Portland, OR: Northwest Regional Educational Laboratory. (http://www.nwrel.org/indianed/cbe.pdf).

Delpit, L. (1995). *Other peoples' children*. New York: The New Press.

Eberhard, D. (1989). American Indian education: A study of dropouts, 1980–1987. *Journal of American Indian Education*, 29(1), 32–40.

George , C., & Just, A. (1992). *Enhanced student outcomes and valuable community resource: Evaluation results about California's Indian education centers.* Report prepared for the California Department of Education.

Goldsmith, S., Howe, L., & Leask, L. (2005). *Anchorage at 90: Changing fast, with more to come—Understanding Alaska research summary No. 4.* Anchorage, AK: Institute of Social and Economic Research, University of Alaska, Anchorage.

Gutiérrez, K., & Rogoff, B. (2003). Cultural ways of learning: Individual traits or repertoires of practice. *Educational Researcher, 32*(5), 19–25.

Lipka, J., with Mohatt, G. V., & the Ciulistet Group. (1998). *Transforming the culture of schools: Yup'ik examples.* Malwah, NJ: Lawrence Erlbaum.

Lipka, J., & Adams, E. (2004). *Culturally Based Math Education as a Way to Improve Alaska Native Students' Math Performance.* The Appalachian Collaborative Center for Learning, Assessment and Instruction in Mathematics Series. Retrieved 1/20/04, from http://acclaim.coe.ohiou.edu/rc/rc_sub/pub/3_wp/list.asp

Lipka, J., Hogan, M., & Parker Webster, J. (2005). Math in a cultural context: Two case studies of a successful culturally based math project. *Anthropology and Education Quarterly, 36*(4), 367–385.

Lipka, J., Parker Webster, J., & Yanez, E. (2005). Special Issue. *Journal of American Indian Education, 44*(3), 1–100.

Lipka, J., Sharp, N., Brenner, B., Yanez, E., & Sharp, F. (2005). The relevance of culturally based curriculum and instruction: The case of Nancy Sharp. *Journal of American Indian Education, 44*(3), 31–54.

National Council of Teachers of Mathematics. (2000). *Curriculum and evaluation standards for school mathematics.* Reston, VA: National Council of Teachers of Mathematics.

Nelson-Barber, S. (2001). Exploring Pacific knowledge and classroom learning in Micronesia: The promise of "cultural considerations." In C. Park, A. Goodwin, & S. Lee (Eds.), *Research on the education of Asian and Pacific Americans.* Greenwich, CT: Information Age Publishing.

Nelson-Barber, S., Villegas, M., & Lipka, J. (2004, April). *The effects of culturally based curriculum on urban Native elementary students in Fairbanks, AK.* Paper presented at the annual meeting of the American Educational Research Association, San Diego, CA.

Ovando, C. (1994). Changes in school and community attitudes in an Athabaskan village. *Peabody Journal of Education, 69*(2), 52–62.

Philips. S. (1983). *The invisible culture.* New York: Longman.

Rickard, A. (2005). Constant perimeter, varying area: A case study of teaching and learning mathematics to design a fish rack. *Journal of American Indian Education, 44*(3), 80–100.

Secada, W. (1992). Race, ethnicity, social class, language, and achievement in mathematics. In D. Grouws (Ed.), *Handbook of research on math teaching and learning* (pp. 623–660). New York: Macmillan.

Smith, L. (1998, Spring). The educational and cultural implications of Maori language revitalization. *Cultural Survival Quarterly*, 27–28.

Smith, D., Leake, D., & Kamekona, N. (1998). Effects of a culturally competent school-based intervention for at-risk Hawaiian students. *Pacific Educational Research Journal*, 9(1), 3–22.

Solano-Flores, G., & Nelson-Barber, S. (2001). On the cultural validity of science assessments. *Journal of Research in Science Teaching, 38*, 1–21.

Steele, C. (1991, April). Race and the schooling of Black Americans. *Atlantic Monthly*, 68–76.

Swisher, K., & Deyhle, D. (1987). Styles of learning and learning of styles: Education conflicts for American Indian/Alaskan Native youth. *Journal of Multilingual and Multicultural Development, 8*(4), 345–360.

Trumbull, E., Nelson-Barber, S., & Mitchell, Jean. (2002). Enhancing mathematics instruction for indigenous American students. In J. Hankes and G. Fast (Eds.), *Changing the faces of mathematics: Perspectives of indigenous people of North America*. Reston, VA: National Council for Teachers of Mathematics.

Trumbull, E., Rothstein-Fisch C., Greenfield, P. M., & Quiroz. B. (2001). *Bridging cultures between home and school: A guide for teachers*. Mahwah, NJ: Lawrence Earlbaum.

Watahomigie, L., & McCarty, T. (1994). Bilingual/bicultural education at Peach Springs: A Hualapai way of schooling. *Peabody Journal of Education*, 69(2), 26–42.

Watson-Gegeo, K. (1989). *The Hawaiian language immersion program: Classroom discourse and children's development of communicative competence*. Paper presented at the Annual Meeting of the National Council of Teachers of English, Baltimore, MD.

Appendix 5.A

Student Interview

1. Tell me about the *Drying Salmon* module. Explain. [If more interesting/fun ask why.]
2. Is this class different from your other (regular) math classes? Explain.
3. What math are you learning? Explain.
4. Does *Drying Salmon* connect to your life or culture? What parts of it? How?

5. (To indigenous students) Do you feel recognized as a Native person through this curriculum? Explain. [Note connections to Native identity, etc.]
6. Have you learned anything about your culture/Alaska Native cultures during the time you have been learning from this module? Explain.
7. Do you work in groups when learning from this curriculum? Explain. [If works alone] Do you prefer to work alone? Explain.
8. Do you like using your hands with the materials?
9. Did you like the story(ies) that were part of the module? [when applicable]
10. What else do you like about this curriculum?
11. What don't you like about this curriculum?
12. Have you learned anything in addition to math when learning from this module?

Teacher Interview

1. What is your response to MCC in general?
2. What do you think of *Drying Salmon*?
3. How does this curriculum engage the students?
4. Does it appear to engage Yup'ik students more than others? Or more than other curricula?
5. Does it engage students not otherwise engaged?
6. For classified students (such as LD), do you see engagement/performance differences? Does the curriculum appear to change their math performance? What exactly about the curriculum seems to make a difference?
7. When you teach *Drying Salmon* does it appear that Native students share information, take leadership roles, or appear to be more engaged?
8. Classroom participation is key to *MCC*. Do you have expectations about everyone participating? How? Do you try to entice everyone to speak or are there other ways to elicit participation?
9. Is there a way of organizing the classroom that seems most effective when teaching the *Drying Salmon* module? (Small groups? Spotlighting?)
10. Do you notice particular interaction patterns among Native students?
11. Do students make reference to personal or cultural experiences? (identity, connections)
12. Do you make reference to personal or cultural experiences?

13. Do you notice Native students using manipulatives, drawings, writings, discussions, etc.?

Endnotes

1. The ideas herein are based in part upon work supported by the National Science Foundation under Grant No. 0138920, U.S. Department of Education award # S356A030033, and the University of Alaska Schools Research Fund. Any opinions, findings, and conclusions or recommendations expressed are those of the authors and do not necessarily reflect the views of the National Science Foundation or the University of Alaska.
2. Acknowledgment: Without the efforts of the following individuals, this chapter would not have been possible. Many elders, Yup'ik teachers, and math educators assisted in the development of *Drying Salmon: Journeys into Proportional and Pre-Algebraic Thinking*, a module in the "Math in a Cultural Context" series. Two individuals were key to its creation. Lead author, Barbara Adams, Ph.D., ran numerous statistical tests to determine the efficacy of the module. Local expert, the late Mary George of Akiachak, Alaska, embodied proportional thinking in her everyday and subsistence-related activities. Her willingness to share this information and her brilliance in being able to integrate Western and Yup'ik knowledge are the foundation for *Drying Salmon*.
3. These authors cite 10 different quasi-experimental studies that identified favorable results for the treatment group, including rural and urban populations.
4. The latter three case studies are found in Lipka, J., Parker Webster, J., & Yanez, E. (Eds.). (2005). *Journal of American Indian Education Special Issue, 44*(3).

Part II

Practice

6

ESL Is Good Teaching "Plus"
Preparing Standard Curriculum Teachers for All Learners

Ester J. de Jong

Candace A. Harper
University of Florida

While the number of culturally and linguistically diverse (CLD) students is increasing rapidly and at a higher rate than the general education population (National Clearinghouse for English Language Acquisition, 2002), there is a critical shortage of specialist bilingual or English as a second language (ESL) teachers (Menken & Antunez, 2001). The majority of CLD pupils with limited English proficiency (English language learners, or ELLs)[1] find themselves in grade-level classrooms taught by teachers with little or no formal professional development in teaching this student population (Barron & Menken, 2002; Kindler, 2002).

This demographic trend is accompanied by a growing assumption that standard curriculum classrooms are optimal learning environments for all students, including CLD students with varying levels of native and second-language proficiency. The focus on standard curriculum classrooms is further reinforced by educational policies at the state and federal levels that stress uniform accountability and assessment systems (Echevarria, Vogt, & Short, 2004; Platt, Harper, & Mendoza, 2003) and that advocate the rapid placement of ELLs in standard curriculum classrooms, such as Proposition 227 in California (e.g., Gándara, 2000; Mora, 2000) or Question 2 in Massachusetts (de Jong, Gort, & Cobb, 2005). Developments within the field of ESL emphasizing language learning through a content-based curriculum (rather than through the study of language itself) have also highlighted the potential of standard curriculum classrooms for ELLs (Crandall, 1995; Snow & Brinton, 1997).

Preparing standard curriculum teachers to work with ELLs should therefore be the concern of all teacher preparation programs. Although some programs offer elective courses specifically related to ELLs, few states require such courses for certification of standard curriculum teachers (Menken & Antunez, 2001). As the demand for teachers prepared to work with ELLs increases, the question arises as to how current general education teacher preparation programs should respond. After providing a rationale for making the linguistic and cultural needs of ELLs visible in teacher preparation, this chapter presents a framework outlining the knowledge, skills, and dispositions that standard curriculum teacher candidates must develop in addition to their general education preparation.

The Need for ELL-Specific Knowledge and Skills

Not everyone agrees that the growing presence of ELLs in standard curriculum classroom settings necessarily requires a change in current teacher preparation practices. As teacher educators, we often hear from our students and faculty colleagues that the educational needs of ELLs are essentially the same as those of native English-speaking students from diverse racial or socioeconomic backgrounds. In this view, teaching ELLs becomes a matter of pedagogical adaptations that can easily be incorporated into a standard curriculum teacher's existing repertoire of "best practices." We have referred to this view as the "just good teaching" (JGT) perspective (de Jong & Harper, 2005).

Many good teaching strategies for diverse students are in fact appropriate for second-language learners. For instance, recommended classroom practices for native English speakers based on constructivist and social interactionist perspectives often correspond with those recommended for the oral language development of ELLs. Practices that support literacy development for native speakers of English, such as guided reading, process writing, and the use of reading strategies to facilitate reading comprehension, can also benefit ELLs (Freeman & Freeman, 2000; Peregoy & Boyle, 2004). Moreover, good teachers make their instruction more accessible through the use of graphic organizers, cooperative learning, hands-on activities, and attention to specialized content-specific vocabulary. They understand that students come to school with a wide range of experiences and they attempt to accommodate these differences, recognizing the danger of stereotypes and inappropriate expectations or interpretations of student behavior. They acknowledge that, like native English speakers, ELLs' background knowledge (or schemata) has been developed through their cultural experiences and that these will influence their conceptual learning and language skills (e.g., vocabulary and reading comprehension). If one accepts that the knowledge and skill base underlying these instructional practices is sufficient to meet the needs of ELLs, there is little reason to reconsider existing teacher preparation programs from an ESL/bilingual perspective. The educational needs of ELLs will be addressed as a natural extension of preparing preservice teachers to work with a diverse group of native English speakers.

The JGT position is problematic for two reasons (for a more detailed discussion, see de Jong & Harper, 2005; see also Clayton, Barnhardt, & Brisk, chapter 2). First, it renders invisible those educational needs that set ELLs apart from U.S.-born, fluent English-speaking students (including vernacular dialect speakers). Second, it leads to classroom practices that, although not necessarily harmful, are not always effective in meeting the needs of ELLs.

The Invisibility of ELLs

By not explicitly acknowledging ELLs, the JGT perspective tends to overlook their specific linguistic and cultural needs. The national standards for core content areas are good examples of the invisibility of ELLs in curriculum planning and implementation (see, for example, National Academy of Sciences, 1995; National Council of Teachers of English [NCTE], 1996; National Council of Teachers of Mathematics, 2000; and National Council for the Social Studies, 1994). These national standards documents provide a comprehensive overview of the disciplinary knowledge base of the content areas and describe effective instructional practices, including using cooperative learning structures, encouraging critical thinking, and building on students' prior knowledge. Though claiming to address "diverse" learners, the standards are primarily directed at a diverse, native English–speaking student population (Dalton, 1998). They tacitly assume that students have mastered sufficient levels of oral language and literacy skills in English to participate meaningfully in content classrooms. Students in these classrooms are expected to learn new information through reading texts, participate actively in class discussions, and demonstrate learning by preparing research papers and presenting oral reports. Whereas most native English speakers are able to take advantage of opportunities for inquiry and discussion (i.e., they can use talk to learn), the standards fail to acknowledge that ELLs face the additional task of mastering the oral language and literacy skills necessary to participate (i.e., they must learn to talk while learning academic content; Gibbons, 2002). These prerequisite language and literacy demands remain invisible in the national standards documents, as do the pedagogical tools that standard curriculum teachers need to provide ELLs with access to high-quality content classrooms (Dalton, 1998).

ELLs are also invisible in teacher education documents, particularly with regard to the linguistic diversity that they add to the classroom. For instance, the guidelines for the preparation of English teachers, while promoting respect for vernacular dialects of English and languages other than English, provide few specifics as to how teachers might include ELLs' native languages (NCTE, 1996). In 2001, following the passage of Proposition 227 limiting services for ELLs to 1-year English immersion programs, the California Council on the Education of Teachers (CCET), the California Association of Teacher Education, and the State of California Association of Teacher Education published a separate document that "translated" or interpreted the California Standards for the Teaching Profession for teacher preparation for ELLs (CCET, 2001), recognizing the significant impact this policy would have on standard curriculum teachers and the different demands it would place on teacher preparation (see also the position paper on diverse learners by the American Association of Colleges for Teacher Education [2002]). Finally, the call for "highly qualified" teachers in the No Child Left Behind (NCLB) legislation excludes bilingual or ESL teachers as core subject area teachers.

These examples illustrate how federal and state educational agendas, while aimed at all students and teachers, tend to exclude ELLs and bilingual and ESL teachers from their initial scope. This exclusion has resulted in the development of separate standards documents (e.g., TESOL PreK–12 Standards for Teacher Education [Teachers of English to Speakers of Other Languages, Inc. (TESOL), 2002]; TESOL Standards for PreK-12 students [TESOL, 1997]) and a series of waivers and "flexibilities" for the assessment of ELLs under the NCLB accountability guidelines. Rather than being included from the outset, ELLs are treated as an afterthought. One exception is a framework proposed by Fillmore & Snow (2002), which specifically includes second language learners. These authors argue that all teachers need to develop a strong foundation in educational linguistics and language and literacy development in order to fulfill their roles as educators, communicators, evaluators, and agents of socialization. Their proposal is an example of how teacher preparation can explicitly address linguistic diversity by thoughtfully integrating such knowledge rather than through an elective, add-on approach that may affect some but not all teacher candidates (Baca & Escamilla, 2002).

JGT in the Classroom

A second reason why the JGT perspective is insufficient for ELLs is because it is grounded in the erroneous assumption that second-language (L2) acquisition and acculturation processes for these students are the same as first-language (L1) acquisition and diverse students' home-school cultural differences. The conclusion is that the linguistic and cultural needs of ELLs are no different than those of native English speakers. JGT teachers who organize their classrooms based on these assumptions may be unaware that their instruction is less than optimal for ELLs (Harper & de Jong, 2004).

JGT and Language and Literacy Instruction   The equation of L1 and L2 acquisition processes frequently leads to the belief that simple exposure to and interaction with native English speakers are sufficient conditions for English language acquisition. As is the case in L1 acquisition, it is assumed that as long as the teacher provides access to native language models (e.g., through comprehensible input, cooperative learning, a print-rich environment, etc.), L2 learners will "pick up" the language naturally (Krashen & Terrell, 1983). However, if a teacher does not go beyond such "laissez-faire" instructional approaches, many ELLs will be unable to take advantage of such unstructured L2 learning opportunities for different reasons. They may have restricted access to the target language because of limited opportunities for student interaction (Harklau, 1999; Harper & Platt, 1998; Valdés, 2001). Native English–speaking peers may have negative attitudes toward ELLs and be unwilling to interact with them (Lindholm, 1990). Finally, ELLs' linguistic inability to participate appropriately (e.g., to question, agree, disagree, or interrupt politely; Coelho, 2004) or the lack of a requirement for each student to contribute to group work (Gibbons, 2002) may also hinder access to L2 input and opportunities for comprehensible output (Swain, 1995).

The danger of equating L1 and L2 acquisition on classroom practices for ELLs also emerges in the area of literacy development when teachers make erroneous assumptions about what works for ELLs. Although oral language is an important foundation for building L2 literacy skills, L2 oral and literacy skills usually develop in a more integrated manner (Freeman & Freeman, 1998; Hudelson, 1984). Delaying the introduction of literacy instruction until students have well-developed oral skills may underestimate (and therefore limit) what ELLs can do. Alternately, teachers of older ELLs may assume that these students bring age-appropriate L1 literacy skills to draw upon and that these skills and strategies will transfer automatically to L2 literacy as students develop oral proficiency in English. While L1 literacy and schooling experiences strongly influence school achievement in English (Cummins, 2000; Thomas & Collier, 2002), Durgunoğlu and Verhoeven (1998) and Jiménez, Garcia, and Pearson (1996) have also shown that transfer is neither guaranteed nor automatic. Further, lack of familiarity with bilingualism may lead standard curriculum teachers to interpret normal bilingual phenomena, such as code-switching, as "language confusion" or, worse, as a language disorder that must be corrected through special needs services.

The JGT perspective also often takes for granted a strong foundation in oral English (i.e., the sound system, vocabulary, grammar, and discourse structures) for literacy development. Assumptions of students' oral proficiency can lead to misdirected L2 reading instruction, such as using nonsense words to teach sound-symbol associations, or inappropriate assessment, such as interpreting a lack of fluency as a lack of reading comprehension. However, ELLs rarely have the same control over the sounds of English and the same access to the target language outside school as native speakers. When an ELL comes across an unknown word, the recommendation to "sound it out" is of limited value if he or she does not already know the meaning of the word orally. In a similar vein, tasks for building phonemic awareness that use minimal pairs to isolate contrasting consonant and vowel sounds (e.g., "bark-park" or "cop-cope") are ineffective if an ELL does not perceive or produce these distinctive contrasts in English (e.g., /l/ may not sound different from /r/, or the vowel sound in "sick" is not distinguished from the vowel sound in "seek") (de Jong & Harper, 2004). Similar assumptions emerge in writing instruction. Prompts commonly used with native speakers such as "Does this word make sense here?" or "Does this sentence sound right?" during teacher-student conferences or written comments at the discourse level that a paragraph is "awkward" will be insufficient for ELLs because they assume the same level of access to native-speaker intuitions regarding English and to fluent L2 language models outside the classroom (Harklau, 1994).

If teachers equate L1 and L2 language development, they may miss opportunities for L2 language and literacy development by failing to support L1 transfer or scaffold appropriate opportunities for ELLs to develop high levels of academic language proficiency. If they are unaware of how instructional practices for L1 speakers rely on a high level of control over the oral language system, they may provide ineffective feedback or fail to mediate the language demands placed on ELLs in their classrooms (Gersten, 1999).

JGT and Cultural Practices   The JGT perspective is not limited to the language domain; it also affects the role of culture in schooling. An awareness of culturally different classroom patterns, such as participation structures and approaches to literacy (Heath, 1983; Michaels, 1981; Nelson-Barber, 1999; Philips, 1983), may increase teachers' sensitivity to cross-cultural differences in expectations. For instance, many ELLs come from cultures in which teachers are considered to be the final authority and questioning the teacher is disrespectful. ELLs may also be less inclined than U.S.-schooled students to publicly display their knowledge (or lack of knowledge) through questioning, answering, or guessing in front of a large group (Au & Carroll, 1997). Differences in nonverbal communication styles (eye gaze, proximity, and physical contact) can also affect student-teacher interactions (e.g., Philips, 1983). Culturally responsive teaching (Gay, 2002) needs to consider cross-cultural communication issues for students other than those who have been born and schooled within the United States.

Even if teacher preparation includes a focus on multicultural education, however, the emphasis on schooling in the United States may overlook issues that specifically affect ELLs. For instance, unlike their U.S.-schooled peers, foreign-born ELLs may be relatively unfamiliar with basic school and classroom routines in American classrooms, such as "dressing out," lining up, or addressing the teacher appropriately (e.g., "Mr. Jones" vs. "Teacher") (Clayton, 1996). Traditional ways of eliciting background knowledge, such as a K-W-L chart, may be ineffective if cross-cultural issues and ELLs' language proficiency are not also taken into account (de Jong & Harper, 2005; Harper & de Jong, 2004). When shared understandings remain unexamined from a bilingual perspective, ELLs may be excluded from sharing their experiences. ELLs, particularly those schooled outside the United States for some time, have rich cultural experiences and skills, but these may not match those developed in American schools. A standard curriculum teacher who uses "Who am I" questions to get to know his or her students may overlook the bilingual and bicultural realities of ELLs (Hornberger & Skilton-Sylvester, 2000; Igoa, 1995) and fail to include questions about language use at home, at school, and in the community (Brisk & Harrington, 2000; Schwarzer, 2001).

Finally, ELLs often find themselves in classrooms that fail to support their bicultural experiences because teachers are unfamiliar with the complex process of bicultural identity development and the sociocultural and sociopolitical pressures that may lead to different acculturation patterns (for more detail on the interaction between identity and schooling, see Clayton, Barnhardt, & Brisk, chapter 2). Teachers may assume that the process of acculturation is linear and a simple matter of choice. For instance, standard curriculum teachers often perceive a student's apparent inability to learn English quickly as a sign of a learning disability or a lack of aptitude for learning a second language. They may interpret students' acting out or tuning out in class as disrespectful behavior. However, some ELLs reject the host culture and language because they see their own identity and language threatened (Portes & Rumbaut, 2001; Rumbaut & Portes, 2001), or they may see learning the L2 as a tacit acceptance of the immigration process, which may have been involuntary and traumatic. Teachers need to understand that their own beliefs and attitudes toward languages other than English and toward multilingualism play an important role in how they facilitate or hinder second-language learners' L2 learning (Baca & Escamilla, 2002; Flores, 2001; Johnson, 1992).

Even the most inclusive constructivist approaches to teaching will be inadequate when they are oriented toward a mainstream student population if they assume that "similarities among students override differences related to ethnicity, primary language, and social class" (Au, 1998, p. 306). Without understanding the process of acculturation and bicultural identity development as well as the sociopolitical and socio-cultural context of language minority education, teachers are likely to fall back on popular myths and personal beliefs about L2 learning and the role of assimilation for school success (Harper & de Jong, 2004; McLaughlin, 1992; Nieto, 2002; Samway & McKeon, 1999).

What Differentiates the ELL Teacher from the Standard Curriculum Teacher?

Standard curriculum teachers who teach in integrated classrooms with ELLs and proficient English speakers find themselves in a unique teaching context that sets them apart from either being a specialist ESL/bilingual teacher or a "regular" grade-level classroom teacher. The need for their preparation has only recently received explicit attention and most teacher education programs have yet to incorporate ELL-related knowledge and skills systematically into their teacher preparation (Menken & Antunez, 2001). The previous section suggested several areas of expertise that standard curricu-lum teachers must develop in order to effectively address the needs of ELLs within their classroom, including:

- ways that L1 and L2 language and literacy development are simi-lar and different
- issues of bilingualism and biculturalism
- the process of acculturation and bicultural identity development
- the sociopolitical context of teaching ELLs.

In this section, we will review studies that have compared the knowledge and skills of ESL/bilingual teachers and standard curriculum teachers and report preliminary findings from our own research in this area.

Comparing ESL/Bilingual Teachers and Standard Curriculum Teachers

Few studies have directly compared the knowledge and skill base of standard curriculum and bilingual/ESL teachers. Quintanar-Sarellana (1991; cited in Grant, 1992) focused on the culture domain. She surveyed bilingual and English-only teachers and found that the former had more-positive attitudes toward the students' native languages and cultures. She proposed that teachers must develop sociocultural knowledge—in other words, "understanding of their own culture, as well as appreciation of other cultures and intercultural knowledge" (p. 21). Constantino (1994), on the other hand, identified key differences in the area of teacher roles and accommodations for different proficiency levels. She interviewed five ESL and six standard curriculum classroom teachers regarding their classroom practices and beliefs toward ELLs. Differences between the two groups were found in several areas, including the extent to which each group perceived their classroom as facilitating language development and the degree to which they made adaptations for ELLs. For example, the regular education teachers did not feel that language development was their responsibility, "they were teaching content not language" (p. 43; emphasis in original). They did not see the need to implement accommodations but, according to Constantino, lowered their expectations instead. As one teacher stated "They have a difficult time understanding me, but I don't treat them any different" (Constantino, 1994, p. 45). In contrast, Constantino found that the ESL teachers considered language explicitly when they planned and implemented their lessons and made more accommodations, particularly in the area of vocabulary development.

Similar differences between ESL and standard curriculum teachers emerged in a pilot study where we asked 12 experienced ESL teachers (the average numbers of years of teaching was 16.5) who were also involved with standard curriculum teacher education to describe what they saw as the key differences between a good ESL teacher and a good standard curriculum teacher. These ESL teachers first of all confirmed Constantino's finding that many standard curriculum teachers do not see language teaching as their responsibility and hence provide few focused or purposeful language development opportunities. Other studies have noted the challenge of shifting roles from content teacher to content *and* language teacher as part of the process of taking responsibility for ELLs and their learning (Mora & Grisham, 2001; Penfield, 1987; Short, 2002). Second, the interviewees stressed the affective domain of teaching ELLs, which often includes an extension of the role of classroom teacher into that of a family member or caregiver. Besides keeping close tabs on their ELLs and their performance in school, many ESL/bilingual teachers take on the role of advocates outside the school setting, helping immigrant families negotiate their new world (Olsen, 1997). Another theme that emerged from these interviews was the lack of standard curriculum teachers' understanding of the process of second-language acquisition. The ESL teachers explained that standard curriculum teachers typically do not recognize the time required for many ELLs to develop high levels of academic language proficiency in English. They assume that second language development will take place quickly and easily, given sufficient amounts of exposure to and use of the language.

What these studies illustrate is that one primary role of the ESL teacher is that of a language teacher—in other words, being able to mediate for comprehensible input and providing appropriate feedback on L2 development and focused instruction as needed (Lightbown, 1986). Assuming that ELLs need support in accomplishing their dual task of language and content development (and that they will not necessarily succeed in this task by osmosis), standard curriculum teachers need to embrace the role of language teacher. They must develop the knowledge and skills that will allow them to carry out this role within their standard curriculum classroom. Insights from teachers working with ELLs in integrated settings illustrate the nature of this role. Gersten (1999) reported that standard curriculum teachers with little to no preparation to work with ELLs were culturally distanced from their students and needed explicit support in how they could guide ELLs' language and literacy development. Brisk, Dawson, Hartgering, MacDonald, and Zehr (2002) described how standard curriculum teachers learned to work with bilingual students. While the teachers commented that they could extend good existing teaching practices to ELLs, they also had to make specific accommodations for their bilingual learners. Based on the four teachers' experiences, the authors conclude that these teachers learned to:

> help the whole class by addressing the bilingual learners' academic needs; make bilingual approaches for bilingual learners part of the class routine; get to know the students; teach bilingual students as bilinguals;

use students' languages and cultures to facilitate acquisition of English; have high expectations for all students; adapt approaches carefully; enlist support from others; and encourage positive attitudes towards bilingualism. (Brisk et al., 2002, p. 112–113)

These studies confirm the importance of understanding the implications of second-language acquisition for instruction, considering the second-language learning process from a bilingual perspective, understanding the role of affective variables in supporting ELLs, and understanding the influence of sociocultural context on schooling practices.

Including ELL-Specific Knowledge in Teacher Preparation

Traditionally, teacher preparation programs have not required ELL-specific course work for general educators, although states have guidelines for ESL or bilingual teacher certification to prepare specialist teachers (Menken & Antunez, 2001). In response to the changing demographics, some states are moving toward including course work related to ELLs in all teacher preparation programs. Florida is one of the few states to mandate such teacher preparation. This requirement was one of the outcomes of a legal challenge that resulted in a consent decree governing the schooling of ELLs in 1990. The Florida Department of Education has outlined specific professional development guidelines for elementary and secondary teachers and, more recently, for counselors and school administrators (online http://www.firn.edu/doe/aala/omsinst.htm). The most common way that colleges of education have met this mandate is by developing ESL-infused teacher preparation programs. In an ESL-infused teacher preparation program, students take two or three ESL-specific courses taught by ESL/bilingual faculty while other state-mandated competencies related to ELLs are infused in the other general education courses. While Florida's universities have implemented ESL-infused programs throughout the state, little is known about their organization or outcomes (but see Morales-Jones, 2003). One of the questions raised by this model is what must be taught in the ELL-specific courses and what will be taught in the general education courses in order to avoid excessive overlap and repetition for students.

As part of an ongoing effort to document the preparedness of elementary teachers to work with ELLs, we have begun a study that attempts to identify the knowledge and skills that elementary teachers must develop in addition to their general education preparation. The study focuses on a 5-year ESL-infused teacher preparation program. The program consists of two ELL-specific courses: one undergraduate course focusing on the foundations of language and culture and one graduate course on ESL curriculum, methods, and assessment. Coverage of state-required ESL competencies, which roughly cluster around issues of culture, language, curriculum, instruction, and assessment, occurs throughout the rest of the program.

A first step in the process of differentiating the content of the ELL-specific courses from the general education courses was to describe the extent to which issues specifically related to ELLs were addressed in general education courses. Sixteen faculty members who were responsible for teaching and coordinating undergraduate courses were asked to identify on a survey which of the state-mandated ESL standards their classes covered and how they addressed these standards. During a 1-hour follow-up interview, more detailed information was obtained from each faculty member. Analysis of the surveys and the interviews showed that the standards related to cultural diversity (e.g., creating a positive learning environment for different learning styles and cultural backgrounds) were addressed more frequently and in more courses than language-related issues or ESL-specific pedagogical issues (e.g., using knowledge of the structure of the English language to adapt instruction for different L2 proficiency levels). In addition, the general education courses assigned few readings or tasks related specifically to ELLs. Finally, issues regarding linguistic diversity were most likely to be included if faculty members themselves were second-language learners or had worked with ELLs.

Another step in this study involved the administration of a student survey in the two ELL-specific courses. The survey asked students to indicate their level of agreement with 20 statements related to language and culture and also included four open-ended questions. For this discussion, the students' responses to a question asking them to describe the difference between teaching a group of native English speakers and teaching an integrated group of native English speakers and ELLs are most relevant. A total of 86 undergraduate students who had completed their first ELL-specific course and a total 128 graduate students in the final semester of their graduate year responded to this question. Most students indicated that they thought accommodations were needed but did not specify the nature of these accommodations. When specific recommendations were included, they mentioned the increased use of visuals, gestures, a slower rate of speech, and more repetition. Some students also referred to accommodating for different learning styles and being aware of differences in general or cultural background knowledge. These findings suggest that the undergraduate preservice students (who had not been exposed to an ESL methods class) perceived teaching ELLs predominantly as a matter of expanding their repertoire of pedagogical tools to accommodate the cultural differences and language demands of instruction for ELLs. Like the standard curriculum teachers in the studies cited earlier, these students do not yet see themselves as language teachers responsible for providing opportunities for language development (see also Mora & Grisham, 2001).

Although the majority of graduate students had completed their pre-practicum, internship, and methods courses by the time they completed the survey, their responses showed similar patterns. They referred to the importance of understanding the stages of oral proficiency and stressed the ability of teachers to make their instruction comprehensible. The generic nature of the graduate students' understanding of the needs of ELLs was confirmed when they engaged in lesson planning. At the beginning of the semester in which they took their second ELL-specific course, 78 students were asked to evaluate a lesson plan developed for a standard curriculum classroom from the perspective of an ELL. They had to indicate whether they thought they would have to make any changes to their instructional objectives, methods, groupings, activities, or assessments and, if so, what kinds of changes. Forty percent of the graduate students indicated they saw no need for a change; they considered their lessons appropriate for ELLs. Those indicating a need for changes suggested the following accommodations: allowing nonverbal instead of verbal responses, pairing an ELL with a native-English speaker, and using visuals or hands-on activities. These results illustrate that even toward the end of their 5-year program, preservice teachers' instructional accommodations focused on comprehensibility. Scaffolding for second-language development remained a relatively invisible component in their lesson planning.

Our research involving both education faculty and preservice teachers indicates, first, that it may be easier to incorporate cultural issues than linguistic issues in teacher education. This finding parallels the relatively minor role that linguistic diversity (particularly as it relates to ELLs) has played in the multicultural literature in contrast to race/ethnicity, class, gender, and special needs (Nieto, 2002). Second, although preservice teachers readily considered strategies to increase comprehensibility of content instruction, the ability to provide sustained and extended opportunities for social and academic language development appears to be the skill area that is most specific to ELLs (see also Gersten, 1999).

Describing the "Plus" of ELL Teaching

Teachers must be able to appropriately differentiate the educational needs of ELLs from those of other students in order to ensure ELLs' equal access to a quality curriculum. To achieve the goal of equal access, educational policy and teacher preparation programs must make the needs of ELLs visible in the broader context of "diversity." In terms of educational policy, it is crucial that ELLs are explicitly included in national content standards, accountability guidelines, and efforts at improving pedagogy. Furthermore, ESL and bilingual teachers should be acknowledged as core subject teachers (TESOL, 2005). Regarding teacher preparation, our study shows that teachers must be able to establish a learning environment based on more than just good teaching. Even very good teachers may fail to support bilingual children adequately in their classrooms if they are unprepared to identify and mediate the specific cultural and linguistic needs of these students. Therefore, teaching fluent English speakers and ELLs is "good teaching plus." Based on our previous discussion, four key areas emerge that describe these knowledge and skills. These include

- Effective teachers of ELLs understand the nature of language in the classroom and make appropriate accommodations for ELLs at different proficiency levels to make content more accessible.
- Effective teachers of ELLs understand the process of second-language acquisition and bilingualism and organize their classrooms to reflect insights from this research.
- Effective teachers of ELLs understand the complex interactions between language, culture, and school and implement a culturally responsive classroom that considers students' bilingual and bicultural realities and the sociocultural foundations of schooling.

- Effective teachers of ELLs understand the dual task that ELLs face in schools and accept responsibility for their language and literacy development, in addition to content teaching.

In short, good teachers of ELLs carefully consider the role of language and culture in schooling from a bilingual and bicultural perspective. This implies that teachers also have the necessary dispositions to translate knowledge and skills into effective instruction. Sonia Nieto (2000) notes that teaching ELLs successfully means "above all challenging one's attitudes toward the students, their languages and cultures, and their communities. Anything short of this will result in repeating the pattern of failure that currently exists" (p. 196). Without also changing teacher candidates' beliefs and attitudes toward ELLs, chances are that their classroom practices will not significantly change.

Conclusion

Teacher preparation programs aim to provide teacher candidates with the knowledge, skills, and dispositions to be effective teachers for all learners. ELLs must become an explicit and visible aspect of the definition of "all learners." Rather than subsuming ELLs under the educational needs of diverse, native-English speaking student populations, teachers must learn to identify and respond to these students' specific linguistic and cultural needs. Without such knowledge, standard curriculum teachers may resort to generic "good teaching" practices that exclude ELLs' strengths and experiences and may result in less than optimal academic and language-learning environments for ELLs (Brisk et al., 2002; Dalton, 1998; Davison, 1999; Grant & Wong, 2003; Harper & Platt, 1998). Rather than closing the existing achievement gap for ELLs, JGT practices risk further widening this gap.

To approach the education of ELLs, standard curriculum teachers must be able to examine monolingual assumptions in educational policy as well as their own practices. Besides recognizing similarities between L1 and L2 acquisition, they must also understand how L2 language development and acculturation differs from L1 acquisition and enculturation (Lessow-Hurley, 2004), particularly for more mature literate and preliterate ELLs. Teachers must not only acknowledge the role of language and culture in schooling, they must also be able to organize their curriculum and instruction to purposefully scaffold (academic) second-language development and support an additive process of bilingualism and biculturalism. The latter requires that teachers move away from a deficit stance that treats ELLs as a problem and toward an additive approach that builds on ELLs' bilingual and bicultural realities, knowledge, and skills. Cummins (2000) argues that effective teachers working with minority language students must operate within a framework of transformative pedagogy. This framework not only provides a collaborative space for the negotiation of identities but also places academic language development at the center of the curriculum. Academic language learning can occur by focusing on meaning (making input comprehensible, developing critical literacy), on language (linguistic awareness and critical analysis of language forms and use), and on use (applying language to generate new knowledge, create literature and art, and act on social realities (Cummins, 2000, pp. 273–280). If teacher preparation programs fail to make bilingual students visible in their curriculum through field experiences, readings, and discussions that explicitly address ELLs, future teachers will continue to evaluate and address the needs of ELLs according to native English-speaking norms and will fail to meet their unique linguistic and cultural needs.

References

American Association of Colleges for Teacher Education. (2002). *Educators' preparation for cultural and linguistic diversity: A call to action.* Retrieved May 2, 2007 from http://www.eric.ed.gov/ERICDocs/data/ ericdocs2/content storage 01/0000000b/80/22/44/a0.pdf

Au, K. H. (1998). Social constructivism and the school literacy learning of students of diverse backgrounds. *Journal of Literacy Research, 30,* 297–319.

Au, K. H., & Carroll, J. H. (1997). Improving literacy achievement through a constructivist approach: The KEEP demonstration classroom project. *Elementary School Journal, 97,* 203–221.

Baca, L., & Escamilla, K. (2002). Educating teachers about language. In C. T. Adger, C. E. Snow, & D. Christian (Eds.), *What teachers need to know about language* (pp. 71–84). Washington, DC: Center for Applied Linguistics and Delta Systems.

Barron, V., & Menken, K. (2002). *What are the characteristics of the short-age of teachers qualified to teach English language learners?* Retrieved May 2, 2007 from http://www.ncela.gwu.edu/pubs/reports/teacher prep/teacherprep.pdf

Brisk, M. E., Dawson, M., Hartgering, M., MacDonald, E., & Zehr, L. (2002). Teaching bilingual students in mainstream classrooms. In Z. F. Beykont (Ed.), *The power of culture: Teaching across language difference* (pp. 89–120). Cambridge, MA: Harvard Education Publishing Group.

Brisk, M. E., & Harrington, M. (2000). *Literacy and bilingualism.* Mahwah, NJ: Lawrence Erlbaum.

California Council on the Education of Teachers. (2001). Success for English language learners: Teacher preparation policies and practices. *Teacher Education Quarterly, 28*(1), 199–208.

Clayton, J. B. (1996). *Your land, my land: Children in the process of acculturation.* Portsmouth, NH: Heinemann.

Coelho, E. (2004). *Adding English: A guide to teaching in multilingual classrooms.* Toronto, Canada: Pippin Publishing.

Constantino R. (1994). A study concerning instruction of ESL students comparing all-English classroom teacher knowledge and English as a second language teacher knowledge. *Journal of Educational Issues of Language Minority Students, 13*, Spring, 37–57.

Crandall, J. A. (Ed.). (1995). *ESL through content-area instruction.* Washington, DC: Center for Applied Linguistics.

Cummins, J. (2000). *Language, power, and pedagogy: Bilingual children in the crossfire.* Clevedon: Multilingual Matters.

Dalton, S. S. (1998). *Pedagogy matters: Standards for effective teaching practice.* Santa Cruz, CA: Center for Research on Education, Diversity & Excellence. Retrieved October 10, 2005, from http://crede.berkeley.edu/pdf/rr04.pdf

Davison, C. (1999). Missing the mark: The problem with the benchmarking of ESL students in Australian schools. *Prospect, 14*(2), 66–76.

de Jong, E. J., Gort, M., & Cobb, C. S. (2005). Bilingual education within the context of English only policies: Three districts' responses to Question 2 in Massachusetts. *Educational Policy, 19*, 595–620.

de Jong, E. J., & Harper, C. A. (2004). Is ESL just good teaching? In M. H. Bigelow & C. L. Walker (Eds.), *Creating teacher community: Selected papers from the third international conference on language teacher education* (pp. 115–131). Minneapolis, Minnesota: Center for Advanced Research on Language Acquisition.

de Jong, E. J., & Harper, C. A. (2005). Preparing mainstream teachers for English language learners: Is being a good teacher good enough? *Teacher Education Quarterly, 32*(2), 101–124.

Durgunoğlu, A. Y., & Verhoeven, L. (1998). *Literacy development in a multilingual context: Cross-cultural perspectives.* Mahwah, NJ: Lawrence Erlbaum.

Echevarria, J., Vogt, M., & Short, D. (2004). *Making content comprehensible for English language learners. The SIOP model* (2nd ed.). Needham Heights, MA: Allyn and Bacon.

Fillmore, L. W., & Snow, C. E. (2002). *What teachers need to know about language.* Washington, DC: ERIC Clearinghouse of Languages and Linguistics.

Flores, B. B. (2001). Bilingual education teachers' beliefs and their relation to self-reported practices. *Bilingual Research Journal, 25,* 251–275.

Freeman, D. E., & Freeman, Y. S. (2000). *Teaching reading in multilingual classrooms.* Portsmouth, NH: Heinemann.

Freeman, Y. S., & Freeman, D. E. (1998). *ESL/EFL teaching: Principles for success.* Portsmouth, NH: Heinemann.

Gándara, P. (2000). In the aftermath of the storm: English learners in the post-227 era. *Bilingual Research Journal, 24*(1&2), 1–14.

Gay, G. (2002). Preparing for culturally responsive teaching. *Journal of Teacher Education, 53,* 106–116.

Gersten, R. (1999). Lost opportunities: Challenges confronting four teachers of English-language learners. *Elementary School Journal, 100*(1), 37–56.

Gibbons, P. (2002). *Scaffolding language, scaffolding learning.* Portsmouth, NH: Heinemann.

Grant, C. A. (1992). Educational research and teacher training for successfully teaching LEP students. *Proceedings of the Second National Research Symposium on Limited English Proficient Student Issues: Focus on Evaluation and Measurement.* Retrieved October 10, 2005, from http://www.ncela.gwu.edu/pubs/symposia/second/vol2/educational.htm

Grant, E. A., & Wong, S. D. (2003). Barriers to literacy for language-minority learners: An argument for change in the literacy education profession. *Journal of Adolescent & Adult Literacy, 46,* 386–394.

Harklau, L. (1994). ESL versus mainstream classes: Contrasting L2 learning environments. *TESOL Quarterly, 28,* 241–272.

Harklau, L. (1999). The ESL learning environment in secondary school. In C. J. Faltis & P. Wolfe (Eds.), *So much to say: Adolescents, bilingualism, & ESL in the secondary school* (pp. 42–60). New York: Teachers College Press.

Harper, C. A., & de Jong, E. J. (2004). Misconceptions about teaching ELLs. *Journal of Adolescent and Adult Literacy, 48,* 152–162.

Harper, C. A., & Platt, E. J. (1998). Full inclusion for secondary school ESOL students: Some concerns from Florida. *TESOL Journal, 7*(5), 30–36.

Heath, S. B. (1983). *Ways with words: Language, life, and work in communities and classrooms.* Cambridge, UK: Cambridge University Press.

Hornberger, N., & Skilton-Sylvester, E. (2000). Revisiting the continua of biliteracy: International and critical perspectives. *Language and Education, 14,* 96–122.

Hudelson, S. (1984). Kan yu ret an rayt in Ingles: Children becoming literate in English as a second language. *TESOL Quarterly, 18,* 221–238.

Igoa, C. (1995). *The inner world of the immigrant child.* Mahwah, NJ: Lawrence Erlbaum.

Jiménez, R. T., Garcia, G. E., & Pearson, D. E. (1996). The reading strategies of bilingual Latina/o students who are successful English readers: Opportunities and obstacles. *Reading Research Quarterly, 31,* 90–112.

Johnson, K. (1992). The relationship between teachers' beliefs and practices during literacy instruction for non-native speakers of English. *Journal of Reading Behavior, 24*(1), 83–108.

Kindler, A. L. (2002). *Survey of the states' limited English proficient students and available educational programs and services. 2000–2001 Summary Report.* Washington, DC: National Clearinghouse for English Language Acquisition & Language Instruction Education Programs.

Krashen, S. D., & Terrell, S. D. (1983). *The natural approach: Language acquisition in the classroom.* New York: Pergamon Press.

Lessow-Hurley, J. (2004). *Foundations of dual language instruction* (4th ed.). Boston, MA: Pearson Education.

Lightbown, P. M. (1986). What's an ESL teacher good for? *TESL Canada Journal,* Special Issue, November, 1–15.

Lindholm, K. J. (1990). Bilingual immersion education: Criteria for program development. In A. M. Padilla, H. H. Fairchild, & C. M. Valadez (Eds.), *Bilingual education: Issues and strategies* (pp. 91–105). Newbury Park: Sage.

McLaughlin, B. (1992). *Myths and misconceptions about second language learning: What every teacher needs to unlearn.* (Educational Practice Rep. No. 5). Washington, DC and Santa Cruz, CA: National Center for Research on Cultural Diversity and Second Language Learning.

Menken, K., & Antunez, B. (2001). *An overview of the preparation and certification of teachers working with limited English proficient (LEP) students.* Washington, DC: National Clearinghouse for Bilingual Education.

Michaels, S. (1981). Sharing time: Children's narrative styles and differential access to literacy. *Language in Society, 10,* 423–442.

Mora, J. K. (2000). Staying the course in times of change. Preparing teachers for language minority education. *Journal of Teacher Education, 51,* 345–357.

Mora, J. K., & Grisham, D. L. (2001). ¡What deliches tortillas! Preparing teachers for literacy instruction in linguistically diverse classrooms. *Teacher Education Quarterly, 28*(4), 51–70.

Morales-Jones, C. A. (2003). Pioneering an elementary/ESOL infused teacher preparation program in Florida. *Sunshine State TESOL Journal 2*(2), 1–8.

National Academy of Sciences. (1995). *National science education standards.* Retrieved October 10, 2005, from http://www.nap.edu/readingroom/books/nses/html/

National Clearinghouse for English Language Acquisition. (2002). *State elementary and secondary LEP enrollment growth and top languages, 1999–2000.* Retrieved October 11, 2004, from http://www.ncela.gwu.edu/pubs/reports/state-data/2000/

National Council for the Social Studies. (1994). *Expectations of excellence: Curriculum standards for social studies.* Waldorf, Maryland: NCSS Publications.

National Council of Teachers of English. (1996). *Guidelines for the preparation of teachers of English language arts.* Urbana, IL: Author.

National Council of Teachers of Mathematics. (2000*). Principles and standards for school mathematics.* Retrieved October 10, 2005, from http://www.nctm.org/standards/

Nelson-Barber, S. (1999). A better education for every child: The dilemma for teachers of culturally and linguistically diverse students. In Mid-continent Research Education and Learning (McREL) (Ed.), *Including culturally and linguistically diverse students in standards-based reform: A report on McREL's diversity roundtable* I. (4-14). Aurora, CO: Author. Retrieved October 10, 2005, from http://www.mcrel.org/PDF/Diversity/5997IR_DiversityRT1.pdf

Nieto, S. (2000). *Affirming diversity: The sociopolitical context of multicultural education* (3rd ed.). New York: Longman.

Nieto, S. (2002). *Language, culture, and teaching. Critical perspectives for a new century.* Mahwah, NJ: Lawrence Erlbaum.

Olsen, L. (1997). *Made in America. Immigrant students in our public schools.* New York: The New Press.

Peregoy, S. F., & Boyle, O. F. (2004). *Reading, writing, and learning in ESL: A resource book for K–8 teachers* (3rd ed.). New York: Longman.

Penfield, J. (1987). ESL: The regular classroom teacher's perspective. *TESOL Quarterly, 21,* 21–39.

Philips, S. U. (1983). *The invisible culture: Communication in classroom and community on the Warm Springs Indian Reservation.* White Plains, NY: Longman.

Platt, E., Harper, C. A., & Mendoza, M. B. (2003). Dueling philosophies: Inclusion or separation for Florida's English language learners? *TESOL Quarterly, 37,* 105–33.

Portes, A., & Rumbaut, R. G. (Eds.). (2001). *Legacies: The story of the immigrant second generation.* Berkeley, CA: University of California Press.

Rumbaut, R. G., & Portes, A. (Eds.), (2001). *Ethnicities: Children of immigrants in America.* Berkeley, CA: University of California Press.

Samway, K. D., & McKeon, D. (1999*). Myths and realities: Best practices for language minority students.* Portsmouth, NH: Heinemann.

Schwarzer, D. (2001). *Noa's ark: One child's voyage into multiliteracy.* Portsmouth, NH: Heinemann.

Short, D. (2002). Language learning in sheltered social studies classes. *TESOL Journal, 11*(1), 18–24.

Snow, M. A., & Brinton, D. M. (1997). *The content-based classroom: Perspectives on integrating language and content.* White Plains, NY: Longman.

Swain, M. (1995). Three functions of output in second language learning. In G. Cook & B. Seidlhofer (Eds.), *Principle and practice in applied linguistics: Studies in honour of H. G. Widdowson* (pp. 125–144). Oxford: Oxford University Press.

Teachers of English to Speakers of Other Languages, Inc. (1997). *TESOL standards for PreK–12 students.* Alexandria, VA: Author.

Teachers of English to Speakers of Other Languages, Inc.. (2002). *TESOL/ NCATE P-12 standards for teacher education programs.* Alexandria, VA: Author.

Teachers of English to Speakers of Other Languages, Inc. (2005). *Position statement on highly qualified teachers under No Child Left Behind.* Retrieved October 10, 2005, from http://www.tesol.org/s_tesol/seccss. asp?CID=32&DID=37

Thomas, W. P., & Collier, V. (2002). *A national study on the school effectiveness for language minority students' long-term academic achievement. Final Report: Project 1.1.* Santa Cruz, CA: Center for Excellence on Education, Diversity, & Excellence. Retrieved on October 10, 2005, from http://www.crede.org/research/llaa/1.1_final.html

Valdés, G. (2001). *Learning and not learning English: Latino students in American schools.* New York: Teachers College Press.

Endnotes

1. Because our chapter focuses on students whose English proficiency levels range from beginner to intermediate/advanced, we will use the term "English language learner" (ELL). The group of CLD students includes ELLs but also students fully proficient in English.

7

Classic
Transforming Hearts and Minds

Socorro G. Herrera

Kevin G. Murry

Della R. Pérez
Kansas State University

Institutions of higher education (IHEs) have been challenged to develop programs for teacher preparation and professional development that better prepare educators to meet the differential language, learning, and socialization needs of culturally and linguistically diverse (CLD) students (Montecinos, 2004; Walton, Baca, & Escamilla, 2002; Wong Fillmore & Snow, 2002). Cognizant of the need to address this challenge, IHEs have responded in broad strokes. Among the many initiatives undertaken by IHE-based programs in teacher preparation and professional development are the following examples: culturally responsive programming initiatives (Phuntsog, 2001); curriculum adaptations designed to encourage teacher research on complex issues of diversity (Nevarez-La Torre & Rolón-Dow, 2000); programs to improve the recruitment and retention of preservice-teacher candidates from underrepresented groups (Murry, 2003); transactional approaches to instruction for teacher preparation (Arias & Poynor, 2001); cross-linguistic relationship- and community-based professional development programs (Beattie, 2002); literacy-based teacher education for linguistic diversity in the classroom (Timperley & Phillips, 2003); and curricular modifications to promote critical thinking models in teacher preparation (Varghese and Stritikus, 2005).

Certainly, these emergent and ongoing innovations in teacher preparation and professional development for classroom diversity are both essential and promising. Nonetheless, little has been done to address those critical capacities that teachers ought to develop and strengthen as goals of their preservice preparation and in-service professional development for linguistic diversity in the classroom (Montecinos, 2004; Varghese & Stritikus, 2005; Walton et al., 2002).

The Accommodation Readiness Spiral

Elsewhere, we have argued that teachers' preparation and professional development for culturally and, in particular, linguistically diverse classrooms should target those capacities represented by the six levels of the *accommodation readiness spiral* (Herrera & Murry, 2005), or ARS (see Figure 7.1). The superordinate goal of this spiral-grounded capacity building for readiness is the mutual accommodation of CLD students.

Unlike the traditional notion of one-way, student-initiated accommodation, *mutual accommodation* describes a reciprocal relationship between teacher and CLD student. In this reciprocal relationship, the teacher and the CLD student collaborate to maximize the resources that each brings to the educational process and to select from among "the best strategies at the disposition of each" (Nieto, 1992, p. 258). As the knowledge that the CLD student brings to the classroom (e.g., bilingualism, cross-national experiences, family resources) is maximized, the teacher's mutually accommodative maximization of those resources increasingly involves the teacher in personal and professional capacity building for diversity.

A Framework of Capacity Building for Diversity

Whether through preservice preparation or through the professional development of practitioners, capacity building for teachers is about readiness for the appropriate accommodation of differential student needs. Teacher readiness to accommodate the CLD student is described by the six levels of the ARS (Herrera & Murry, 2005). The spiral is an emergent framework of teacher readiness for classroom diversity and is based on more than 10 years of field experience and evolving research (Herrera & Murry, 2005; Murry & Herrera, 1999). The six levels of the accommodation readiness spiral are illustrated in Figure 7.1. They range from Level One, *readiness for critical reflection on practice*, to Level Six, *readiness for application and advocacy*.

A spiral best represents teachers' preparedness for accommodation readiness because the process of capacity building for each subsequent level is progressive; however, regression to a prior level is always a possibility. For example, the attainment of Level One readiness, *readiness for critical reflection on practice*, serves as essential preparation for Level Two readiness, *readiness for CLD students and families*. A foundation of reflective capacities is essential to progress along the spiral because effective and productive interactions with CLD students and families require *reflection* (validity testing) on the range of cross-cultural assumptions that teachers may hold as they interact with individuals of a culture (or a language) different from their own. Similarly, such interactions also require a capacity for *critical reflection* (testing the influences of one's socialization biography).

This is so because it is one's prior socialization in a particular culture (especially a culture different from that of the CLD student) that is typically at the core of misconceptions and inaccurate assumptions about CLD students or their family members. By the time that most graduates of teacher preparation programs begin their instruction in diverse classrooms, they have already experienced 20 or more years of primary and secondary socialization in the dominant culture (Montecinos, 2004; Walton et al., 2002; Wong Fillmore & Snow, 2002). Many of their professional experiences with CLD students will not match the expectations that are part and parcel of that socialization. A capacity for reflection on those mismatches is, therefore, critical to the teacher's readiness for classroom effectiveness with increasing numbers of these students.

As teachers learn from, and build readiness for, their cross-linguistic and intercultural interactions with CLD students and families, regression along the many levels of the spiral tends to become incrementally less recurrent. These teachers are building the capacities over time to critically reflect on the complexities of each level of the ARS.

As illustrated in Figure 7.1, the ARS is also a double helix because a teacher's readiness for accommodation can be either apparent or demonstrable. *Apparent readiness* is indicative of what the educator says, and may believe, about her or his level of readiness for accommodation. Apparent readiness operates at the conscious level and may vary considerably in

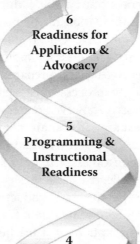

ESPOUSED ⟶   ⟵ PRACTICAL

Figure 7.1

response to new information, training, or ideas. Although the educator may believe that apparent readiness guides his or her actions, a closer examination of practices may suggest discrepancies.

Demonstrable readiness, on the other hand, is so deeply ingrained in the teacher's consciousness that she or he may not be able to fully articulate the nature of that readiness. Unlike apparent readiness, an individual's level of demonstrable readiness is formulated over years of socialization before and during professional practice. Accordingly, a teacher's level of demonstrable readiness is not so easily recognized or changed.

In contrast to demonstrable capacities, apparent (or espoused) readiness among teachers is sometimes unfortunately indicative of unchecked or unreflective assumptions and beliefs of primary socialization that tend to limit effectiveness in practice with CLD students. Not surprisingly, then, a particular teacher's level of demonstrable capacities may not support his or her apparent (or espoused) degree of readiness for accommodation.

Quality programs of teacher preparation and professional development should guide teachers in both recognizing such discrepancies and in building capacities for more reflective (assumption-checking) practices. When discrepancies exist between these two types of readiness, deeply ingrained and unchecked assumptions born of socio-historical perspectives on teaching tend to prevent new intentions of apparent readiness from appropriately guiding the educator's professional actions in practice. If the discrepancy between the two types of readiness grows sufficiently large, the double helix of the ARS soon becomes so distorted that the spiral collapses. Such a situation often suggests the teacher's need to personally and professionally rethink and reconstruct his or her readiness for the appropriate accommodation of CLD students and families.

Levels of Teacher Readiness for Diversity

Each of the six levels of the ARS is progressive and increasingly indicative of the teacher's capacity building for effective praxis with CLD students. As illustrated in Figure 7.1, the first level of the spiral describes the teacher's readiness to surface assumptions about practice with cultural and linguistic diversity, test the validity of those assumptions, and examine whether their origin lies in the teacher's prior socialization in a culture different from that of the student. The second level of the spiral highlights the teacher's readiness to recognize, explore, and maximize those resources, those funds of knowledge (e.g., value placed on education, bilingualism, cross-cultural biography) that CLD students and their immediate or extended family members may bring to the learning environment. The third level of the spiral describes the teacher's capacity to preassess, monitor, and make the most of both the internal environment (e.g., environmental print, classroom arrangement, literacy support) and external environment (e.g., status of CLD students' native languages in the community, family or community involvement) for language and academic learning. The fourth level of the spiral explores the teacher's readiness to emphasize those curriculum essentials (e.g., the adopted curriculum, knowledge of standards or benchmarks, access to the curriculum) that are critical to the classroom success of CLD students. The fifth level of the spiral describes the teacher's readiness to evaluate the efficacy of programming (e.g., bilingual, dual language, English as a second language [ESL]) for CLD students and to differentiate classroom instruction (e.g., process and product, preinstructional and postinstructional assessment) for them. Ultimately, the sixth level of the spiral describes the teacher's readiness to advocate for the rights of, differentiated practices with, and appropriate services for CLD students and families.

Building Readiness: Program Implementation and Research

To reiterate, the ARS (Herrera & Murry, 2005) serves as an emergent framework for capacity building among educators of CLD students. This capacity building is especially focused on efficacy in practice with classroom diversity. This chapter will explore the efforts of one Midwestern university to implement professional development that was designed to target and develop accommodation readiness among in-service teachers of CLD students. The model of professional development implemented (hereinafter referred to as the Differentiated Professional Development [DPD] Model) has been developed and refined over the past 10 years. It has served as the cornerstone of professional development for more than 2,500 in-service teachers in five states. Among specific emphases of the DPD Model is the professional development of grade-level, classroom teachers for linguistic diversity in the classroom, including attainment of the ESL endorsement.

Of particular concern to this exploration of professional development for accommodation readiness were two critical research questions: (a) What are the key challenges of fostering accommodation readiness through targeted professional development? and (b) What perspectives on capacity building for accommodation readiness, at each of the six levels of the ARS, emerge as in-service teachers participate in this professional development? Participant teachers included 200 grade-level educators from nine rural and five urban school districts in two Midwestern states. These practicing teachers were enrolled in professional development toward the ESL endorsement (15 credit hours), including courses in: (a) ESL methods, linguistics, and assessment; (b) multicultural education emphasizing cross-linguistic interactions; and (c) a portfolio-based practicum experience.

Of the 200 participating teachers, 89% self-classified their ethnicity as European American, 5% as African American, 4% as Asian American, and 2% as Mexican American. This stratification was consistent with typical faculty distributions for participating Midwestern school districts. Among these participating educators, 92% were female, 8% were male; 77% were elementary educators and 23% were middle or high school teachers. Of the 200 research participants, 24% were *new to the profession*; 22% possessed 1 to 2 years of teaching experience; 17%, 3 to 5 years; 18%, 6 to 10 years; and 9%, more than 10 years of service.

The outcomes of professional development undertaken according to the DPD Model were explored ethnographically through participant reflection journals, course products, participant artifacts, field observations, and snowball interviews. Such interviews are appropriate as necessary to follow up on, or fill gaps in, patterns of qualitative data (Creswell, 1998). The ARS served as the substantive theoretical framework for this exploration of professional development for accommodation readiness. Data were collected over a 2.5-year period and analyzed as received according to etic and emic coding methods. Thematic patterns in emic findings were directly associated with the six levels of the ARS for purposes of program improvement and refinement.

Program Professional Development Model

Teachers' capacity building for accommodation readiness in this case was grounded in the DPD Model of professional development. Not surprisingly, the DPD Model places a superordinate emphasis on capacity building for *critically reflective practice.* The diverse group of languages and cultures represented in post-modern classrooms is matched only by the lack of diversity among the nation's population of in-service teachers (National Center for Educational Statistics, 2001). Therefore, capacity building for critical reflection is essential to effectiveness in teaching practice, given the many cross-linguistic and cross-cultural differences extant in American classrooms.

Site-specific dynamics are also an intentional focus of professional development conducted according to the DPD Model. Today, the dynamics of teaching praxis vary markedly according to the idiosyncratic sociocultural and sociopolitical contexts of communities, districts, and schools. Practitioners need the capacities to effectively adapt the theories, concepts, and strategies they learn to the site-specific dynamics of their professional practice.

Cross-cultural and cross-linguistic competencies guide teachers in the development of capacities for empathy and an affirmation of the value of diversity in the classroom and in our society. Accordingly, the DPD Model targets the nurturance of these competencies in order to enable more inclusive and constructivist perspectives among teachers.

Through *needs-based education,* the DPD Model helps teachers evaluate and align multiple curricular initiatives with their own classroom population. Such alignment reduces redundancy and enhances instructional flexibility, while maintaining high standards for professional development and best practice.

Finally, the DPD Model targets accommodation readiness through its emphasis on perspectives of *lifelong and collegial learning* among teachers of CLD students. To this end, the DPD Model organizes teachers into collegial groups who collaborate in theory-into-practice applications of their professional development (according to site- and region-specific dynamics).

Outcomes of Program/Professional Development Implementation

The discussion that follows summarizes the major outcomes of the program implementation. That is, it answers the question: What were the significant findings of this effort to provide and research targeted professional development designed to enhance teachers' readiness for the appropriate classroom accommodation of CLD student needs? Consistent with a focus on readiness, these outcomes are presented and discussed in terms of the six levels of the ARS. For each of these levels, this summary is organized according to the two research questions that guided the study. Therefore, presentation and discussion at each ARS level addresses: (1) *shared perspectives of participant teachers* on capacity building for readiness and (2) *key program implementation challenges* of targeting accommodation readiness through differentiated professional development.

ARS Level One: Readiness for Critical Reflection on Practice　For the teachers who participated in this program implementation, readiness for critical reflection on professional practice with CLD students was all about time. Building this capacity was, for many participant teachers, a difficult and longitudinal process of transcending both primary socialization in the dominant culture and secondary socialization for a homogenous classroom that is no longer the reality of their schools. Most promising for these teachers was the shared perspective of *emergent realizations* about the value of critical reflection on one's practices with CLD students. The following excerpt from a teacher's reflection journal is exemplary of this shared perspective:

> I guess I'm just beginning to realize that I've never thought much about how and why I have some of the biases and feelings toward groups and individuals that I have apparently had for a long time. These are qualities that I bring to each and every teaching situation with me on a daily basis. (MNS04CS)

This teacher's comments, like that of others, reflect the realizations that are possible when teachers are encouraged to critically reflect on their biases and assumptions in practice (in this case, through an *in-service* program of professional development). Moreover, because this teacher is in the fourth course of her five-course (15-hour) professional development sequence, the phrase "I'm just beginning to realize" indicates that her capacity building for critical reflection is emergent and has also taken some time (2 years, in fact) to develop.

Similarly, time was also the most challenging and frustrating aspect of professional development and program implementation at this level of the ARS. Few of these educators had received capacity building for critically reflective practice during their teacher preparation (*preservice*) programs. Therefore, developing participating teachers to the point of emergent realizations was, for facilitators, a time-consuming, sometimes frustrating process of patient facilitation, coaching, and mentorship in capacity building for critical reflection. Yet, without this capacity, teachers will not build the foundation for progress along the helices of the ARS.

ARS Level Two: Readiness for CLD Students and Families   Readiness for CLD students and families is often an unfamiliar issue for many rural and some urban, in-service teachers in the Midwest. Yet, although linguistic diversity in these classrooms is a comparatively new phenomenon for these teachers, certain regions of the rural Midwest have witnessed more than a 150% increase in the number of CLD students who have enrolled in the past 10 years (Johnson-Webb, 2001).

A recurrent theme among the Midwestern teachers of this program implementation was a shared perspective of the *separation of content and language learning.* For example, many of these teachers, despite what they espoused to the contrary, tended to assume in practice that CLD students were not capable of grade-level, content-area learning because of their limited English proficiency. Others tended to assume that second language development was an instructional issue to be pursued separate and apart from content-area learning; the prevalence of ESL pull-out programming in the target region contributed to this perspective. The following remarks of a participating teacher are indicative of this shared perspective:

> I used to regard ELL [CLD] students as a challenge and another burden placed upon teachers. I felt that I was overwhelmed enough teaching the content that I didn't have the time or energy to devote to the added stress of working with the development of their language. I now realize that it was my own feeling of inadequacy that led me to believe these things. I had never taken the time to prepare myself to handle ELL students in my classroom. I felt guilty because I knew that if I had an ELL student, they would not have the support from me because of my biases and my inadequacies. (JDF03RW)

Through critical reflection on the assumptions she was making about the linguistic and content-area abilities of her students, this educator came to realize: (a) that her own biases and feelings of inadequacy were negatively impacting her readiness to mutually accommodate her CLD students and (b) that her feelings of inadequacy often related to her lack of preparedness to appropriately differentiate her teaching practices (e.g., develop separate language and content objectives) for a classroom that did not meet the expectations borne of her *pre-service* teaching experiences. Over time, teachers who shared this perspective often gained the readiness necessary to combine content-area learning and English-language acquisition through highly differentiated and sheltered instruction.

Among the challenges of program implementation at this level of the ARS, perhaps none was more formidable than that of convincing participating teachers that home visits to the families of CLD students were integral to mutual accommodation. Elsewhere, Herrera and Murry (2005) have detailed the many advantages of home visits in the mutual accommodation of CLD student needs and in the effective promotion of CLD family involvement. In brief, home visits afford the visiting teacher opportunities to: (a) partner with student caregivers, (b) collaborate with extended family members, (c) encourage native language support, and (d) better understand home cultural mores and expectations. In this case, participating teachers, through home visits, eventually built the capacity to involve the family in helping CLD students simultaneously build increasing proficiencies in both their first and second languages. Long-standing research has shown that such an approach not only encourages first and second language development but also tends to improve classroom performance in the content areas (Collier, 1995).

ARS Level Three: Environmental Readiness Somewhat striking among teachers' perspectives on readiness for CLD students was the reminder that an ideology of *Americanization* (Appadurai, 1990) is alive and well among educators of the Midwest. Just as it was at the turn of the 20th century, so it is, again, in the 21st. The prevalence of this ideology that CLD students and families should be assimilated to the language, tenets, and mores of the dominant culture, especially the so-called *American ideal* was, in turn, a reminder that the sociopolitical contexts (external environment) of schooling may exert a powerful influence on teachers' perspectives despite the curricula of their preservice, teacher preparation programs. In fact, this perspective of an *Americanization redux,* shared among teachers in this study, also tended to divide school faculties about whether accommodation for CLD students should be one-way or mutual (two-way) in nature. Indicative of this perspective is the following excerpt taken from a participant teacher's course assignment:

> I would say that about one third of the teachers in my school understand the need to support the native language development and home culture of our CLD students. But, the rest of our teachers think that these students are in the United States now so they need to learn to be American—and that starts with learning to speak English only! As a teacher of the first group, my goal is to encourage more professional development for our teachers to help them see that we are helping our students be "American." But, that does not mean that they cannot maintain their native language and culture in order to be "American." (IAS02JL)

For this teacher, and others like her who are building the capacities for accommodation readiness, acculturation to life and productivity in America need not necessitate monolingualism or the loss of one's cultural identity (Americanization/assimilation). Furthermore, his discourse reflects a willingness to advocate for the professional development of fellow teachers toward the consideration of alternative perspectives on acculturation. This teacher is aware that CLD students can achieve successful acculturation without assimilation. That is, CLD students who *adjust* to a new language and culture may be successful in their acculturation to new schools and their matriculation to the workplace without the disenfranchising effects of assimilation. Nonetheless, this sociopolitical issue of the external environment is serving to both divide the school faculty over perspectives on accommodation and to disrupt the mutually beneficial learning dynamics that might take place between teachers and their CLD students.

Of course, many of the critical challenges of professional development at this level of the ARS were also found to be sociopolitical in nature. For example, it was not uncommon for a rural superintendent to telephone a program director with the complaint that this brand of professional development tended to promote radicalism among teachers. Among other challenges noted were: (a) the difficulties of persuading teachers that variables arising outside their classroom often had a determinate influence on their degree of success in the classroom and (b) that reflection on the internal environment of the classroom must encompass more than a summary consideration of the physical layout and tangible hallmarks of the classroom.

ARS Level Four: Curricular Readiness   Certainly, no theme in teachers' perspectives on accommodation readiness was any more unexpected than that associated with curricular readiness. As professional developers, we were startled that more than 40% of participating teachers reported that they had never really thought about the need to adapt their classroom curriculum for changing student populations. In fact, the indications were that this *never-really-thought-about-it* perspective in teacher's curricular practices had remained unchanged despite steadily increasing numbers of CLD students in their classrooms. In addition, analysis of data in this case indicated that this professional development (DPD Model) implementation was one of a very few (including teachers' preparatory field experiences) that had prompted any systematic reflection on the notion of meaningful curriculum adaptation in the classroom. The characteristic vernacular of this perspective on curriculum adaptation is evident in the following transcribed excerpt of a snowball interview with a participating elementary school teacher:

> I know where you're coming from ... and, I have made some big changes.... In fact ... well, I hate to admit it ... but there was a time, not too long ago ... when ah, well, the curriculum was just the curriculum. Ya see, it had always worked just fine, and ... I just never had to worry about changing it.... Even when I began to get the language learners [CLD students], I just always assumed that they'd get a different one [curriculum] ... you know, one that they worked on in ESL pullout ... to learn English.... To tell ya the truth, I never really thought they could handle the regular curriculum, much less learn English with it.... Anyway, these days, my bilingual para [paraprofessional] and I work together ... ya know, on ways to like shelter it [the curriculum] and scaffold what we do in the class [classroom].... It really does work.... Back when I started [the professional development sequence], *I never would have believed it ... or really have thought about it. (SIVF04LS)*

Most importantly, this teacher's remarks indicate that she has, in collaboration with a bilingual paraprofessional, begun to regularly adapt and modify her classroom curriculum for the needs of CLD and other students. On the other hand, her comments also reflect the shared perspective among some participating teachers that systematic reflection on curriculum adaptation had not been a significant part of their prior classroom practices or their preservice preparation for teaching as a profession. For her, and others like her, "the curriculum was just the curriculum." However, through differentiated professional development, this teacher and her paraprofessional are now pooling their resources to both "shelter" the curriculum for variant student needs and "scaffold" instruction to increase the comprehensibility of content-area learning. Such changes are a frequent outcome of systematic reflection on previously unchecked assumptions (e.g., *the curriculum is the curriculum*) of professional practice with diverse student populations (Herrera & Murry, 2005; Murry & Herrera, 2005).

Consistent with this perspective in teachers' classroom practices, one of the key challenges of program implementation at this level of the ARS was grounded in teachers' curricular approaches to CLD students. Specifically, this challenge involved persuading practitioners that the grade-level curriculum could be utilized as the basis for both content-area learning and second language acquisition among CLD students. Other challenges associated with professional development for curricular readiness included: (a) the complexity of facilitating teachers in their navigations of multiple, unrelated curricular and instructional agendas taking place in their schools (e.g., Success for All, CORI, PWIM, Reading Recovery, Balanced Literacy) and (b) convincing teachers that they possess the knowledge and resources to initiate appropriate curricular accommodations for CLD students.

ARS Level Five: Programming and Instructional Readiness   One of the many advantages of differentiated professional development for classroom diversity is that it encourages reflection on and collaborative dialogue about site-specific dynamics at the district and building levels. So, it was not necessarily unexpected that program participants would begin to share and discuss, in collaborative and site-based groups, their viewpoints about site-specific professional practice and their emergent realizations arising from critical reflection on that practice (as well as reflection on their *preservice* preparation for that practice).

From these discussions emerged a recurrent willingness among participating teachers to *question the unquestioned*. This theme was especially prevalent where their dialogue turned to questions of appropriate programming for language acquisition among CLD students. Field observation of participant dialogue during collaborative group discussions and activities yielded the following excerpt of teacher discourse. This excerpt is exemplary of this *questioning-the-unquestioned* perspective shared among participating teachers:

I just don't get it! Our school is way beyond pull-out [ESL pullout]. Our numbers of ESL [CLD] kids have grown so fast in the last 9 months.... The ESL teacher pulls out more kids every day than I have left in the classroom.... Soon, I'll have no kids left to pullout. What is she [the school administrator] thinking? We've got to look at some other way to educate these children.... They've got to get more contact time than what they're getting in ESL pullout. (FOS04JM)

The comments of this teacher surface a number of contextual and sociohistorical issues that are, in many ways, the basis of this shared participant perspective on language programming.

First, her discourse reflects the growing degree of linguistic diversity in classrooms (such as those in her school) that were, heretofore, largely homogeneous with respect to both language and home culture. This is a growing trend for both classrooms of the Midwest and the nation (Johnson-Webb, 2001; U.S. Department of Education, 2002).

Second, her comment that, "our school is way beyond pullout," suggests: (a) that her school employs the ESL pullout model of programming for second language acquisition and (b) that the school has continued to utilize the model in the face of changing classroom demographics. This arrangement is not atypical among schools and school districts of the Midwest and several other regions of the nation (Herrera & Murry, 2005). In fact, more than 65% of participating teachers began this iteration of differentiated professional development in schools where ESL pullout was the predominant programming model for second language acquisition among CLD students.

Third, her comments indicate that she has begun to question the validity of adhering to this long-standing model of language programming (ESL pullout) as the student populations in the classrooms of her school become increasingly diverse. In fact, among schools that participated in this professional development, this model of language programming was not only predominant but had, in the case of many schools, been the only model used for decades. Finally, her discourse indicates that this teacher is beginning to question (in light of emergent school demographics) her school administrator's willingness to persist in the continued utilization of this ESL pullout programming model.

ESL pullout is a programming model that removes ("pulls out") the CLD student from the grade-level classroom for some portion of the school day (each day) to receive auxiliary language instruction. Such instruction is typically delivered by a dedicated or itinerant ESL pullout teacher who may serve one or multiple schools within a school district. This pullout instruction emphasizes second language learning in the target language (English) and typically provides no support to CLD students for ongoing development in the native language.

Unfortunately, as the teachers who share the *questioning-the-unquestioned* perspective are aware, long-standing, longitudinal research has repeatedly demonstrated that ESL pullout is one of the least effective language programming models for CLD students (Thomas & Collier, 1995, 2002). Among other problems and deficiencies that have been associated with use of the model in rural and urban classrooms are: (a) Contrary to conventional thinking, ESL pullout is one of the most expensive models to implement because it does not maximize the use of resident, grade-level teachers for the language and content-area instruction of CLD students (Thomas & Collier, 1995, 2002); (b) Increasing numbers of target students soon render the model unrealistic to implement (Herrera & Murry, in press); and (c) The model tends to stigmatize CLD students who are *pulled out* (Collier, 1995; Herrera & Murry, 2005).

In point of fact, the participant teachers who share the *questioning-the-unquestioned* perspective on appropriate programming for CLD students have some very compelling rationales for their newfound voice. Indeed, many are, as in-service versus preservice teachers, just beginning to build the capacities, programming, and instructional readiness to think critically about long-standing traditions in policy and practice.

Perhaps the most problematic challenge of professional development for programming readiness was the difficulty of persuading participant teachers to consider programming alternatives that included some degree of native language support for CLD students. Native language support is critical for these students because of the notion of *common underlying proficiency* (CUP). Like a computer's operating system, CUP (Cummins, 2001) connects first and second language acquisition efforts among CLD students. This connection is crucial because development in either language is ongoing, into adulthood (Cummins, 2001). This CUP connection between the two language acquisition efforts ensures that the prior knowledge and academic skills acquired in one language are transferable to constructivist learning and performance in the other. Without ongoing native language support, students lose the capacity for these synergistic transfers of knowledge, skills, and capacities.

Many participating schools, because of the dearth of available bilingual personnel, were compelled to consider only ESL programming alternatives. ESL instruction need not preclude provisions for native language support. For example, among the resources and strategies that grade-level teachers may maximize to provide native language support, along with ESL programming in the classroom, are: (a) encouraging home language use in the home, (b) previewing lessons in the native language via a bilingual paraprofessional, (c) building a bilingual classroom library, and (d) grouping students by differential native and second language abilities in cooperative learning activities.

Among other challenges of program and professional development implementation associated with this level of the ARS are: (a) persuading teachers of the many benefits to learning and to productivity of bilingualism among CLD students and (b) encouraging theory-into-practice applications of content learned toward differentiated classroom instruction for CLD students.

ARS Level Six: Readiness for Application and Advocacy   As participant teachers progressed along the ARS and enhanced their readiness for application and advocacy, one particularly recurrent perspective among these educators was that of *knowledge building*. This perspective was especially salient for those teachers who taught in school districts with very limited services for their CLD students.

As those teachers who held this perspective completed the various courses of their in-service professional development, opportunities for advocacy tended to surround their experiences with CLD students. Concomitantly, many of these teachers came to the realization that certain interventions for advocacy were needed in their schools.

However, the nature of their advocacy actions tended to be very delimited. In fact, teachers who held this perspective tended to maintain that their advocacy actions were, at this point in their professional development, best limited to *knowledge building* about CLD students, CLD families, appropriate practices for linguistic diversity, and so forth. The following excerpt taken from one teacher's response to a course assignment is typical of this theme in teachers' discourse:

> I'm very limited in what I can do for these students [CLD students] right now because their needs are very different than those that I usually address in my classroom. I am not an ESL teacher [ESL pullout teacher] and have limited exposure to second language learners in an ESL program. Many of my students are Native American, but few have language-learning issues. Most of what problems they have in my classroom relate to how other students perceive members of their culture as lazy and uneducated.... By educating myself on the necessary and proper programs to help these [CLD] kids develop their skills, I am preparing myself to be a better advocate for their needs. (CAS03MH)

To the extent that this teacher is expanding her knowledge base and extending her repertoire of skills applicable to the needs of (and on behalf of) CLD students, this teacher is *knowledge building* for advocacy. This is so because we may describe an advocate as "one who defends, pleads, or maintains the cause of another, a proposal, or a program" (Herrera & Murry, 1999, p. 114).

Nonetheless, her remarks, as indicative of a shared perspective among teachers, do not suggest *advocacy actions* toward specific applications of the theory, content, and strategies offered by either this professional development sequence or any advocacy curricula of teachers' preparatory programs. Instead, her emphasis is on self-education (knowledge building) to address the needs of "ESL" students, to the exclusion of the Native American, CLD students already in her classroom. That is, her perspective is less focused on actions and applications designed to address inequities (such as the attributions experienced by her Native American students) than it is on self-education as a means of knowledge building. In this respect, the comparison of *talking the talk* versus *walking the walk* comes to mind.

Elsewhere, Herrera & Murry (2005) have argued that effective advocacy for CLD students must involve more than just knowledge building (currency). Advocacy should also encompass the capacity to cogently defend one's differentiated practices for CLD students (defensibility) and the readiness to act on opportunities to improve practices for, change policy applicable to, or intervene on behalf of CLD students and families (futurity).

As one might expect, therefore, the greatest challenges of program implementation for advocacy and application readiness lie in: (a) educating these in-service teachers about those critical aspects of advocacy for which their preservice experiences have not prepared them and (b) helping teachers understand advocacy as an application or action component of capacity building for accommodation. Of these challenges, the latter was by far the more formidable.

Findings and Implications

The focus of this research was the study of professional development designed to foster increasing accommodation readiness among teachers of CLD students. The framework for this capacity building was, in turn, designed to address the lack of scholarship on critical capacities that teachers should develop as goals of teacher preparation and professional development.

The major findings of this research indicate that the ARS provides a useful framework for both professional development and for research in teacher education. Specifically, these findings, at each of the six levels of the ARS suggest: (a) notable similarities between what teachers espouse about their perspectives and practices with CLD students and the capacities that teacher preparation programs expect of their graduates, (b) marked dissimilarities between what teachers espouse about best practices for CLD students and what perspectives they hold on such practice (and what capacities they exhibit) in situ, and (c) implications as to what capacities teacher education faculty must demonstrate in order to close the gap between what candidates as teachers espouse and what they are able to demonstrate in practice.

Table 7.1 summarizes these findings and these implications according to the six levels of the ARS and the six themes in participant voice identified by this research. For example, row one of the figure is a summary for the sixth and highest level of the ARS—*Readiness for Application and Advocacy*. Column one of that row identifies the ARS level as six and summarizes the theme in research findings for that level of the ARS—*Knowledge Building*. At this level of the ARS, teachers often espouse what they were prepared to articulate as *candidates* or preservice teachers (column two)—that is, that they are prepared to practice according to what is pedagogically and ethically sound for CLD students. On the other hand, these same teachers as *candidates in practice* (column three), or in-service teachers, are (according to the theme for this level of the ARS) continuing to build the knowledge for advocacy (see column one). Therefore,

TABLE 7.1 Table of Summarized Findings and Implications

Level of Accommodation Readiness	University Preparation/Apparent Readiness Candidates	Classroom Practice with Diversity/Demonstrable Readiness Candidates as Teachers	Faculty Capacities Needed to Align Apparent & Demonstrable Readiness Teacher Preparation Faculty
Readiness for Application and Advocacy **Theme in Findings [TIF]: Knowledge Building**	Are prepared to practice according to what is ethically and pedagogically best for CLD and other students Emphasize theory into practice applications in field experiences	Exhibit limited understanding of what it means to be an advocate Demonstrate limited capacities for theory into practice applications for advocacy and for social justice	Model advocacy and social justice in their own practice Teach advocacy and social justice strategies as a component of the ethics curriculum Develop course projects that benefit school communities
Programming and Instructional Readiness **TIF: Question the Unquestioned**	Are aware that a range of language programming models exist for use with CLD students Utilize action research as a preinstructional and postinstructional assessment tool	Are reluctant to pilot language program models (e.g., Sheltered ESL) that are more specific to the needs of the classroom population served Are unable to discuss (with key stakeholders) the limited theoretical and research bases for inappropriate language programming practices	Better prepare candidates to: (a) defend their program practices (and arguments for change) with theory and current research and (b) utilize action research to assess the efficacy of pilot programming
Curricular Readiness **TIF: Never Really Thought About It**	Understand constructivist learning and the learning styles through which students may comprehend key curricular concepts Understand how standards and benchmarks may be used to assess student progress in learning the core curriculum.	Are unable to differentiate their core curriculum and materials for variant student assets, needs, and backgrounds in the classroom Are often unable to translate preservice preparation and in-service professional development into meaningful curricular adaptations for site-specific student populations	Better prepare candidates to target both content learning and language acquisition objectives for CLD students, via the core curriculum Offer candidates enrichment courses (e.g., ESL endorsement classes) that prepare them for the differential assets and needs of students who are acquiring English as a second language

Environmental Readiness TIF: Americanization Redux	Understand ways to enhance and maximize the learning environment of the classroom Are able to discuss the range of multiple cultures and languages that may be represented in the classroom and in a school's (external) community Are typically afforded preclinical and student teaching experiences with diverse student populations	Are unable to recognize the value of integration (or acculturation) as a superior goal for CLD students (and families) versus the assimilation (or Americanization) of these students Often neither value native language support for CLD students (e.g., through external, family, or community resources) nor believe that it is possible unless the teacher is bilingual	Approach candidate capacity building for diversity as a recurrent thread in preservice curricula and experiences Structure projects and field experiences that encourage candidates to explore and learn about the cultures, languages, and communities that are external to the school of experience
Readiness for CLD Students and Families TIF: Separation of Content and Language Learning	Understand key precepts that apply to CLD students and their families Have teacher expectations that influence student success Find parental involvement to be key Believe classroom environments should reflect the cultures and languages of students	Neither value, nor are prepared to conduct, purposive home visits as capacity building for diversity Frequently engage in inappropriate assumptions about CLD students and families (as a product or outcome of prior socialization) Believe that limited English ability predicts poor academic achievement	Build the capacities to offer candidates the following range of differential experiences: community-based teaching; oral history development in students' homes; international experiences that are relevant to target teaching populations
Readiness for Critical Reflection on Practice TIF: Emergent Realizations	Comprehend the notion of reflective practice Are provided with experiences that encourage reflective practice in lesson planning, delivery, and evaluation	Misunderstand the alignment of their diversity perspectives with CLD student views, including invalid and insensitive assumptions about: Commonalities in home and school socialization experiences; the value of retaining one's home culture and language; equality versus equity of treatment	Provide candidates transcurricular and structured formats for reflection that encourage assumption surfacing and validity testing, of the influence of one's prior socialization, on actions and efficacy in current practice with CLD students

according to various subthemes in findings (see column three) these teachers, in practice with CLD students, discuss and exhibit limited understanding of advocacy and limited theory-into-practice applications for advocacy. Naturally, this discrepancy between apparent and demonstrable readiness (column one vs. column three) begs the question: What can teacher education faculty do to better prepare these candidates for the reality side of professional practice with student diversity.

Consequently, column four of row one offers a sample set of targets (implications) for capacity building among teacher education faculty who seek to better prepare candidates for cultural and linguistic diversity in the classroom. That is to say, these faculty will better prepare candidates for applications and advocacy for CLD students and families (level six of the ARS and row one of the table) if they, as mentors, build the capacities to: (a) model advocacy and social justice, (b) teach advocacy strategies, and (c) develop course projects that emphasize advocacy and social justice, in action. Graphically, and in this manner, Table 7.1 summarizes such findings and implications for each of the six levels of the ARS.

Conclusions

The findings and implications of this research suggest that graduates of teacher preparation programs are frequently able to articulate and espouse sound pedagogy and best practices for the education of diverse student populations. Yet, pedagogy is not enough. Too powerful and pervasive are the social, political, and symbolic influences of our school cultures and our society's influences that often serve to reeducate or diseducate candidate teachers and those who are in the first years of their profession.

To combat these influences, candidates must build certain *critical capacities,* the most crucial of which, is the capacity for *critical reflection* upon these influences and the fallacious perspectives and assumptions that they may foster. Candidates who demonstrate readiness for the mutual accommodation of, and advocacy for, CLD students and families also exhibit the capacity to critically reflect on their own socialization and the ways in which that socialization can filter and distort their perceptions, expectations, actions, and inaction as professionals in schools with high levels of student diversity.

Hence, ongoing capacity building among teacher education faculty members is integral to the adequate preparation of candidates for diverse classrooms. Among the unit-wide strategies that teacher education programs may utilize to encourage this goal are:

- program- and college-wide diversity initiatives
- faculty institutes that feature expert speakers who focus on strategies for curriculum adaptation and instructional differentiation
- differential faculty incentives and opportunities that reward capacity building, curricular revisions and updates, and the restructuring of field experiences.

Among department-level initiatives that may build the appropriate capacities among faculty members are: (a) faculty retreats that emphasize transcurricular improvements in the preparation of candidates for student diversity, (b) workshops where faculty collaborate with a diversity specialist to develop preclinical and field experiences and formats that target capacity building for critical reflection among candidate teachers, and (c) peer or mentor coaching of junior faculty with an emphasis on modeling appropriate strategies for diverse school classrooms (modeling, that is first initiated in the teacher preparation classroom).

Ultimately, effective professional development for candidates and faculty that is responsive to increasing classroom diversity begins and ends with empathy (walking in the CLD student's shoes). Courses and sequences of teacher education that fail to reach the prior socialization of candidate teachers are unlikely to touch the *hearts and minds* of those who must empathize with students and families in order to judiciously comprehend the often unanticipated differences that students can bring to the classroom. Instead, caring professional development persuades and reminds teachers that they are capable of reaching, educating, and transforming the lives of both students like them and students who are culturally and linguistically different.

References

Appadurai, A. (1990). Disjuncture and difference in the global cultural economy. *Theory, Culture, and Society, 7*(2), 295–310.

Arias, M. B., & Poynor, L. (2001). A good start: Transactional approach to diversity in pre-service teacher education. *Bilingual Research Journal, 25*(4), 417–434.

Beattie, M. (2002). Finding new words for old songs: Creating relationships and community in teacher education. In H. Christiansen & S. Ramadevi (Eds.), *Reeducating the educator: Global perspectives on community building* (pp. 17–38). Albany: State University of New York Press.

Collier, V. P. (1995). *Promoting academic success for ESL students: Understanding second language acquisition for school.* Elizabeth: New Jersey Teachers of English to Speakers of Other Languages-Bilingual Educators.

Creswell, J. (1998). *Qualitative inquiry and research design: Choosing among five traditions.* Thousand Oaks, CA: Sage.

Cummins, J. (2001). *Language, power, and pedagogy: Bilingual children in the crossfire.* Philadelphia: Multicultural Matters.

Herrera, S., & Murry, K. G. (1999). In the aftermath of Unz. *Bilingual Research Journal, 23*(2–3), 113–132.

Herrera, S., & Murry, K. (2005). *Mastering ESL and bilingual methods: Differentiated instruction for culturally and linguistically diverse (CLD) students.* Boston: Allyn and Bacon.

Herrera, S., & Murry, K. (in press). *ESL pull-out: A persistent programming paradox for teachers and administrators.* Manuscript submitted for publication.

Johnson-Webb, K. D. (2001). Midwest rural communities in transition: Hispanic immigrants. *Rural Development News, 25*(1), 4-5.

Montecinos, C. (2004). Paradoxes in multicultural teacher education research: Students of color positioned as objects while ignored as subjects. *International Journal of Qualitative Studies in Education, 17*(2), 167–181.

Murry, K. (2003, January). *The journey: Transitions in higher education.* Presentation at the annual conference of the National Association for Bilingual Education, New Orleans, LA.

Murry, K., & Herrera, S. (1999). CLASSIC impacts: A qualitative study of ESL/BLED programming. *Educational Considerations, 26*(2), 11–19.

Murry, K., & Herrera, S. (2005). *Readiness for accommodation?: Teachers and their CLD students.* Paper presented at the annual meeting of the American Educational Research Association, Montreal, Canada.

National Center for Educational Statistics. (2001). *Teacher preparation and professional development: 2000.* Retrieved July 14, 2004, from http://nces.ed.gov/pubs2001/2001088.pdf

Nevarez-La Torre, A., & Rolón-Dow, R. (2000). Teacher research as professional development. In D. J. McIntyre & D. M. Byrd (Eds.), *Research on effective models for teacher education* (pp. 78–96). Thousand Oaks, CA: Corwin Press.

Nieto, S. (1992). *Affirming diversity: The sociopolitical context of multicultural education.* New York: Longman.

Phuntsog, N. (2001). Culturally responsive teaching: What do selected United States elementary school teachers think? *Intercultural Education, 12*(1), 51–64.

Thomas, W., & Collier, V. (1995). Language-minority student achievement and program effectiveness studies support native language development. *NABE News, 18*(8), 5, 12.

Thomas, W. P., & Collier, V. P. (2002). *A national study of school effectiveness for language minority students' long-term academic achievement.* Santa Cruz, CA: CREDE. Retrieved February 5, 2003, from www. crede.ucsc.edu/research/llaa/1.1_final.html

Timperley, H. S., & Phillips, G. (2003). Changing and sustaining educators' expectations through professional development in literacy. *Teaching and Teacher Education, 19,* 627–641.

U.S. Department of Education. (2002). *Survey of the states' limited English proficient students & available educational programs and services 1999–2000 summary report.* Washington, DC: Office for English Language Acquisition.

Varghese, M., & Stritikus, T. (2005). "*Nadie me dijó* (nobody told me)": Language policy negotiation and implications for teacher education. *Journal of Teacher Education, 56*(1), 73–87.

Walton, P. H., Baca, L., & Escamilla, K. (2002). *A national study of teacher education preparation for diverse student populations: Final report.* Boulder, CO: Center for Research on Education, Diversity & Excellence.

Wong Filmore, L., & Snow, C. E. (2002). What teachers need to know about language. In C. T. Adger, C. E. Snow, & D. Christian (Eds.), *What teachers need to know about language* (pp. 7–54). Washington, DC: Center for Applied Linguistics.

8

Highly Qualified Teachers for Our Schools
Developing Knowledge, Skills, and Dispositions to Teach Culturally and Linguistically Diverse Students

Jorgelina Abbate-Vaughn
University of Massachusetts–Boston

The discussion of what it means to be a highly qualified teacher has paid scarce attention to the specific knowledge, skills, and dispositions teachers need to work effectively with culturally and linguistically diverse (CLD) students in urban schools. Although CLD students' presence has increased in both suburban and urban school districts, I locate this discussion of strategies to help mainstream preservice teachers (PTs) become effective instructors of CLD students within the context of an urban school setting. This approach should not be interpreted as conceding more importance to issues of diversity in urban settings because all CLD students, regardless of geographic and socioeconomic location, are entitled to the benefits of well-prepared teachers. The use of an urban school district as the implementation site for a comprehensive approach to preparing PTs for diversity has to do with the compelling percentage of such populations in urban sites (Antunez, 2003) and the potential for PTs' close interaction with CLD students and families.

In this chapter, I propose a model designed to align comprehensive urban field experiences with coursework to help PTs develop the sensitivities and practice the performances necessary to work with CLD learners. The underlying assumption of such design and implementation in teacher education is that by acquiring fluency in the prevailing customs, belief systems, values, and language resources of communities different from their own, PTs are best equipped to understand and access students' background knowledge and make meaningful connections between the students' existing prior knowledge and any given curriculum. Two coursework strategies are described in detail: one is process writing as the methodology to facilitate PTs' social (re)construction of knowledge in regard to previously held notions about diverse communities; the other is the use of ethnic autobiographical literature to increase PTs' understanding of the people whose children they teach. Implications for teacher education policy stemming from the implementation of both approaches are offered.

Personal Background

My sister and I grew up in the same household in South America, were exposed to similar experiences while growing up, earned college degrees, and came to the United States as adult "voluntary" immigrants (Ogbu, 1987). We are both married to white males, American-born and raised, and holders of graduate degrees. Not long ago, we were all watching *Saturday Night Live* (*SNL*). An opening skit loaded with cultural references elicited a good laugh from the men and me, while my sister exhibited no reaction. After a little probing, it became evident that she was unfamiliar with the "prior knowledge" necessary to make sense of the skit.

My sister has lived in American suburbia for more than 5 years as a full-time homemaker. She and her family spend time with a close-knit circle of South American families in which the females raise the children and the husbands, all professionals, work long hours. All of those families enjoy an upper-middle-class socioeconomic status. Although all the adults and children are fully bilingual, Spanish is the language widely used at social gatherings. The wives typically gather and share parenting tips, while the men talk business. The women are all assertive in securing the best educational options for their children, whether in choosing of schools or selecting the most appropriate enrichment activities beyond school. A pervasive nostalgia for the native land becomes evident after following a few of the women's conversations, which often involve accounts of the frequent visits they all pay to the motherland as well as the consistent preference they exhibit for its specific cultural artifacts, such as food, apparel, and music.

My assimilation process was quite different. I have lived in this country for more than 10 years in three different large urban centers and always held full-time professional jobs while completing graduate work. I have spent most of my work and spare time in the company of a variety of groups—African American, Latino, Asian, gay and lesbian, as well as mainstream—in middle- and low-income neighborhoods. Due to the close contact with such a mixture of people and cultures, I have incorporated into my "knowledge base" a considerable reservoir of the cultural references necessary to make meaning of what is being said explicitly and tacitly in various settings. It is also worth pointing out that my immersion into American urban public schools as a teacher has left its imprint on what I now know. Cultural phenomena I would have probably learned only if growing up here are evident in my current cultural capital—for instance, my detailed understanding of the origin and meaning of each American holiday—because I learned them to teach my students.

Thus, we have two siblings with almost identical experiences well into adulthood, including that of voluntary immigration. Yet, using the *SNL* skit as an analogy to what happens in classrooms, one successfully "absorbs" the content being delivered whereas the other remains oblivious to it. My sister's experience somehow mimics those of most CLD students. The *SNL* skit writer neither has a command of the ethnic cultural references necessary to capture my sister's attention nor succeeds in engaging her with the mainstream ones. Teachers in this country, particularly in urban settings, confront a similar challenge on a daily basis.

Proficiency in the mainstream's cultural references, language, and available cultural capital (Bourdieu & Passeron, 1977) plays an important role in school success. CLD students, who are often perceived to be unmotivated, at-risk, or just simply unable to "get it" based on their limited prior knowledge of the cultural references or complex English structures necessary to make sense of the school's daily curriculum, are less likely to experience equity of access to the benefits of a public education. As Trueba (1999) points out, from a Vygotskian perspective, "children who are socialized in a new linguistic and cultural environment cannot get the assistance that is congruent with their zones of proximal development and their linguistic and cognitive skills" (p. 134), urging educational reformers to prepare teachers that can successfully work with diverse populations. This in no way undermines the fact that some CLD students from every socioeconomic background might experience processes of assimilation similar to my own. Yet, in urban centers where opportunity attracts low-income and immigrant families alike, schools face the daunting task of educating highly diverse groups of children whose cultural and linguistic prior knowledge differs markedly from that of the mainstream population (Antunez, 2003; Rivera-Batiz, 1996; Suárez-Orozco & Suárez-Orozco, 2001).

An explicit assumption of this work is that PTs can be best equipped to understand and access students' background knowledge and make meaningful connections between the students' existing prior knowledge and any given curriculum if they become "fluent" in the prevailing customs and belief systems of communities different from their own (Gay, 2002). It is also helpful that PTs exhibit an interest in understanding the language structures in which the newcomers are fluent.

Theoretical Background

My quest to help contribute to improving the preparation of teachers who can capably work with CLD students draws from research on the multicultural education of PTs and urban education. Whether stressing the importance of parental and community involvement in schooling or raising awareness about the relevance of preparing culturally competent teachers by providing carefully aligned learning experiences that consider urban families and community as resources, those interested in the urban public school challenge of educating large numbers of low-income and CLD children have produced important studies (see, for instance, Comer & Maholmes, 1999; Haberman, 1996; Hollins, 1995; Oakes, Franke, Quartz, & Rogers, 2002; Weiner, 1999).

Also in response to this urban challenge, a small but growing number of schools of education (SoEs) have implemented programs specifically geared toward preparing prospective teachers to work with the large numbers of CLD families that most urban centers now house. A variety of top-ranked, large, private universities; small private colleges; and land-grant state institutions alike have developed unique urban teacher education programs (UTEPs)[1] to help prospective teachers develop the skills and sensitivities needed to work with diverse constituencies. Efforts leading to the specialization of UTEPs as an area of teacher education that tackles at the importance of diverse school contexts are well grounded in the statistics of student population trends described in chapter 2 of this book.

An analysis of large urban centers indicates that minority group segregation to urban public schools is alarmingly high. For instance, African American children compose between 81% and 96% of the public school population in eight large cities.[2] In addition, Latino children compose school population majorities between 51% and 71% in seven large cities.[3] Also significant is that, although more than 35% of today's school children are of color, only approximately 13% of the teachers belong to minority groups (National Center for Education Statistics, 1997). The cultural mismatch between a largely mainstream teacher force and an increasingly diverse student body has preoccupied researchers for a while.[4]

Research indicates that white PTs manifest little interest in working in diverse settings (Zeichner & Melnick, 1996; Zimpher & Ashburn, 1992) and that, when they do, deficit perspectives of diverse students prevail among them (Delgado-Gaitan & Trueba, 1991; Irvine, 1990; Lopez, 1999; Valdés, 1996; Valenzuela, 1999). Problems also arise when SoEs either "do" diversity as add-on curricula, rather than promote an awareness of and appreciation for cultural diversity as a central mission (Gollnick, 1992; Villegas & Lucas, 2002), or approach cultural diversity as something worth studying but with which it is not necessary to interact (Zeichner & Hoeft, 1996). With regard to socioeconomic diversity, the challenge is magnified. Whereas most PTs come from a range of middle-class backgrounds or social groups who hold "enough capitals of the right currency" (Ball, 2003), the CLD families with which their work unfolds rarely possess the "know-how" to secure the best educational opportunities available for their offspring.

A sizeable amount of research has centered on the many aspects involved in "multiculturalizing" teacher education through academic work and diverse school placements (Banks, 1991; Gay, 1993; Ladson-Billings, 1991). Since the early 1990s, an increasing emphasis on taking PTs' preparation beyond the boundaries of the school building—drawing in part from what is known about service learning—has fueled a considerable amount of empirical and conceptual research (Aguilar & Pohan, 1998; Boyle-Baise, 2002; Cooper, Beare, & Thomas, 1990; Mahan & Stachowski, 1994; Noordhoff & Kleinfield, 1993; Tellez, Hlebowitsh, Cohen, & Norwood, 1995; Zeichner

& Melnick, 1996) and reviews of studies (Root & Furco, 2001; Wade, 2000) that analyze the outcomes and challenges such implementations pose.

By increasing PTs' understanding of diverse learners' contexts, the quality of connections that teachers can make between curricula and children's prior knowledge is maximized. Additionally, fostering relationships between CLD parents and students, community agencies, and PTs enables the latter to become knowledgeable of and empathetic about the prevailing "ways of doing" in the settings where their students are reared, while promoting involvement with the families served by those schools. In the same way that minority students often become cultural and language brokers between school and home (Gentemann, 1983; Tse, 1995), PTs can be prepared to broker the relationship between public schools and diverse home cultures (Gay, 2002; Goodwin, 2000).

Putting together what is known about preparing teachers for urban settings, Murrell (2001) describes several conditions that need to be met in preparing what he calls the "community teacher." This preparation enables PTs to become well-rounded professionals who are keen to collaborate with colleagues, understand teaching as a lifelong commitment to learning with humility, and endeavor to reach "fluency" in the existing knowledge base of diverse communities. Murrell is not alone in proposing that teacher educators design collaborative efforts with the adult members of a given community to help scaffold PTs' understanding of that community. Similar ideas are discussed in Boyle-Baise and Sleeter (2000) and Boyle-Baise (2002). In sum, the need for educating competent teachers for an increasingly diverse student body calls for a more committed relationship with the communities involved. While fieldwork in the CLD community provides a fecund ground to "experience" some of the knowledge gained in university courses and practice pedagogically relevant skills, the field-support coursework enable PTs to refine the dispositions to excel in such settings.

Linking Coursework to Fieldwork in CLD Settings

The complexity of developing context knowledge is mediated by our own identities and life circumstances as they impact that understanding (Gee, 2001) and has specific links to the "knower's" racial and ethnic locations (Diaz-Rico, 1998; Helms, 1990; Tatum, 1992). Many mainstream PTs are first acquainted with CLD children when they complete field experiences at their clinical workplaces in urban districts. It is at this point when PTs either attempt to understand the phenomena around utilizing schemata from their own mainstream upbringings or resort to the stereotyped images from the media. Both strategies often reinforce negative views of minorities (Cortes, 2000). Additionally, PTs may be exposed to contradictory versions about CLD students as held by teachers with differing ideological stances (Abbate-Vaughn, 2004). The process of teacher socialization (Zeichner & Gore, 1990) into workplaces where staff hold deficient views of CLD students can be enduring, particularly because cultural and linguistic diversity are also often associated with poverty. Even if they are among the lowest-salaried professionals, most teachers enjoy a middle-class socioeconomic status and may not understand the extent to which poverty magnifies the challenges experienced by CLD students who are expected to master a mainstream curriculum and ways of "doing school." Low expectations of success—or in Merton's (1948) words, the "self-fulfilling prophecy" of low achievement—when teaching poor and CLD students are widespread and resilient among school staff.

On a side note, I would also argue that a significant fraction of those of us preparing teachers also enjoy lives far removed from the everyday struggles of poverty and that it may not be enough to hire faculty from diverse national origins, races, and ethnic groups to "tackle" the diversity challenge. Proximity to low socioeconomic status CLD families clustered in large urban areas cannot be thought of as something only middle-class mainstream families avoid by fleeing to the comfort of the suburbs. Anecdotal evidence suggests that university faculty, mainstream and minority alike, exhibit a disparaging lack of awareness with regard to CLD populations in general and low-income CLD students in particular. Indeed, in preparing PTs to effectively deal with CLD populations, the hands-on activist could potentially be a resource more credible than the scholar isolated in theoretical pursuits (Kiang, 2001). Ideally, both faculty and schoolteachers sharing the task of preparing urban teachers should have an extensive understanding of CLD communities in context through research, activism, and teaching.

The Study

How can a CLD community—as a source of knowledge for teaching—be imbricated in teacher preparation programs to inform PTs' dispositional approaches to work with diverse students? To answer this question, I draw from a year-long study that documented how the strategies of process-writing and ethnic literature discussion circles play out in PT education. Among the goals in implementing such strategies were to help PTs (a) "de-otherize" CLD students and (b) theorize the outcomes of their own practices. The outcome of the year-long experience for the PTs was completion of an inquiry project that paralleled requirements for a master's thesis.

Data collected over two academic semesters included products from 16 PTs, including journals and ongoing drafts of their inquiry projects, field notes, and email exchanges between instructor and students. The setting for the field placement was a small urban cluster nestled by farms I call "Windmill."

Prospective teachers' journal entries and ongoing drafts were scrutinized using a discourse analysis technique, which enabled the researcher to identify the underlying assumptions behind specific issues (Potter, 1996). This part of the analysis was not intended to provide unequivocal answers but to force the continuing questioning of what appeared to shape PTs' ideas about CLD students. All data were also read chronologically by participant and by data source across participants and analyzed and coded for emerging themes by the researcher and a "critical friend" (Stenhouse, 1975) with ample familiarity with the community setting. Peer debriefing supports the credibility of the data analysis in qualitative research and lays the groundwork to support the trustworthiness of the findings (Spall, 1998).

The next sections provide a definition of process writing and ethnic literature discussion circles and a description of the ways in which they were used—in conjunction with urban field experiences—to address the lack of familiarity most participants initially exhibited with regard to the underserved children of poverty in general and CLD communities specifically. Those strategies provided a venue for systematic peer sharing, guided reflection, and feedback on events witnessed during their stay in Windmill.

Strategy # 1: Process Writing

In process writing (Graves, 1983), pupils write a series of successive drafts that are constructively scrutinized and enhanced by peer and instructor comments and suggestions, until the written product is deemed ready for publication. Lannon (2004) points out that good writing can "move readers to act or reconsider their biases" (p. 3). In the same manner, process writing might help the writers themselves work on their biases. Extremely popular at the elementary grades with emerging writers, this approach can be used in college-level course-work to promote a well-documented reflection about the biases or misunderstandings that PTs encounter at the workplace or in society at large with regard to CLD communities. The pupils' own interests typically generate the topics for process writing, but topics can also be "induced" by the teacher who suggests writing prompts. For the participants in this study, process writing facilitated a thoroughly monitored process of ongoing self-analysis, as well as an opportunity for me as the instructor to continuously assess my students' evolving conceptualizations and adjust my instruction accordingly. Occasion-ally, I resorted to writing prompts when a given issue was not clearly fleshed out and there was an obvious need for further exploration.

The expectation was that process writing could lead PTs to incrementally gain an appreciation for the role their own identi-ties play—particularly for those of middle- and upper-middle-class background—in making sense of the often overlapping contexts of poverty and cultural and linguistic diversity. Process writing, or as Richardson (2000) calls it, "writing as inquiry," provided a com-plementary pedagogical approach in my quest for developing PTs' awareness of their underlying assumptions about marginalized groups. The reflective nature of process writing—that of successive drafts polished with the help of peers and instructor—also enabled PTs to undergo a rethinking of their roles as cultural brokers between schools and CLD communities, while engaging in alternative peda-gogies that take advantage of CLD students' prior knowledge and maximize their academic and social achievement.

PTs' Journals, Field Notes, and Drafts   Prospective teachers doc-umented their evolving understandings through journals and field notes that they later incorporated into their ongoing drafts leading to the final project. As the year-long urban field placement provided the ground for building meaningful interactions with diverse families, PTs were asked to document through periodic journaling their reactions to such interactions. The journals were used in their successive drafts as a data source that enabled PTs to unpack their raw reactions to events in the field. They also kept field notes of actual conversations and interactions with students, teachers, and families that were meant to cover "the facts" (Faulk & Blumenreich, 2005). Within the confines of a community of peers-learners, PTs reflected collaboratively and provided constructive criticism of their peers' work through process writing. To illustrate the evolution of PTs' conceptualization of CLD students and their contexts, I present Sonia, a participant of the study and representative of the larger sample, and excerpts from her evolving drafts leading to the final inquiry project.

Sonia started the year with deep doubts about her students' potential for success. Earlier in the year, her journal included this depiction of the context responsible for the low academic performance of one of her students:

> Families like Analia's struggle just to provide food for their children, which does not leave room for many material possessions. Many families live with relatives just to make ends meet. Some families are even unable to provide basic needs for their children, such as beds or clothing. On top of everything these children are lacking what they need most, parental involvement.

Confused or uncomfortable with the initially accurate description of poverty and its links to preparedness for school, Sonia's interpretation of Analia's plight quickly fell back on familiar terrain—that of blaming the parents for their perceived indifference to school matters. From then on, Sonia's portrait of Analia relied on a deficit perspective and on middle-class assumptions to assess CLD families' concerns:

> These children are often times left at home without any parents to even help them with homework. Often, those who do not work cannot speak English either. As a result, students are faced with the hardship of poverty and language barriers, and therefore, school becomes a second priority.

Sonia assumed that parental absence in school meetings, scarce time to help with homework and lack of fluency in English equate to lack of interest in academic achievement. She further expanded on this perspective during the seminar session where initial drafts were discussed:

> I went to an urban school, and we were kind of poor, and my mother always made sure that I got proper schooling. She found the best school

in the city and made sure that I was accepted. I went to a performing arts school like Fame's. So if my mother could do this, what prevents other parents from having the same commitment to their kid's education?

Although certainly valid as an emic perspective on urban schools' potential to successfully educate students from working-class families, Sonia failed to define what "kind of poor" meant, while pointing that her father worked hard so her mother "could stay home to raise the children."

Topical Writing Prompts to Aid Reflection   Writing prompts can be used to elicit further reflection on latent topics in PTs' oral or written contributions that are not appropriately fleshed out. With Sonia's latent but barely articulated concern about the relationship between socioeconomic status and school success, in a subsequent seminar session, I proposed a writing prompt to help PTs explore the multiplicity of meanings involved in "being rich." Expectedly, a range of existing middle-class values emerged, as "being rich" went from having a summerhouse and frequent shopping trips to New York to owning a boat and a plane to travel the world. Subsequently, PTs were asked to gather in small groups and continue to scrutinize their most current drafts for assumptions related to socioeconomic status.

Additional Factors Impacting Sonia's Thinking and Writing   Sonia's cooperating teacher Mrs. Lee, under whose guidance she spent a good part of the day, markedly shaped Sonia's impressions of the challenges posed in urban teaching. During supervisory visits, Mrs. Lee was quick to point to the difficulty of teaching reading to "kids who know so little English" and who "lack adult role models who value education." This perception of parental involvement as a problem mirrors trends of teachers' perceptions in high-poverty and high-minority schools across the nation (Park, 2003) and crystallizes the notion that linguistic diversity and low-income status are handicaps that threaten a school's mission.

Changing Thinking through Peer-Sharing, Field Interactions, and Writing   Through ongoing small-group sharing of writing and peer and instructor feedback, Sonia's approach to CLD students changed significantly. Several factors intervened to make this possible. First, a close writing partnership with another student, Holly, may have been helpful in her rethinking of the impact of context in assessing strengths and needs for CLD learners. Holly had first-hand experience with linguistic diversity because she grew up in a middle-class home led by a single parent who was also foreign-born. She exhibited a heightened degree of empathy for immigrant families with whom schools often find it difficult to communicate. Second, Sonia's experiences with students and families outside of school appeared to tamper with some of her prior beliefs. She soon elaborated on how fortunate her "kind of poor" upbringing had been in comparison to the deprivations some of the families in her field placement endure, as she began frequenting a neighborhood community center located in one of the most impoverished areas of the town. Sonia's comment in class was testimony to that change:

> Compared to my friends in college, my upbringing seems kind of poor. I mean, here I am one of the few people who didn't grow up in a big house with two cars and a manicured lawn. Yet, if I compare my life to the kids I'm teaching now, you can probably see a thick line between "working-class" upbringings like mine and poor like theirs.

Third, because of active encouragement inherent to the expanded field experience approach, Sonia developed a close relationship with a sixth grader, Carina, and her extended family of eight siblings. She set up a volunteer tutor situation that enabled her access to Carina's home. While acknowledging that there were not many resources in a small apartment with 10 mouths to feed, Sonia was quick to point out that the scarcity of material wealth did not prevent the parents from instilling "good values" to their offspring.

Drawing on the enrichment opportunities for learning facilitated by expanded field placements and the reflection promoted and feedback obtained through process writing, Sonia's final interpretation of home environments such as Analia's revealed noteworthy adjustments:

> Like many students in Windmill, Analia is both tired and hungry. She is also a second language learner and so she must keep up in school coursework while learning English. At the end of the class I inquire why she is sleeping in class. She informs me that she does not have a bed, and sleeps on a broken recliner in her living room. At the tender age of ten she has taken on the role of a mom for her younger sibling while her mother works. Analia has taken on the responsibilities of feeding and comforting her infant brother. Like many children in Windmill, Analia faces poverty in her everyday life. Families like Analia's struggle just to provide food for their children, which does not leave room for many material possessions. Many families live with relatives just to make ends meet. Some families are even unable to provide basic needs for their children, such as beds or clothing.

Sonia introduced Windmill as a context that mattered in order to understand Analia's family location. Through their engagement in the community, PTs had benefited from various sources of information about the town, its history, and power holders as aids to assess the variables that impacted CLD communities and gain a better understanding of the economies of poor families that often rendered older siblings as caretakers of the younger ones.

Holly's insistence in suggesting ways to write about the parents' life circumstances without "taking away their dignity" became evident in Sonia's remaining paragraphs:

> Parents are involved in the education of their kids in ways teachers often do not see. Parents may not be able to help their kids with homework when too many jobs prevent them from even seeing their children. Some have parents available at home but who might not be yet fluent in English. As a result, students are faced with the hardships of poverty and language barriers, and therefore, *teachers must find new ways to reach them* (emphasis added).

In addition to benefiting from peer modeling of humanizing depictions of diverse families, Sonia's portrayal of Analia's family life incorporated the notion of families' lack of English proficiency as a temporary barrier ("parents might not yet be fluent"), instead of being an indicator of unavoidable academic failure. The most compelling change, however, was the affirmation that teachers, rather than students, bore the burden of bridging the potential mismatch between home resources and school expectations.

The evolution of Sonia's ideas crystallized in her ongoing drafts suggest that PTs benefit from phased academic work in which their written assumptions are scrutinized and alternative views are pondered for potential incorporation. The stages of Sonia's own *writing as inquiry* (Richardson, 2000) can be best appreciated when accounted for as part of a series of academic and field-based events that helped Sonia and like peers problematize their initial deficit views of low-income, CLD families. Additional insights from this intervention are available elsewhere (Abbate-Vaughn, 2005a).

Although I do not argue here that teacher education programs should incorporate core coursework requirements to account for all possible unfamiliar contexts, I do contend that PTs should be consistently provided with opportunities to experience how contexts and life circumstances other than those privy to mainstream and middle-class families affect pupils' standing in schools. Prospective teachers should be expected to master the epistemological stance of questioning their own assumptions about unfamiliar populations through applied research within those populations and utilize this epistemology with the subsequent diverse communities in which their work as teachers may engage them. Drawing on Cochran-Smith and Lytle's (1999) conceptualization of local knowledge as a socially constructed "process of building, interrogating, elaborating and critiquing conceptual frameworks that link action and problem posing to the immediate context as well as to larger social, cultural, and political issues" (p. 292), the approach described in this chapter ultimately stems from a commitment to CLD pupils and their right to equal access to a public education. It should also be underscored that PTs with diverse backgrounds—such as Holly and her experience with linguistic diversity in this case—can act as scaffolds for their mainstream counterparts. Thus, a concerted effort to recruit and retain a diverse PT population should also be high in teacher preparation programs' agendas.

Strategy # 2: Ethnic Literature Discussion Circles

In order for schools to equalize access to the curriculum, teachers ought to be able to design and implement lessons whose objectives can be mastered by all students. To accomplish this, teachers need some familiarity with the cultural references likely to engage CLD students' attention and must be able to maximize students' connection to prior knowledge they may have on the subject being taught. The discussion of ethnic literature and the histories of diverse groups can help PTs gain that familiarity. As virtually all students attending public schools are taught about Martin Luther King in the context of the Civil Rights Movement—unarguably one of the most important points of 20th century American history—teachers of Nicaraguan immigrants or Vietnamese refugees should strive to attain a working knowledge of the figures revered by those groups with a similar comfort level, given that those are the references to which students and their families are likely to relate.

Along with process writing as a methodology for reflection, the ethnic literature discussion circles enabled PTs to have a glimpse of LD pupils' lives, helping the PTs compare and contrast the similarities and differences between their own contexts and those of diverse "others." Traditionally, education at the K–12 levels has promoted an array of Western cultural artifacts—literature, art, and the repetitive account of Western achievements—underpinning the validity of the school curriculum. Mainstream values and culture are what schools help reproduce. Most prospective teachers experience difficulty in embracing diversity, even if exposed to related fieldwork (Ladson-Billings, 1995). This may be due in part to their lack of familiarity with the values and achievements of the diverse groups in question, for which society at large may rely on stereotypes (Nieto, 2000) and distorted media images (Cortes, 2000). By acquainting themselves with ethnic groups different from their own, PTs are more likely to engage in meaningful interactions with members of the group with which they are newly acquainted, through activities such as frequenting their stores and participating in their cultural activities, which in turn may lead to the development of empathy (McAllister, 2002). In the same manner, PTs can develop familiarity with what the after-school lives of their CLD students may be through ethnic literature which, in conjunction with relevant field experiences, can become an instrumental experience in helping "de-otherize" CLD communities.

Throughout the year, coursework requirements for the same participants included reading a series of autobiographical works penned by well-known ethnic authors, discussing those works in class, and incorporating that new knowledge into such activities as lesson planning and implementation and in their developing relationships with students and parents in the urban CLD community. My goal here was to develop a diverse "cultural literacy," with a reading list tailored to the specific community in which the PTs were involved. The majority of CLD pupils in Windmill were Puerto Rican (some long established, some recent arrivals), Dominican (mostly recent arrivals, some documented), or Mexican (mostly migrant, undocumented farm workers). There were also small numbers of children from various areas of the world whose parents held appointments at the nearby university.

Multicultural education advocates have long called for the use of ethnic literature in diverse classrooms, so that children are taught with materials to which they can relate (Au, 1993; Harris, 1992). Many school districts around the nation have adopted mandatory and suggested reading lists for each grade level that include literature from diverse ethnic groups. This argument for the use of multicultural literature can be easily transferred to the education of prospective teachers who, in the span of their careers, will witness the dramatic transformation of the school population's landscape.

Due to space limitations, I share a few of the works specifically selected for PTs serving low-income Latino pupils in Windmill, while accounting for some of the insights PTs gained from reading and discussing those works. Four different types of books were utilized. The first type was included to continue an informed conversation about poverty, cultural diversity, and perceptions of potential for school success, due to PTs' initial indictments of children reared in housing developments as prone to taking the "wrong turn." *Project Girl*, an autobiography penned by an African-American female writer (McDonald, 1999), describes the author's painful experiences while growing up in economic deprivation and cultural marginality, falling early prey to the temporary relief drugs seemed to provide. Now a successful author living abroad and defying stereotypical forecasts of poor children of color, McDonald's work helped PTs move beyond their quick judgments to imagine the promise held in many of those "written off" low-income students. *Project Girl* helped some to question the loaded assumptions of helplessness that middle-class individuals tend to endorse to those living in poverty and was summarized in a statement from Gerry, a PT completing her year-long field experience in Windmill with secondary students at an in-school suspension program:

> This sort of makes you rethink who you're really dealing with. So far I've been unable to think "poor," "drugs," and "potential" in the same sentence, but that's only [when I am] at Windmill. Then, I know guys who do drugs in college and I never thought of them as completely lost. Then again, [these are] White guys from what I've so far thought of as good families.

In this reflection, Gerry was pointing to the irony that her previous assessment of certain actions by young males was linked to socioeconomic status and imposed middle-class biases on those outside of her circle.

In addition to hinting at the connection between color and socioeconomics in impacting how we assess students' potential, Gerry decided to share *Project Girl* with some of her secondary students in the in-school suspension program. The rationale for doing so-sharing with her students artifacts that aided in her own evolving thoughts about people whose backgrounds differed from hers—

contributed to building an atmosphere of trust in Gerry's classroom and, by her own reporting, a more enjoyable experience for all.

A second type of reading was similar to *Project Girl* in its intimate depictions of low-income families' daily lives but was also informative of the impact cultural and linguistic diversity has on the children of immigrants in and outside of school. Also autobiographical, the intimate details of the upbringings of three Puerto Rican authors— *Down These Mean Streets* (Thomas, 1974), *El Bronx Remembered* (Mohr, 1986), and *Almost a Woman* (Santiago, 1998)—turned out to develop in some cases, and strengthen in others, empathy toward the challenges faced by poor students whose families endured society's stereotyping based on skin shade, perceived linguistic shortcomings, and customs that differed from those of mainstream society. Rainy, a PT who assisted ninth-grade struggling readers placed in the lowest track of the high school, found *Down These Mean Streets* especially useful in grappling with certain implicit codes for settling scores held by her Latino students. As she compared the ways in which middle- and upper-class families deal with altercations or differences—often resorting to arbitrators, attorneys, or mental health providers, depending on the situation—the book helped Rainy to identify means through which low-income students—particularly young males—may learn to define and defend their territory. Rainy documented in her journal a fight in which one of her students, when provoked by another, took part: "When I asked Juan why he couldn't have just walked away when the student shoved him, he said he couldn't and he had to fight him. He looked at me like I was crazy when I asked him that."

As an engaging depiction of low-income Latino youth growing up in the crowded Spanish Harlem of the 1960s, Thomas' writing vividly transports the reader into physical confrontation among male adolescents as a means to "gain respect" from one's peers. Rainy took it upon herself to have her own student read the novel so she could then engage him in a book discussion of "street etiquette." Over time she proudly reported that her classes were "a lot more relaxed," a likely consequence of a more empathetic attitude on Rainy's part, as students appreciated her efforts to "see things" from their perspective.

Down These Mean Streets and *Almost a Woman* touch upon different perspectives related to skin color common among Latino communities. One is of rejection, as Thomas refers to his own relatives' denial of the existence of African blood within the family despite

Thomas' dark skin. The other is of acceptance, as Santiago herself responds to the nickname of *"Negri"* (which translates as "little Black") by her family as a neutral reference to her darker skin shade. Many prospective teachers had heard the word "prieto" used by their Puerto Rican and Dominican students as a pejorative term but felt ambivalent about articulating skin color as an issue in their journals. With the two different perspectives on color offered in Thomas' and Santiago's autobiographies as an issue relevant to understanding Latino students' contexts in relation to skin color, discussions about its impact in Latino interrelationships took a promising turn, as PTs pondered the pervasiveness of intragroup discrimination even within minority communities who, as a whole, face discrimination.

Dolly, a PT who spent most of her Windmill's field placement in a bilingual second grade, mentally canvassed her classroom offering the following reflection:

> The most popular girl in the classroom appears to be Jamie. Every boy wants to sit next to her, and all the girls want to be Jamie's friend. She doesn't have an amazing personality or anything like that, but she's really pretty: green eyes, tiny nose, and dark blond curls. Now, there are two other girls, Lucia and Giselle, that are smarter, definitely funnier, and cute in their own ways—long dark shiny hair, big brown eyes, million dollar smiles—but they are nowhere close as popular as Jamie. It's so hard to think that seven-year-olds can have these ideas about color.... I think teachers are so uncomfortable about this that they wouldn't even try to address it.

The implication stemming from Dolly's observation was that CLD children must be exposed to multicultural education as well since all groups, regardless of status within a society, tend to be monocultural (Nieto, 2000) and limited by the worldview of those who rear and surround them.

A third type of reading was selected to foster an informed discussion on the advantages and disadvantages posed by assimilation to the mainstream. The controversial autobiography *Hunger of Memory*, penned by Mexican American author Richard Rodríguez (1983), lent itself to this sort of debate, since a large number of book reviews from scholars and the lay public alike are available on the Internet. *Hunger of Memory* depicts assimilation and the learning of English as the unavoidable step in becoming somebody, a person with a "public" identity, as opposed to the private identity nurtured by the author's parents in his Spanish-speaking home prior to the children's schooling. Prospective teachers reacted positively to Rodríguez's pro-assimilation story, perhaps because of his success as a writer and cultural commentator. Simultaneously, they also grappled with the opposing arguments set forth by supporters of native language maintenance in regard to the benefits of becoming biliterate and bicultural (Brisk, 1998; Valdés, 1997). Polly, a PT whose own research had taken her to interview some of Windmill's Latino "key informants," expressed her amazement in regard to how common the experiences and contradictory feelings from Rodríguez's book were in many of the conversations she held with her interviewees:

> I definitely think that when I'm talking to these folks I have Rodríguez's book in mind, so my questions aren't innocent in a sense.… But for example Ms. Peralta [a teacher aid], she's young, she's halfway into her degree, and she talks about the same things.… Not being able to answer to her grandma in Spanish, having relatives who'd prefer she get married rather than going to college … being alien to the pride her folks hold in being Latino by having her own sense of accomplishment anchored in her college career and her being fully fluent in English … having come out of a high school where most of her friends had long become dropouts and teenage moms.

The last type of reading strayed from the autobiographical and individual to address cultural and linguistic diversity in relation to a group's historical and political contexts. Rather than using the well-known autobiographical work by Dominican author Julia Alvarez (1992) *How the Garcia Girls Lost Their Accents*, this last discussion circle centered on the same author's fictionalized account of the fated quest for freedom in which the Mirabal sisters died in the hands of dictator Trujillo, masterfully recreated in the novel *In the Time of the Butterflies* (Alvarez, 1994). This choice was influenced by my own personal experience coming of age during a 7-year long military dictatorship in South America and by anecdotal evidence suggesting that PTs in general did not exhibit an understanding of how the absence of democratic institutions impact people's beliefs and behaviors.

The Mirabal sisters—known as the "Butterflies"—were insurgents against dictator Trujillo, who ordered their assassination in 1960. The Mirabal sisters had grown up in a middle-upper-class Dominican family. Although the sisters are known for their fight against the oppression of the dictatorship, the fact remains that a large segment of the Dominican society was rule-abiding and very afraid of the repercussions of opposing the speaking up against the government. The implications of growing up in households where the adults themselves were the survivors of totalitarian governments had not escaped Susan, a PT completing her Windmill internship at the high-school level. After several strategies to manage the behavior of Daniel, a disruptive Dominican male student, Susan resorted to calling home. Daniel's father showed up for the parent conference and utilized threatening language with his son that Susan found unacceptable. Yet, after witnessing the positive change in Daniel's behavior thereafter, Susan felt a guilty sense of relief:

> Daniel says his dad is "old school." I asked what this means to Mr. Diaz, one of the lunch monitors. Mr. Diaz said it's got to do with the use of the belt on the parent's part. I'd hate to learn that he got a beating after our conference, but truth is … I can teach the whole lesson now and Daniel won't disrupt.

Although teachers are by law mandated to report signs of child abuse, the line demarcating the extent of parents' rights to discipline their children varies across cultures and the very notion of abuse is subject to cultural scrutiny. Portes and Rumbaut (2001) discuss this very issue when presenting the story of an immigrant Dominican father witnessing the erosion of his own authority as his son mingles with gang members from the neighborhood. Torn between potentially losing the adolescent to the street and sending him back to the motherland, where the youth would be raised with the necessary amount of adult authority in a less-limiting setting, the man and his wife chose the latter. This makes the discussion more layered and complex, as respect for cultural differences is not always aligned with the procedural—and even legal—demands of teachers' work.

In a more positive outcome, Susan made sense of her troublesome experience with Daniel by resorting to knowledge gained from viewing the film version of *In the Time of the Butterflies*. Drawing on the history of authoritarian rule undergone by the Dominican people, Susan initiated a reflective process of gauging how "the history of the place in which we grow up shapes what we believe in."

Gerry, Rainy, Dolly, Polly, and Susan provide representative examples of how PTs utilized ethnic literature as an alternative lens through which they could reflect on their own experiences in and around school life in Windmill. Their willingness to incorporate resources and strategies modeled in college coursework into their own practice suggests that they internalized the relevance of such approaches when working with CLD students A more detailed description of this intervention is available elsewhere (Abbate-Vaughn, 2005b). Ethnic literature discussion circles appeared to have provided an efficient forum to "normalize" others' lives and ways of looking at the world that significantly differed from those of the PTs involved.

Highly Qualified Teachers Redefined: Including Knowledge of CLD Learners As An Integral Part of Teachers' Preparation

The proposal that teacher educators might only provide meaningful experiences for PTs to work effectively with CLD students when all learning opportunities are synchronized—coursework and field placements where the instructors are familiar with the ways of the schools and those of the communities served—might certainly be problematic for institutions to embrace. Implementation of the strategies described in this chapter—using process writing as a reflective methodology for making sense of an expanded urban field experience, while drawing on ethnic literature as a way for PTs to develop the multicultural literacy needed to strive in such settings—requires heavy involvement in the field not only on the part of those planning and teaching courses but also of those supervising field experiences. From the faculty perspective, coupled with the demands of publishing, teaching, and committee service, extended field involvement may be difficult for both those struggling to survive the tenure process and those who have established high visibility careers with professional commitments geographically apart from the university.

Yet, regardless of those difficulties institutions may experience to prepare culturally sensitive and responsive teachers for CLD students, policy makers might not prioritize the same aims for teacher education. As defined by the *No Child Left Behind Act* of 2001 (NCLB), the federal government's requirements for highly qualified teachers include a deep understanding of subject matter "proven" through passing scores in the state's licensing exam and full state certification obtained through various routes. Little is noted about the necessity for those teachers to develop the understanding of diverse learners' contexts, designing lessons from state-mandated curricula that incorporate students' experiences, or addressing the stereotypical notions about low-income, CLD communities that many new teachers carry to their first jobs. The notion that a solid knowledge of content area is all a teacher needs to educate children is fallacious and yet permeates the agenda of NCLB.

Four implications for policy-making in relation to teacher education can be drawn from this chapter. First, that student-teaching, additional fieldwork, and coursework aligned to appropriately process those experiences should remain a central part of the process of learning to teach. Second, mandatory experiences in diverse settings would cement the principle that teachers are to be bastions of democracy and equal access and not the up-keepers of segregationist practices that overwhelmingly affect CLD learners. This is commonly the case when PTs who have enjoyed comfortable upbringings complete teacher education programs in which all field experiences mirror those of their upbringings and issues of social justice are addressed only in theory. Third, and given what we know about the pervasive biases that the typical middle-class PT holds about poverty and diversity, coursework and aligned field experiences to process conflicting views of diverse communities should also be an expected feature in any degree-bearing program. Fourth, an expanded conceptualization of the types of knowledge necessary for teaching is also called for. Command of subject matter is unarguably one of the pillars of good teaching, but a deep understanding of the "objects" of teaching—the learners—is extremely important, more so when learners' languages and cultures are increasingly different from those of the graduating pools of new teachers. Additionally, teacher education programs should include not only curricula that enable PTs to understand diverse learners but also other types of experiences that increase their awareness of their role in a racialized society (Rosenberg, 1997; Sleeter, 2001) and strive to interrogate their multicultural education strands in ways that facilitate difficult discussions of race, ethnicity, socioeconomics, and language differences.

In addition to the indigenous CLD groups, more than 34 million immigrants (legal and undocumented) currently live on U.S. soil. They account for 12% of the total population and typically speak languages other than English at home. Forty-five percent of those immigrant families live in or near poverty (Camarota, 2004). Teacher education cannot afford to underestimate the impact that such diversity of values, beliefs, forms of communication, and ways of knowing bears on 21st century classrooms. A proactive collaborative effort of teacher education programs, state teacher licensing divisions, teacher education accreditation agencies, and federal policies to vehemently press for a broader conceptualization of the knowledge, skills, and dispositions necessary to teach in today's diverse classrooms is imperative if teachers are to be prepared to serve all learners.

References

Abbate-Vaughn, J. (2004). The things they carry: Ideology in an urban teacher professional community. *Urban Review, 36*(4), 227–249.

Abbate-Vaughn, J. (2005a). *Acción y reflexión hacia la praxis: Un enfoque freireano en la preparación de maestros para la enseñanza en comunidades biculturales marginalizadas.* REICE (Revista Electrónica Iberoamericana sobre Calidad, Eficacia, y Cambio en Educación), *3*(1), 541–551. Available at http://www.ice.deusto. es/RINACE/reice/

Abbate-Vaughn, J. (2005b). "They are just like any of us": Improving teaching students' understanding of marginalized urban pupils through the use of contextualized literature. *Improving Schools, 8*(2), 133–151.

Aguilar, T. E., & Pohan, C. A. (1998). A cultural immersion experience to enhance cross-cultural competence. *Sociotam, 8*(1), 29–49.

Alvarez, J. (1992). *How the García girls lost their accents.* New York: Plume.

Alvarez, J. (1994). *In the time of the butterflies.* Chapel Hill, NC: Algonquin Books.

Antunez, B. (2003). *English language learners in the great city schools: Survey results on students, languages, and programs.* Washington, DC: Council of the Great City Schools. Retrieved November 20, 2004, from http://www.cgcs.org/pdfs/surveyfinalreport.pdf

Au, K. (1993). *Literacy instruction in multicultural settings.* Forth Worth: Harcourt Brace College Publishers.

Ball, S. J. (2003). *Class strategies and the education market: The middle classes and social advantage.* New York: Routledge Falmer.

Banks, J. A. (1991). Teaching multicultural literacy to teachers. *Teacher Education, 4*, 135–144.

Bourdieu, P., & Passeron, J. C. (1977). *Reproduction in education, society, and culture.* Beverly Hills, CA: Sage Publications.

Boyle-Baise, M. (2002). *Multicultural service learning: Educating teachers in diverse communities.* New York: Teachers College Press.

Boyle-Baise, M., & Sleeter, C. (2000). Community-based service learning for multicultural teacher education. *Educational Foundations, 14*(2), 33–50.

Brisk, M. E. (1998). *Bilingual education: From compensatory to quality schooling.* Mahwah, NJ: Lawrence Erlbaum Associates Publishers.

Camarota, S. (2004). *Economy slowed, but immigration didn't: The foreign-born population, 2000–2004.* Washington, DC: Center for Immigration Studies. Retrieved on March 26, 2007, from http://www.cis.org/articles/2004/back1204.pdf

Cochran-Smith, M., & Lytle, S. (1999). Relationships of knowledge and practice: Teacher learning in communities. In A. Iran-Nejad & C. D. Pearson (Eds.), *Review of research in education* (Vol. 24). Washington, DC: American Educational Research Association.

Comer, J. P., & Maholmes, V. (1999). Creating schools of child development and education in the USA: Teacher preparation for urban schools. *Journal of Education for Teaching, 25*(1), 3–15.

Cooper, A., Beare, P., & Thomas, J. (1990). Preparing teachers for diversity: A comparison of student teaching experiences in Minnesota and South Texas. *Action in Teacher Education, 12*(3), 1–4.

Cortes, C. E. (2000). *Our children are watching: How media teach about diversity.* New York: Teachers College Press.

Delgado-Gaitan, C., & Trueba, E. (1991). *Crossing cultural borders.* Bristol, PA: Falmer Press.

Diaz-Rico, L. T. (1998). Towards a just society: Recalibrating multicultural teachers. In R. Chavez-Chavez & J. O'Donnell (Eds.), *Speaking the unpleasant: The politics of (non)engagement in the multicultural education terrain.* Albany, NJ: State University of New York Press.

Faulk, B., & Blumenreich, M. (2005). *The power of questions: A guide to teacher and student research* (pp. 91–114). Portsmouth, NH: Heinemann.

Gay, G. (1993). Building cultural bridges: A bold proposal for teacher education. *Education and Urban Society, 25*(3), 285–289.

Gay, G. (2002). Preparing for culturally responsive teaching. *Journal of Teacher Education, 53*(2), 106–116.

Gee, J. P. (2001). Identity as an analytic lens for research in education. In W. G. Secada (Ed.), *Review of research in education* (Vol. 25, pp. 99–125). Washington, DC: American Educational Research Association.

Gentemann, K. M. (1983). The cultural broker concept in bicultural education. *Journal of Negro Education, 52*(2), 118–129.

Gollnick, D. (1992). Multicultural education: Policies and practices in teacher education. In C. Grant (Ed.), *Research and multicultural education: From the margins to the mainstream* (pp. 218–239). London: Falmer Press.

Goodwin, L. (2000). Teachers as (multi)cultural agents in schools. In R. Carter (Ed.), *Addressing cultural issues in organizations: Beyond the corporate context* (pp. 104–114). Thousand Oaks, CA: Sage.

Graves, D. H. (1983). *Writing: Teachers and children at work*. Portsmouth, NH: Heinemann Educational Books.

Haberman, M. (1996). Selecting and preparing culturally competent teachers for urban schools. In J. Sikula, T. Buttery, & E. Guyton (Eds.), *Handbook of research on teacher education* (2nd ed., pp. 747–760). New York: MacMillan.

Harris, V. J. (1992). *Teaching multicultural literature in grades K–8*. Norwood, MA: Christopher-Gordon.

Helms, J. E. (1990). *Black and white racial identity: Theory, research, and practice*. Westport, CT: Greenwood Press.

Hollins, E. R. (1995). Revealing the deep meaning of culture in school learning: Framing a new paradigm for teacher preparation. *Action in Teacher Education, 17*(1), 70–79.

Irvine, J. J. (1990). *Black students and school failure*. New York: Greenwood Press.

Kiang, P. N. (2001). Teaching, tenure, and institutional transformation: Reflections on race, culture, and resilience at an urban university. In E. Kingston-Mann & T. Sieber (Eds.), *Achieving against the odds* (pp. 125–140). Philadelphia: Temple University Press.

Ladson-Billings, G. (1991). Culturally relevant teaching: The key to making multicultural education work. In C. A. Grant (Ed.), *Research and multicultural education: From the margins to the mainstream* (pp. 106–121). Bristol, PA: Falmer Press.

Ladson-Billings, G. (1995). Multicultural teacher education: Research, practice, and policy. In J. A. Banks & C. A. Banks (Eds.), *Handbook of research on multicultural education* (pp. 747–761). New York: Macmillan.

Lannon, J. M. (2004). *The writing process: A concise rhetoric, reader, and handbook* (8th ed.). New York: Pearson Longman.

Lopez, M. E. (1999). *When discourses collide: An ethnography of migrant children at home and in school*. New York: Peter Lang.

Mahan, J. M., & Stachowski, L. (1994). Diverse, previously un-cited sources of professional learning reported by student teachers serving in culturally different communities. *National Forum for Teacher Education Journal, 3*(1), 21–28.

McAllister, G. (2002). The role of empathy in teaching culturally diverse students: A qualitative study of teachers' beliefs. *Journal of Teacher Education, 53*(5), 433–443.

McDonald, J. (1999). *Project girl*. New York: Farrar, Straus and Giroux.

Merton, R. (1948). *The self-fulfilling prophecy*. Antioch Review, *8*, 193–210.

Mohr, N. (1986). *El Bronx remembered*. Houston: Arte Público Press.

Murrell, P. (2001). *The community teacher: A new framework for effective urban teaching*. New York: Teachers College Press.

National Center for Education Statistics. (1997). *Condition of education, 1997.* Washington, DC: U.S. Department of Education.

Nieto, S. (2000). *Affirming diversity: The sociopolitical context of multicultural education* (3rd ed., Rev.). New York: Longman.

Noordhoff, K., & Kleinfield, J. (1993). Preparing teachers for multicultural classrooms. *Teaching and Teacher Education,* 9(1), 27–39.

Oakes, J., Franke, M. L., Quartz, K. H., & Rogers, J. (2002). Research for high-quality urban teaching: Defining it, developing it, assessing it. *Journal of Teacher Education, 53*(3), 228–234.

Ogbu, J. (1987). Variability in minority school performance: A problem in search of an explanation. *Anthropology and Education Quarterly, 18*(4), 312–334.

Park, J. (2003). *Deciding factors.* Education Week, 22(17), 17–18, January 19, 2005. Retrieved March 26, 2007, from http://counts.edweek.org/sreports/qc03/templates/article.cfm?slug=17divide-s1.h22

Portes, A., & Rumbaut, R. G. (2001). *Legacies: The story of the immigrant second generation.* Berkeley, CA: University of California Press.

Potter, J. (1996). *Representing reality: Discourse, rhetoric, and social construction.* London: Sage.

Richardson, L. (2000). Writing: A method of inquiry. In N. K. Denzin & Y. S. Lincoln (Eds.), *Handbook of qualitative research* (2nd ed., pp. 923–948). Thousand Oaks: Sage Publications.

Rivera-Batiz, F. L. (1996). *The education of immigrant children: The case of New York City.* New York: The New School for Social Research. Retrieved on November 20, 2004, from http://www.columbia.edu/~flr9/immigedu.pdf

Rodríguez, R. (1983). *Hunger of memory: The education of Richard Rodríguez.* New York: Bantam Publishers.

Root, S., & Furco, A. (2001). A review of research on service learning in preservice teacher education. In J. B. Anderson, K. J. Swick, & J. Yff (Eds.), *Service learning in teacher education: Enhancing the growth of new teachers, their students, and communities* (pp. 86–101). Washington, DC: AACTE Publications.

Rosenberg, P. M. (1997). Underground discourses: Exploring whiteness in teacher education. In M. Fine, L. Weiss, L. Powell, & M. Wong, *Off-white: Readings on race, power, and society.* New York: Routledge.

Santiago, E. (1998). *Almost a woman.* New York: Vintage Books.

Sleeter, C. E. (2001). Preparing teachers for culturally diverse schools: Research and the overwhelming presence of whiteness. *Journal of Teacher Education,* 52(2), 94–106.

Spall, S. (1998). Peer debriefing in qualitative research: Emerging operational models. *Qualitative Inquiry,* 4(2), 280–292.

Stenhouse, L. (1975). *An introduction to curriculum research and development*. London: Heinemann Educational.

Suárez-Orozco, C., & Suárez-Orozco, M. M. (2001). *Children of immigration*. Cambridge, MA: Harvard University Press.

Tatum, B. D. (1992). Talking about race, learning about racism: The application of racial identity development theory in the classroom. *Harvard Education Review 62*(1), 1–24.

Tellez, K., Hlebowitsh, P., Cohen, M., & Norwood, P. (1995). Social service field experiences and teacher education. In J. Larkin & C. Sleeter (Eds.), *Developing multicultural teacher education curricula* (pp. 65–78). Albany: State University of New York Press.

Thomas, P. (1974). *Down these mean streets*. New York: Vintage Books.

Trueba, E. (1999). *Latinos unidos: From cultural diversity to the politics of solidarity*. Lanham, MD: Rowman & Littlefield Publishers, Inc.

Tse, L. (1995). Language brokering among Latino adolescents: Prevalence, attitudes, and school performance. *Hispanic Journal of Behavioral Sciences, 12*(3), 256–276.

Valdés, G. (1996). *Con respeto: Bridging the distances between culturally diverse families and schools*. New York: Teachers College Press.

Valdés, G. (1997). Dual language immersion programs: A cautionary note concerning the education of language minority students. *Harvard Educational Review, 67*(3), 391–429.

Valenzuela, A. (1999). *Subtractive schooling: U.S.-Mexican youth and the politics of caring*. Albany: State University of New York Press.

Villegas, A., & Lucas, T. (2002). *Educating culturally responsive teachers: A coherent approach*. Albany: State University of New York Press.

Wade, R. C. (2000). Service learning for multicultural teaching competency: Insights from the literature for teacher educators. *Equity & Excellence in Education, 33*(3), 21–29.

Weiner, L. (1999). *Urban teaching: The essentials*. New York: Teachers College Press.

Zeichner, K. M., & Gore, J. M. (1990). Teacher socialization. In W. R. Houston (Ed.), *Handbook of research on teacher education* (pp. 329–348). New York: Macmillan.

Zeichner, K., & Hoeft, K. (1996). Teacher socialization for cultural diversity. In J. Sikula, T. Buttery, & E. Guyton (Eds.), *Handbook of research on teacher education*, 2nd ed., (Vol. 525–547). New York: Macmillan.

Zeichner, K., & Melnick, S. (1996). The role of community field experiences in preparing teachers for cultural diversity. In K. Zeichner, S. Melnick, & M. L. Gomez (Eds.), *Currents of reform in preservice teacher education* (pp. 176–198). New York: Teachers College Press.

Zimpher, N. L., & Ashburn, E. A. (1992). Countering parochialism in teacher candidates. In M. Dilworth (Ed.), *Diversity in teacher education* (pp. 40–62). San Francisco: Jossey-Bass.

Endnotes

1. A Web search yields that SoEs identify their urban teacher preparation programs with such acronyms as UTE, LUTE, UTP, UTCP, and UETR.
2. In percentages: Atlanta, GA, 89; Baltimore, MD, 88; Birmingham, AL, 96; Detroit, IL, 91; New Orleans, LA, 93; Richmond, VA, 91; St. Louis, MO, 81; Washington, DC, 84.
3. In percentages: Providence, RI, 52; Miami, FL, 58; Los Angeles, CA, 71; Fresno, CA, 51; Denver, CO, 55; Dallas, TX, 57; Albuquerque, NM, 51.
4. As early as 1980, the American Association of Colleges of Teacher Education (AACTE) issued a report in which the issue of equity was raised (in Baptiste, H. and Baptiste, M. [1980], Competencies toward multiculturalism, in H. Baptiste, M. Baptiste, & D. Gollnick, Multicultural teacher education: Preparing teacher educators to provide educational equity [Vol. 1]. Washington DC: AACTE).

9

Teacher Education to Serve a Native Hawaiian Community

Lessons Learned

Kathryn H. Au
University of Hawaii–Manoa

Yvonne Kaulukane Lefcourt
University of Illinois

Alice J. Kawakami
University of Hawaii

The Ka Lama Teacher Education Initiative (Ka Lama, for short) aims to help Native Hawaiians become teachers in schools in their own communities. Native Hawaiians are the descendants of the original Polynesian inhabitants of the Hawaiian Islands. In the Hawaiian language, the phrase *ka lama* means "the light," and the connotation is that teachers bring the light of knowledge to their students. Native Hawaiians are underrepresented in the teaching population in Hawaii, accounting for only 10.2% of teachers, compared to 26.1% of students (State of Hawaii Department of Education, 2004). The purpose of this chapter is to describe the principles that have guided the Ka Lama Teacher Education Initiative, as well as the procedures found to be successful over the course of its 10-year evolution. We begin by exploring underlying concepts and by describing the particular community served by Ka Lama. We then discuss the development of Ka Lama in terms of five lessons learned along the way. We offer these lessons as ideas that others interested in developing teacher education programs for diverse communities may wish to pursue.

Underlying Concepts and Program Design

Two Perspectives on Community

The notion of community is subject to various interpretations, and the development of Ka Lama has been guided by concepts of community deriving from two different perspectives. The first perspective comes from the work of McKnight (1995) in his book entitled *The Careless Society: Community and Its Counterfeits*. McKnight defines community as the site for the relationships among citizens. These relationships lead to care, which McKnight regards as "the consenting commitment of citizens to one another" (p. x). McKnight argues that society has become careless in the sense that citizens have come to doubt their capacity to care. As a result, McKnight suggests, citizens have abdicated this responsibility in the belief that care is best delivered by social service institutions.

We designed Ka Lama to fit with McKnight's thesis that communities need to recover their capacity to care. One of the guiding principles of Ka Lama is that teacher education and school reform should be seen as part and parcel of a community's own efforts to provide care. Although Ka Lama has received considerable support from outside experts and mainstream institutions, it has always been seen as part of the community's own efforts to advance itself and care for its young people.

The second perspective on community comes from the work of Wenger, who studied what he termed "communities of practice." In his book, *Communities of Practice: Learning, Meaning, and Identity*, Wenger (1998) defines community as "the social configurations in which our enterprises are defined as worth pursuing and our participation is recognizable as competence" (p. 5). Each of us belongs to many communities of practice, such as families, informal networks of friends, professional organizations, sports teams, and religious groups. Each community of practice has its own rituals and routines, discourse and stories, artifacts and symbols. All those contributing to Ka Lama—preservice teachers, mentor teachers, teachers who have graduated from the program, university instructors, community leaders, and others—have been seen as forming a community of practice. This community of practice has needed to coordinate its energies and activities to address issues posed by the social, economic, and political context of the area it seeks to serve. Connections of this community of practice to the historical past—that is, to the community of practice formed by Native Hawaiian teachers in the 19th century—are discussed elsewhere (Au, 2000). In this chapter, we describe the present workings of Ka Lama as a community of practice as well as plans made for its continuation into the future.

Program Design

These concepts of community, along with the very idea of teacher education in service to Native Hawaiian communities, are in striking contrast to mainstream perspectives on teacher education (Au, 2002). Teacher education programs conducted from a mainstream perspective commonly pursue the goal of preparing "good teachers for all children," in keeping with what Haberman (1996) termed "the universal perspective." While this universal view of the purpose of teacher education appears to make sense, it means in practice that many teacher education programs end up preparing mainstream teachers to teach mainstream students. Students of diverse cultural and linguistic backgrounds are rendered invisible in such universal views of teacher education and, as a result, many beginning teachers may not be prepared to bring these students to high levels of achievement.

We deliberately designed Ka Lama to differ from mainstream teacher education efforts in several ways (Au, 2002). First, we established Ka Lama with the goal of preparing teachers to meet the challenges of diversity found in a Native Hawaiian community, rather than preparing teachers in a general way. Second, we aimed to have Ka Lama build on resources within this community, rather than assuming a lack of resources or interest within the community. Third, we kept the interests of the community at the forefront.

The community in this case is the Wai'anae Coast of the island of O'ahu, an area approximately a 45-minute drive from downtown Honolulu. Most residents consider the Wai'anae Coast to begin at Kahe Point, a popular surfing spot and the site of the largest electrical power plant on the island. The community extends up the coastline and into the valleys, a largely rural area with most commercial activity confined to spots along a single highway. About 30,000 Native Hawaiians reside on the Wai'anae Coast, some in Hawaiian homesteads in Nanakuli, Lualualei, and Wai'anae valleys. The area has a higher percentage of school-aged children than the state of Hawaii as a whole, a higher percentage of families headed by single mothers, and a lower median household income. Homeless families can often be seen camping or living in cars on the beach.

There are seven elementary schools on the Wai'anae Coast. Historically, achievement test scores at these schools have been among the lowest in the state. In the typical classroom, about two-thirds of the children are of Hawaiian ancestry, with the remainder composed of a mix of children of other ethnicities, including Filipino, Samoan, and White. More than 80% of the children are eligible for free- or reduced-cost lunch, an indication that they come from low-income families. The vast majority of children speak Hawaii Creole English (a nonmainstream variety of English) as their first language, while only about 5% speak a first language other than English. These demographics do not tell the whole story. Most teachers describe the children in their classrooms as bright, affectionate, and appreciative of the help they receive.

The approach we used to keep the interests of the community at the forefront of Ka Lama was somewhat unusual and merits further explanation. From its inception, Ka Lama has been coordinated by a nonprofit Hawaiian educational services organization, the Institute for Native Pacific Education and Culture (INPEACE), led by Native Hawaiian educator and then–executive director Sherlyn Franklin Goo. Teacher education initiatives are almost always coordinated by universities, and the College of Education at the University of Hawaii at Manoa (UHM) has certainly been a key player in Ka Lama. Preservice teachers who enter the Ka Lama preservice cohort are enrolled in the elementary and early childhood education program in the College of Education, and they take courses within this program to earn bachelor's degrees in elementary education. However, INPEACE convenes the community advisory board that sets policy directions for Ka Lama, prepares grant proposals, and receives all external funding for the operations of Ka Lama. In addition to the College of Education, key partners include the local community college (Leeward Community College) and public schools in the community.

This arrangement with INPEACE has enabled Ka Lama to thrive, despite the fact that the Ka Lama preservice cohort receives no funding from the UHM College of Education beyond that provided to all other cohorts. In our experience, Ka Lama and similar teacher education efforts may not succeed if they rely only on the support of a university, without close ties to community organizations such as INPEACE. The reason is that a college of education within a state university is likely to see its mission as preparing teachers for the whole state. Administrators may express the view that the college of education cannot be seen as preparing teachers to serve any particular community and group of children but must be seen as preparing teachers to teach all children, everywhere in the state. Obviously, this approach amounts to preparing "good teachers for all children," as discussed above, with its attendant weaknesses. In short, to maintain a focus on teacher preparation in service of diverse communities, it may be important for the teacher education initiative to be run in close collaboration with a community organization rather than based entirely in a university.

Figure 9.1 shows the three components of the Ka Lama Teacher Education Initiative, which began with just the 2-year preservice teacher education cohort, shown in the box in the center of the second row. As discussed below, the other two components, the education academy and the leadership network, were added later. Students who participated in the cohort are referred to as *preservice teachers*. A cohort graduated with bachelor's degrees in elementary education every 2 years beginning in 1998. The first cohort is referred to as Ka Lama I, the cohort that graduated in 2000 as Ka Lama II, and so on.

Lessons Learned

We discuss five lessons learned. These lessons are:

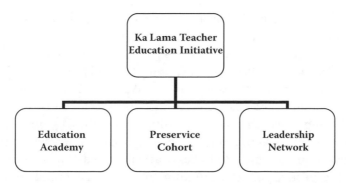

Figure 9.1

1. Establish an ongoing connection to the community.
2. Create your own pipeline.
3. Help students understand education as a process of social change and the importance of culturally responsive instruction.
4. Place preservice teachers with mentor teachers who exemplify successful practices.
5. Build a leadership network.

First Lesson: Establish an Ongoing Connection to the Community

In the fall of 1995, Kathryn Au began work as a professor in the UHM College of Education. For the previous 15 years, Au had worked in elementary schools on the Wai'anae Coast. Through her research, she had gained a good understanding of how teachers could bring these elementary school students to high levels of literacy (Au & Carroll, 1997). As a professor in the College of Education, she hoped to put this knowledge to practical use by establishing a teacher education initiative for the Wai'anae Coast.

Efforts to bring innovative practices into the schools on the Wai'anae Coast were often stymied by the high rate of teacher turnover. Many new teachers obtained their first teaching jobs in classrooms on the Wai'anae Coast. After 3 years, when they received tenure, these teachers often transferred to schools closer to their homes in the suburbs of Honolulu. Teachers moved in and out of schools on the Wai'anae Coast as if through a revolving door, and it was not uncommon for an elementary school to lose one-third of its teachers in a single year. Au reasoned that one way to stabilize the teaching force in these schools would be to recruit community residents, especially Native Hawaiians, to become teachers.

Did community leaders on the Wai'anae Coast see the needs of the schools in the same way? While Au began preliminary arrangements within the College of Education, Sherlyn Franklin Goo began contacting community leaders on the Wai'anae Coast. Goo found that community leaders were enthusiastic about the prospects of establishing a teacher education initiative for the Wai'anae Coast. Mililani Allen, a community leader and respected teacher of traditional Hawaiian dance and chant, accompanied Goo to meetings with prospective funders. Funding from the first grant, from the Hawai'i Community Foundation, was used to establish a community advisory board to develop policies to guide Ka Lama, as well as to involve instructors from the community in teaching courses.

The Ka Lama community advisory board, headed by Goo, began meeting once per semester, a pattern that continued in the years to come. The board included community leaders, principals of public schools on the Waiʻanae Coast, and graduates and present participants of the Ka Lama preservice cohort. The group also had representatives from the UHM College of Education, Leeward Community College, and INPEACE.

From the start, the community advisory board provided valuable advice and resources. Au wanted to teach education courses on the Waiʻanae Coast, rather than on the UHM campus, an hour's drive away. She arranged to teach these courses after school in the library at one of the elementary schools. However, this arrangement proved inconvenient for the school, which needed the library for such events as faculty meetings and book fairs. When Au raised the problem at an advisory board meeting, one of the members secured the use of a large conference room in the offices of a nonprofit organization in the community. Later, another member suggested that Au move her classes to the satellite campus of Leeward Community College located in the business district of Waiʻanae (LCC-W). This last arrangement proved beneficial in allowing the Ka Lama preservice teachers to serve as role models for the community college students and to let them see that UHM education courses were being taught in the community.

One of the most significant meetings of the advisory board took place in May 1998. Members of the first Ka Lama preservice cohort graduated that month, and the second cohort was admitted at about the same time. Au had seen a disappointing pattern in enrollment: Only 6 of the 29 students in the first cohort were residents of the Waiʻanae Coast, and only 4 of 26 in the second cohort. At the advisory board meeting, Au described how she had been unable to bring more residents into the preservice cohort, despite having held several well-attended recruitment meetings in the community. Advisory board members readily identified probable obstacles, including a low rate of high school graduation and the small number of residents who had the opportunity to advance to higher education, often due to financial need and family responsibilities. Advisory board members cautioned that Ka Lama could not wait for qualified students to come through the pipeline. Instead, they recommended that Ka Lama create its own pipeline.

Second Lesson: Create Your Own Pipeline

Acting on the advice of the advisory board, Au took the lead in preparing a grant proposal to the U.S. Administration for Native Americans (ANA) for the Ka Lama Education Academy. This proposal was successful, and the Education Academy opened its doors in the fall of 1998 (the education academy is shown as the first box in the second row of Figure 9.1). Most funding for the academy came from the ANA, with some monies from the state Office of Hawaiian Affairs. The Atherton Family Foundation provided funds that allowed academy counselors to provide services to non-Hawaiian residents of the community.

The purpose of the academy was to recruit and then assist residents of the Wai'anae Coast to become teachers. Although the Education Academy emphasized recruitment and services for Native Hawaiians, community residents of other cultural backgrounds were welcomed as well. Education Academy counselors assisted residents with the process of enrolling at LCC-W. A similar effort at this campus, one that prepared students for careers in health care, had served as the model for the Education Academy. Education Academy counselors helped residents plan the courses they would take so that they earned associate of arts degrees from LCC-W, while at the same time fulfilling the course requirements for admission as juniors to the UHM College of Education.

Larrilynn Holu Tamashiro, a Native Hawaiian Ka Lama I graduate, served as the lead coordinator and counselor for the Education Academy from its inception. Holu Tamashiro was raised on the Wai'anae Coast, graduated from Wai'anae High School, and had a wide network of family and friends in the community. Her background enabled her to understand the issues students faced, whether academic, financial, social, or emotional. Holu Tamashiro and her fellow counselors—who included Barbra Kaimuloa Bates, a Ka Lama II graduate, and Ray Jeanine Pikelny, a Ka Lama IV graduate—provided a variety of services that included directing students to sources of financial aid, making arrangements for students to meet with tutors, and helping students to complete application forms for the UHM College of Education.

After Education Academy students were admitted to the College of Education, Holu Tamashiro and other counselors continued to monitor their progress. Keeping up with the demands of the full-time, 2-year preservice teacher education program was a challenge for many who came through the Education Academy. For this 2-year period, preservice teachers were on a tight schedule with a heavy load of courses. This schedule was in contrast to that of the community college, where many students had taken just one or two courses a semester and had the time to hold down full-time jobs as well as meet family responsibilities. Once they entered the cohort, preservice teachers had to develop the skills to juggle school, work, and family responsibilities successfully.

Preservice teachers who came through the pipeline provided by the Education Academy were always grateful for the help they had received. Many believed that they would not have advanced to the College of Education without the help of the Education Academy. The academy showed particular success with recruitment and counseling of Ka Lama IV, the cohort that graduated in May 2004. This cohort of 21 included 11 Native Hawaiian residents of the Wai'anae Coast.

The Education Academy certainly showed success in increasing the number of residents entering the preservice teacher education cohort. The combination of the Education Academy and the preservice cohort worked well to produce a small and steady flow of well-qualified teachers, residents of the community, for the schools on the Wai'anae Coast. However, Holu Tamashiro and other advisory board members saw the need for a much larger number of residents to become teachers. By the fall of 2004, approximately 35 Ka Lama graduates were teaching in classrooms in elementary schools on the Wai'anae Coast, 20 of them residents of the community. Ka Lama graduates only accounted for 11% of the 318 teachers in the seven elementary schools on the coast. A generous estimate would indicate that perhaps 15% of all teachers were residents of the community. Furthermore, no attempt had been made to expand Ka Lama's services to residents wishing to become teachers at the intermediate and high school levels.

Holu Tamashiro expressed the belief that the goal should be for residents of the community to make up one-half of teachers in public schools on the Wai'anae Coast. Reaching this goal would mean doubling the number of residents entering teaching through the Ka Lama Education Academy and preservice cohort. What prevented more residents from entering the preservice cohort? Holu Tamashiro and Pikelny observed that the design of the preservice cohort introduced an economic barrier because it did not allow participants to hold full-time jobs. A possible solution under investigation involved redesigning the curriculum to include a combination of evening, weekend, and online courses. Another idea being explored was to have participants employed as paraprofessional aides in elementary schools, as a way of allowing them to fulfill field experience requirements while still earning income.

Third Lesson: Help Students Understand Education as a Process of Social Change and the Importance of Culturally Responsive Instruction

Preservice teachers in Ka Lama were introduced at the outset to critical theory and the notion that education should be a process of social change, not one of reproducing the existing social order (McLaren, 1989). Critical theory provided a lens through which preservice teachers could understand that the detrimental conditions in schools on the Wai'anae Coast—such as high rates of teacher turnover and reading programs that neglected comprehension and higher level thinking—were not matters of happenstance but persistent patterns found in many schools in diverse, low-income communities. The Ka Lama preservice teachers learned that the secret to improving education on the Wai'anae Coast was to put favorable new patterns in place.

In a two-semester sequence of language arts courses, Au emphasized the remedies to two negative patterns: (1) students' limited access to instruction in higher level thinking and (2) their lack of engagement with classroom learning activities. Preservice teachers learned to apply critical theory to see that an overemphasis on instruction in basic skills had the likely effect of preparing students to become workers but not leaders and thinkers (Delpit, 1991). They also learned that students' lack of engagement commonly resulted from the teacher's failure to help them make meaningful, personal connections to the content or activity at hand. Au taught the preservice teachers to promote higher level thinking and student engagement by using the process approach to writing and the writers' workshop, along with literature-based instruction and the readers' workshop (Au, Carroll, & Scheu, 2001). Previous studies demonstrated the effectiveness of these approaches in improving the literacy learning of Hawaiian children (Au & Carroll, 1997). No studies could be conducted of the effectiveness of Ka Lama graduates in using these same approaches because schools on the Waiʻanae Coast were under a mandate to implement reading programs that did not incorporate all of the features of instruction previously found to be critical to students' learning.

Au introduced the preservice teachers as well to the importance of culturally responsive instruction, defined as teaching that builds on the values and knowledge students bring from the home in order to promote academic learning (Au & Maaka, 2001). Culturally responsive instruction has two dimensions, and bringing these two dimensions together is likely to have a positive effect on the engagement and academic performance of students of diverse cultural and linguistic backgrounds. The first dimension has to do with the process of instruction, whereas the second concerns the content of instruction.

In terms of the process dimension, Au acquainted the preservice teachers with three major findings from the research base on culturally responsive instruction for Native Hawaiian students. The first finding had to do with structuring interaction with students in a culturally responsive manner through the use of participation structures similar to those in talk story, a common speech event in the Hawaiian community (Au, 1980). In talk story, speakers collaborate to produce a narrative, speaking in rhythmic alternation (Watson, 1974). Studies showed that, when Hawaiian students participated in talk story–like reading lessons, they showed higher levels of on-task behavior, discussed more text ideas, and made more logical inferences than when they participated in lessons structured following conventional western rules for classroom recitation (Au & Mason, 1981).

A second finding was that of using a classroom management style described as the "smile with teeth," the metaphor developed by the anthropologist John D'Amato (1986) to describe teachers successful in classrooms with Hawaiian students. These teachers exuded warmth, caring, and respect for students (the smile), while demanding high levels of academic performance, orderly behavior, and consideration of others.

The third finding had to do with the value of peer work groups in which students were allowed to teach and to learn from one another (Jordan, 1985). This approach was consistent with the emphasis placed in many Hawaiian households on sibling caretaking and contributing to the well being of the group or family.

Less research has been completed on the benefits of the second dimension of culturally responsive instruction, using Hawaiian studies content in lessons. However, attention to content is no less important than attention to processes of instruction. As a non-Hawaiian, Au relied on colleagues to guide the Ka Lama preservice teachers in this regard.

Julie Kaomea, a UHM professor of Native Hawaiian ancestry, taught the two-semester sequence of courses on the teaching of mathematics in the elementary school to several Ka Lama preservice cohorts. Kaomea (personal communication, May 8, 2004) gave the following example of how she incorporated Hawaiian studies content in her math methods courses. Kaomea taught the preservice teachers that early civilizations relied on body parts as nonstandard units of measurement. The ancient Hawaiians used such units as the *anana* (the distance between the tips of the longest fingers, when a person's arms were extended to either side), the *pi'a* (the length of one hand), and the *kiko'o* (the distance between the tip of the thumb and tip of the index finger). Kaomea let the preservice teachers know that these forms of measurement were still being used by some Hawaiian craftspeople. Through hands-on activities, elementary students might learn how to measure length using nonstandard units, such as the *pi'a* and *kiko'o*, and eventually gain a deeper understanding of why units such as inches and meters had evolved.

However, few university instructors had the depth of knowledge necessary to show the preservice teachers the possibilities for making Hawaiian studies content central to the elementary school curriculum. For this reason, Au sought to involve cultural experts from the community to provide the preservice teachers with a richer background. She designed a course on Hawaiian and American foundations of education, which was substituted for a required course on the foundations of education typically taught from a mainstream perspective. Eric Enos, a community leader and expert in Hawaiian culture, served as Au's coinstructor for this course with three preservice cohorts: Ka Lama II, III, and IV. An overarching goal of this course was to emphasize the intellectual content of Hawaiian studies, including the values and worldview underlying cultural practices, and to challenge negative stereotypes about Hawaiian culture.

Enos engaged the preservice teachers in questioning commonly held assumptions about Hawaiian culture and what it meant to be Hawaiian. He served as director of the Cultural Learning Center at

Ka'ala, a site that allowed the preservice teachers to gain some sense of Hawaiian culture before Western contact. For example, in a unit on cultural geology, the preservice teachers collected black and white pebbles from the beaches as markers for *konane,* a Hawaiian strategy game. They used hammerstones to shape rocks into puck-shaped disks called *'ulu maika.* In the game of *maika,* the object is to roll these disks through stakes set in the ground.

In reflecting on their experiences at the Cultural Learning Center at Ka'ala, most of the non-Hawaiian preservice teachers indicated that they had not previously understood the depth of Hawaiian culture, especially its spiritual nature, or the ingenuity of Hawaiians in making use of the natural materials available to them. Most of the Hawaiian preservice teachers came away with a greater pride in their culture and respect for the intelligence of their ancestors.

In Hawaiian studies units created as part of the course with Au and Enos, most of the preservice teachers showed that they could apply what they had learned. For example, two preservice teachers working with sixth-grade classes created a social studies unit centering on Hawaiian and Western perspectives on the uses of land. The unit focused on issues raised by protests at Mākua Valley on the Wai'anae Coast, long a site for military training activities using live ordnance. The sixth graders had the opportunity to evaluate the perspectives of Native Hawaiian activists, who wanted the scarring of the land to end, and of military officials, who justified the training activities in the interests of national security. Students heard speakers on both sides of the issues, analyzed the arguments, and debated the issues themselves.

As this sample unit suggests, bringing Hawaiian studies to a central position in the elementary school curriculum—as part of the core subjects of language arts, mathematics, science, and social studies—involves intellectual rigor and a firm understanding of Hawaiian cultural perspectives on the part of teachers. For teachers of mainstream backgrounds, it may take several years beyond the preservice level to feel comfortable with culturally responsive instruction (Au & Blake, 2003). Culturally responsive instruction should be emphasized in preservice courses when preparing teachers to work in classrooms in diverse communities such as the Wai'anae Coast and should remain an emphasis in ongoing professional development for experienced teachers.

Fourth Lesson: Place Preservice Teachers with Mentor Teachers Who Exemplify Successful Practices

Studies indicate that field experiences in schools exert a powerful effect on preservice teachers, often considerably more powerful than the effect of academic courses (Cruickshank & Armaline, 1986). One of the reasons beginning teachers experience difficulty teaching effectively in classrooms with many students of diverse cultural and linguistic backgrounds is that they were not placed in such classrooms during their preservice field experiences and so did not have the opportunity to develop the teaching skills to meet the needs of these students. Obviously, it is highly important that preservice teachers' field experiences as well as academic coursework prepare them to teach in classrooms with students of diverse backgrounds. Because the intention of Ka Lama was to prepare teachers to be successful in classroom on the Wai'anae Coast, the preservice teachers were placed in the classrooms of mentor teachers in schools in the area.

Ka Lama mentor teachers were selected on the basis of recommendations by principals and colleagues, especially other mentor teachers familiar with the philosophy and instructional approaches emphasized in Ka Lama. With Ka Lama V, about half the mentor teachers were themselves Ka Lama graduates. Native Hawaiians and residents of the community were overrepresented as Ka Lama mentor teachers, when compared to their presence in the schools as a whole.

Most community residents who entered the Ka Lama cohort as preservice teachers knew the public schools well from their own personal experience. They began with a good working knowledge of the culture of schools on the Wai'anae Coast that helped them adjust quickly to managing the classroom and relating to students. Barbra Bates Kaimuloa, a Ka Lama II graduate mentioned earlier, was mentored by her former sixth-grade teacher during student teaching. Other residents also had the opportunity to work as preservice teachers with mentor teachers in their former elementary schools.

The picture was quite different for Ka Lama preservice teachers from outside the community, even those who were Native Hawaiians. Some Native Hawaiians outsiders felt a cultural connection to the students, but at the same time, they sensed a separation from the students due to differences of social class and often came to recognize the privileged nature of their own upbringing (Au & Blake, 2003). At the same time, many felt a strong calling to teach in a Hawaiian community where they could make a difference in the lives of their students.

Non-Hawaiian preservice teachers who were outsiders to the community were likely to experience culture shock. A Japanese American preservice teacher, who had attended a private school in Honolulu, wrote of her surprise at seeing the students on the first day of her field experience in a Wai'anae Coast elementary school. Not until that moment had she realized that she was accustomed to being in classrooms with Asian American and European American students, not Hawaiian students. Another Japanese American preservice teacher, also educated in a private school, discussed how she had been extremely apprehensive about having her field experience in a school on the Wai'anae Coast because of the negative stereotypes about the community. During the first week of her field experience, she changed her attitude completely. She found the students to be friendly and eager to learn, and she described her mentor teacher, a Ka Lama graduate and Native Hawaiian resident of the community, as "awesome."

The Ka Lama preservice teachers spent at least 10 hours per week in the classrooms of their mentor teachers during the first three semesters in the elementary education program and spent more than 40 hours per week during the fourth, or student teaching, semester. They devoted much more time to working alongside their mentor teachers than they did to classes with any of their university instructors, and the mentor teachers were often able to provide the preservice teachers with more immediate and specific guidance than the university instructors. Having well-qualified mentor teachers was essential to the development of the preservice teachers' management and instructional skills as well as to their professional dispositions.

In our experience, good field placements for the Ka Lama preservice teachers were located by following the strategy of identifying successful teachers to serve as mentors across a number of schools. This strategy was in contrast to trying to establish a professional development school and placing all the Ka Lama preservice teachers at this one site. At various points in time, Ka Lama preservice teachers were placed in all seven of the elementary schools on the Wai'anae Coast. In a given year, we found that a single school typically had only 6 to 8 tenured teachers with both the qualifications and willingness to serve as mentors to Ka Lama preservice teachers. A high rate of teacher turnover was one reason that some schools could not develop a large pool of mentor teachers. Other factors affecting the availability of mentor teachers included administrative and leadership difficulties, such as a new principal who wished to move the school in a different direction; the mandating of new programs in reading, math, and other areas; and the numerous demands placed on experienced teachers to serve as grade level chairs, head committees, and lead new initiatives in the school. Fortunately, these negative factors had little impact on the willingness of Ka Lama graduates to serve as mentor teachers, perhaps because of their close personal connections to the program.

Of course, Ka Lama graduates who served as mentor teachers were sometimes able to model successful practices, such as the process approach to writing and literature-based instruction, that preservice teachers were learning about in their university courses. The preservice teachers were always heartened to see mentor teachers implementing approaches such as shared reading, guided reading, and book clubs. However, mentor teachers' ability to use balanced literacy instruction was often affected by accountability pressures brought on by state and federal legislation. In an effort to raise test scores, the district issued a mandate requiring elementary schools on the Wai'anae Coast to adopt packaged programs. One school adopted a highly scripted reading program that severely restricted mentor teachers' ability to use practices—such as literature-based instruction—that could contribute to students' higher level thinking about text and enjoyment of reading.

Au followed a policy of placing Ka Lama preservice teachers at all schools with qualified mentor teachers, even when the reading program ran counter to the philosophy of Ka Lama by not promoting higher level thinking and student engagement. She reasoned that the preservice teachers needed to be exposed to the range of programs likely to impact schools on the Wai'anae Coast and to judge for themselves which had positive effects on children's learning. Similarly, Au believed it was important to keep in the pool some mentor teachers who favored traditional rather than innovative teaching practices but who could model successful classroom management practices and warm relationships with children. She thought that the preservice teachers would benefit from seeing a range of teaching styles and philosophies in the process of developing their own professional stances and identities.

Fifth Lesson: Build a Leadership Network

The need for a leadership component of Ka Lama became apparent shortly after work with the first preservice cohort began. The work that teachers do is affected by the larger context of the schools in which they work, and that context is shaped not just by teachers but by district administrators, principals, curriculum coordinators, resource teachers, and others. Au and others believed that, once Ka Lama graduates became teachers, they should be encouraged to advance to a variety of leadership roles (Au & Maaka, 2001).

Originally, an attempt was made to fill the need for leadership development by organizing a cohort of Ka Lama graduates who would progress through the master's program in curriculum and instruction at the UHM College of Education. This plan proved difficult to carry out. Although several Ka Lama graduates did benefit from this arrangement and complete master's degrees—including Ka Lama I graduate Yvonne Lefcourt—only one was a Native Hawaiian resident of the Wai'anae Coast. Three obstacles seemed to block the success of an approach centered on a master's degree cohort. First, the schedule and location of classes was inconvenient for many community residents. Almost all master's courses were taught at the UHM campus during evening hours, a situation that presented difficulties for women with families. Second, paying for graduate courses proved to be an obstacle. While enrolled full-time in the Ka Lama preservice cohort, Native Hawaiians had access to ample scholarship funds and stipends. Once they took jobs as public school teachers, these same individuals could only take graduate courses on a part-time basis, and no programs offered scholarships or tuition assistance to part-time students. Third, the content of master's courses did not address the Ka Lama graduates' professional interests as future leaders. Courses in the master's program in curriculum and instruction gave the Ka Lama graduates the knowledge needed to improve their practices as teachers and teacher researchers but not the knowledge needed to work beyond the classroom level and to lead educational change efforts.

In 2001, Au and Marci Sarsona, a Ka Lama I graduate who had become the associate executive director of INPEACE, made a second attempt to organize a leadership network within Ka Lama. This time, Au worked with Holu Tamashiro to identify two or three potential community leaders from each Ka Lama cohort. All the participants were residents of the Waiʻanae Coast or had been educated on the coast and maintained close ties to the area, and all were teachers in public schools on the coast or planning to become teachers there. Although these individuals knew one another, they had not worked closely together on any projects. Au suggested that participants view themselves as a network that might stay together for two or three decades, if necessary, to bring about substantial improvements in education in Waiʻanae Coast schools.

Au and Sarsona sought to design an approach to leadership development to overcome the obstacles encountered earlier. Grant monies were used to sponsor workshops, at no expense to the participants. Sarsona worked with participants to identify the areas of leadership expertise they felt they needed, and these areas included strategic planning, grant writing, networking, and public speaking. Among other activities, Sarsona conducted a workshop on strategic planning in which she guided participants through the process of developing a mission statement for the leadership network. She also arranged a grant writing workshop for participants. However, scheduling issues proved to be a continuing obstacle. It proved difficult to find times when the majority of participants could meet and, as of this writing, the leadership network had not been mobilized to work on any particular projects. The network might be expected to evolve in the future, as participants advance to leadership roles, have more opportunities to meet, and identify issues of common concern.

Conclusion

The purpose of the Ka Lama Teacher Education Initiative is to improve education by preparing teachers for schools in a specific, diverse community. Furthermore, Ka Lama focuses on preparing Native Hawaiian residents to become teachers. A commonly asked question has to do with the implications of this effort for teachers who are from outside the community and teachers who are not from the same cultural background as their students. In many classrooms in urban districts, the majority of teachers are monolingual speakers of English, from mainstream backgrounds, who do not reside in the communities in which they teach (Au & Raphael, 2000). What the work of Ka Lama suggests is that mainstream teachers can be prepared to teach successfully in classrooms with students whose cultural and linguistic backgrounds do not match their own (Au & Blake, 2003; cf. Ladson-Billings, 1994). Certainly, any teacher education initiative designed to serve a diverse community must recognize the positive role that can be played by teachers who are outsiders to the community and whose backgrounds do not match those of the majority of students. This recognition is in keeping with the finding that the population of teachers in the United States is growing less diverse, at a time when the diversity of the student population is increasing dramatically (Au & Raphael, 2000).

The work of Ka Lama is not intended to downplay the role of teachers from outside the community, but it does seek to emphasize the valuable contributions that can be made by teachers who reside in the community, especially in situations where residents are underrepresented as teachers. An important factor to be considered is that residents are far more likely, than even dedicated outsiders, to devote their careers to teaching in schools in the community.

Some findings from the Ka Lama Teacher Education Initiative, as summarized in the five lessons learned, may well be applicable to other settings. First, much may be gained by viewing teacher education in relationship to processes of community development. Programs with the aim of preparing teachers to work effectively with students in diverse communities might find considerable value in establishing an ongoing connection to these communities. While this connection may be achieved in a variety of ways, we have suggested two possibilities: a community advisory board and long-term relationships with mentor teachers who reside in the community.

Second, recruiting and preparing teachers from the community may require creating a pipeline, rather than waiting for potential candidates to come through existing systems. Such a pipeline may be necessary in low-income communities where residents interested in becoming teachers may be nontraditional, first-generation college students, lacking access to information about higher education, such as how to apply for admission and financial aid. The pipeline could help residents gain an associate of arts degree through a community college, as many residents may be high-school graduates with few or no college credits. With an associate's degree in hand, residents are prepared to transfer to an undergraduate teacher education program.

Third, the teacher education program may be strengthened by emphasizing a critical perspective, so that preservice teachers preparing to work in diverse communities learn to see education as a process of social change. Preservice teachers benefit when they gain the ability to spot negative patterns that typically serve to limit the school achievement of students of diverse backgrounds, such as programs that emphasize lower level skills at the expense of higher level thinking. Over time, as the program's graduates gain influence in schools in the community, they will have the knowledge, awareness, and commitment to create conditions that improve the quality of teaching and learning while avoiding typical pitfalls.

Fourth, an effort should be made to identify experienced teachers who can model effective practices in classrooms in the community and to recruit these teachers to serve as mentors. Preservice teachers typically develop close working relationships with their mentor teachers, who may exert a stronger influence on their professional growth than university instructors. If mentor teachers reside in the community, they can serve as role models for preservice teachers who are insiders to the community, and they can impart valuable knowledge about the setting to preservice teachers who are outsiders to the community.

Fifth, building a leadership network of program participants and graduates from the community may be an important step toward reinforcing school improvement efforts. Schools serving students of diverse backgrounds in low-income communities are commonly under pressure to raise test scores, resulting in a constant search for a ready-made solution or quick fix. Yet research suggests that it is not a packaged program or other quick fix but long-term, home-grown solutions that may be the surer route to improved results for students (Au, 2006; Lipson, Mosenthal, Mekkelsen, & Russ, 2004). Significant change can come about through the efforts of a network of educational leaders from the community who can work collaboratively, keep the best interests of the students in mind, and take the long view.

Synergies develop once these different pieces of a teacher initiative fall into place. For example, the Ka Lama community advisory board helped to identify locations in the community where courses for the preservice cohort could be taught. Ka Lama graduates who became teachers referred educational assistants in their schools to the education academy. Ka Lama graduates become mentor teachers to help those in the preservice cohort advance in their teaching careers, just as they themselves had once been helped.

After a decade we can look back and see how far the Ka Lama Teacher Education Initiative has come, as well as what its future directions should be.

In terms of accomplishments, Ka Lama succeeded in developing a means of preparing beginning teachers to work effectively in classrooms on the Waiʻanae Coast. Ka Lama graduates earned a reputation for being well prepared to meet the challenges of classroom teaching and were often recruited by principals. Furthermore, the positive effects of involvement with Ka Lama extended beyond preparation for elementary school teaching. Graduates noted the mentorship provided by Ka Lama faculty members, such as Au and Margaret Maaka. For example, Ka Lama I graduate Yvonne Lefcourt received support to conduct research and to present her findings at a national conference. Lefcourt went on to earn a doctoral degree in curriculum and instruction.

Another of the accomplishments of Ka Lama was its firm base in the community of the Waiʻanae Coast, and this close involvement helps to shape future efforts. Although Ka Lama's focus is teacher education, it has not been viewed as a stand-alone effort but has sought to contribute to long-term goals of community development. In 2005, a transition to Native Hawaiian leadership was made in Ka Lama, with two educators of Hawaiian ancestry, Sarsona and Alice Kawakami, assuming responsibility for the Education Academy and preservice cohort, respectively, with continued guidance from the community advisory board.

Future directions include developing a teacher education program that will reduce economic biases. At present, residents must attend the university full-time for 2 years and are unable to continue full-time employment during this period. Estimates indicate that the number of residents who enter teaching might double under a 3-year program with evening, weekend, and online classes that permits continued full-time employment. Another possibility for the future is to establish working relationships with high schools in the community, for the purpose of identifying teens who might be interested in careers in teaching. Finally, there is interest in extending the Ka Lama model to other communities and to target candidates of other ethnicities, especially Filipino Americans, another group significantly underrepresented as teachers in the Hawaii public schools. Clearly, while much has been accomplished, many opportunities lie ahead.

References

Au, K. H. (1980). Participation structures in a reading lesson with Hawaiian children: Analysis of a culturally appropriate instructional event. *Anthropology and Education Quarterly, 11*(2), 91–115.

Au, K. H. (2000). Literacy education in the process of community development. In T. Shanahan & F. Rodriquez-Brown (Eds.), *Forty-ninth yearbook of the National Reading Conference* (pp. 61–77). Chicago, IL: National Reading Conference.

Au, K. H. (2002). Communities of practice: Engagement, imagination, and alignment in research on teacher education. *Journal of Teacher Education, 53*(3), 222–227.

Au, K. H. (2006). Negotiating the slippery slope: School change and literacy achievement. *Journal of Literacy Research, 37*(3), 267–286.

Au, K. H., & Blake, K. M. (2003). Cultural identity and learning to teach in a diverse community. *Journal of Teacher Education, 54*(3), 192–205.

Au, K. H., & Carroll, J. H. (1997). Improving literacy achievement through a constructivist approach: The KEEP Demonstration Classroom Project. *Elementary School Journal, 97*(3), 203–221.

Au, K. H., Carroll, J. H., & Scheu, J. A. (2001). *Balanced literacy instruction: A teacher's resource book* (2nd ed.). Norwood, MA: Christopher-Gordon.

Au, K. H., & Maaka, M. J. (2001). Teacher education, diversity, and literacy. In C. M. Roller (Ed.), *Learning to teach reading: Setting the research agenda* (pp. 136–148). Newark DE: International Reading Association.

Au, K. H., & Mason, J. M. (1981). Social organizational factors in learning to read: The balance of rights hypothesis. *Reading Research Quarterly, 17*(1), 115–152.

Au, K. H., & Raphael, T. E. (2000). Equity and literacy in the next millennium. *Reading Research Quarterly, 35*(1), 170–188.

Cruickshank, D., & Armaline, W. (1986). Field experiences in teacher education: Considerations and recommendations. *Journal of Teacher Education, 37*(3), 34–40.

D'Amato, J. (1986). *"We cool, tha's why:" A study of personhood and place in a class of Hawaiian second graders.* Unpublished doctoral dissertation, University of Hawaii, Honolulu.

Delpit, L. D. (1991). A conversation with Lisa Delpit. *Language Arts, 68*(7), 541–547.

Haberman, M. (1996). Selecting and preparing culturally competent teachers for urban schools. In J. Sikula, T. J. Buttery, & E. Guyton (Eds.), *Handbook of research on teacher education* (2nd ed., pp. 747–760). New York: Macmillan.

Jordan, C. (1985). Translating culture: From ethnographic information to educational program. *Anthropology and Education Quarterly, 16,* 105–123.

Ladson-Billings, G. (1994). *The dreamkeepers: Successful teachers of African American children.* San Francisco: Jossey-Bass.

Lipson, M. Y., Mosenthal, J. H., Mekkelsen, J., & Russ, B. (2004). Building knowledge and fashioning success one school at a time. *The Reading Teacher, 57*(6), 534–542.

McKnight, J. (1995). *The careless society: Community and its counterfeits.* New York, NY: Basic Books.

McLaren, P. (1989). *Life in schools: An introduction to critical pedagogy in the foundations of education.* New York: Longman.

State of Hawaii Department of Education. (2004). *Superintendent's 15th Annual Report.* State of Hawaii Department of Education. Retrieved February 5, 2006, from http://doe.k12.hi.us/reports/suptsannualreport

Watson, K. A. (1974). Transferable communicative routines: Strategies and group identity in two speech events. *Language in Society, 4,* 53–72.

Wenger, E. (1998). *Communities of practice: Learning, meaning, and identity.* Cambridge, UK: Cambridge University Press.

10

"Does She Speak English?"
Hmong Educators in Western Wisconsin

Ronald S. Rochon[1]
Buffalo State College

Clifton S. Tanabe
University of Hawaii–Manoa

Tamara H. Horstman-Riphahn
University of Wisconsin–La Crosse

> No matter how long you are here in America you will always be an Asian, always an outsider. Not an American.
>
> Ronald Takaki

The title for this chapter, "Does She Speak English?," was taken from a formal interview we conducted with an elementary school principal from a midsized western Wisconsin school district. During our interview, the principal was explaining a specific interaction she had had with a parent who learned that his child was placed in the classroom of a new teacher. The new teacher happened to be of Hmong descent and the parent reacted to this fact by approaching the principal and asking if this Hmong American teacher spoke English.

When this situation is unpacked, it reveals several powerful implications. First, this parent's question shows a tremendous lack of faith in the teacher education process. After all, any process that would end up placing a teacher who could not speak English in an elementary classroom in a predominantly white and English-speaking Wisconsin school district is a process that is not worthy of confidence.

We believe that the teacher education process in Wisconsin would never result in the placement of a non-English-speaking teacher and are troubled that this parent genuinely worried that his school district might have hired a second-grade teacher who is unable to speak any English.

This parent's reaction forces us to ask what experiences or perspectives led him to his misguided concern. Does he truly feel that it is possible that the teacher training and selection process could result in the placement of utterly unqualified teachers—teachers that cannot even communicate in the language their student's speak and understand?

Second, this situation reveals the depth and complexity of the stereotypes faced by teachers of Hmong descent in western Wisconsin; stereotypes that have not been overcome despite the fact that there are and have been thousands of Hmong families in western Wisconsin for nearly 30 years. The fact that people who have lived side by side with generations of Hmong families still wonder whether a young teacher of Hmong descent is capable of speaking English is a potent reminder that merely living in a diverse community is not enough to cause meaningful cross-cultural interactions and awareness.

Third, this situation reveals the types of obstacles that teachers of Hmong descent face before and after they enter the school building. For example, university admissions officers and teacher education program directors hold their own deeply entrenched prejudices and stereotypes, which may prevent them from envisioning a young Hmong man as a credible and competent elementary school teacher. Even if this Hmong man manages to convince a university to help him become a certified teacher, he is likely to face further obstacles because school administrators have their own prejudices. And, if he manages to land a teaching position, the parents of his students will also come with prejudices, his fellow teachers and administrators will come with prejudices and, most hurtfully, his own young students will come with prejudices.

In this chapter, we examine the ways in which successful educators of Hmong descent have prepared themselves to deal with prejudices and how they have overcome the effects of sometimes devastating stereotypes in their quest to become fully certified public school teachers in Wisconsin. Finally, it is our intention that this chapter furthers the conversation regarding the advancement of Hmong educators and other language minority teachers nationwide.

We begin by outlining the relevant research regarding the experiences of Hmong educators and follow this with the articulation of a collection of observations gathered through a series of formal interviews we conducted with several educators of Hmong descent as well as the school administrators who worked with them.

History and Background of the Hmong Community

In 1975, as the "secret war" conducted by the United States in the mountains of Laos was coming to an end, thousands of Hmong refugees were pushed out of Laos by the North Vietnamese and Pathet Lao government. Prior to fleeing their homes, the Hmong citizens who had been recruited by the U.S. government to assist in the Vietnam War were promised protection and assistance, yet they were initially abandoned as they fled for their lives to camps in Thailand (Sacramento Hmong Refugee Task Force, 2004). Eventually, many of these refugees were accepted into other countries, with some resettling in France, Australia, Canada, and the United States; however, many others remained stranded in temporary relocation camps in Thailand (Quincy, 1995). In 1990, the Thai camps began to close and those Hmong who were forced out sought refuge in other parts of Thailand and also at the inadequately equipped Wat Tham Krabok, a former monastery where they survived awful conditions without any type of citizenry for over a decade (Sacramento Hmong Refugee Task Force, 2004). In 2003, a second wave of Hmong refugees were allowed to join their families in the United States.

To understand Hmong American history, one must to distinguish the refugee status of first generation people of Hmong descent in the United States from the nonrefugee status of other groups. The Hmong in America are not immigrants. They were forced out of their homeland under the threat of death and, as a result, have a perspective of their relocation that differs immensely from that of other immigrant groups who have come to America (Berkson, 1997).

First-generation Hmong who arrived in the United States faced many basic challenges. They didn't speak English and did not have a firm understanding of American customs (Fadiman, 1997). Second and third generations of Hmong Americans faced struggles of a different type. While these individuals grapple with some of the same issues as their predecessors (such as high rates of poverty), they also deal with significant social and educational barriers (Lee, 2001). Socially, Hmong Americans are often viewed as culturally different foreigners and therefore "un-American" (Lee, 2002, p. 238). This has led to a debilitating secondary educational effect; Hmong American students are viewed as outside the traditional responsibility of local school districts (Lee, 2002).

In addition to the issues associated with their refugee status and difficulty in being treated and viewed as "American," people of Hmong descent have also faced the issue of ongoing relocation (Yang, 2001). By 1999, an estimated 200,000 Hmong refugees had settled primarily in three states: California, Minnesota, and Wisconsin (Yang, 2001). Because members of extended families within the Hmong community are often spread between each of these three states, individuals spend decades acquiring the resources needed to bring family members together in one location.

In California and Minnesota, the Hmong are concentrated in one or two urban centers, but in Wisconsin they have settled in several medium-sized communities, such as Eau Claire, Green Bay, La Crosse, Menomonie, Oshkosh, Stevens Point, Wausau, and Wisconsin Rapids. Hutchison (1994) asserts that Wisconsin's Hmong population pattern was largely the result of church-based (Catholic and Lutheran) sponsorships, a U.S. policy to limit resettlement in California, and the secondary migration that allowed for the reunification of clans.

When considering the history of the Hmong community in the United States, we want to caution the reader against giving in to knee-jerk assumptions regarding the primitiveness of Hmong culture. Through personal experiences, each of us has learned that Hmong language, culture, and historical traditions are rich and deeply complex. In a fundamental sense, they dwarf the history and traditions developed in the United States. After all, Hmong history dates back 2,000 years to the central plains of ancient China. The ancient Hmong folktales and songs have only recently been documented, but the values and history that they convey present a strong sense of the depth and sophistication of Hmong culture.

Hmong Children and Education

There are several components to consider when discussing the educational experiences of students of Hmong descent. As described in this section, research shows that many Hmong elementary, middle, and high school students are faced with distinctive challenges not experienced by their non-Hmong peers. Along with the common challenges of studying and test taking, students of Hmong descent also face imbalanced societal labels and a severely homogenous set of teacher role models who do not resemble them.

Model Minority Myth

Historically, the term "model minority" has been used to refer to Asian Americans—predominantly Japanese or Chinese Americans—who are said to have risen above the prejudice accompanying their minority status to become good, educationally prosperous, model citizens without needing legal support or "special" treatment (Brand, 1987; Peterson, 1966). Wu's (2002) sketch of the ideal "model minority" describes hard-working Asian Americans who are self-reliant, obedient, motivated toward study rather than play, brainy, compliant, controlled, quiet and, above all, successful without government assistance or special minority status. This depiction may sound like the "American dream," but Wu (2002) points out that the "model minority" myth is destructive not only in that it is a "gross simplification" (p. 49) but also in that it conceals behind a mythical story of "success-in-the-face-of-adversity" the fact that Asian Americans do experience racial discrimination, poverty, and academic failure.

In addition, inherent in the "model minority" theory is the notion that Asian Americans who do not fit this stereotype are delinquents and that other groups of color who have not been as successful are simply not working hard enough. In particular, the question is raised as to why African Americans cannot succeed when Asian Americans have. This assessment undercuts the assertion that racism contributes to the failures and struggles of other groups of color (Wu, 2002).

As recent immigrants to the United States, Hmong Americans are also subjected to the "model minority" label. Lee (2001) asserts that many Hmong American youth are "stereotyped by the popular press as either high-achieving 'model minorities' or low-achieving 'delinquents'" (p. 1). The students she interviewed expressed frustration at being labeled as either fully "good" (hard working and studious) or fully "bad" (truant gangsters) and explained that this type of stereotyping increased their already tenuous relationship with teachers and administrators, to whom most of them already felt disconnected (Lee, 2001). By limiting the Hmong American student experience in this manner, the diversity of individual experiences is ignored, voices are silenced, and identities (sex, age, culture, socioeconomic status) are erased (Lee, 1996).

Delpit (1995) stresses that the "model minority" myth creates an environment in which teachers and administrators ignore Asian American students and overlook their academic needs. The "model minority" stereotype supports the concept of whiteness as desirable and valuable in that it suggests that educationally successful Asian Americans are overcoming the struggle of being nonwhite and are "outwhiting whites" (Lee, 1996, p. 5). It can also be used to argue that claims of racial inequality are misguided and that social mobility and equality are possible for those individuals who are willing to strive to achieve the (European) American ideal (Lee, 1996). The idea that Asian Americans are inherently academically successful may seem complimentary; however, it contributes to the silencing of those individuals who it appears to admire (Lee, 1996). Students identified as part of the "model minority" may begin to disassociate themselves from the connections (language, family, and cultural traditions and practices) that hold them as foreigners and instead work to live up to the standards of a Eurocentric America. Hmong American children are faced with the challenge of assimilating into and adapting to a predominately White culture in order to succeed in America while attempting to maintain their culture and history, which is not often reflected in mainstream American schools or society.

Delpit (1995), Gay (2002), and Lee (2002) report that, contrary to the "model minority" myth, some scholars state that students of color, including low-achieving students of Hmong descent, are viewed as biologically disadvantaged when it comes to educational achievement and therefore they cannot be expected to succeed at the level of other "mainstream" children. Because of this theory, many students of color are marginalized, blamed for their low learning performance, and not academically challenged (Gay, 2002). Recent interview data with Hmong American students in La Crosse, Wisconsin, indicate that the students recognize an obvious correlation between the problems they encounter in school and the dominance of white teachers in those schools (DePouw, 2003). The students interviewed seem to not only feel alienated from their teachers and schools but also as if they were constantly struggling against subtle forms of inequity and disrespect that made them "feel less and less a part of school" (DePouw, 2003, p. 9).

Parental/Guardian School and Student Involvement

It is not an unfamiliar notion that parent involvement is key to student success, although this endeavor is often viewed as extremely challenging for busy, working parents who are juggling a variety of responsibilities. Research shows that parent involvement by parents who speak little or no English, and are not familiar with the structure of the American school system, can make the difference between student success and student failure (Thao, Y. J., 2003). More specifically, teachers and parents both believe that parental association with and involvement in the school assists students of Hmong descent in becoming stronger students (Thao, Y. J., 2003). However, these same teachers are quick to put the blame on certain families for their inability to utilize school resources, rather than spreading some of this blame to specific schools for failing to find ways to communicate effectively with parents of Hmong descent (Thao, Y. J., 2003). Language differences and a minimal understanding of school systems—not a lack of interest in education—are two primary reasons for Hmong parents' separation from the school environment. Teachers and school administrators who do not take the time to recognize the struggle and conflicts encountered by Hmong families in dealing with the educational system are underserving members of this community and alienating them from participating in their children's education.

Role Model Diversity

Many scholars (such as Delpit [1995], DePouw [2003], Gay [2002], Lee [2001]) who research Hmong education highlight the difficulties these students have in coping with the variance between their home and school cultures. Students of Hmong descent come from families that were forced to relocate to the United States in order to save their lives and must now learn techniques for assimilating into a new culture while simultaneously working to maintain a connection to the traditions of their ancestry (McInnis, 1991). Interview data has revealed that societal racism, along with the struggle to meet parental and cultural expectations, can alienate students from their educational settings (DePouw, 2003). Hmong children are torn between the expectations and customs of school, society, and their families (McInnis, 1991; Thao, Y. J., 2003), and they lack role models and allies who understand and resemble them and who are also in positions of power and leadership (Delpit, 1995; Tanabe, Rochon, Root, & Root, 2001). Delpit (1995) asserts that a diversification of teaching professionals can help to alleviate misunderstandings, create role models, enhance comfort levels, reduce feelings of isolation, and increase participation.

Gay (2002) determines that "students should be routinely surrounded by images, sounds, and symbols of their ethnic and cultural diversity," and that "tremendously powerful lessons are taught by and through what is on display in the classroom" (p. 621). These are compelling assertions that speak to the importance and constructive effect of having educators of diverse backgrounds working with children. All students can benefit from exposure to the vastness of the world through diversity in their classrooms. When students encounter individuals from diverse backgrounds who exemplify a wide range of achievements, leadership, power, and success, they develop a broader vision of what they are capable of as well as what they can expect or hope for from others (Gay, 2002).

In order for students to feel comfortable reaching out to educational professionals, there must be a valid connector, a transition, between their home and school environments. Students who are not able to find connections between curriculum and school settings and their cultural and family associations struggle to succeed academically (Thao, Y. J., 2003).

Hmong Liaisons and Translators

Hones (1999) effectively illustrates the value of having an individual of Hmong descent within the schools; yet, his research supports the assistance of Hmong liaisons without examining the power and pay differential between support staff and teachers. In addition, he does not fully consider the benefits for children to have a *teacher* role model who looks and potentially "thinks" like them. Hones presents the idea of Hmong liaisons as "peacemakers," a concept that hints that liaisons smooth over student and family issues for teachers but have no direct input into the policy and structure of the students' education (though, as an individual having the ability to speak directly to families in their own language, one can easily discern that the liaison would understand their needs more deeply).

Tanabe et al. (2001) examine the low ratio of Hmong teachers to Hmong students. They remind us that there is an overdependence on Hmong translators who are not long-term employees and are not provided opportunities for advancement, yet serve as the only school personnel who correspond with students and families in their native language. These aides are usually hired only to translate and are not able to contribute to school decisions or policy making. The subordinate status of aides not only limits the individual aides as professionals but can also contribute to the future professional expectations that students of Hmong descent have for themselves by witnessing the status of Hmong adults in the classroom.

Culturally Responsive Pedagogy

According to Gay (2002), stereotypes about people of color commonly lead to the placement of those children in special education classes. She emphasizes that a "culturally responsive" and "developmentally appropriate" educational setting utilizes the students' cultural and ethnic backgrounds to facilitate learning (Gay, 2002, p. 614). In order to implement a culturally responsive curriculum, educators must recognize and challenge the assertions and negative attitudes and expectations that they may have regarding students of color. According to Ronald Rochon, cofounder and former director of the Research Center for Cultural Diversity and Community Renewal (CDCR), "There's no complete school without complete representation of the people in the community. There's no learning process or effective learning process in place until children have an opportunity to learn from all of its members," (*Campus Connection*, 1999, p. 1). Teachers commonly have a tendency to search for and sometimes expect student weaknesses rather than to learn and support their strengths, which leads to a "teaching-down" approach for those who have been labeled as low-level learners (Delpit, 1995). In order to locate and reach out to students from communities separate from their own, teachers of all ethnicities must learn about their students' lives outside of school.

Curriculum changes designed to meet the needs of a growing multicultural community most commonly include the simple addition of one or two "diversity" courses (Villegas & Lucas, 2001). Gay (2002) notes that our school systems tend to resist diversity while teaching children to ignore, distrust, or diminish the importance of differences among individuals and groups in an effort to encourage everyone to act, think, and choose values in the same way. Unfortunately, within this structure, teachers who are not familiar with a nonwhite child's background or upbringing may become resentful that the child is not "mainstream" (i.e., not acting white) and are prone to blame the child for not learning (Gay, 2002). A culturally responsive classroom, on the other hand, includes a multiplicity of learning and communication styles; recognizes levels of ethnic and cultural identity and affiliation; understands various student experiences, perspectives, and traits as contributions to the learning process; and helps students to recognize themselves as capable of acting as agents of change (Gay, 2002; Villegas & Lucas, 2001). In addition, culturally responsive schools and communities encourage and strive for the inclusion of both parents/guardians and teachers, prepare educators for teaching a diverse group of students, and focus on hiring educators with whom the students can relate (Gay, 2002; Thao, Y. J., 2003; University of Wisconsin–Extension, 2002). It is vital that educators of European descent understand the influences of race, culture, and ethnicity on learning and teaching and remain critical and conscious of their own perceptions and behaviors as well as truly care for and believe in the children with whom they work (Gay, 2002). A culturally deliberate classroom can strengthen a sense of community and responsibility among children through personal connections and an interlacing of the lives of people of diverse identities.

Hmong Teacher Preparation Program

Background

Like other culturally and linguistically diverse groups, many Hmong Americans have worked hard to obtain English proficiency while also maintaining and passing on fluency in the Hmong language. Initially, most first-generation Hmong men and women had a very limited grasp of English; therefore, in many communities, English classes were created during the daytime. Because most Hmong women were not employed, they were able to attend classes while their husbands worked (Root, Rudawski, Taylor, & Rochon, 2003). Over time, the English language skills of some of the women quickly surpassed the skills of the men. Once armed with adequate English language skills, women sought employment and left their children in the care of grandparents, who generally did not speak English (Mason-Chagil, 1999).

The result was that many second-generation Hmong children were raised, in large part, by non-English-speaking grandparents. These children often had limited English exposure prior to attending school. Thus, a significant number of Hmong students needed assistance in school to acquire English language skills. In 2000, according to a report produced by the Wisconsin Department of Public Instruction, Hmong students composed more than 70% of the nearly 11,000 students who were identified as having limited English proficiency (University of Wisconsin–Extension, 2000). This report showed that more than 16,000 Hmong children attended public schools in Wisconsin, but very few Hmong teachers, counselors, or administrators were hired in these schools. Although most of the school districts in these areas have hired a significant number of Hmong paraprofessionals to be teacher assistants or translators, these paraprofessionals hold almost no authority because they are not certified and have no direct input into policy or curriculum development.

Project Teach and Project Forward

The CDCR was founded in 1997 at the University of Wisconsin (UW)–La Crosse. It serves as the center for two large, federally funded initiatives (Project Teach and Project Forward) that are designed to assist recent high-school graduates and working paraprofessionals of Hmong descent in becoming K–12 teacher educators or administrators. These programs operate across several campuses within the UW System, including UW–La Crosse, UW–Eau Claire, UW–Stout, UW–Stevens Point, and UW–Marathon County. Each of these programs furthers CDCR's mission to promote culturally responsive teacher education, and a more thorough discussion of these programs and their educational impact will make up the second half of this chapter.

Since their inceptions, many Project Teach and Project Forward graduates have earned jobs as teachers in Wisconsin schools. One has gone on to become the first principal of Hmong descent in the state of Wisconsin. Others have gone on to pursue masters and doctoral degrees. The hope was that these programs, by increasing the pool of available certified teachers of Hmong descent, would have a positive influence on the schools, communities, students, and curricula and potentially on the way in which we as citizens think about teaching and learning as well as race relations within our neighborhoods. Specifically, the projects' aims included the following goals: (1) increase Hmong student language skills, (2) increase positive identity formation for students, (3) reduce Hmong gang participation, (4) diversify school personnel in a way that more accurately reflects the community, (5) reduce conflict between Hmong and non-Hmong youth and adults, (6) increase understanding of Hmong culture for Hmong and non-Hmong students, (7) increase role models for Hmong youth, and (8) include a diversity component for schools and students (Tanabe et al., 2001).

In an effort to follow the results of these projects, CDCR has engaged in an ongoing data collection effort. Specifically, the Center has interviewed various participants and graduates of the projects as well as other teachers and administrators that have worked and are working with these participants and graduates. Here, we draw out some of the key aspects of data drawn from interviews with two Project Teach graduates and the principals at the schools wherein they first taught. We seek to highlight the complexities faced by teachers of Hmong descent as well as specific key insights of successful Hmong educators. In addition, we compare our data and analysis to the observations and statements of other researchers and scholars.

Key Observations

Through an ongoing interview and data collection project focused on the experiences and perceptions of recent graduates from Project Teach and Project Forward, we have gathered a set of key observations, which will be presented in this section. Among the issues addressed by our interview subjects is the idea that, despite excelling in their teacher education programs, receiving full certification, and obtaining full-time teaching positions, several of our recent graduates feel an especially high level of pressure to prove themselves as competent professional educators. In addition, these recent educators of Hmong descent report that their success in a particular school often depends on their ability ease their colleagues[1] and their students' parents' discomfort with their specific racial and ethnic background. Finally, our interview process revealed an interesting perspective concerning the normalizing results of having young children exposed to teachers of Hmong descent.

Each of the subsections below captures a specific issue related to the obstacles faced by newly hired teachers of Hmong descent. We believe that, combined, these observations and experiences reveal the dual burden felt by teachers of Hmong descent. This burden includes the normal adjustments all new teachers face when making the transition from student to professional educator; however, for our interview subjects, the burden is exacerbated by an additional set of specific institutional obstacles that are directly associated with their being Hmong.

"I Had to Prove Myself" Our data reveal a certain internalized pressure felt by recently hired teachers of Hmong descent to prove to their colleagues and to the parents of their students that they are legitimate educators. While this echoes other recent research (Thao, B., 2003), our interview data add to the research base by identifying specific ways in which this pressure is particularly demoralizing. The teachers of Hmong descent in our interview pool, most of whom are first-generation college attendees, have strived to obtain full certification but are crushed to learn that in the schools such an accomplishment does not bring with it the immediate assumption that they are legitimate and competent educators.

One of our interview subjects, a western Wisconsin district superintendent of European descent, has worked with and hired teachers of Hmong descent. When asked about the specific challenges faced by newly hired teachers of Hmong descent, he suggested that such teachers are treated just like other non-Hmong teachers. When pressed about the claim that Hmong teachers feel the need to prove themselves as legitimate, he explained that this is not unusual and that many teachers are often required to prove themselves before their colleagues accept them as competent educators. He stated, "I think that it takes a number of years to learn all the ins and outs."

In direct contradiction, several of our Hmong interviewees reported feeling a form of pressure that goes beyond what might be called a "traditional hazing period," where new hires are taken at face value as legitimate members of the profession but are then put through a series of informal character tests. Rather, our interview subjects described themselves as being placed in the position of having to first show that they even deserve to be taken as legitimate members of the profession. In effect, they suggest that because they are not immediately recognized as legitimate members of the profession, they are not yet even eligible to be "hazed" by their colleagues—a process that, although not desirable, reveals a certain acceptance that is not immediately offered to the Hmong teachers we interviewed. The end result is that these teachers tend to be marginalized from the start and must work "up the ladder" from a "rung" that is lower than the "rung" from which other teachers start. One Hmong teacher we interviewed explained that this result is intensified by the fact that he grew up in a cultural tradition that frowned upon the act of questioning elders and superiors. "I think ... [because I am] Hmong ... [I] was always brought up with respecting the elders. And that was really difficult for me to speak up against somebody who I have differences in opinion."

In addition to this, our interview subjects reported that they felt the need to prove themselves to the parents of their students and their teaching colleagues. One teacher stated, "I feel like I am proving myself to the parents every year. I do. I will be honest about that." When this same teacher was asked why she thinks she was tested by the parents of her students, she responded by saying, "I think because ... I don't really want to say this but ... because I am a minority.... I think they want to test [teachers of Hmong descent] to see if [they are] capable of teaching their child."

One particularly worrisome and potentially humiliating result of working with parents who do not immediately accept them as legitimate is that these teachers find that they even have to prove themselves to their own students. The mistrust conveyed by the parents is captured by their children and the children bring this wariness to the classroom. A male third-grade elementary teacher of Hmong descent said, "Yeah, my first year the kids looked at me like 'Who are you?' They were so curious because they, you know, they would think that I would be a T.A. [teacher assistant] versus a teacher. They look at you and they're like, 'Who are you and what are you doing here?'" One of the administrators that we interviewed confirmed this impression when she asserted that, in the school districts of western Wisconsin, teachers (and administrators) of color must work twice as hard to assure their colleagues and "clients" that they are worthy.

While having to prove oneself in this manner may be hurtful and disadvantaging for teachers of color, it is an unwitting problem for their nonminority colleagues as well. Because teachers of color are required to spend so much effort on proving themselves and on making their colleagues and others comfortable with their "Hmongness," it is a long time before they are able, allowed, and willing to share with their colleagues their own unique personal and pedagogical understandings and skills. In regards to this, one Hmong teacher said, "I want more experience so that they can say, 'Oh this person has this much experience and she knows what she is talking about.'"

"We Need Teachers Who Speak Hmong" One administrator explained that his interest in hiring a teacher of Hmong descent stemmed from his concern that many of the Hmong parents connected to his school did not speak English. Clearly, this administrator's view is that Hmong teachers who are able to speak Hmong deserve a spot in schools where there are Hmong children who have parents that do not speak English. This position raises an interesting question as to whether this administrator believes that such teachers belong in schools where there are Hmong and non-Hmong parents that *do* speak English. When the administrator was asked this question, he responded by changing the subject.

This administrator's opinion raises an interesting dilemma. We are encouraged by his efforts (and the efforts of others like him) to diversify his teaching staff and his interest in hiring teachers with whom students of color can identify. However, we are concerned that his perceptions reinforce a dominant and problematic ideology—namely, that having Hmong children in our schools is a *problem* because they and their parents may not speak English. Moreover, this ideology seems to ignore the fact that students of Hmong descent bring much more than a language difference to the schools. They bring a deep and rich cultural perspective that helps to broaden the experiences and awareness of all students.

Although this administrator clearly understands that the Hmong teacher he hired was fluent in English, he stated that the overriding reason he hired this teacher was simply because he also spoke Hmong. The problem with this reasoning is that the parents of the non-Hmong children in this new teacher's classroom may pick up the administrator's perspective and become concerned. In particular, they may worry that because this teacher was hired specifically because he speaks Hmong (rather than because he is a competent fifth-grade teacher), he may not be a very good teacher or he may not speak English very well. In effect, the principal's perspective trickles down to the parents and students and results in a degrading, potentially devastating, and patently false assumption that this young, competent, bilingual, energetic, intelligent, and highly trained educator might not be prepared to teach their children. Ultimately, this appears to be one key source of the mistrust previously described that some non-Hmong parents have of Hmong teachers.

It must be noted that not all of the principals we interviewed struggled with a limited view of Hmong teachers. In fact, one principal shook us to our cores when she described a wonderful, young teacher that she could not keep at her school because of district-wide budget cuts. She explained that even though this teacher had been a recent hire, other more senior faculty members were in awe of her teaching prowess and held her in high esteem. The principal went on to explain how this young teacher shared her intelligence and enthusiasm with every member of the school community. This teacher's desire and passion for education were infectious. The principal also noted that, although the other teachers in her school building are, in general, extremely well educated (most had graduate degrees; some were seeking doctorates), no other faculty member matched the intellectual and educational impact made by this young teacher. Then, on tape, during our formal interview, this principal choked up. She explained that losing this teacher was devastating. She put her hand to her face to wipe away the tears that were rolling down her cheeks and revealed that this individual was the first Hmong teacher with whom she had ever worked.

Humbly, and with a touch of pride, we want our readers to know that this teacher was a member of the very first cohort of students to graduate from Project Teach.

Teaching with Hmong Food   One of our interview subjects related a situation that took place in the teacher's lounge at her school. She began by recounting the ways in which an incredibly talented, young teacher of Hmong descent worked to put her non-Hmong colleagues at ease. This Hmong teacher accepted the burden of engaging her colleagues in a manner that allowed them to feel more comfortable with her, while she also strove to perform her normal teaching duties at the highest level.

Among the many creative and inspiring things this teacher did was to share with her colleagues the Hmong food she brought in for lunch each week. At first, her fellow teachers were skeptical and occasionally repelled by these dishes, but she turned the lunch hour into a sort of lesson-time for her peers. Her principal, remembering this, recounted the effort this way: "When she would have lunch in the lounge, she would bring her authentic Hmong foods ... and these are things my staff had never seen before ... then she would go on to teaching lessons.... [She] is always teaching and learning.... She started bringing, I think, a personal scope to the Hmong culture." The effect of this practice was that it provided this Hmong teacher's colleagues with the opportunity to see her as an individual, rather than as a stereotype. It allowed her to have control over this part of herself that was revealed and scrutinized and made it possible for her to discuss herself in the first person, rather than as a member of an oppressed group. This young teacher's wisdom worked so well that some of her colleagues soon became comfortable enough to ask her for teaching tips and curricula advice.

The prospect of making one's colleagues comfortable with one's "Hmongness," as well as with one's newness, is daunting. Achieving it is a tremendous success. However, it comes with a high price. Part of that price is the immense time and effort it takes to bring one's colleagues around. This is time and effort spent over and above that which is needed to cover the normal responsibilities as a full-time elementary school teacher. Although many teachers find the task of meeting their everyday responsibilities daunting, Hmong teachers must meet these responsibilities and, in addition, work overtime to make their white colleagues comfortable with their presence.

Hmong teachers also pay a psychological and emotional price. When coming to the realization that they will not be accepted simply for who they are, young Hmong teachers find themselves in a very difficult situation. Those who decide to address this situation often determine that they must exploit one aspect of their culture and reduce it to a "bite-sized slice." In other words, they pull one small feature of Hmong culture out of context, convey it in easily understood terms, and present it to their non-Hmong colleagues in a manner that is as nonthreatening as possible. Anyone who has engaged in this process recognizes that it does not happen without a tinge of humiliation. After all, Hmong culture (like other cultures) is infinitely more complex and rich than one plate of Hmong food. This price makes the profession of teaching very, very expensive for Hmong teachers.

"Yeah, Ya"   One of our interview subjects described the ongoing issue of being viewed as an "outsider" or a stranger in her institution. This alienation was captured by an interesting interaction in which she took part. One day, in the teacher's lounge, while taking part in a group conversation, this young Hmong teacher asked her colleagues a question about the daily schedule. One of her colleagues quickly responded to the question by saying, "Yeah, Ya." When pronounced quickly, the word "yeah" sounds very much like the pronunciation of this Hmong teacher's first name, which is "Ya." In effect, it *sounded* like this teacher was making fun of this teacher's Hmong name. Suddenly, the non-Hmong teacher realized how this sounded and she became horrified by the idea that Ya might have interpreted her response as an off-handed attempt to make fun of her name. Thus, she immediately blurted out, "I shouldn't have said that. I'm sorry." In fact, the non-Hmong teacher was not making fun of this Hmong name and Ya did not initially interpret her response in that manner. For this young Hmong teacher, the situation served as a powerful reminder that her cultural and ethnic identity can still make her colleagues very uncomfortable. For her colleague, this situation reinforced a worry that her ignorance of Hmong culture reflects a subtle racism on her part.

The question we want to consider is why this small and harmless incident resulted in such deep and troubling concerns. The answer is located in the context in which this non-Hmong teacher and her young Hmong colleague find themselves. They are in an environment wherein the Hmong teacher has always been and still is understood as an outsider—"the other." And, in this context, the otherwise innocuous words, "Yeah, Ya," have the capacity to convey deep and powerful messages about belonging, professional acceptance, and racial prejudice. Perhaps, if Ya were no longer considered an outsider, but rather as someone who belonged, as someone who was no longer the potential object of exclusion and discrimination, the non-Hmong teacher would not have had a second thought about the way the words, "Yeah, Ya," sounded or about how they might be interpreted.

"It Just Became Normal" During one of our interviews, a graduate of the Project Teach program, who is now a kindergarten teacher in western Wisconsin, expressed her frustration with the prevalent and unfortunate view that cultural diversity education is only introduced into the classroom during "Diversity Week." She noted that, at best, a month may be devoted to a particular segment of society. She describes her own classroom as an environment in which cultural learning is interwoven and modeled through each activity of every school day. Her young students develop an awareness of different cultures by learning to count not only in English but also in German, Spanish, Hmong, Swahili, and Arabic. The books they read include stories and pictures of individuals and families from many different ethnic backgrounds. Perhaps the most remarkable characteristic of this young teacher's cultural guidance is that she so naturally and effectively leads by example. As a result, her students begin to perceive cultural learning as an everyday occurrence and consider the infusion of many customs into their environment as something natural and expected.

Perhaps there is a lesson to be learned from the young students of another Hmong teacher we interviewed. This teacher said, "It was interesting how the following year I have not heard any kids say anything like [why do I have a Hmong teacher]. They come up to you and just talk to you on a normal basis." These young children were able to extend the hand of acceptance, and they did so in a way that was natural and complete. We can only imagine the day when adults may follow this example.

Conclusion

This experience has taught us the important and ancient lesson of sacrifice. It has taught us the lesson of parental love and respect for children. It has taught us the lesson of connectedness. We are truly one. We wrote these grants, and everyday we are thanked by Hmong students and educators throughout the state for these grants. But when we are honest with ourselves, we recognize with humility and sincerity that we have received far more than we were able to give.

Perhaps most importantly, our projects and our research have revealed to us that Hmong teachers who are able to teach their students in a way that makes diversity a normal aspect of schooling are extremely valuable to a healthy school environment. They reveal that individuals of Hmong descent are not outsiders whose experiences and aspirations are unrelated and detached from "ours." Rather, these individuals are very much involved in shaping the face of our nation's history and society. The presence of teachers of Hmong descent is essential not only for the sake of those children who resemble them but also for the ethical development of culturally and educationally responsive children of all ethnicities and backgrounds. As institutions devoted to shaping and guiding each generation's youth, schools must step to the forefront in striving to create educational environments that welcome and support teachers of diverse backgrounds. In this way, our nation's schools will be more prepared to graduate leaders who are committed to designing a more just and ethical society.

References

Berkson, H. (1997). Labor-force participation among Southeast Asian refugee immigrants: An update on 1975 to 1984 entrants. *Hmong Studies Journal, 1*(2), pp. 1–27.

Brand, D. (1987, August 31). The new whiz kids. *Time, 130I*(9), 42–51.

Delpit, L. (1995). *Other people's children: Cultural conflict in the classroom.* New York: New Press.

DePouw, C. (2003, April). *Familiar foreign: Hmong American students engaging and resisting America.* Paper presented at the annual meeting of the American Educational Research Association, Chicago, IL.

Fadiman, A. (1997). *The spirit catches you and you fall down.* New York: Farrah, Straus and Giroux.

Gay, G. (2002). Culturally responsive teaching in special education for ethnically diverse students: Setting the stage. *Qualitative Studies in Education, 15*(6), 613–629.

Hones, D. F. (1999). Making peace: A narrative study of a bilingual liaison, a school, and a community. *Teachers College Press, 101*(1), 106–134.

Hutchison, R. (1994). English language use in the Hmong community. In A. White-Parks, D. D. Buffton, U. Chiu, C. M. Currier, C. G. Manrique, & M. M. Piehl (Eds.), *A gathering of voices on the Asian American experience* (pp. 9–16). Fort Atkinson, WI: Highsmith Press.

Largest single grant promotes Hmong educators. (1999, September). *Campus Connection, 1,* 2.

Lee, S. (1996). *Unraveling the "model minority" stereotype: Listening to Asian American youth.* New York: Teachers College Press.

Lee, S. (2001). More than "model minorities" or "delinquents": A look at Hmong American high school students. *Harvard Educational Review, 71*(3), 505–528.

Lee, S. (2002). Learning "America": Hmong American high school students. *Education and Urban Society, 34*(2), 233–246.

Mason-Chagil, G. P. (1999). *Hmong parents' perspectives on the role of schools in raising and educating children in the United States.* Unpublished doctoral dissertation, University of Minnesota–Twin Cities, Minneapolis-St. Paul, Minnesota.

McInnis, K. (1991). Ethnic-sensitive work with Hmong refugee children. *Child Welfare, 70*(5), 571–581.

Peterson, W. (1966, January 9). Success story, Japanese-American style. *The New York Times Magazine,* 20–43.

Quincy, K. (1995). *Hmong: History of a people.* Cheney, WA: Eastern Washington University Press.

Root, S., Rudawski, A., Taylor, M., & Rochon, R. (2003). Attrition of Hmong students in teacher education programs. *Bilingual Research Journal, 27*(1), 137–148.

Sacramento Hmong Refugee Task Force. (2004, June). *A special report: A coordinated network of support for Hmong refugees to Sacramento County.* Accessed online March 5, 2005, at http://www.centralcallegal.org/hrtf/reports/final.html

Tanabe, C., Rochon, R. S., Root, S., & Root, K. (2001, April). *Assisting Hmong educational paraprofessionals obtain certification: Applied Sociology at the University of Wisconsin–La Crosse.* Paper presented the annual meeting of the Midwest Sociological Society, St. Louis, MO.

Thao, B. (2003, June 17). Reality check: How Hmong American students are doing in K 12 education. Testimony prepared for "Evaluation of Asian Pacific Americans in Education" forum. Accessed online March 4, 2004, at http://www.hndlink.org/Education.6.17.03%20testimony.htm

Thao, Y. J. (2003). Empowering Mong students: Home and school factors. *Urban Review, 35*(1), 25–42.

University of Wisconsin–Extension. (2000). *Wisconsin's Hmong population: Census 2000 population and other demographic trends. Accessed online January, 15, 2003, at* http://www.ssc.wisc.edu/poplab/reports/HmongChartbook.pdf.

University of Wisconsin–Extension. (2002). *Hmong educational needs assessment project. Brown, Dane, Eau Claire, La Crosse, Marathon, Milwaukee, Outagamie, Portage, Sheboygan, and Winnebago counties.* Accessed online [1/15/03]: http://www.uwex.edu/ces/hmong/documents/assessment.pdf.

Villegas, A. M., & Lucas, T. (2001, April). *Preparing culturally responsive teachers: How can we teach what we don't know?* Paper presented at the annual meeting of the American Educational Association, Seattle, WA.

Wu, F. (2002). *Yellow: Race in America beyond black and white.* New York: Basic Books.

Yang, K. (2001). The Hmong in America: Twenty-five years after the U.S. secret war in Laos. *Journal of Asian American Studies, 4*(2), 165–174.

Endnotes

1. The order of the authors' names is random and does not reflect differing levels of contribution. Each author contributed equally to the chapter.

11

Program and Faculty Transformation
Enhancing Teacher Preparation

María Estela Brisk
Boston College

Transforming faculty and programs to address the education of culturally and linguistic diverse (CLD) students requires special attention to language and culture and to the historical-political events impacting such populations and the schools that serve them. Research on teacher preparation to work with CLD students has mainly focused on knowledge, beliefs, and attitudes teachers need to have and on processes to help teachers acquire them to work effectively with CLD populations. Faculty teaching bilingual or multicultural courses have traditionally carried out this work. There has been limited effort to involve teacher education faculty as whole in this type of teacher preparation.

This chapter illustrates a faculty development project carried out at a private university. This ongoing development project aims to change the expertise of faculty and the curriculum content within a teacher education department in order to better prepare graduates of the program to work with CLD students in their classrooms. The chapter concentrates on how the professional component of faculty development, particularly the teaching content and delivery, was conceived and implemented. The chapter first reports on the findings of the literature with respect to the scope, type, and process of faculty development as well as factors impacting such efforts. This discussion is followed by a description of the process of faculty development and the activities that supported institutionalized changes to the teacher education program. The last part of the chapter isolates factors that affected the project. Institutional context plays an important role in the nature of faculty development programs.

Therefore, each institution needs to analyze how to best carry out faculty development within its own context. Keep in mind that the programs described in this chapter, as well as those in chapter 11, provide ideas and not a blueprint.

Transforming Teacher Education

The steady increase of immigrant students entering U.S. schools at the turn of the 21st century has heightened the awareness among educators to prepare teachers to serve these populations. Moreover, movements to eliminate bilingual education make even more important the need to have mainstream teachers ready to serve bilingual students. These external events are pressuring teacher education programs to graduate teachers with the skills and dispositions needed to serve the numerous CLD students found in U.S. classrooms. Previous research on faculty development has pointed at the need to be aware of external influences (Walvoord, Carey, Smith, Soled, Way, & Zorn, 2000).

Professional development in institutions of higher education is multidimensional. Transformation occurs at three levels: personal knowledge, individual courses, and program (Costa, McPhail, Smith, & Brisk, 2005). To build confidence to change, faculty need to develop expertise in the area. As Anstrom (2004) notes, "Faculty can't be expected to teach what they don't know" (p. xi). A field such as education of CLD students includes knowledge that may not be part of the scholarship or experience of faculty who do not teach bilingual or multicultural courses. Knowledge and awareness of language and culture are needed to transcend isolated courses or isolated themes within courses and to create an inclusive, in-depth transformation in teacher education with respect to addressing the needs of CLD learners (Costa et al., 2005; Nevarez, Sanford, & Parker, 1997). Once faculty acquire an understanding of the effects of language and culture on CLD learners, they are better able to embed that knowledge within the theme of their courses; they can challenge preservice teachers' attitudes toward, beliefs about, and expectations of CLD populations; and they can provide aspiring teachers with the tools to teach and assess CLD students and to work with their families. Faculty development programs that seek to transform teacher education curricula from within can have a highly valued, powerful impact on the institution, faculty, and students involved (Wheeler & Schuster, 1990). Coordination among faculty and support from administrators provide the final touch for a cohesive new program. Successful programs are those that are initiated by faculty and supported by the central administration (Aleamoni, 1997; Gaff & Simpson, 1994).

Other principles critical to the process of faculty development include starting small and gradually expanding the range of change over time (Cochran-Smith, 2003; Nevarez et al., 1997; Wheeler & Schuster, 1990). Involving all faculty, or at least a core number, is essential to support change. Impetus for transformation comes from the collective effort of a group of individuals. Curriculum change requires faculty to work together to see individual interests in the context of the entire department (Gaff & Simpson, 1994). Having a common goal facilitates faculty working together despite differences in perspectives and disciplines (Anstrom, 2004; Cochran-Smith et al., 1999).

Faculty and administrators trying to bring needed change must be aware of the culture of the academic department, including collegiality among members, autonomy and academic freedom, expertise among faculty, trust, and values within the department (Walvoord et al., 2000).

Activities

Activities of the project reported in this chapter have evolved over 4 years, responding to perceived needs and prompted by faculty initiative. The initial effort aimed to make faculty familiar with the educational needs of CLD learners in order to find fitting themes to be included in the various teacher education courses. To this end, faculty seminars were implemented for 2 consecutive years. Each seminar ended with a summer institute to recap what was learned and discuss course and program changes. Equipped with this new knowledge, the program entered a new phase wherein individuals initiated more in-depth projects. These initiatives had a wide impact on faculty as well as on preservice and in-service teachers (see Figure 11.1). The last phase, which is still ongoing in the fourth year of the project, focuses on sustainability of efforts to ensure that the changes remain independent from the individuals who initiated them.

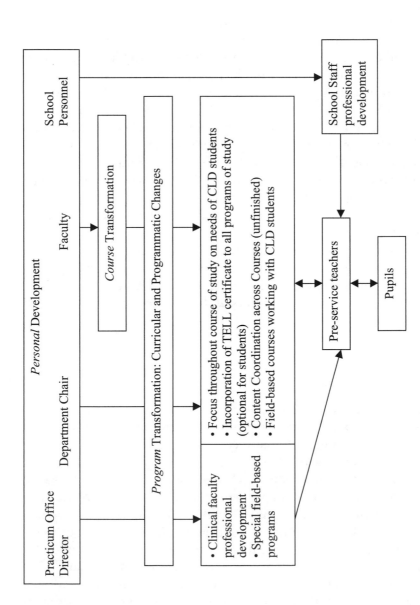

Figure 11.1

Development of Faculty Expertise: Seminars

Faculty, the chair of teacher education, field office administrators, clinical faculty, and doctoral students who were course instructors were invited to attend a semester-long seminar. This seminar was repeated the following year in order to include most faculty instructing teacher certification courses. Seminar participation was voluntary. A federal grant allowed for participants to receive a small stipend. Three spaces in the seminars were designated for staff from partner schools.[1] Participants received a notebook with a syllabus and readings. The syllabus included broad social issues, characteristics of a good school that includes CLD students, and classroom practices related to language, literacy, and various content areas. Participants met with a faculty facilitator six times every other week for 90 minutes. Questions generated small-group and whole-group discussions. Other activities included viewing and discussing videos, reporting on school visits, and listening to guest speakers. Videos of exemplary classroom practices elicited discussion on facilitating comprehensibility of input and second language learners' participation. For example, a video of a lesson taught in Farsi helped faculty understand the difficulties of receiving instruction in an unknown language. School visits made faculty aware of the difficulties teachers face when working with students of many different cultural backgrounds and varied language proficiency levels. Guest speakers were helpful in raising issues to the larger university and public school community. The first year, the guest speaker replaced a seminar meeting. Some seminar participants were critical because they felt that the time together was more useful. Subsequent years, guest speakers were scheduled as a separate activity, which increased their success and attracted faculty from other education departments and other colleges within the university as well as neighboring universities. Teachers from neighboring school systems also attended.

To address the common belief that all we need to do is to have good education to address the needs of second language students, an academic language analysis activity was carried out to make faculty aware of the language difficulties encountered by second language learners. Participants, working in small groups, were asked to analyze short texts drawn from various content area books and standardized tests at the elementary and secondary levels. They were to isolate elements of language that they deemed would be difficult for second language learners. Participants commented on the fact that they had never thought about the notion of academic English or about language difficulties beyond vocabulary.

Scaffolding Change: Individual Meetings   In addition to building content expertise, the seminar also aimed for participants to change the syllabus of at least one of their courses. To facilitate the process, the seminar facilitator met individually with participants to discuss their ideas and make additional suggestions for content and readings. These meetings took place before the end of the seminar. A number of faculty commented that they already addressed issues related to CLD learners, but this was typically done in one class toward the end of the semester. The modifications included addressing these issues throughout the course, assigning relevant readings, and requiring attention to CLD learners in the course assignments. For example, faculty teaching methods courses required students to propose sample unit adaptations to address the needs of second language learners or propose language objectives in addition to content objectives for their lessons.

Some faculty redesigned their syllabi by the end of the seminar; others worked during the summer and had them ready for the following fall. In addition to the scheduled individual meeting, faculty stopped by the facilitator's office to request ideas on possible readings for their courses, to share articles they had found, or to ask specific questions. The participating school personnel proposed their own professional development plans. One of the principals included strategies to support second language learners in her plans for teacher evaluation and coaching.

Coordinating Change: Summer Institute

One problem with individual faculty efforts is that everybody may include the same type of content in their courses. To address complementarity and depth of content, a whole-day meeting immediately after each seminar brought all the participants together to discuss individual course plans as well as programmatic changes. Individual course changes shared by the faculty were posted on chart paper around the room. A discussion ensued that led to the creation of a list of key issues. For the second-year summer institute, the key issues were revisited, revised, and grouped into three categories: knowledge, attitudes and beliefs and teachers' tool kit. A matrix with necessary competencies and course offerings for the teacher education majors was produced. The group identified which competencies were going to be covered by which courses.

Although these 1-day institutes carried out after each seminar began the discussion of coordination and helped build program and course continuity, it was evident that more time and effort were needed to achieve full coordination.

Focused Activities: Widespread Impact

In the third year of the program, participants of the seminars initiated a series of activities. These activities helped spread the effort of making the education of CLD learners an important aspect of teacher preparation at the college. Initiatives implemented during this period include collaboration with the "Methods of Science" course; language and content team work; the Read Aloud project; additional professional development of clinical faculty, prepracticum supervisors, teachers in partner schools, and induction teachers; and integration of the Teaching English Language Learners (TELL) certificate program to the various teacher education master's programs at the School of Education.

The professor and graduate assistant teaching the "Methods of Science" course teamed with the seminar facilitator and a doctoral student versed in second language teaching. Together, they infused the "Methods of Science" course with issues of second language and literacy. In addition, the doctoral student with expertise in second language attended the science course and added to the discussion as appropriate. The course was field based so the team ran a special institute for cooperating teachers on teaching science as well as literacy in the second language. To build expertise, the science graduate student enrolled in an advanced course on bilingualism and second language learning and has been reviewing the literature on teaching science to second language learners. The methods course has also experimented with various field placements, including an after-school program in which all the children are bilingual, some very recent arrivals, thus challenging the preservice teachers to teach science to second language students.

Work with the faculty in the seminars revealed that the most "foreign" concept was language and the development of language objectives. The facilitator convened a small group of faculty and doctoral students with training in language to work on language in the content areas. With an initial focus on science, the group explored the literature on the language used in science, isolated specific issues, and developed sample text sets of children's literature with different degrees of language difficulty for elementary and secondary levels. These books also had stories that related to various cultures. Other material to be shared with faculty teaching methods courses included sample lessons with language objectives emerging from lesson materials, themes and activities addressing issues important for CLD learners to be included in methods courses, and specific skills demanded by academic English to be taught to CLD learners through the various content areas. The product of this work is being revised and expanded in the next phase of the project.

The Read Aloud project reached all preservice undergraduates and graduates majoring in elementary education. As part of their teacher preparation program, these students spend one day a week in the partner schools. While in their assigned classrooms, they read aloud books with a CLD learner. Students and supervisors received instruction on how to read aloud with CLD learners, including choosing books, teaching vocabulary, addressing issues of language and culture, and so on. A similar project with instructional strategies appropriate for high-school students is in the planning stages.

To expand the preparation beyond the faculty seminars, professional development was carried out with other constituencies. Two of the faculty experts on the education of CLD students have conducted professional development with clinical faculty, prepracticum supervisors, induction candidates, and teachers in the partner schools. Faculty and doctoral students conducted professional development for the staff of several partner schools aligned with the state demands to prepare mainstream teachers to teach bilingual learners in their classrooms. This professional development supports the preparation of the preservice teachers because many of the teachers participating in this professional development also host the program's preservice students.

The teacher education department has strongly supported the development of the TELL certificate. Students majoring in the various fields in teacher education can add certificate courses to their program to fulfill the state's competency requirements for qualified teachers of English language learners. Programs of study are planned to embed these courses without extending the program. Faculty advisors have encouraged students to add these courses given the increase of bilingual learners in both urban and suburban school districts.

In Progress: Sustainability and Impact of the Program

Several of the initiatives of the third year of the program have become institutionalized. The attention to second language learners has become a feature of the courses of faculty who have participated in the activities of the first 3 years. The Read Aloud project continues to be required during the field experience for early childhood and elementary majors. The practicum office has hired a clinical faculty member with expertise in CLD education. Part of the role of this person is to continue the professional development with all supervisors. Institutes on teaching CLD learners are now part of the menu offered in the summer induction program.

Because much of the flurry of activities and support emanated from the particular faculty members involved in the project, one dilemma of change relates to how efforts can be sustained and become less dependent on the individuals involved in the change. To this end, the seminar facilitator, faculty, and doctoral students with expertise in CLD education are pursuing two strategies. First, the development of web-based resources for faculty as well as preservice and in-service teachers that are part of the university community concerned with the education of CLD learners. This resource will include sample lessons in various content areas addressing language objectives, text sets and other instructional resources, readings for various teacher education (TE) courses, and exemplars of model teachers who address language within their content teaching. As their work continues, this team of faculty and students will update this web resource. Faculty will be introduced to this resource at a future TE department meeting. A larger event is planned for the university and school communities in general. Comments and suggestions will serve as catalysts for improvement and additions.

Second, faculty will be convened to reflect on the changes in the curriculum and to discuss the knowledge that preservice teachers require to better serve CLD students and where this knowledge is being covered. Course content guidelines will be developed to inform future faculty as well as part-time faculty when developing their courses. These guidelines will be added to the web resources.

Critical Elements and Impact on Faculty and Program

As the process of faculty development and transformation occurred, it became evident that the success of the program was contingent on a number of critical elements impacting process, faculty, and program. These elements include:

- Context
- Structure
- Knowledge building
- Constructivist approach
- Meaningful content
- Leadership support.

The process continues to move toward development and sustainability of a coherent program. The long-term impact of the program eventually will be best measured in the ability of the graduates to effectively teach CLD students.

Context

Politics at the state level (with respect to educating students not fluent in English), the mission of the university, and priorities of the TE department provided a favorable context to carry out the project. In addition, the TE department had recently hired a senior faculty member who was an expert in the education of CLD students. The presence of this faculty member permitted this initiative to come from within the department.

New state policies have greatly affected the education of bilingual learners during the past few years in the state where the institution is located. Dismantling of bilingual education brought about urgency to establish policies that address the education of students for whom English is a second language. State administrators, principals, and teachers realized that no special programs would be available to serve these students. Thus, mainstream teachers would be responsible for educating them. With this added responsibility came the need for professional development for teachers. The TE program concluded that graduates of its program should have that knowledge as well.

These changes in legislation and program structure has heightened the awareness of the presence of bilingual students in schools, but the actual impetus to learn how to work with them comes from the introduction of the issue in the various courses. These two forces feed each other, increasing the motivation of faculty and students in TE to embrace the mission of educating CLD students rather than leaving it up to specialized courses or personnel.

The TE program is housed at a private catholic university with a strong commitment to social justice that serves schools in the nearby communities, including urban and suburban school systems with considerable numbers of CLD students. A few years before this project started, the TE faculty agreed on five unifying themes carried out throughout the courses; two of them include: "promoting social justice" and "accommodating diversity." In addition, the semester preceding the start of the project, the department as a whole agreed that addressing the needs of CLD learners would be a programmatic focus for the upcoming year. Faculty also agreed to support a proposal to the U.S. Department of Education to secure funding to help accomplish such a goal for the department and expressed interest in participating in a faculty seminar. The grant provided a stipend for faculty and school staff participating in the seminars.

The facilitator for the various activities is a faculty member at the university and an expert on the topic of CLD learners, bilingual education, and teacher preparation for multilingual classrooms. She is a full professor with tenure and author of many articles and books and is well respected and recognized nationally and internationally. The status of the facilitator avoided the awkwardness of faculty with lesser status instructing those with more status. The facilitator provided expertise and guidance in navigating the theoretical and practical knowledge about educating CLD students as well as a plan for enacting concrete change across the curriculum. In addition, having an expert within the faculty facilitated continuous casual interaction with the faculty as they were considering changes within their courses.

Structure

The structure of the project had all the characteristics recommended for successful faculty development. It was inclusive, the change was incremental, the change came from within, and the faculty took ownership of the project (Cochran-Smith, 2003; Nevarez et al, 1997; Wheeler & Schuster, 1990).

The program started with a small number of faculty, administrators, doctoral students, and partner school members. Their work impacted a small numbers of key courses, including some of the foundation and methods courses. By the second seminar, almost the entire full-time faculty involved in teacher education courses for licensure had participated. The third and fourth years involved both activities with more breath of reach as well as others with more depth. Through these activities, more preservice and in-service teachers were reached. The knowledge of language and how to incorporate it into TE courses and classroom practices is still being established through intensive work with specific faculty and doctoral students with expertise in language or in the content area. These teams work together to create concrete examples of language issues, lesson or unit plans with language instruction included, and other resources.

The participation in all of these activities has always been voluntary on the part of the faculty. Initially, the activities were planned and encouraged by the facilitator. In the third and fourth year, faculty and administrators have initiated activities themselves. Except for the one-to-one discussion on specific changes in the syllabi between the facilitator and faculty, all the activities have been collaborative, including faculty, doctoral students and, in many cases, partner school personnel.

Knowledge Building Faculty acquired knowledge on research, policies, and practices impacting CLD students through the seminar activities. Faculty found the time to read, discuss, and reflect, which was essential for them to develop the confidence to make changes in their courses. This newly developed expertise allowed the topic to transpire throughout their classes, rather than just be limited to one class. The impact also went beyond their courses. One of the faculty commented that this knowledge allowed her to be more critical in writing a review of a volume in her field of expertise that included a chapter on bilingual learners.

Of particular importance were topics related to language and culture. Language policies in school, attitudes toward language varieties, use of heritage and second language in the curriculum, and classroom practice to enhance the acquisition of academic language were topics somewhat unfamiliar to faculty. The demands of academic language, specifically those related to different content areas, were of particular interest and faculty felt it is quite significant for preservice teachers because:

> It is through language that school subjects are taught and through language that students' understanding of concepts is displayed and evaluated in school contexts.... In other words, the content, as well as the medium, of schooling is, to a large extent, language. (Schleppegrell, 2004, pp. 1–2)

Culture and identity are two additional topics that need to be built in the TE curriculum (see Clayton, Barnhardt, & Brisk, chapter 2). Culture has been part of the scholarship of a number of faculty members and needed less in-depth exploration.

Constructivist Approach

The facilitator did not use her rank to impose her ideas but rather used a constructivist approach to conducting the activities, consistent with the teaching culture of the department. Using this approach in the seminar, summer institutes, and other activities, the facilitator demonstrated flexibility organizing and adapting activities and acceptance of the variety of experiences and points of view relative to CLD that participants' brought to the activities. Participants influenced the process and the content of the activities. The facilitator balanced the need for participants to have a voice in the discussions with maintaining the central questions of the session. Evaluations and comments on first-year activities served as the basis to modify second-year plans. Participants, including doctoral students and school personnel, felt respected as capable adults. They all felt they had something to contribute to everybody's learning.

This collaborative atmosphere contributed to the general feeling that the project was a department effort, an essential feature for successful change (Cochran-Smith, 2003; Nevarez et al., 1997). As a result, faculty and administrators initiated several of the third-year activities.

Meaningful Content

The intellectual endeavors of the faculty seminar were complemented with practical resources and ideas to support change. The course syllabi became valuable tools that TE faculty members compared, shared, and integrated into their efforts to infuse knowledge about CLD students across the curriculum. The syllabus is the "link between individual courses and the mission pursued by the wider curriculum" (Strada, 2001, p. 209). Focusing on the syllabus made participants think about whether they were addressing the education of CLD learners and the ways in which they were addressing it. For example, participants mentioned that, in the current design of many syllabi, these issues are most often scheduled at the end of the semester and are shortened or skipped over if other curricular topics take more time than planned. Adaptations made to courses included addition of appropriate readings, activities focusing on teaching CLD students, and assignments that included attention to CLD students. Moreover, CLD issues were covered throughout the course rather than in one class.

The greatest demand from the faculty in the process of modifying syllabi was readings that they could use in their courses. Including such readings in the seminar encouraged faculty to read them and discuss them. This in turn made them familiar with the content. Many of the readings used in the seminars became part of the course requirements. An article on working with immigrant parents turned up in a "Social Context of Education" class. Faculty teaching methods courses included readings connected with that discipline. These readings had been included in the faculty seminars to stimulate the discussion of academic language. Foundation courses adapted readings used during the discussion of sociopolitical issues. Even a principal and teachers from a high school who participated in the seminar used the readings to organize their own professional development at their school. The range of readings provided something for everyone.

Practical ideas used as tools during the seminars served as models for use in the classrooms. Analysis of academic text in different disciplines translated into reviewing lessons or units to include opportunities to teach language and add language objectives. A video of a class taught in Farsi without subtitles made faculty aware of the experience of attending classes in a language that one has not mastered. As a result, several faculty members who taught methods courses incorporated the idea of teaching in a different language or reflecting a different culture. For example, the methods of science professor asked a Korean doctoral student to teach a science class in Korean. Equipped with science textbooks and worksheets from Korea, the student taught a 20-minute lesson, demanding interaction, reading, and writing from preservice teachers enrolled in the course. The reflections that followed raised most of the relevant challenges encountered by CLD learners in mainstream American classrooms. The course participants evaluated this activity highly in the end-of-semester evaluation.

Thus, the seminars provided knowledge, instructional ideas, and readings that had immediate use for the participants. Faculty were able to do it without additional work and apply it directly to their syllabi, their course planning tools. Eventually, many commented that their syllabi did not reflect the amount of coverage that took place in their courses. Class discussions and student work were spaces where the needs of CLD students was constantly addressed.

Leadership Support

TE leadership got personally involved. Both the department chair and the director and associate director of the Practicum Office participated in the initial seminars and have maintained the topic in their agenda over the years. They have facilitated the follow-up activities and programmatic decisions brought about. Both the department chair and director of the Practicum Office keep the topic of CLD students present in their agendas, encouraging the integration of the curriculum and meaningful field experiences for preservice teachers. Leadership support has been essential for sustainability and expansion of the project. It has made the issue of educating CLD a department agenda rather than an individual faculty agenda.

Conclusion

According to Fillmore and Snow (2002):

> As a society, we expect teachers to educate whoever shows up at the schoolhouse, to provide their students the language and literacy skills to survive in school and later on in jobs, to teach them all of the school subjects that they will need to know about as adults, and to prepare them in other ways for higher education and for the workplace. (p. 42)

Such expectations demand that TE education programs support pre-service and in-service teachers with needed content. Teacher education programs have no choice but to change to better prepare their students to work in schools with increasing diversity among their students.

This chapter indicates that program transformation is a long process that starts with faculty transformation and must seek program coherence and sustainability. Change was possible because faculty were provided with the knowledge and tools to carry out the work in a context supported by internal and external forces. For program change to have quality impact, it must be coherent and in depth. The teacher education department must collaborate to establish coordination across the curriculum of the themes addressing CLD students to avoid repetition and ensure that teacher knowledge goes beyond the surface level. These 4 years of intense work must be followed by reflection and review to achieve such coherence.

Much of the activities and support emanates from the particular faculty involved in the development of the program. The dilemma of change is how efforts can be made sustainable and become less dependent on the people involved in the change. Two features of the program may facilitate sustainability: the involvement of young, recently hired faculty with backgrounds in and commitment to CLD education and the interest in social justice deeply edged in the mission of the university.

References

Aleamoni, L. M. (1997). Issues in linking instructional-improvement research to faculty development in higher education. *Journal of Personnel Evaluation in Education, 11*, 31–37.

Anstrom, K. (2004). Introduction to preparing all educators for student diversity: Lessons for higher education. In K. Anstrom, J. Glazier, P. Sanchez, V. Sardi, P. Schwallie-Giddis, & P. Tate (Eds.), *Preparing All Educators for Student Diversity: Lessons for Higher Education*. Washington, DC: *Institute for education policy studies Graduate School of Education and Human Development, The George Washington University.*

Cochran-Smith, M. (2003). Learning and unlearning: the education of teacher educators. *Teaching and Teacher Education, 19,* 5–28.

Cochran-Smith, M., Albert, L., DiMattia, P., Freedman, S., Jackson, R., Mooney, J., et al. (1999). Seeking social justice: A teacher education faculty's self-study. *International Journal of Leadership in Education: Theory and Practice, 2*(3), 229–253.

Costa, J., McPhail, G., Smith, J., & Brisk, M. E. (2005). Faculty first: The challenge of infusing the teacher education curriculum with scholarship on English language learners. *Journal of Teacher Education, 56*(2), 104–118.

Fillmore, L. W., & Snow, C. (2002). What teachers need to know about language. In C. T. Adger, C. Snow, & D. Christian (Eds.), *What teachers need to know about language* (pp. 7–54). McHenry, IL: Center for Applied Linguistics.

Gaff, J. G., & Simpson, R. D. (1994). Faculty development in the United States. *Innovative Higher Education, 18*(3), 167–176.

Nevarez, A. A., Sanford, J. S., & Parker, L. (1997). Do the right thing: Transformative multicultural education in teacher preparation. *Journal for a Just and Caring Education, 3*(2), 160–179.

Schleppegrell, M. (2004). *The language of schooling: A functional linguistics perspective.* Mahwah, NJ: Lawrence Erlbaum Associates.

Strada, M. J. (2001). The case for sophisticated course syllabi. In D. Lieberman & C. Wehlburg (Eds.), *To improve the academy: Vol. 4. Resources for faculty, instructional and organizational development.* Bolton, MA: Anker Publishing.

Walvoord, B. E., Carey, A. K., Smith, H. L., Soled, S. W., Way, P. K., & Zorn, D. (2000). *Academic departments: How they work, how they change* (ASHE-ERIC Higher Education Report, Vol. 27, No. 8). San Francisco: Jossey-Bass.

Wheeler, D. W., & Schuster, J. H. (1990). Building comprehensive programs to enhance faculty development. In J. H. Schuster & D. W. Wheeler (Eds.), *Enhancing faculty careers* (pp. 275–297). San Francisco: Jossey-Bass.

Endnotes

1. These schools work in close connection with the university. University students are placed for supervised practica, they volunteer in in-school and after-school programs. Faculty provide professional development and carry out other projects at the schools. In turn, teachers from the schools serve as part-time and clinical faculty.

12

Faculty Perspectives on Integrating Linguistic Diversity Issues into an Urban Teacher Education Program

Aida A. Nevárez-La Torre
Fordham University

Jayminn S. Sanford-DeShields

Catherine Soundy

Jaqueline Leonard

Christine Woyshner
Temple University

A current and ongoing challenge for teacher education programs across universities in the United States has been to change the traditional approach to teacher education, from a narrow focus on a monocultural and monolinguistic student population to a broader approach that recognizes and values cultural and linguistic diversity. For more than a decade, scholars have called attention to the changing faces of students and the implications for teacher preparation (Banks, 1998; Darling-Hammond & Youngs, 2002; Ladson-Billings, 2000; Nevárez, Sanford, & Parker, 1997; Nieto, 2000). Their writings have documented efforts to weave multicultural education into the curricular fabric of teacher education. Ways in which race, class, and gender influence educational processes and outcomes have been well documented (Gollnick & Chinn, 2005; Nieto, 2000; Shapiro, Sewell, & DuCette, 1995). However, until recently, the exploration of ways in which linguistic diversity influences learning and teaching has been scarce in mainstream research literature (Beykont, 2002; Téllez & Waxman, 2004). Voices calling for the integration of linguistic diversity issues in the preparation of all teachers, not just bilingual and English as a Second Language (ESL) teachers, are gradually emerging (Adger, Snow, & Christian, 2002; Friedman, 2002; Gándara & Maxwell-Jolly, 2003; García, 2001).

As authors of this chapter, we contend that changing demographics (Gándara & Maxwell-Jolly, 2003; MSNBC News, 2004; President's Advisory Commission on Educational Excellence for Hispanic Americans, 2003) and the low academic performance of English language learners (ELLs) (American Federation of Teachers, 2004; CNN.com, 2005; Gersten & Jiménez, 1998; Gibbons, 2002; Waxman & Téllez, 2004) require that preservice and in-service teachers develop knowledge about language differences and about effective pedagogy to address the linguistic needs of all their students. Although improving the education of ELLs has been proposed as a pressing national educational priority (Waxman & Téllez, 2004), many teachers are not adequately prepared to work with a linguistically diverse student population (American Federation of Teachers, 2004; Fillmore & Snow, 2002; Gándara & Maxwell-Jolly, 2003; Menken & Antunez, 2001; Nieto 2003). The issue addressed in this chapter, then, is how to build the capacity of teacher education programs in colleges and universities to "prepare educators who have the competencies and dispositions to work effectively with [linguistically] diverse students" (Anstrom, 2004, p. vii).

The first purpose of the chapter is to describe the Faculty Linguistic Diversity Academy (the Academy) as a professional development tool to build the knowledge about linguistic diversity of faculty in an urban university. The Academy is an effort to ensure high-quality teacher preparation through the examination of language diversity across the curriculum. The second important purpose is to discuss the perspectives of a group of faculty, members of the Academy, who are striving to introduce the exploration of language diversity issues into teacher education courses. This information is relevant to all teachers and teacher educators whose work may have an impact on the lives of the increasing number of children in U.S. schools who speak a language other than English.

We explore three questions:

1. How can the capacity of faculty in an urban teacher education program be built to identify promising pedagogies that use language diversity as a key element for implementation in today's K–12 classrooms?
2. How has a group of faculty infused knowledge about linguistic diversity into teacher education methods courses?
3. How have faculty perspectives on educating teachers about the diverse linguistic capital in schools evolved to innovate teacher education in an urban university?

The chapter is divided into three sections. In the first section, the authors present a research context by reviewing the literature on educating all teachers for a linguistically diverse student population. In the second section, we describe the structure of the Academy and the professional activities that guided a group of faculty to inculcate knowledge about linguistic diversity into pedagogy courses. Specifically, four faculty members of the Academy voice their perspectives on infusing courses in their respective disciplines—multicultural education, early childhood education, mathematics education, and social studies education. Finally, in the third section, we specify conclusions and implications by discussing the potential of our work to create long-term change in teacher education.

Research Context: New Demands in Teacher Education

It has been argued that to change the present state of teacher education, institutions of higher learning should implement two interconnected initiatives: (1) redesign curricula and (2) support the professional development of faculty (American Federation of Teachers, 1999; Cochran-Smith, 2003; Gándara & Maxwell-Jolly, 2003; García, 2001; Minaya-Rowe, 2003; National Council for Accreditation of Teacher Education [as cited in Anstrom, 2004]; Nevárez et al., 1997; Quintanar-Sarallana, 1997). The redesign of curricula calls for the inclusion of specialized courses that deal with the education of ELLs and bilingual students (Hamayan, 1990) as well as an integration into the pedagogy courses of knowledge and experiences in essential domains such as: (1) second language (L2) development in the content areas; (2) bilingualism and biliteracy; (3) language development, acquisition and use, and cultural patterns for language; (4) culturally responsive pedagogy; (5) administrators' roles in responding to the instructional needs of ELLs; and (6) ways of partnering with linguistically diverse parents and their communities (Adger et al., 2002; Beykont, 2002; Nieto, 2003, Valdés, Bunch, Snow, Lee, & Matos, 2005).

The focus of this chapter is on the second important initiative, building the capacity of faculty in teacher education. Descriptions of faculty development projects for diverse education are scarce in the research literature (Anstrom, 2004). The examples found center their discussion on multicultural education, with a few commenting on linguistic diversity. However, they all agree that a long-term goal of this venture should be to create forums where faculty can gradually change personal and professional beliefs as well as practices. Their recommendations emphasize that faculty professional development should be shaped to include workshops, conference attendance and presentations, self-directed projects, inquiry and problem-solving activities, opportunities for reflective and critical thought through experiential learning, discussions of research literature, ongoing feedback and consultation with experts, peer support groups, and open dialogue in a safe environment (Bristor, Pelaez, & Crawley, 2000; Dillard, 1997; King, Hollins, & Hayman, 1997; Pang, Anderson, Martuza, 1997; Wilson & Berne [as cited in Anstrom, 2004]). As we describe later in this chapter, these recommendations were integrated into the capacity-building activities offered by the Academy.

The new demands imposed on school districts and states regarding teacher preparation and achievement accountability by the No Child Left Behind Act of 2001 (NCLB) strongly suggest a need to restructure teacher education following the two interconnected initiatives mentioned above. NCLB mandates that "every state must ensure that there is a qualified teacher in every classroom by the 2005–2006 school year" (President's Advisory Commission on Educational Excellence for Hispanic Americans, 2003, p. 21). The concept of "highly qualified teachers" narrowly refers to the percentage of fully certified and properly assigned classroom teachers (Pennsylvania Department of Education [PDE}, 2003). However, teacher education programs must not only educate teachers to respond to the requirements of certification but also equip them with the experiences, knowledge, skills, and attitudes to successfully promote the educational success of all children, including ELLs (Gándara & Maxwell-Jolly, 2003).

The Faculty Linguistic Diversity Academy

Our university is located in a major city in the northeastern part of the United States. Historically, it has prepared school teachers, principals, psychologists, and counselors with a focus on the urban center. Part of the college's mission is to value diversity. Conventionally, this mission has been implemented by having all undergraduates take a course on race and the impact of racism on society. In addition, all education majors must take a multicultural education course. A recent change in curricula pays attention to the initiative of redesigning curricula by offering undergraduate preservice teachers the choice of *adding* to their program an ESL Program Specialist Certificate (requires 12 additional credit hours on second language education).[1] At the graduate level, the College of Education's Teaching English to Speakers of Other Languages (TESOL) Program has national and international recognition for preparing professionals to work with college level and adult ELLs. The ESL Specialist Certificate is also available at this level.

Currently in our institution, a project that gives specific attention to educating professionals to work in K–12 schools with a linguistically and culturally diverse student population is the Career Advancement for Paraprofessionals in Education (Project CAPE). It is funded through a Title VII federal grant from the U.S. Department of Education.[2] To address the second initiative in reforming teacher education, a unique component of this project is the Faculty Linguistic Diversity Academy (the Academy). Instituted in 2001, the Academy has worked to familiarize teacher education faculty with ways to integrate issues of linguistic diversity in undergraduate and graduate teacher education courses.

The two facilitators of the Academy are faculty members who are experts in the field of language education and literacy. The purpose of the Academy is to create opportunities for teacher education faculty to critically reflect on language difference and ways it can shape educational achievement across different content areas. Our discussions explore teaching strategies and approaches that aspiring teachers can use to facilitate the acquisition of ESL in cognitively demanding academic tasks in content area classes (Hamayan, 1990). We design professional activities to innovate teacher education through the integration of knowledge about language and language learning into undergraduate and graduate education pedagogy courses.

Over the past 3 years, the Academy has developed several components to achieve our purpose. The components were designed using the available research on professional development that is conducive to changing teachers' beliefs and instructional practices. First, it has worked with a total of 11 full-time professors (representing one-third of faculty in the teacher education program), a cohort of five faculty members the first year and a cohort of six during the second year. These faculty members teach pedagogy courses at the undergraduate and graduate levels, covering such disciplines as mathematics education, science education, language arts, literacy, English education, early childhood education, multicultural education, and educational technology. Second, it has held regular interactive and participatory meetings with members of the Academy to discuss the complexities of teaching in schools with rich linguistic backgrounds and to investigate strategies for integrating these concepts into their courses. The group critically reflects on experiences with bilingual and ELLs students and problem solves real situations shared by members.

Third, we coordinated the Linguistic Diversity Forum, where renowned local, national, and international experts in the fields of ESL and bilingual education offer seminars and workshops to faculty and teacher education students. The knowledge base discussed in the monthly meetings and Forum series was identified from the essential domains of knowledge about linguistic diversity mentioned in the literature (see above), as well as from suggestions given by individual Academy members. Specifically, we learned about the research being conducted by experts in the areas of (1) language learning theories; (2) multilingualism, bilingualism, and biliteracy development; (3) bilingual education and ESL program models and approaches; (4) L2 development in the content area; (5) academic vocabulary development in L2; (6) writing in L2; (7) bilingualism and special education; (8) bilingualism and peace education; (9) promising practices and policies when "teaching across language difference" (Beykont, 2002); and (10) the politics of language and language policy.

Fourth, faculty developed their own self-directed projects on infusion and the facilitators gave ongoing feedback. Through one-on-one meetings, we provided individual assistance to faculty in changing their syllabus to reflect this new knowledge base. Fifth, it offered a stipend for members of the Academy to buy books and other resources to assist in the infusion process.

The members of the Academy are expected to attend all monthly meetings, seminars, and workshops as well as to infuse at least one course during the 1-year intensive program. In the initial year of participation in the Academy, each member is given a binder with research-based readings on the topic of linguistic diversity to be discussed during the monthly lunch meetings. To remain active after the first year, the members of the Academy are expected to attend once-a-semester seminar meetings to discuss progress and participate in the Academy Forum.

Members documented growth in infusing courses by completing a questionnaire at the beginning of their participation and by writing a reflective essay (due at the end of their initial year) that addressed some of the same issues included in the initial questionnaire (Appendix 12.A includes a sample of the questionnaire). Faculty members also developed portfolios to showcase artifacts that depict course innovations, including the changed syllabus, lecture notes, student assignments, and samples of preservice and in-service teachers' work (Appendix 12.B includes guidelines for portfolio development).

One of the authors of this manuscript is the principal investigator of the grant, and the other authors are participants of the Academy. All of the authors are females, two are Caucasian, two are African American, and one is Latina. Only one of the authors speaks two languages fluently. To help the reader understand the scope of our work, it is important to mention two limitations of this documentary account. One is that, at the time, no class observations were conducted to examine the implementation of infusion activities described in the altered syllabi. Also, it is beyond the scope of this chapter to explore the impact of infused activities on the develop ing teaching philosophies and practice of preservice and in-service teachers. Limitations in the capacity of the current project prevented us from pursuing these lines of research. We plan to seek funding to explore these areas in the future.

The work of the Academy presented here, however, does illustrate a process of faculty professional development. In the next section, we identify the activities that Academy members implemented to incorporate linguistic diversity into teacher education courses at our institution. More specifically, we explore faculty perspectives on changing the way we prepare prospective teachers. After a brief description of infusion activities, four Academy members describe the learnings and challenges they experienced.

Initial Exploration of Infusion Activities

Early discussions among faculty during the Academy's monthly meetings revealed three facts about our teacher education program. First, faculty were personally interested in the topic of language difference and were curious about the process of infusion. This was evident because the faculty members of the Academy volunteered to participate.

Second, although most of these professors explored issues of multicultural education in their courses, they did not discuss linguistic diversity issues. One professor explained, "I do not get any questions about linguistic diversity from preservice teachers. Until now, I do not get any questions, and I have not brought it for discussion either. I think that they see the subject matter of the course within a box separate from language development. Some of my students are not even aware that this is part of teaching."

Third, faculty members lacked the knowledge necessary to discuss these issues in teacher education courses. Professors brought to the meetings some key and practical questions: What resources exist in the subject matter of my course related to language diversity? How can teachers teach content when students are not fluent in the language used to teach? How can I present information about language difference in my course? How can I infuse more information into an already crowded syllabus? How can I integrate this topic throughout the course rather than as a separate and isolated topic?

Through Academy activities such as reflective readings of the research literature and discussions with experts in the field, we provided insight into these questions and some possible answers. The challenge, then, was for professors to apply this knowledge in pedagogy courses.

Academy members designed and implemented activities for one course they taught that reflected their newly acquired understanding about language difference and effective practices educating ELLs. Syllabi of the pedagogy courses, both before and after becoming members of the Academy, were examined to determine infusion through type and quantity of changes in instructional activities. Essays written as part of portfolios were also read to identify infused activities. Finally, samples of preservice teachers' course work included in the portfolios were reviewed to confirm integration of activities. The criteria used to consider the activity part of the infusion process were three: (1) The activity was never used in the course before, (2) the activity reflected new understanding on the part of the professor about language diversity in the subject matter, and (3) the activity reflected an increase in the number of sessions (discussion time) and resources used to explore this topic in the specific course. Although a minimum of one criterion was needed to satisfy the requirement of infusion, the majority of professors (10 out of 11) satisfied at least two criteria in the redeveloped courses.

Documentation collected for 3 consecutive years suggests that professors designed and implemented various activities to incorporate discussions about language difference into pedagogy courses. Among the instructional activities that consistently (meaning two or more semesters) have been implemented in courses are: (1) include course readings on linguistic diversity in general or in ways that language difference issues connect with the specific subject matter of the course; (2) require preservice and in-service teachers to observe a classroom with ELLs and report findings following specific guidelines provided by the professor; (3) include a list of resources relevant to the course content (i.e., children's books, websites) that reflect the languages and cultures of students taught; (4) search research literature for articles exploring linguistic diversity issues relevant to the course content and summarize findings; (5) demonstrate and discuss best practices in educating language diverse students (demonstrations were done by the professor, guest speakers, and experienced in-service teachers or shown through videos); (6) incorporate language diversity throughout the semester when discussing other topics, such as special needs, assessment, and best practices relevant to the course content; (7) assign practical projects (i.e., lesson plans, thematic units) that require students to design or adapt instruction for ELLs; (8) assign small-group interactive activities (i.e., discussion circles, poster sessions) to explore issues about language difference in depth; (9) use personal and professional experiences to model critical reflection about linguistic diversity issues relevant to the content area taught (modeling was done by professor); and (10) include linguistic diversity issues in the assessment of course content.

The breadth of instructional activities listed here suggests that Academy members acquired new knowledge about language diversity and were diligent in infusing this knowledge into four methods courses. However, it is clear that they are just beginning to alter the content and instructional process by creating forums in the courses where issues of teaching across language difference are reflected on and discussed in sensitive and meaningful ways. Thus, a closer look at how this knowledge was built and enacted is necessary. How did faculty come to their individual understanding of diversity issues? How did they decide to infuse this knowledge? What facilitated or impeded their trajectory in changing the courses? These questions are addressed in the next section of the chapter.

We present the perspectives of four professors on changing pedagogy courses in an urban institution of higher learning. Their documentary accounts give a more detailed description and analysis of the successes and challenges they faced in educating a group of preservice teachers to effectively work in culturally and linguistically diverse environments. The first two professors participated in the first cohort (2001–2002), and they teach courses in multicultural education and early childhood education. The last two participated in the second cohort (2002–2003), and they teach mathematics education and social studies education courses. Their accounts reveal a range of infused activities and a detailed discussion of their implementation. They write about their new insights, changes made to their syllabi, and the resulting response from preservice and in-service teachers taking their courses. To ascertain the development of the new knowledge base, the four faculty documented class discussions and examined course assignments. Several samples of preservice and in-service teachers' work are used in the discussion as evidence of the emerging curricular changes in their courses.

Faculty Perspectives

Inclusive Education for a Diverse Society

One of the first courses I began to infuse with information about linguistic diversity was Education 652 (Ed 652), the graduate version of *Inclusive Education for a Diverse Society*. The purpose of the course is to facilitate students' developing awareness of the roles of culture in educational systems in the United States. The course's primary goal is to identify and capitalize upon ways in which culture impacts teaching and learning. The main objectives include promoting the valuing of diversity, understanding the influence of culture, learning culturally responsive teaching strategies, and thinking transformatively about educational systems and practices.

I started attending meetings of the Academy in the 2001–2002 academic year and, since then, I have transformed two areas of the course, its conceptual framework as well as the pedagogy used to teach it. Originally in Ed 652, language was introduced in this course as one of several components of culture to be discussed theoretically and explored in practical application throughout the semester. My participation in the Academy expanded this knowledge base and provided a more in-depth understanding of its rich connection to other components of culture. For example, initially in the course, I introduced the topic of second language acquisition from a research perspective. I thought that by doing this I had achieved the integration of linguistic diversity into the discussion of culture. However, the Academy challenged me to take a second look at the course and reconsider what I saw as integration of language as a component of culture. Thus, I started to discuss with my students the conceptual framework of the course—that is, the intersection of economics, gender, and other social factors with language.

The Academy also provided the opportunity to make changes in the pedagogy used in this course. Initially, reading and discussion were the primary pedagogical activities I used with my graduate students. In addition, the viewing of videotapes supplemented the analysis of culture. Students were also required to write a reflective paper individually in response to five of the assigned readings or videos.

After several luncheon meetings with Academy members, I decided to integrate several class activities that require students to work in pairs or in small groups to explore the intersection of several components of culture, including language, race, gender, sexual orientation, ethnicity, economic and social class, nationality, and religion. I became more sensitive to the fact that language as an obvious component of culture demanded a more careful exploration for its impact in education.

In this course, the engagement process—to learn, reflect, introspect, and incorporate these new ideas into preservice and in-service teachers' actions in their classrooms—is the most important outcome. The process of engaging with culture—that is, learning about unfamiliar aspects of diversity; considering alternatives; establishing fit, reflecting, and incorporating new knowledge into an emerging pedagogy—is life long. Consequently, the highest rewards in Ed 652 are earned by those who best tackle the various forms of resistance to the engagement process. The Academy sensitized me to model for my students the engagement process by exploring linguistic diversity. Thus, a second area of change was to use modeling as a pedagogical tool to reintroduce and engage my students in a process of thinking about a less familiar component of culture in education, language.

Through modeling, I presented what I knew about the inclusion of bilingual and ELL children and families in discussions about diversity. During the semester, I was honest about what I was learning about language and culture and the reasons why this interested me. I specifically showed them how to incorporate new learning into teaching. In this graduate class, I "thought aloud," one way in which an educator can read and think and pose questions and adapt while teaching. I wanted them to see that in teaching one can think in public. My goal was to show students that effective teaching demands educators to grapple with their ignorance and biases and confront societal inequities related to language and culture.

In the past year, my third as a member of the Academy, I have become more comfortable with integration and modeling as well as with the material about linguistic diversity that I have incorporated into the class. I use oral and written students' reflections and responses to the material specifically to gauge the degree to which they are engaging in a process of transforming their developing teaching philosophy and practice. The following excerpts are representative student reflections. They illustrate students' engagement with information about linguistic diversity and different degrees of understanding and ability to incorporate the information into their practice (some students in this graduate course are in-service teachers).

I considered the first student's reflection to illustrate an initial degree of engagement in that the student describes a somewhat simplistic view of the incorporation of linguistic diversity in the classroom. Still, the introduction of simple phrases is not a bad idea. The student does understand a pedagogical emphasis on diversity as being a teacher's responsibility and also includes the importance of family and community in the process:

> Student 1: Teachers can show their students how to gain an appreciation for different languages by welcoming multilingualism in their classroom. Maybe by just teaching simple phrases from an array of languages or allowing students to teach their classmates different language phrases.... Lastly, work with students' parents to help stimulate a positive learning experience for their child.

In the second reflection, the student repeats factual information that has been presented. She explores the relationship of dialect to language and is able to make strong, albeit impersonal statements about systemic reform:

> Student 2: Dialects which differ from that of "standard" language are looked down upon in the classroom. Bilingual students, for instance, are quickly corrected when they improperly pronounce words. Their dialect is perceived as evidence of lack of intelligence or ignorance. In textbooks, "standard" language is the only one discussed while variations of language are perceived as slang or improper. Textbooks discourage different forms of syntax, grammar, semantics or various morphemes.... Different dialects should be embraced and perceived as linguistic learning opportunities.... Schools should hire bilingual instructors who understand the integration of English along with another language. Textbooks should be updated and modified so that misconceptions regarding dialects can be eradicated from pedagogy and the school environment.

In the third reflection, I assessed an increased degree of awareness and knowledge from that of the first two students. The student describes the value that linguistically diverse students add to the classroom and the responsibility of the teacher to provide opportunities for students to volunteer to bring that value into the teaching and learning process:

> Student 3: Students who speak another language or dialect can add to the classroom environment. They often bring with them different experiences and cultural values which can enhance the education of all of the students in the class. It is up to the teacher to make sure these students are seen as valuable, intelligent members of the classroom who have different experiences to share with their classmates on a voluntary basis.

I considered the last excerpt to best illustrate a high degree of engagement in that the student describes the relationship of language and culture, custom, and community:

> Student 4: Language and dialect serve as a focal point for cultural identity.... It provides a common bond for individuals with the same linguistic heritage. Language shapes cultural and personal identity.... Language is much more than just a means of communication. It is used to socialize children into their linguistic and cultural communities, developing patterns that distinguished one community from another. Native speakers of a language unconsciously know and obey the rules and customs of their language community.

Incorporating knowledge into practice is the final and very important step in the engagement process. In the following excerpts from students' reflective papers, two in-service teachers describe how they were able to apply information taken from readings and class discussions about linguistic diversity into their teaching process:

> Student 5: As a teacher, I know that I am guilty of buying into the stereotypes that society and the media help to create and maintain. I have one student this year from Eastern Europe who struggles with speaking English and even more so with writing it. I cannot determine if he has low ability or if there is a language barrier preventing him from achieving his potential. I worry that I enable him by "letting go" his horrible spelling or grammar or by not calling on him in class. I know he cannot write well yet, however, will he ever learn if I continually let it go? How will he be perceived in society later down the line? I don't want to embarrass him by making him speak in class, but will he ever gain confidence in or command of the language by avoiding it?... I am more aware now of my own biases and have already noticed a change in my thinking. I am hoping that soon the changes in thinking will translate into a change in my behavior and pedagogy, so that all of my students benefit from a more accepting, fair, and enriching environment.
>
> Student 6: A new student, Tony has just enrolled in my class. He is from Texas and has moved to the area because of his father's job. Although he looks like all of the other students, his dialect is different. His accent is heavy, and his "vocab" is nothing like that of my urban students. His dialect could probably be labeled as southwestern. Each time he speaks it is hard for the students and I to understand. The result is laughter, mocking, and name-calling. Consequently, his grades have suffered. He realizes this and is extremely frustrated. Currently, he is in my honors class. Advice from my colleagues has been to put him in a lower track. I did not. Intellectually, he is capable of handling the work. Bad grades, I believe, are a consequence of the way he is being treated. The most difficult part for me is trying to make his transition much easier. Currently, I have been working with him after school, so that he does not feel intimidated by the other students.... I realized I could use Tony's dialectical differences to make things easier for him.... I do not believe my students are cruel. I believe they are unaware of how different the world is outside of their neighborhood. Educators can do a lot to make a difference.... One way to achieve this is to have the student share where they are from and how they used to live. For example, I had Tony describe for the class what school was like for him in Texas. I also had him tell the students his hobbies, likes and dislikes, and what he thought about Philadelphia. During the class, I had students describe similarities and differences between languages.

Information I learned from the Academy's speaker forum assisted me in analyzing the students' reflections. Specifically, the difference between reflective and transformative practice was a critical concept to incorporate into my lens as a teacher. Student five is able to view herself as having "bought into" stereotypes. She is aware of stereotypes that affect her teaching and where those stereotypical images of students come from. She knows that the difference in achievement may be due to language. However, she views one of her student's language as a "barrier preventing him from achieving his potential." She has assigned a value judgment to the student's work, viewing his spelling and grammar as "horrible." She views herself as having two choices, either "letting it go" or "embarrassing him in public." Further, the student seems to feel that the changes in her thinking will by themselves translate into changes in her pedagogy. She does not express an understanding that she will have to actively change her own behavior. However, she does realize that addressing bias will result in a more "… fair and enriching [classroom] environment."

Student six is further along in that she has begun to translate language acquisition theory into practical classroom application. She examines dialect as linguistic diversity. She has put into action her belief that intellectual capacity can be obscured by language acquisition. She has taken it upon herself to work with the student individually. She has brought the student's cultural experiences into her classroom and structured students' responses for him.

The above student reflections document emerging changes in pre-service and in-service teachers who have taken Ed 652. They are also evidence that my infusion efforts are not complete or sufficient to engage all students who take this course in learning about linguistic diversity. I plan to expand my professional knowledge about linguistic diversity in the upcoming academic year (my fourth as part of the Academy) through the more in-depth study of language loss and dialect as a language.

Linguistic Diversity in Early Childhood

I have participated in the Academy for 3 consecutive years. During my tenure in the Academy, I have come to realize that the integration of ethnic and multicultural content into undergraduate curricula must be interwoven throughout the entire 12-hour block of early childhood courses at our institution. Multiple exposures to real-life examples over the period of several semesters promote a deeper understanding of the language and culture of diverse learners. During an extended time frame, prospective teachers have more opportunities to build a stronger repertoire of successful classroom strategies and to develop an informed perspective on all children and their learning potentials. Instructors have many class sessions in which to create an enlightened vision in the minds of preservice teachers, establishing a paradigm that guides them toward genuine appreciation of the native cultures and languages of people not born into the dominant culture.

Traditionally, early childhood educators have believed that a "caring person" mindset provides the necessary impetus for acting on their beliefs and values about people who are different from them or from the mainstream. My perspective now challenges that conventional view. I believe that preservice and in-service teachers must expand their knowledge base to ensure effective early childhood education for all students. In this section, I discuss some of the new thoughts I gained from my participation in the Academy and identify specific changes that I have made in my early childhood courses to promote understandings in linguistic diversity. I also reflect on how students have reacted to these changes and to the challenges of educating ELL students.

Although early childhood teachers are generally responsible for all areas of the curriculum, a strong need exists for ways to improve the early literacy learning of students from diverse linguistic backgrounds. For this reason, many initial changes to my syllabus were designed to help prospective teachers improve the literacy outcomes of young learners. In planning for my targeted areas of change, I selected five key factors from research-based studies to guide the integration of new content and experiences into early childhood courses:

1. Encourage children and their parents to bring their cultural values and languages into the classroom. For example, Cummins (1986) suggested the linguistic interdependence principle, which accounts for the fact that the more children's home language is developed, the better their chances for true mastery of a second language. Children could make an easier and faster transition into another language (and into early reading) if their own language is well developed and they have positive self-regard and strong family support.

2. Recruit parent volunteers who are native speakers of languages represented in your classrooms. Monolingual preschool teachers need to be diligent in reaching out to parents and community members to help tutor young literacy learners (National Association for the Education of Young Children, 1995). These parents can be trained on ways to implement developmentally

appropriate practices in your classroom. Parents who have well developed oral and written skills in their native language will be able to provide the best language and literacy role models for children (Crawford, 1993).

3. Choose curriculum materials that reflect the language and culture of the population to be served. The current topic of study should be supported with a wide selection of materials: multicultural books, posters, videos, and displays; crayons of various flesh tones; dolls and people figures from different ethnic backgrounds and racial groups; and charts around the classroom in different languages (Derman-Sparks, 1989).

4. Adapt practices to create a climate within the classroom and school wherein children feel comfortable and confident and a respect for each other's languages and cultures is constantly being developed. Early childhood staff must assume a sensitive, positive role in their attempt to scaffold and support their bilingual learners' oral development. Adult-dominated talk commonly leaves young children with insufficient opportunities to initiate and extend their personal meaning. All adults must search for the most effective ways of giving children "a voice" in the classroom (Au, 1993; Strickland, 1998).

5. Speak with administrators and policy-makers to help them understand the value of proficiency in the first language to gaining proficiency in the second language, English. They should be informed of the ultimate benefits that being a balanced bilingual brings in educational terms. The "English only" prejudice in this society has to be dealt with before parents will stop urging their children and pressuring their teachers to speak and teach in English at school (Brisk & Harrington, 2000).

The research findings on best practices in literacy guided me in restructuring *ECH ED* 0320: Curriculum Development and Implementation in Early Childhood Programs. This three-credit course is the first of four taken by undergraduates who are working toward certification in early childhood education and provides an introduction to the field of early education. The syllabus includes the following course description: "Students learn how to organize the classroom and plan educationally appropriate experiences for infants, toddlers, and young children. Practicum experiences in local schools and centers provide opportunities for students to implement curricular activities in areas such as language and literacy, mathematics, science, social studies, expressive arts, and play."

The structure of the course includes four field experiences: two observations in student-selected early childhood centers and two direct teaching experiences in instructor-chosen Head Start programs located in close proximity to the campus. Emphasis is placed on how the content of the curriculum is actualized in classrooms containing three-, four-, and five-year-old children. In addition, students are expected to construct teacher-made instructional materials in two different curriculum areas and prepare for a midterm and final exam.

Several of the above-mentioned practices learned during the 1st year of study in the Academy were included in my introductory early childhood course. One modification occurred in the practicum requirement. For the observation assignment, students were asked to choose an early childhood center in a Latino community or other setting containing children whose culture and language are different from the dominant culture. Observational guidelines were adjusted from previous semesters to include a section on exploring what experienced preschool teachers do to facilitate the development of bilingualism. Students were directed to look for the integration of bilingual images, curricular materials, and practices in the classroom. The following suggestions provided a starting point for their observations: (1) Record all types of multicultural images, such as dolls or people figures from different ethnic backgrounds and racial groups; (2) observe circle or whole group time and watch to see if teachers incorporate oral participation in children's literacy and numeracy awareness in the minority language alongside the majority culture; (3) note the availability of dual-language and first-language books, especially in the classroom literacy corner; and (4) identify any evidence of first-language print materials from the home environment that are visible in the classroom, such as newspapers, calendars, postcards, recipes, and other artifacts.

The second assignment modification occurred with the resource project. Preservice teachers were asked to create opportunities for children to work with their home languages and literacies in supportive mainstream classroom environments. As they constructed their teacher-made instructional materials and teaching units, they were asked to incorporate multicultural children's books, songs, dances, and other elements into their plans and to include ten suggested readings about this topic for other interested colleagues. The underlying purpose was for students to compile examples of successful classroom practice regarding bilingual work with language minority children in mainstream preschools. During class presentations, all students were asked to think about ways to create a classroom climate that promotes positive intercultural interactions between students.

After a full year of reflecting on linguistic diversity, I made additional refinements to this course. I wanted prospective teachers to acquire a rich repertoire of opportunities for children to study their home literacy during regular classroom time. To this end, during the last 2 years of participation in the Academy, I demonstrated specific approaches, such as Morning Message, a unique activity developed to integrate the teaching of reading and writing (Crowell, Kawakami, & Wong, 1986). Students were introduced to ways for ELLs to connect this activity from the usual circle time setting to language and literacy learnings in a broader array of classroom life. I also added an assignment in which students select one article to review other successful approaches teachers have found to welcome linguistic diversity. Students are provided a list of suggested practitioner-based journals known for publishing articles on organizing classrooms to promote multicultural environments and curriculum.

The following excerpts from student-authored observational reports reflect a heightened awareness of objectives that educators of ELL students need to keep in mind. For this assignment, students visited two different preschool sites in Latino neighborhoods and noted the materials in the environment and teacher practices that fostered diversity in all its forms. In addition to the general reporting of the availability of materials and practices that encourage teachers to value languages and cultures, early childhood preservice teachers took the next step and asked questions to supplement their areas of inquiry. The following comments were typical of those found in the observation reports that students submitted after their visitations:

- I scrutinized the classroom libraries for children's books written in minority languages and for dual-language books. I asked if bilingual libraries for parents were available on-site.
- At the two centers I visited, charts and posters were visible in the classroom in both Spanish and English. According to the head teacher, almost all written communication (from school to home) is available in Spanish. I inquired whether translators were present to help monolingual teachers communicate with Spanish-speaking parents and grandparents.

- I observed as children enjoyed ethnic foods during snack and lunchtime, (e.g., pita bread, bean dip, and tacos), and I asked if parents volunteered to prepare family heritage dishes.
- I observed circle time and heard songs and rhymes recited in Spanish by all the children. I looked in the listening centers to see if cassette tapes of children's books and songs were available in Spanish.
- I didn't observe any differences in communication patterns with bilingual children and teachers. I asked the teacher whether special language activities were implemented to develop extended conversation in the dominant language with bilingual children.

Students enjoyed comparing findings from their observations. Their initial fears of not being able to communicate with parents and children were replaced with a "can do" attitude. Prospective teachers learned that young children quickly learn enough English to be able to navigate the classroom. They also became comfortable with children and adults using the child's first language in the classroom. These observations and follow-up classroom discussions, in combination with readings on how to infuse classrooms with culturally sensitive materials, proved to be important tools for equipping and inspiring prospective teachers for their future work with diversity and language.

Once students began to develop their resource projects, they had enough knowledge to create instructional materials tailored to second language learners. Many of their teacher-made resources included matching games such as picture lotto, specifically constructed so that children can join in using nonverbal action. And students spent more time discussing their plans to include illustrated sequential cards, counting games, cutting and pasting activities, and puzzles, activities that afford successful early learning experiences for increased numbers of ELL children. Students not only included titles of multicultural children's books in their suggested resource lists, but they also began to talk about the lack of books that feature second language learners as main characters.

Although attributing changed perspectives to any one particular course is difficult, preservice teachers taking this revised early childhood course showed signs of acquiring the skills needed to honor children's linguistic and cultural heritage. The work submitted in class suggests that they are better prepared than earlier groups for developing an early childhood curriculum and teaching philosophy that supports and affirms children's cultural and linguistic identities and backgrounds.

My goal for early childhood classes is to expose all preservice teachers to the central tenet: effective learning environments may start with a "caring teacher" mindset, but the desirable ending point requires well-trained early childhood teachers who are able to create environments that are representative of the social world of all children and support their ways of making sense of the world. Through my continued participation in the Academy, I am eager to learn more about practical ways teachers have found to welcome linguistic diversity and to develop the distinctive voices of their multilingual students. I plan to investigate early language programs that introduce mono-English speaking children to second languages. Perhaps more concerted efforts need to be made to begin second language learning in the preschool years rather than the upper-elementary and middle-school years. At any rate, it's exciting to be a part of the changing classroom context for children who live in a bilingual reality to one that nurtures both language and cultures. And it is equally satisfying to watch as classrooms become supportive communities in which all children apply their growing knowledge of letter-sound correspondences in meaningful literary contexts.

Second Language Connections in Mathematics Education

When I was approached by the Academy to participate in the program, I believed I was already doing a great deal of diversity work. However, as a result of the meetings and workshops held by the Academy in 2002–2003 and the articles that I had been reading on diversity for my own research agenda, I discovered that my concept of diversity was narrow. I understood diversity in terms of race, ethnicity, gender, sexual orientation, and disability. However, I neglected to understand diversity in terms of language. In particular, language was an oversight because English is my first and only language, and I have had very little experience with non-English speakers.

Being familiar with the Black dialect and participating in code-switching (the ability to adequately use both Standard and non-Standard English) with family and close friends, I understood the power of language to communicate one's thoughts and feelings. I used formal English at work and in public places. However, with my "home girls," I used Black English because it allowed me to express myself more fully in terms that everyone familiar with the dialect understood. Therefore, I thought I could learn more about language diversity and the specific issues that second language learners dealt with on a regular basis.

The Academy further influenced my thinking by inviting several renowned speakers to present papers and talk with the faculty informally about diversity issues. The speakers were excellent and a strong point of the Academy. I learned the meaning of several terms, such as "English as a second language," "English language learners," "second language learners," and "bilingual education," and how these terms have different meanings. In addition, I learned that some states had abolished bilingual education programs for "English-only" programs. In the school district our College of Education serves, I also learned there were a limited number of bilingual education teachers who were fluent in two or more languages to address the needs of a diverse group of students who collectively spoke more than 100 languages. These conditions raised my social consciousness and prompted me to understand the dilemmas of second language learners in terms of critical race theory (CRT; Ladson-Billings, 1998; Rousseau & Tate, 2003).

CRT begins with the premise that racism is the norm in the United States (Ladson-Billings, 1998). There are systemic and institutional forces at work that continue to oppress persons of color. Race becomes a metaphorical way of "referring to and disguising forces, events, classes, and expressions of social decay and economic division" (Morrison, 1992, p. 63). The Academy speakers illuminated this by explaining how accents and other cultural traits impacted ELL students in the context of an economic, political, and social arena such as a classroom or society at large. For example, some L2 students could be treated differently by teachers or those with White (monolingual) privilege because of their limited English or thick accents. The speakers helped me to understand how prejudice can be inflicted on those who speak a second language just as easily as it can be inflicted on those with darker skin tones. More impressive, however, was the message of peace that some speakers brought, especially one speaker from the Middle East who discussed how students of Palestinian and Israeli backgrounds coexisted in one elementary school. Listening to this particular speaker, I realized just how far the United States still needs to come in regard to equity. Everyone does not have equal protection under the law, and everyone cannot pursue life, liberty, and happiness to the same degree.

Persons of color are often marginalized and prevented from the pursuit of happiness because of unequal facilities and lack of opportunity to learn. Extraordinary teachers such as Jaime Escalante and Bob Moses have shown that students of Mexican and African descent, respectively, can learn the mathematics needed to gain access to higher education and high-quality jobs. Although these cases have been documented in California and Mississippi, respectively, the models have not been widely used with minority populations across the United States. Focus has primarily been on standards-based learning, which deals with the use of certain curriculum or teaching practices to improve students' mathematical achievement (Collopy, 2003; Remillard, 1999). Despite current calls to connect mathematics teaching to the culture of the community (Leonard & Dantley, 2005), emphasis on accountability and outcomes that measure achievement based solely on standardized test scores limits the activities that teachers do in their classrooms.

During the summer of 2003, I decided to explore ways to connect the teaching of mathematics to the culture of the students. I changed the syllabus in Teaching Children Mathematics N-6 (MTH ED 462), a graduate-level pedagogy course, by requiring preservice and in-service teachers to write lesson plans that took language and cultural diversity into account. This was the first time I required students to do this. In this particular course, students transformed their lessons to include language diversity in the following ways: (1) translating Arabic numbers into Swahili counting numbers, (2) using diverse children's literature books to reflect on various cultures, and (3) using materials such as tangrams, kites, quilts, and origami to get ideas and mathematical concepts across to students. One student wrote a unit plan about the Japanese contribution to baseball. Another wrote a unit about the African American art of quilting. Some of the books that were considered to give children a glimpse of diverse language and culture included *Sadeko, The Three Little Javelinas, Mufaro's Beautiful Daughters, The Spider Weaver, One Grain of Rice, Two of Everything,* and *Grandfather Tang's Story.*

In addition to the lesson plans, I also changed the reading assignments in MTH ED 462. Journal articles that related to linguistically diverse cultures were included in the course pack. Two of these articles were "Examining language in context: The need for new research and practice paradigms in the testing of English-language learners" (Solano-Flores & Trumbull, 2003) and "Culturally relevant mathematics teaching in a Mexican American context" (Gutstein, Lipman, Hernández, & de los Reyes, 1997). In the Solano-Flores and Trumbull article, the authors find that assessment commonly confounds the language skills of students with their academic aptitudes and contend that existing approaches to testing ELLs do not ensure equitable and valid outcomes (Solano-Flores & Trumbull, 2003).

In the second article, Gutstein and colleagues (1997) build on Ladson-Billings' (1994) theory of culturally relevant teaching and apply it to mathematics teaching in a Mexican immigrant community. The authors found that teachers made connections to mathematics and social activism. Two teachers, in particular, helped prepare students to be leaders of their people and society. Moreover, teachers built on students' first language as a means of empowering them and as a way to promote cultural excellence and biculturalism.

In addition to these readings, students had to write a precultural and postcultural autobiography. This assignment requires students to write about their lives in terms of their views of mathematics, culture, and their intersections. They write an autobiography at the beginning of the course and a revised one at the end of the course. The initial version of the cultural biography assignment revealed some prospective teachers' lack of understanding about language and culture and their connection to mathematics equity and access. In reading their work, I learned there was some resistance from students around the issue of diversity (Leonard & Dantley, 2005). One preservice teacher wrote, "I am tired of hearing diversity mentioned in all of my classes."

I also learned some of my students believed mathematics is acultural. Another preservice teacher said: "Math is math, period! How can a link be made between culture and math?" Mathematics was seen by some as acquiring the procedural knowledge needed to carry out operations and not as an invitation to engage in higher-order thinking skills and decision-making relative to culture (Blagmon & Murray, 2004). Moreover, I learned that some of my students adhered to a deficit model for teaching minority students (Ladson-Billings, 1998), which focuses on the skills that teachers perceive students lack instead of the mathematics they need to succeed in life. Another prospective teacher wrote, "I believe that some groups are simply not as intelligent as others. It is clear by standardized test scores that certain students simply cannot learn." Sadly, this in-service teacher worked in a classroom with ELLs. However, other preservice teachers were less resistant and more supportive of the notion that mathematics and culture were not mutually exclusive. One student remarked, "It is only natural that children with different backgrounds will have different learning styles, and these differences should be investigated and documented."

With this initial data about preservice and in-service teachers' understanding in my class, I proceeded to include specific readings and discussions about the connections of mathematics to culture and language throughout the semester. This proved to be challenging and rewarding for me and my students. After the class read an article about issues of culture and mathematics by Malloy and Malloy (1998), some preservice teachers understood how cultural barriers contributed to inequities in education whereas others did not fully understand the ramifications of culture and race as it related to learning mathematics. One student stated, "A person's culture is part of everything they do, including mathematics." However, another student failed to see how her Jewish culture impacted her learning of mathematics. Yet, mathematics is used in a particular way to define Jewish culture, such as observing the Sabbath on the 7th day of the week or lighting candles for a certain number of days during Chanukah. Even in a small way, rituals and experiences such as these contribute to an understanding of number and numeracy in a young child.

The connections became more apparent for my class when they read multicultural literature books and additional articles (Leonard & Guha, 2002; Strutchens, 2002) that linked children's literature with mathematics. The postautobiographies revealed a change in some preservice teachers' attitudes about culture, language, and mathematics. Examples of these are found in two preservice teachers' reflection papers:

Excerpt 1

In order to make learning more pertinent to a diverse class, teachers must filter the information to their students through their cultural frames of reference. Teachers must establish challenging and relevant expectations that are developed through meaningful activities that reflect students' backgrounds. For example, in a math class on geometry, incorporating patterns from African kente cloth or Mexican pottery makes the content more meaningful to students represented by those cultural groups. Another teaching practice could be including culturally relevant literature in math lessons. By using themes that are reflected in students' cultures, we empower them by affirming their backgrounds and experiences (Irvine & Armento, 2001).

Excerpt 2

Cultural diversity can be addressed in the classroom in all academic areas, including mathematics. For example, because mathematical situations are often embedded in the social and cultural contexts provided by literature, children's multicultural literature is the perfect medium for including culture-related activities in mathematics lessons (Strutchens, 2002). Thus mathematics can be used as a tool in exposing students to cultures other than their own. In addition, by including aspects of the students' culture in mathematical problems, students and teachers are able to value the culture of community; for framing mathematical problems in a cultural context exposes students to problem solving from many perspectives (Leonard & Guha, 2002). Hence, mathematics, as well as all academic areas, can be utilized to promote cultural awareness and sensitivity in the classroom.

While I believe that the aforementioned activities, such as reading multicultural literature, reading and discussing articles about diverse language learners, and writing cultural autobiographies, are a good first step, they only begin to scratch the surface in making second language connections in mathematics classrooms. When prospective teachers come together to learn about their differences and to interact in ways that enhance understanding to work against racism, classism, elitism, and so on, we can foster a climate of peace and mutual respect. This ideal is captured by a third preservice teacher who wrote the following statement in a reflection paper:

Excerpt 3

It is very important for all teachers to understand that multicultural diversity in the classroom is not a *surface* activity. In other words, it's not enough to bring in chopsticks when the Chinese New Year rolls around, talk about Dr. Martin Luther King for the months of January and February, to talk to a Native American storyteller in November, and put up shamrocks and talk about leprechauns in March. Learning about the children you teach and the people with whom you share this country is a lifelong endeavor. It should be approached with zeal and enthusiasm— when it is, everyone becomes engaged in an educational experience that will last for a lifetime. [Emphasis added]

Because of the discourse that emerged around the topic of multiculturalism in mathematics education, I have included articles on culture, culturally relevant teaching, and language diversity in all of my graduate education courses in mathematics education since 2003. One of the ways I integrate culture and language diversity into mathematics is through problem solving. Students project their own culture and worldview onto the problems they solve (Solano-Flores & Trumbull, 2003). Children's literature books provide an excellent resource to help bridge the connection between culture and problem solving. I continue to add new books to my collection to emphasize this point. In addition to expanding my syllabus to include issues of language diversity in my mathematics methods course, I plan to address the issue as part of my scholarship by researching cultural relevance and computer-assisted instruction. Plans are underway to examine the use of culture and language in learning mathematics and science among Latino and African American students. Mathematics can only become a universal language when everyone is empowered to use it to improve their lot in life. Inherently, dismantling the master's house can only be done with the master's tools (Audre Lorde [as cited in Ladson-Billings, 1998]). Those tools include mathematics.

Linguistic Diversity in the Social Studies

The field of social studies has a long tradition of focusing on issues of diversity, globalism, and culture. In fact, shortly after the creation of the National Council for the Social Studies (NCSS) in 1924, one of its early leaders, Rachel Davis DuBois, spearheaded the intercultural education movement in the Northeastern United States. DuBois' goal, beginning in the 1930s, was to create a better sense of cultural awareness and valuing of differences through school initiatives (DuBois, 1984; Montalto, 1982). In the 1970s, another leader of cultural understanding emerged: James Banks (1975). His important works in ethnic studies and social studies education promote a pedagogy of understanding cultural differences. However, so far little attention has been paid to linguistic diversity in social studies.

The emphasis on diversity and cultural awareness as a foundation of social studies make it an important subject area through which to teach about and explore linguistic diversity and support the education of ELLs. Such an approach, while worthwhile, can be complicated by the discourse use and the sensitive aspects of the content. For one thing, social studies instruction can present additional challenges. As Jones, Pang, and Rodríguez (2001) point out, "In terms of social studies, students must learn not just the content knowledge but also the oral and written discourse features of the social sciences if they are to attain the level of competency they need at the high school and college level" (p. 40; see also Delpit [1988]). Heath (1996) explains that working with linguistically diverse students is "further compounded by having to address issues related to social awareness, prejudice, and peer acceptance among the students in the process of implementing the curriculum" (p. 106). Nonetheless, social studies teachers have many opportunities, due to the nature of this subject area's content, to teach to and for linguistic diversity.

As a member of the Academy during the 2002–2003 school year, I sought to explore how to incorporate linguistic diversity issues into the graduate elementary social studies pedagogy courses I taught. Thus, I perused the literature on the topic. My search for studies on linguistic diversity in the social studies turned up little, which surprised me, given what I viewed as the natural fit between the content area and ELL issues.[3] Most of what I located in the key national social studies journals entailed suggestions for teachers on teaching to linguistic diversity, which included oral history projects, the use of video technology, and direct language instruction (DeCoker, 1989; Heath, 1996; Milligan & Ruff, 1990; Olmedo, 1996). While these strategies appear to be useful, more empirical research in this area is needed.

For the remainder of this section, I reflect on my self-directed project as a member of the Academy. We were asked to focus on one course to explore issues in linguistic diversity. I chose my graduate elementary course, since I feel this course is the most fully developed in my repertoire. Each class typically has twenty-five students, most of whom are already in elementary school classrooms as long-term substitutes, full-time teachers, or literacy interns. In my discussion below, I reflect on a moment of insight related to a paper I assigned my students.

Many challenges face those who instruct preservice and in-service teachers in social studies methods, issues, and curricula. In my graduate elementary education courses, my greatest obstacle is convincing prospective teachers that social studies is indeed an important subject. I am not alone in this quest. Social studies scholarship documents the common barriers in teaching social studies at the elementary level that include lack of time in an overburdened curriculum; an increasing emphasis on literacy, numeracy, and science skills; and standardized tests that reinforce the importance of teaching these subjects (Stanley, 2001). Nonetheless, I believe I am successful when

I make the case that social studies content is found in every dimension of the school curriculum, explicit and hidden, and is linked in an integral way to reading, writing, listening, and speaking. That is, social studies topics such as culture, families, change over time, self-growth, and communities are enduring themes in literacy and oracy instruction at the elementary level.[4]

If we were to continue this line of thinking, we would come to see that social studies necessarily bring language and literacy out of the realm of individual growth and development and into the arena of the social and interactive. We do not learn another language to use it with ourselves, but to communicate with others. Therefore, linguistic diversity becomes an integral part of social studies, because we need to acknowledge and understand others' and our own different types of speech, vernacular, colloquialisms, and culture. We need to appreciate linguistic diversity in order to best become social and civic beings. Yet, this is not as easy as it may appear, given the history of dissent around language diversity issues in this country. As Portland school teacher Linda Christensen (1994) reminds us, "Grammar [is typically viewed as] an indication of class and cultural background in the United States and ... there is a bias against people who don't use language 'correctly'" (p. 142).

The ways that two students responded to a writing assignment serve to illustrate the direct action elementary school teachers can take to highlight the importance of linguistic diversity awareness and respect for all students in social studies lessons. I asked my students to choose a children's storybook to review and critique in terms of its use in teaching social studies concepts and themes. I directed my students to use the Ten Thematic Strands of the NCSS as a guide. The year I became a member of the Academy I modified the task by encouraging my students to consider linguistic diversity when preparing their brief papers. This was an optional part of the assignment.

For the course session where we discussed students' projects, I drew on readings that dealt with the importance of language and an appreciation of linguistic diversity in social studies. We read Paul Skilton-Sylvester's (1994) journal article "Elementary School Curricula and Urban Transformation" and an article in the journal *Theory Into Practice* titled "Social Studies in the Elementary Classroom: Culture Matters" (Jones et al., 2001). Skilton-Sylvester (1994) writes that in his third-grade classroom he "wanted to raise my students' awareness of the role that language differences play in social situations, but … do so in a way that did not demean the language style used in their homes" (p. 317). In so doing, he worked with his students to create two charts of Standard and non-Standard English to which the students added phrases throughout the school year.

In our discussion, I also employed three principles from critical theory outlined by Jones and colleagues (2001) that speak to linguistic diversity: status equalization, bicultural affirmation, and codes of power. Language use plays a central role in each of these three. The valuing of different languages had an effect in Skilton-Sylvester's classroom of equalizing the status placed on languages. In his classroom, the students learned that Black Vernacular English and Standard English were both valued and used in certain contexts and not others. Bicultural affirmation resulted when children learned that the various languages and vernaculars they spoke were valued. His students also learned about the importance of using certain types of language in certain situations in order to achieve success socially and economically.

One in-service teacher in my course, Kendra, decided to use a book by Leventhal (1999) called *What Is Your Language?* Kendra, in taking on my challenge, addressed the concept that people speak different languages in her paper. More importantly, she also later taught this lesson in her second-grade classroom. She identified five of the NCSS's Thematic Strands that she felt addressed linguistic diversity: culture; people, places, and environments; individual development and identity; individuals, groups, and institutions; and global connections.

Kendra's central goal in using *What Is Your Language?* in her classroom was to heighten her students' awareness of linguistic diversity and to teach them to value different languages (she teaches early childhood children). Therefore, the lesson she designed was for all students, not just the ELLs. Her activities included having the students repeat words in various languages after her and thinking about which language sounds appealed to them. This activity removed language from the ownership usually attributed to it (as Spanish is María's language, and English is Tom's language) and helped her students understand that languages sound different and that they might think about speaking another language. As Skilton-Sylvester (1994) taught his students about language use in different contexts, the activity Kendra designed works in a similar way by helping facilitate discussions among children about the language choices they make in the social studies curriculum.

When analyzing the next paper, I discovered it indirectly addressed issues of status equalization and bicultural affirmation discussed in class. Another student, Candace, was working as a literacy intern in the city during the semester she was in my methods course.[5] Candace did not need much prodding to prepare her paper on a children's book and incorporate linguistic diversity issues. She used this assignment as an opportunity to reflect on something that had happened with her second grade ELL students. Candace read a book she had purchased the previous year but had not yet used, *My Dog Is Lost,* by Ezra Jack Keats and Pat Cherr (1999), which is written in Spanish and English. Candace, a native English speaker, had read the book and emphasized the social studies themes of notions of difference, the importance of friends, and the definition of community in addition to working on reading skills. She did not anticipate her students' powerful response to this book:

> As I read it, I do recall the look on my ELL students' faces when I said these Spanish words. They just flipped! Suddenly, my Spanish speaking children became very knowledgeable, *and then* we all had to learn what the same words meant in the native languages of all the other students!![emphasis added]

Candace took a risk in letting her students teach her and others about Spanish and other languages, and she was able to involve all students in the discussion. The lessons of difference, friendship, and community took on new meaning through this discussion. Her insight, unlike Kendra's, was less a part of the design of her lesson and more a result of her ability to recognize what is colloquially known among educators as "the teachable moment." Candace's actions equalized the status in her classroom as it affirmed the culture and language of her ESOL students by her willingness to learn and speak their language and let them teach her.

The papers of Kendra and Candace help reveal the importance of attending to linguistic diversity in the social studies curriculum. Additionally, the fact that both my students taught lessons based on this assignment suggests the positive impact that the readings on this topic and related class discussions had on their teaching practice. In our increasingly diverse classrooms, teachers need to be more aware, educated, and sensitive to linguistic diversity. In so doing, they emphasize the central goals in the social studies: respect for diversity and civic and social competence (Woyshner, 2003).

The scholarship in social studies, although it has been inclusive of multicultural education, has yet to fully consider issues of linguistic diversity. As these examples show, myriad opportunities exist in the social studies curriculum to address, support, and nurture linguistic diversity. The dearth of scholarship is surprising given social studies' focus on culture, diversity, citizenship, and multiculturalism. The danger lies in rendering students of color and ELLs invisible in their own classrooms. Likewise, students who are English-only speakers can learn much through the activities described in this section.

The 2 years I participated in the Academy has influenced my own practice. Linguistic diversity has become part of my teaching repertoire. The idea remains in my syllabus as one of the teaching objectives of each course. I continue to raise the issue with students in class discussions about difference and diversity and when we seek out resources that support teachers' awareness of linguistic diversity issues. However, I want to explore additional questions that have emerged from the Academy for me in social studies, such as how to support L2 learners through the challenges of reading primary sources and ways to extend preservice teachers' understanding of Black Vernacular English. With increased sensitivity to linguistic diversity in the social studies, all students may come to realize the goals of civic and social education.

Conclusions

In response to the dearth of scholarly discussions about language in teacher education, the authors of this chapter documented the perspectives of a group of faculty who have integrated linguistic diversity issues into subject area pedagogy courses in an urban teacher education program. The effort of the Academy revealed that preparing teachers for linguistic diversity demands a comprehensive approach that designs specialized courses on language difference and infuses the study of language across all pedagogy courses. Our work exposed an emerging but insightful research literature that discusses the knowledge base all teachers should develop about the kind of language use and development important for ELLs to be successful in schools (Valdés et al., 2005). In addition, we identified those elements that seem to make a difference in edifying the knowledge base of future educators related to language and content learning in mainstream classrooms (Coady, Hamann, Harrington, Pacheco, Pho, & Yedling, 2003).

The authors contend that a key step in this endeavor is to build the capacity of professors to integrate issues of linguistic diversity across the entire teacher education curriculum. Our project exemplifies how interdisciplinary collaboration can work to educate preservice and in-service teachers in addressing the language and content learning needs of ELLs. The documentary account presented in the second part of the chapter describes what happened when a group of faculty from different disciplines came together to gain knowledge about language difference and its impact on learning across different content areas. The perspectives of the faculty discussed here point to a complex process of personal and professional change that shaped curricular infusion at our teacher preparation program. We depict our process through five components that reflect progressive learning as well as intricacy in the infusion process:

- *Heightened awareness and change in attitude.* As evident from essays written by Academy members and their changed syllabi, professors increased their sensitivity and understanding about language difference issues. Faculty specified that they gained knowledge about terminology, theories, best practices, and debates relevant to teaching about language use and development. As members of the Academy became aware of their own cultural and linguistic identities, they also faced some personal biases and narrow worldviews. We realized that this level of change is crucial to more in-depth and continued transformation of courses. In the past 3 years, this level of change has been experienced at different points by all Academy members, and they discuss it as a sign of personal and professional growth. As one professor stated,

  My attitude has been challenged. This is not an area of "special issues" but rather a dimension of operating a classroom that is truly speaking to social justice, priorities, values and language respect that will impact the next generation. Clearly, the attitude on my part will hopefully impact the attitude that characterizes the young teacher-to-be. I must infuse within the topical discussions these elements of sound pedagogy which embellish the learning of the multilingual student.

- *Add assignments in the syllabus that required prospective teachers to consider language diversity in their instruction.* The changed syllabi of members of the Academy included specific activities that for the first time required preservice and in-service teachers to ponder their own linguistic self. The inclusion of assignments such as adaptation of lessons and identification of multicultural children's literature guided prospective teachers to consider ways of creating the best learning environment for ELL students. These assignments constitute beginning steps toward the integration of linguistic diversity into pedagogy courses. However, the emergent quality of this level of infusion is revealed through the lack of connections between assignments to the ongoing themes and to other instructional activities within courses. One possible reason for the use of the "added assignments" approach to change was that participants had a short time participating in the Academy. Typically, this approach was used when faculty had participated in the Academy the least (1 year or less). Interviews suggest that a lack of resources specific to content areas or a lack of exposure to the few resources available might have also contributed to this more-superficial implementation of infusion. Faculty who used this approach pointed out that they found a scarcity of scholarly discussions about teaching ELLs in their discipline (i.e., math, social studies). It was also noted that, given time limitations, their search for resources was not comprehensive enough. The overall lack of scholarly sources on the exploration of language and content integration and its infusion into teacher preparation is confirmed by experts in the field of second language (Téllez & Waxman, 2004; Valdés et al., 2005). However, recent publications in the content area of science (i.e., Lee, 2004, 2005; Lee & Avalos, 2002; Stoddard, Pinal, & Latzke, 2002) and pedagogical discussions for working with ELLs in mainstream classrooms (Adamson, 2005; Gibbons, 2002) suggests a promising turn of attention to this field.

- *Make linguistic diversity a central theme of courses by including it in the course objectives and through required class readings, discussions, and assessment.* This more thorough treatment of infusion was evident in syllabi from professors who have participated in the Academy the longest (between 2 and 3 years) and professors in fields that are giving increased attention to this topic (i.e., multicultural education and early childhood). Some faculty identified multiple sources in the literature that discuss research-based instruction in specific pedagogical areas (i.e., early childhood, literacy) and others explored language difference in light of known theories (i.e., CRT). This component was also visible in syllabi that met two or more of the criteria for infusion used in this project. Faculty's perspectives reveal this level of change to provide a more cohesive and structured approach to infusion, which might be more helpful in preparing all teachers to work effectively in linguistically diverse educational contexts. Preservice and in-service teachers can perceive the importance of this topic in learning the pedagogy of a particular content area because they see it as a main objective in the course, they have to critically reflect on it through a variety of interconnected class discussions and assignments, it is modeled for them by faculty, and they observe it in the field placement settings they visit. The documentary accounts indicate that this level of infusion helps prospective teachers recognize key connections between this topic and specific content areas beyond the superficial discussions of multiculturalism in education. They are presented with opportunities to problematize their own knowledge about language and its implications for developing self-identity, for recognizing the language demands of particular curricula, and for ultimately facilitating the academic learning of ELLs. The fact that a few of the in-service teachers taking courses with Academy members carried this newly acquired knowledge into their own teaching practice suggests the efficacy potential in reaching this level of infusion.

- *Design research projects that help professors explore questions related to linguistic diversity in different pedagogy courses.* An advanced level of faculty involvement in the infusion process is suggested when Academy members reflect on their own questions and design investigations to answer them. Documentary accounts ascertain that faculty members want to further explore the connections of language diversity to teaching and learning in their different disciplines. Academy members want to investigate issues of language loss, language challenges of reading primary sources, ways to extend preservice teachers' understanding of Black Vernacular English, examine the use of culture and language in learning mathematics and science among Latino and African American students, and effective early language programs for monolingual children. They also have started to infuse other courses they teach. Faculty perspectives explored here strongly suggest, then, that conditions for the long-term sustenance of infusing this topic into teacher education are best when teaching and scholarship influence one another. Thus, we believe there is much hope for this to happen in our institution as a result of professors' participation in the Academy.

- *Have faculty share their experience of infusion.* Dissemination of learning is a key part of scholarship and curriculum transformation. Faculty in the Academy have met every month and now meet once a semester to share insights about educating prospective teachers in language diversity. They have also presented at professional conferences to share their learning with colleagues outside our university. Through publishing and presentations we can share critical knowledge about the infusion process and dialogue with a wider teacher education audience. Although the documentary account about the Academy is not presented as a program model, some of the lessons learned can be shared with other teacher education programs that want to pursue similar goals. Thus far, we have discovered that in order to effectively plan for curricular change and faculty professional development, programs should examine the attitudes, interest, and curiosity of faculty; the knowledge base faculty already have about linguistic diversity and infusion across the curriculum; the resources available to meet, learn together, and collaborate; the institutional support for sustained comprehensive curricular change; and the scope of the intended change (i.e., general education courses, pedagogy courses, field experience courses).

Implications for Further Research

Further scrutiny of infusion in these classrooms is needed to establish sustainability of the new knowledge base and identify factors that impede or facilitate it. Equally important is to differentiate among those activities that are more effective in transmitting the new knowledge to preservice teachers. To this end, future research should be conducted to observe the pedagogy courses and document the revised practices implemented by professors. Finally, the efficacy of the Academy efforts could be identified by establishing its long-term effects. This can be done by documenting the learning trajectory of preservice teachers from when they take methods courses to after graduation, when they teach in their own classrooms. Important then will be to explore how recent graduates, who took these courses, implement the learned best practices in their own linguistically diverse classrooms and what is needed to further support their efforts.

We expect that the work of the Academy will facilitate the institutionalization of infusion practices to prepare all educators to work with linguistically diverse students at our university. With this in mind, the Academy wants to expand and refine the dialogue and collaborative work among faculty. In addition to other instructors teaching pedagogy courses, it will be important to invite professors teaching general education as well as field experience courses to join the Academy. The scope of the Academy's discussions should also be expanded to explore: (1) ways to communicate with linguistically diverse parents and their community to improve education, (2) the impact of language difference on assessment and the need to redesign the assessment agenda in schools, and (3) key information for the preparation and professional development of school administrators who work in linguistically diverse contexts.

The Academy members have learned that to achieve higher levels of excellence, prospective teachers now need several types of direct experiences that demonstrate how to welcome linguistic diversity in their classrooms and improve their educational opportunities. Preservice and in-service teachers also need support in developing a professional teaching philosophy that captures the best thinking in teaching and learning in order to guide their decisions in the linguistically diverse classroom. The faculty perspectives presented in this chapter argue that the skills needed for integrating multicultural and multilingual content into the curricula need to be interwoven throughout a teacher education program for lasting change to occur.

References

Adamson, H. D. (2005). *Language minority students in American schools: An education in English*. Mahwah, NJ: Lawrence Earlbaum Associates.

Adger, C. T., Snow, C., & Christian, D. (Eds.). (2002). *What teachers need to know about language*. McHenry, IL: Center for Applied Linguistics and Delta Systems Co.

American Federation of Teachers. (1999). *Teaching reading IS rocket science: What expert teachers of reading should know and be able to do*. Washington, DC: AFT Educational Issues Publications.

American Federation of Teachers. (2004). Bilingual education 30 years later. *AFT on Campus, 3*(6), 6.

Anstrom, K. (2004). Introduction. In K. Anstrom, J. Glazier, P. Sanchez, V. Sardi, P. Schwallie-Giddis, & P. Tate, *Preparing all educators for student diversity: Lessons for higher education* (pp. vii–xvii). Washington, DC: Institute for Education Policy Studies, Graduate School of Education and Human Development, The George Washington University.

Au, K. H. (1993*). Literacy instruction in multicultural settings*. Fort Worth, TX: Harcourt Brace Jovanovich.

Banks, J. A. (1975). *Teaching strategies for ethnic studies.* Boston, MA: Allyn & Bacon.

Banks, J. A. (1998). *Multiethnic education: Theory and practice.* Second Edition. Boston: Allyn and Bacon.

Beykont, Z.F. (Ed.) (2002). The power of culture: Teaching across language differences. Cambridge, MA: Harvard Education Publishing Group.

Blagmon, J. L., & Murray, N. M. (2004, April). *Connections and conflicts between math methods courses and classroom practice.* Paper presented at the National Council of Teachers of Mathematics Research Panel, Philadelphia, PA.

Brisk, M. E., & Harrington, M. H. (2000). *Literacy and bilingualism: A handbook for all teachers.* Mahwah, NJ: Lawrence Erlbaum.

Bristor, V. J., Pelaez, G. M., & Crawley, S. (2000). An integrated elementary education/ESOL teacher preparation program. *Action in Teacher Education, 22*(2), 25–32.

Christensen, L. (1994). Whose standard? Teaching Standard English. In B. Bigelow & B. Peterson (Eds.), *Rethinking our classrooms: Teaching for equity and justice* (pp. 142–145). Milwaukee, WI: Rethinking Schools.

CNN.com. (2005). Report: High school exit exams pressuring limited-English students. Retrieved August 2005, from www.cnn.com/2005/education/08/16/graduation.exams.ap/index.html

Coady, M., Hamann, E. T., Harrington, M., Pacheco, M., Pho, S., & Yedling, J. (Eds.). (2003). *Claiming opportunities: A handbook for improving education for English language learners through comprehensive school reform.* Providence, RI: The Education Alliance at Brown University, Northeast and Islands Regional Laboratory (LAB).

Cochran-Smith, M. (2003). Learning and unlearning: The education of teacher educators. *Teaching and Teacher Education, 19,* 5–28.

Collopy, R. (2003). Curriculum materials as a professional development tool: How a mathematics textbook affected two teachers' learning. *Elementary School Journal, 103,* 287.

Crawford, L. W. (1993). *Language and literacy learning in multicultural classrooms.* Boston, MA: Allyn & Bacon.

Crowell, D. C., Kawakami, A. J., & Wong, J. L. (1986). Emerging literacy: Reading-writing experiences in a kindergarten classroom. *The Reading Teacher, 40,* 144–149.

Cummins, J. (1986). *Empowering minority students: A framework for intervention.* Harvard Educational Review. (Reprint in Minami and Kennedy 1991)

Darling-Hammond, L., & Youngs, P. (2002). Defining highly qualified teachers: What does scientifically based research actually tell us? *Educational Researcher, 31*(9), 13–25.

DeCoker, G. (1989, November). Bringing foreign languages into the social studies classroom. *The Social Studies,* 219–224.

Delpit, L. (1988). The silenced dialogue: Power and pedagogy in educating other people's children. *Harvard Educational Review, 58*(3) 280–298.

Derman-Sparks, L. (1989). *Anti-bias curriculum: Tools for empowering your children.* Washington, DC: National Association for the Education of Young Children.

Dillard, C. B. (1997). Placing student language, literacy, and culture at the center of teacher education reform. In J. King, E. R. Hollins, & W. C. Hayman (Eds.), *Preparing teachers for cultural diversity* (pp. 40–52). New York: Teachers College Press.

DuBois, R. D., with K. Okorodudu. (1984). *All this and something more: Pioneering in intercultural education: A biography.* Bryn Mawr, PA: Dorrance.

Fillmore, L. W., & Snow, C. E. (2002). What teachers need to know about language. In C. T. Adger, C. Snow, & D. Christian (Eds.), *What teachers need to know about language* (pp. 7–54). McHenry, IL: Center for Applied Linguistics and Delta Systems Co.

Friedman, A. A. (2002). What we would have liked to know: Preservice teachers' perspectives on effective teacher preparation. In Z. F. Beykont (Ed.), *The power of culture: Teaching across language difference* (pp. 193–218). Cambridge, MA: Harvard Education Publishing Group.

Gándara, P., & Maxwell-Jolly, J. (2003, November). *Critical issues in developing the teacher corps for English learners.* Paper prepared for the National Invitational Conference on Improving Teacher Quality for English Language Learners. U.S. Department of Education and the Laboratory for Students Success, Mid-Atlantic Regional Educational Laboratory at Temple University, Arlington, VA.

García, E. E. (2001). *Hispanic education in the United States: Raices y alas.* Lanham, MD: Rowman and Littlefield Publishers.

Gersten, R. & Jiménez, R.T. (1998). Modulating instruction for language minority students. In E. J. Kameenui & D. W. Carnine (Eds.), *Effective teaching strategies that accommodate diverse learners.* Columbus, OH: Merrill.

Gibbons, P. (2002). *Scaffolding language, Scaffolding learning: Teaching second language learners in the mainstream classroom.* Portsmouth, NH: Heinemann.

Gollnick, D. M., & Chinn, P. C. (2005). *Multicultural education in a pluralistic society* (6th ed.). New York, NY: Maxwell Macmillan International.

Gutstein, E., Lipman, P., Hernández, P., & de los Reyes, R. (1997). Culturally relevant mathematics teaching in a Mexican American context. *Journal for Research in Mathematics Education, 28*(6), 709–737.

Hamayan, E. V. (1990). Preparing mainstream classroom teachers to teach potentially English proficient students. *Proceedings of the first research symposium on limited English proficient students' issues.* Washington, DC: Office of Bilingual Education and Minority Language Affairs.

Heath, I. A. (1996). The social studies video project: A holistic approach for teaching linguistically and culturally diverse students. *The Social Studies, 87*(3), 106–112.

Irvine, J. J., & Armento, B. J. (2001). *Culturally responsive teaching: Lesson planning for elementary and middle grades.* New York: McGraw-Hill Companies, Inc.

Jones, E. V., Pang, V. O., & Rodríguez, J. L. (2001). Social studies in the elementary classroom: Culture matters. *Theory Into Practice, 40*(1), 35–41.

Keats, E. J., & Cherr, P. (1999). *My dog is lost.* New York, NY: Puffin.

King, J., Hollins, E. R., & Hayman, W. C. (Eds.). (1997). *Preparing teachers for cultural diversity.* New York: Teachers College Press.

Ladson-Billings, G. (1994). *The dreamkeepers: Successful teachers of African American children.* San Francisco, CA: Jossey-Bass.

Ladson-Billings, G. (1998). Just what is critical race theory, and what's it doing in a nice field like education? *Qualitative Studies in Education, 11*(1), 7–24.

Ladson-Billings, G. (2000). Fighting for our lives: Preparing teachers to teach African American students. *Journal of Teacher Education, 52,* 206–214.

Lee, O. (2004). Teacher change in beliefs and practices in science and literacy instruction with English language learners. *Journal of Research in Science Teaching, 41*(1), 65–93.

Lee, O. (2005). Science education and student diversity: Synthesis and research agenda. *Journal of Education for Students Placed at Risk, 10*(4), 431–440.

Lee, O., & Avalos, M. (2002). Promoting science instruction and assessment for English language learners. *Electronic Journal of Science Education, 7*(2), 99–122.

Leonard, J., & Dantley, S. (2005). Breaking through the ice: Dealing with issues of diversity in mathematics and science education courses. In A. J. Rodriguez & R. Kitchen (Eds.), *Preparing prospective mathematics and science teachers to teach for diversity: Promising strategies for transformative action* (pp. 87–117). Mahweh, NJ: Lawrence Erlbaum.

Leonard, J., & Guha, S. (2002). Creating cultural relevance in teaching and learning mathematics. *Teaching Children Mathematics, 9*(2), 114–118.

Leventhal, D. (1999). *What is your language?* New York, NY: Scholastic.

Malloy, C. E., & Malloy, W. M. (1998). Issues of culture in mathematics teaching and learning. *The Urban Review, 30*(3), 245–257.

Menken, K., & Antunez, B., (2001). An overview of the preparation and certification of teachers working with limited English proficient students. Washington, DC, National Clearinghouse of Bilingual Education. Retrieved March 1, 2004, from http://www.ericsp.org/pages/digests/ncbe.pdf

Milligan, J. L., & Ruff, T. P. (1990, September). A linguistic approach to social studies vocabulary development. *The Social Studies,* 218–220.

Minaya-Rowe, L. (2003). *Training teachers through their students' first language.* Paper prepared for the National Invitational Conference on Improving Teacher Quality for English Language Learners. U.S. Department of Education and the Laboratory for Students Success, the Mid-Atlantic Regional Educational Laboratory at Temple University, Arlington, VA.

Montalto, N. V. (1982). *A history of the intercultural education movement, 1924–1941.* New York, NY: Garland Publishing.

Morrison, T. (1992). *Playing in the dark: Whiteness and the literacy imagination.* Cambridge, MA: Harvard University Press.

MSNBC News. (2004). *U. S. 2050: Asians, Hispanics will triple.* Retrieved March 18, 2004, from http://www.msnbc.msn.com/id/4547427

National Association for the Education of Young Children (1995). Responding to linguistically and cultural diversity: Recommendations for effective early childhood education. Position Statement. Washington, DC: Author.

National Council for the Social Studies. (1994). *Expectations of excellence.* Washington, DC: Author.

Nevárez, A. A., Sanford, J. S., & Parker, L. (1997). Do the right thing: Transformative multicultural education in teacher preparation. *Journal for a Just and Caring Education, 3*(2), 160–179.

Nieto, S. (2000). *Affirming diversity: A sociopolitical context of multicultural education.* (3rd ed.). White Plains, NY: Longman.

Nieto, S. (2003). Challenging current notions of "highly qualified teachers" through work in a teachers' inquiry group. *Journal of Teacher Education, 54*(5), 386–398.

Olmedo, I. M. (1996). Creating contexts for studying history with students learning English. *The Social Studies, 87*(1), 39–43.

Pang, V. O., Anderson, M. G., & Martuza, V. (1997). Removing the mask of academia: Institutions collaborating in the struggle for equity. In J. King, E. R. Hollins, & W.C. Hayman (Eds.), *Preparing teachers for cultural diversity* (pp. 53–72). New York: Teachers College Press.

Pennsylvania Department of Education. (2001a). *Basic education circulars (Pennsylvania code)*. Retrieved March 1, 2004, from http://www.pde.state.pa.us

Pennsylvania Department of Education. (2001b). *Pennsylvania accountability system*. Retrieved March 1, 2004, from http://www.pde.state.pa.us

Pennsylvania Department of Education. (2003). *Pennsylvania accountability system: About the State Report Card 2003*. Retrieved March 1, 2004, from http://www.pde.state.pa.us

Pennsylvania Department of Education. (2004). *LEP counts by school 2002–2003*. Retrieved March 1, 2004, from http://www.pde.state.pa.us

President's Advisory Commission on Educational Excellence for Hispanic Americans. (2003). From risk to opportunity: Fulfilling the educational needs of Hispanic Americans in the 21st century. *The Final Report of the President's Advisory Commission on Educational Excellence for Hispanic Americans*. Washington, DC: Author.

Quintanar-Sarallana, R. (1997). Culturally relevant teacher preparation and teachers' perceptions of the language and culture of linguistic minority students. In J. King, E. R. Hollins, & W.C. Hayman (Eds.), *Preparing teachers for cultural diversity* (pp. 40–52). New York, NY: Teachers' College Press.

Remillard, J. (1999). Curriculum materials in mathematics education reform: A framework for examining teachers' curriculum development. *Curriculum Inquiry, 100*(4), 315–341.

Rousseau, C., & Tate, W. F. (2003). No time like the present: Reflecting on equity in school mathematics. *Theory Into Practice, 43*(3), 210–216.

Shapiro, J. P., Sewell, T. E., & DuCette, J. P. (1995). *Reframing diversity in education: Educational leadership for the 21st century*. (W. J. Bailey, Ed.). Lancaster, PA: Technomic Publishing Company.

Skilton-Sylvester, P. (1994). Elementary school curricula and urban transformation. *Harvard Educational Review, 64*(3), 309–331.

Solano-Flores, G., & Trumbull, E. (2003). Examining language in context: The need for new research and practice paradigms in the testing of English-language learners. *Educational Researcher, 32*(2), 3–13.

Stanley, W. B. (2001). *Critical issues in social studies research for the 21st century*. Greenwich, CT: Information Age Publishing.

Stoddard, T. Pinal, A., & Latzke, M. (2002). Integrating inquiry science and language development for English language learners. *Journal of Research in Science Teaching, 39*(8), 664–687.

Strickland, D.S. (1998). Education of African American learners at risk: Finding a better way. In M. G. Optiz (Ed.), *Literacy instruction for culturally and linguistically diverse students* (pp. 71–80). Newark, DE: International Reading Association.

Strutchens, M. E. (2002). Multicultural literature as a context for problem solving: Children and parents learning together. *Teaching Children Mathematics, 8*(8), 448–454.

Tate, W. F. (1995). Returning to the root: A culturally relevant approach to mathematics pedagogy. *Theory into Practice, 34*(3), 166–173.

Téllez, K., & Waxman, H. (2004). *Quality teachers for English language learners: A research synthesis.* Publication Series #2. Laboratory for Students Success, The Mid-Atlantic Regional Educational Laboratory at Temple University, Philadelphia, PA..

Valdés, G., Bunch, G., Snow, C., Lee, C., & Matos, L. (2005). Enhancing the development of students' language. In L. Darling-Hammond & J. Bransford (Eds.), *Preparing teachers for a changing world: What teachers should learn and be able to do* (pp.). San Francisco, CA: Jossey-Bass.

Waxman, H., & Téllez, K. (2004). Publication Series #2. Laboratory for Students Success, The Mid-Atlantic Regional Educational Laboratory at Temple University.

Woyshner, C. (2003). *Social studies: A chapter of the curriculum handbook.* Washington, DC: Association for Supervision and Curriculum Development.

Appendix 12.A: Faculty Linguistic Diversity
Academy Faculty Questionnaire

1. What questions about linguistic diversity would you like to explore in the Academy?
2. What questions do preservice teachers taking your course ask about working with language minority students?
3. What questions do you have about the infusion of issues related to linguistic diversity into your course?
4. What course do you plan to infuse? Which semester?
5. What resources and activities related to linguistic diversity have you used in this course before?
6. What support or resources do you think you will need in order to effectively infuse this course?

Appendix 12.B: Faculty Linguistic Diversity Academy Portfolio Guidelines

The portfolio documenting the infusion process in your course should include:

1. Copy of original syllabus and revised syllabus
2. Copy of handouts related to linguistic diversity given to preservice teachers
3. Sample of preservice teachers work related to linguistic diversity
4. Reflective paper (and relevant documentation from course) discussing the following ideas:
   - original question and assumptions about linguistic diversity
   - original focus of course
   - areas of change in knowledge base and assumptions
   - changes made to course and why
   - tensions, questions, and problems encountered in the infusion process
   - reaction and responses of preservice teachers to the infusion of linguistic diversity issues into the course
   - knowledge acquired through the Academy
   - current question and tensions
   - future changes to course way in which the Academy could assist you in implementing future changes and answering current questions.

Endnotes

1. Some faculty in the teacher education program joined efforts from across our state to advocate for the design of an ESL teacher certification. Before 2002, our state's department of education did not offer any specific guidance on the recruitment and preparation of teachers to work with ELLs and it did not specify minimum standards for certification. After many years of advocacy, the state recently enacted the ESL Program Specialist Certificate and approved our institution as a provider. In the 3 years since the inception of the Academy, through the grant, we designed and piloted three new courses. These courses discuss (1) knowledge of program models and promising pedagogy for educating ELLs, (2) knowledge of sociocultural and political context for language learning and cultural patterns for language, and (3) knowledge of language devel-

opment in the content areas and bilingualism and biliteracy. They are part now part of the ESL Program Specialist Certificate at both undergraduate and graduate levels.

2. Since 2000, Project CAPE has been supported through U.S. Department of Education Title VII and Title III grants. The three main goals of the teacher training grant are: (1) expand the capacity and diversity of the teaching force in urban schools, (2) build the knowledge and skills of bilingual paraprofessionals, and (3) facilitate the development in teaching subject matter knowledge, bilingualism, classroom management, and interpersonal capacities of the participants to promote their role of teachers as agents of change.

   CAPE, guided by a central goal of providing effective preparation of all teachers to work with linguistically diverse students, accomplishes change through a variety of components. First, the project pays for tuition and books for bilingual paraprofessionals toward their completion of an undergraduate or graduate degree in early childhood or elementary education. CAPE students need to complete the regular program requirements in undergraduate or graduate teacher education at our university. Second, CAPE students need to take three additional courses on bilingualism, second language learning, and pedagogy to better equip them as bilingual practitioners. Until recently, these courses were only offered to the students in CAPE. Beginning in the fall of 2004, they became requirements for all teacher education students who want to complete an ESL Program Specialist Certificate. Third, it recruits high-school students into professions in education through Project Path and the Bilingual Young Scholar Summer Academy. Fourth, it acquired a collection of books, videos, and other materials available to faculty and students as resources on language diversity. Fifth, it instituted the Faculty Academy for Linguistic Diversity.

3. I scanned the indices of four major social studies journals: *The History Teacher, Theory and Research in Social Education, The Social Studies,* and *Social Education*.

4. One of the ways to support and encourage preservice teachers to locate social studies themes is to work with the ten thematic strands of the National Council for the Social Studies (NCSS). See NCSS, Expectations of Excellence, Washington, DC, 1994.

5. Literacy internships were designed and funded by the Philadelphia Education Fund to support and increase literacy instruction in elementary classrooms in the Philadelphia schools. Interns worked alongside classroom teachers as part of the Graduate Certification Program at Temple.

Part III

Policy

13

Educational Policy and Linguistic Diversity
A Critical Analysis of Teacher Certification Requirements

Lisa Patel Stevens
Boston College

In education, daily classroom practices are the result of myriad influences, pressures, and innovations that have bearing on teaching and learning. For example, imagine that a secondary science teacher is grading some of her students' papers, including work by students who speak languages other than English and nonstandard varieties of English. In grading their work, the teacher decides to deduct points for students' patterns that differ from Standard English conventions. Is this decision a reflection of mainstream ideology about the "proper," or inherent correctness of Standard English? Is it reflective of a personal professional belief that students must see their work corrected to grown in their fluency in academic English? Is it the result of her school or district's policy around writing and assessment? Or perhaps it is reflective of what this teacher learned or did not learn through her teacher licensure program. Any and all of these factors are possible points of influence upon the daily decision-making found within a classroom. What further complicates the consideration of the influences on language and culture in the classroom is that these influences do not work in isolation from each other. A teacher's own cultural background interplays with teacher education experiences; requirements for certification; and state, district, and school policies, to name just a few possibly idiosyncratic presences at work in the system of beliefs and practices. Given the complex and interrelated nature of these influences, a comprehensive consideration of culturally responsive teaching must consider not just existing research and practices but also policy sources as a potential constraint or support of pedagogy that affirms students' diverse backgrounds. At the same time, no single analysis of influence can consider all of these possible pressures. Although personal proclivities always play significant roles, we can purposefully focus some analytic lenses on another source of influence: policy that influences classroom pedagogy. One such policy source is the requirements that preservice teachers must complete along the road to certification. Encompassed within these requirements are, purportedly, the knowledges, skills, and attitudes toward language and culture that prospective teachers are to explore to then enact these orientations in their classroom pedagogy. As such, the teacher certification requirements offer one location to explore what is influencing and what could possibly differently influence classroom practices with language and culture. To build an agenda for culturally relevant pedagogy in teacher education, one must consider not only what existing research demonstrates as areas of need but also what policies are in place that might address this bank of skills, knowledges, and attitudes. Teacher certification requirements offer one such pressure point—a site where current areas of priority are apparent and also a site that can be adjusted to better meet the needs of linguistically diverse students learning academic English.

Specifically, the requirements for secondary teacher certification are reviewed. This focus is to draw particular attention to an area of Standard English, academic English used in secondary contexts, where the conventions, structures, and semantics offer uniquely challenging linguistic and cultural patterns (e.g., Lemke, 1990). For example, science teachers, just like other teachers, face the challenges of making their curricular objectives accessible and achievable to students in increasingly high-stakes assessment contexts. Therefore, although science has always been a field of English usage marked by complex structures and patterns that have particular meanings in scientific discourse, supporting linguistically diverse students' abilities to navigate these patterns is particularly imperative with the advent of high-stakes assessments determining, among other consequences, funding, promotion through school grades, and high school graduation. The same is true in terms of challenges and uniqueness in the other academic disciplines that characterize secondary education in the United States (Vacca & Vacca, 1999). In this current context, language can and does act as both a potential mediator for access and exclusion.

In this chapter, a critical policy analysis is used to examine what priorities, beliefs, and influences are found in contemporary secondary teacher certification requirements in the United States. A review of certification requirements is provided, followed by a critical analysis of these policies and recommendations for future certification policies.

Educational Policy and Critical Analysis

Policy serves to communicate values (Stone, 1997). Policy analysis, examining the purpose, fruition, and other aspects of policy, runs the gamut from simple cost-benefit analyses to complex questions of inducements, rules, facts, rights, and powers (Edmondson, 2004; Stone, 1997). We can read and interpret policies, such as certification requirements, as a snapshot of contemporary values, priorities, and beliefs toward teachers and children from linguistically and culturally diverse backgrounds and the responsibility of schools to meet their needs within a larger social landscape. The crystallization of values in policy is brought to fruition in both explicit and implicit ways. Explicit statements about what counts as teacher skill and knowledge, goals in creating highly qualified teachers, and related guidelines about assessment and reporting all comprise readily accessible language policies. From a critical perspectives, these explicit and implicit sources communicate messages about what is possible, what is not possible, by whom, and on whose behalf, combining in various ways to exert pressure and influence on daily classroom practices. Within a critical policy analysis, then, is the need to examine what is discussed but also what is not discussed or required, as silences speak as loudly as explicit requirements. These analyses are necessary because policies can simultaneously limit our options as teachers and open up possibilities for pedagogy and curriculum. The analysis within this chapter is done from an ideological standpoint and research base that privileges the education of linguistically diverse children in ways that affirms their home languages and cultures while providing them with materially significant knowledge to access the cultural capital needed for success in U.S. society and culture. Simply put, this analysis is done from a perspective that values additive and scaffolded language practices. In this section, we discuss the results of a systematic review of linguistic requirements to become a teacher in the 50 states.*

Review of State Requirements Relevant to Supporting Language

In devising the survey for educational linguistics, or the unique aspects of language found and potentially taught in schools, in secondary teacher education, this analysis sought to cast a wide net, not only inquiring about explicit requirements for linguistics but also searching for openings where this topic might be addressed, including methods courses, linguistics courses, and courses specific to language and literacy. From this reasoning, three key areas of inquiry were identified: linguistics, content area literacy, and bilingualism/teaching English as a second language (ESL). Although the first area would mark a clear potential arena for addressing educational linguistics, more states were likely to require a content area literacy component or an ESL component for secondary teachers. Although it is by no means probable that educational linguistics (inclusive of attitudes and research toward second language acquisition) would be addressed within a content area literacy or ESL course, the likelihood is higher than without this requirement, and these types of course might, again, serve as potential sites for the infusion of culturally responsive linguistic practices into existing pedagogical content knowledge.

In their 1996 survey of reading coursework requirements for middle- and high-school content area teachers, Romine, McKenna, and Robinson found that a total of 37 states, plus the District of Columbia, reported at least one course for middle- or high-school certification in one or more content subjects. This survey, however, did not discern if any requirements existed regarding linguistics. Furthermore, this study did not distinguish between the requirements for secondary teaching and pedagogical knowledge for other academic disciplines. However, the 1996 survey provides an historical referent point, showing that while linguistics may not have been a priority or explicit agenda item for teacher education, some conversations have taken place about the particular nature of texts in the content areas. The survey for this inquiry, into the place of culturally relevant

---

* Special thanks to Stacy Kaczmarek for her research of the states' requirements.

language practices in teacher education, was designed to specifically address this topic while also accounting for other requirements that might address the concepts.

Because states vary in their specificity about both competencies and course requirements, we asked questions regarding the state's requirements for teacher competencies and if these competencies were specifically required through prescribed coursework and we compiled results from either source as an indication of current priorities for teacher competencies. Also, because certification requirements for teachers differ from state to state, all 50 state departments of education and that of the District of Columbia were surveyed. In reviewing of the certification requirements, each state department's website was consulted for an initial review of the requirements of linguistic knowledge. This electronic review was then followed up with phone interviews with certification specialists in each state. The information obtained via the website was first confirmed, and all specialists were then interviewed using a standard protocol of the following questions:

1. What are the exact requirements for secondary teacher licensure? Do they include an educational linguistics component or a course in content area literacy?
2. What standards, specific to linguistics or content area literacy, must be met in order for a teacher education program to become a state-approved program?
3. Once a teacher has been practicing for several years, must he or she complete any professional development workshops or courses in educational linguistics or content area literacy?
4. Do any state-wide initiatives address bilingualism for teachers or students?
5. Have there been any conversations about changing these requirements for educational linguistics or bilingual education for teacher candidates?

This review focused primarily on secondary certification requirements, as most of the studies that address second language acquisition and academic learning stem from secondary contexts (Lee, 2005). State teacher licensure requirements, through both traditional, 4-year programs and guidelines for alternative licensure, were reviewed, particularly for requirements that may lead to knowledge about linguistics, including any requirements for content area literacy or the linguistic needs of a diverse school population. For the most part, the departments' websites and the certification specialists addressed the competencies that typically fell into tertiary coursework. In some instances, certification specialists indicated that knowledge about language acquisition and linguistics was expected to be addressed under content area literacy courses; in these cases, this requirement was counted under the content area literacy requirement but not as a specific requirement of linguistically supportive practices, including the explicit use of educational linguistics.

Results

In general, the results from the review of teacher certification requirements in the 50 states revealed a mixed view of requirements, recommendations, and priorities toward educational linguistics (see Table 13.1 for a concise overview of requirements and states). Very few states (six) specifically address educational linguistics as a source of competency for some of its teachers. Furthermore, only one state, California, requires all K–12 teachers to meet a "Developing English Language Skills requirement by completing a comprehensive course in reading instruction that includes: systematic study of phonemic awareness, phonics, decoding, literature, language, comprehension, diagnostic, and early intervention techniques" (California Department of Education, 2005). However, as detailed as this list of requirements is, none of these areas is synonymous with the field of second language acquisition or with educational linguistics. Much more prevalent was the requirement that teacher candidates be able to address reading and writing in the content areas.

Educational Linguistic Requirements   Of the 50 states surveyed, 5 states (Louisiana, Mississippi, Missouri, Pennsylvania, and Vermont) had specific requirements for teacher candidates to take a course in linguistics in pursuit of their certification. Of these 5 states, Louisiana, Pennsylvania, and Vermont maintained this requirement for teacher candidates pursuing a specialization to work with English language learners (ELLs). Mississippi required all English language arts teachers to complete a course in linguistics, and Missouri maintained this requirement for its teachers certified to teach English at the secondary level.

TABLE 13.1   Literacy Requirements of Secondary Education Teacher Preparation Programs by State

State	Course in Linguistics	Content Area Literacy/Reading	Working with English Language Learners
Alabama			
Alaska			
Arizona			
Arkansas		x	x
California			
Colorado			
Connecticut		x	
Delaware		x	
Florida			
Georgia			
Hawaii			
Idaho		x	
Illinois		x	
Indiana			
Iowa		x	
Kansas		x	x
Kentucky		x	x
Louisana		x	
Maine			x
Maryland		x	
Michigan		x	
Minnesota		x	x
Mississippi		x	x
Missouri		x	
Montana		x	
Nebraska			
Nevada		x	
New Hampshire			
New Jersey		x	
New Mexico		x	x
New York		x	x
North Carolina		x	x
North Dakota			
Ohio		x	
Oklahoma			
Oregon		x	
Pennsylvania			
Rhode Island			
South Carolina		x	
South Dakota			
Tennessee			
Texas			
Utah		x	
Vermont			
Virginia			
Washington			
West Virginia		x	
Wisconsin		x	
Wyoming		x	x

Content Area Literacy   Thirty-one states and the District of Columbia required some or all of its teacher candidates to complete specific coursework in content area literacy or addressed content area literacy as a competency expected of teachers. Of these states, 12 maintained this requirement for secondary education majors, 15 states mandated this knowledge for all of its teacher candidates, and only 3 required content area literacy knowledge of its elementary teachers.

The results from this survey show a decrease of six states from the previous study of content area literacy requirements (Romine, McKenna, & Robinson, 1996). In speaking with the certification specialists in these states, the competencies were shifted due to changes in state demographics and other requirements for teacher candidates. In one case, the content area literacy requirement was eliminated to make room for specific coursework in multicultural education. In three other cases, the certification specialist expressed a belief that all teachers would be expected to learn about literacy pedagogy throughout all of their methods coursework. Although this may or may not be the case in practice within various teacher education programs, these requirements provide a partial potential picture of the place of educational linguistics within teacher education.

English Language Learner Component   In addition to specific requirements in linguistics and content area literacy, teacher education programs might also address the linguistic needs of ELLs within courses addressing linguistic diversity or bilingualism. Of the states surveyed, all had certification requirements for teachers wishing to become specialists deemed highly qualified to work with ELLs. However, four states (Arizona, California, Minnesota, and New York) also required knowledge of the needs of linguistically diverse students for all of their teachers. Additionally, certification specialists in seven states (Kansas, Kentucky, Maine, Mississippi, New Mexico, Wisconsin, and Wyoming) cited their states' requirements within multicultural or diversity education as a potential area where teacher candidates might learn about the particular linguistic needs of students learning academic English.

Analysis: What Is Present

At best, the results of this survey of state departments of education show an uneven status of culturally responsive practices that support ELLs in secondary learning. The most direct and explicit item reviewed, the requirement of a course or specific competency in educational linguistics, yielded only a handful of states with this requirement. Further complicating this specific inquiry, though, is what type of orientation toward second language acquisition and what role linguistics might be incorporated through coursework or professional development addressing the requirement. The prospect of addressing linguistic variety is daunting enough for most teachers who might not even see themselves as particularly oriented to macro features of text. Simply put, most secondary teachers see themselves as content experts, not as knowledgeable within the field of language diversity or second language acquisition. In consideration of this population and mindset found within most teacher education programs, the prospect of adding in the nuances of linguistics structures, semantics, and features found in academic texts and conceptual and pedagogical discourses further complicates the ways in which linguistics might be addressed.

In addition to the specific requirements for competencies in second language acquisition and applied linguistics, courses in content area literacy are another potential, albeit delimited, site to address language issues and challenges in secondary academic learning for diverse students. Content area literacy and reading have not historically addressed, in specific detail, linguistic diversity. More common to this area of scholarship, practice and policy are textual reading strategies, such as prereading activities, approaches to teaching content vocabulary, and comprehension strategies (e.g., Readence, Bean, & Baldwin, 2006). Although many of these strategies are helpful to some bilingual children and their needs, this is not true across the range of strategies. For example, using a discussion strategy that asks students to first respond in writing to a text and then to share this writing aloud may or may not specify how to consider the needs of a recently immigrated student who may still be in a silent phase of second language reception.

Moreover, content area literacy courses are not specifically required to address linguistic structures found within different content areas, including the variances that occur across the sciences and the humanities (Unsworth, 1999). As has been discussed, though, the particular structures, semantics, and patterns found within secondary academic discourse (print, oral, and multimodal) present unique meaning-making challenges (Martin & Veel, 1998). While specific linguistic analyses and pedagogical explorations of explicit teaching linguistic structures may be taken up within the context of a content area literacy course, this is up to the discretion of the program and instructor and is not compelled by certification requirements. It is, therefore, at best an idiosyncratic practice that has yet to systematically effect classroom practices that support linguistically diverse children.

A similar de facto limitation is found within requirements for working with linguistically diverse students. Often couched under course requirements or competencies associated with multiculturalism, diversity, or inclusion, these arenas again have the potential to address the specific educational linguistics as a pedagogical and curricular feature to be considered and incorporated into planning for learning within secondary academic areas. However, the chances are much more likely that such courses address more sociocultural elements of classroom instruction, attending to such macro features as creating an inclusive classroom community, tapping students' funds of knowledges, and including references to multicultural sources of information and texts. As such, the analysis of content area literacy and ESL courses provides, perhaps, a possible entry point for considering where these issues can be explored by secondary teachers as well as the purposeful exploration of educational linguistics within teacher education.

Analysis: Silences in Teacher Education Requirements

The dearth of requirements in educational linguistics poses several questions worth exploring. Does this lack of attention communicate an inattention to ELLs and their linguistic needs? Does education consider this to be the domain of a specialist rather than a mainstream classroom teacher? Or is the prospect of addressing educational linguistics too daunting for teacher education programs that are pushing at their seams with the existing requirements for methods and survey courses? All of these are likely reasons for a current list of priorities that does not adequately include educational linguistics as a necessity for teachers' pedagogical content knowledge and skills. While numerous interpretations can and should be made about the gaps in knowledge shown through survey, I aver that the profound silence of language knowledge and research required for secondary teachers speaks to an irrelevant, outdated, and unrealistic view of who is found within contemporary classrooms in the United States.

Today's classrooms represent unprecedented levels of cultural and linguistic diversity in the United States (see chapter 2 of this volume for demographical and statistical information). Although one could argue that even mainstream, monolingual English speakers who can easily access the standard variety could benefit from specific attention to discussion and teaching around language in secondary classrooms, the need for purposeful attention to today's learners necessitates in-depth knowledge about the intersections of language, culture, and knowledge. The current requirements for teacher certification and education in the curricular areas of secondary schooling do not systematically address language. This does nothing to address the significant challenges experienced by both the largely monolingual, monocultural teaching force and the linguistically and culturally diverse students in today's classrooms. In fact, this silence and lack of knowledge requirement dangerously work to deepen the gap between these cultural groups. And while this gap is obviously uncomfortable and disconcerting for teachers who wish to best serve their students, the gap is more than uncomfortable for children from nonmainstream backgrounds. It works to keep linguistically diverse students from expert pedagogy that can support their abilities to be fluent code-switchers across language and registers, including academic English. In this way, this gap reflects a reference to a time, formerly real or just imagined, when monolingual students were the primary concern. However, this reference is clearly insufficient for today's classrooms.

However, the antidote to this misplaced and ill-conceived referent point is not as simple as the injection of a number of linguistics courses into existing teacher education programs. Some researchers have argued that a number of linguistics courses would be required to address the knowledge gap in linguistics (Fillmore & Snow, 2002); however, this prospect is an incomplete solution to the situated nature of language within content learning. Considered alongside the growing cultural mismatch between today's linguistically and culturally diverse students and the largely white, monolingual, and female teacher profession (Sleeter, 2001), addressing linguistic diversity cannot be conceptualized as a simple add-on. Incorporating module-like formats onto existing frames of knowledge found within teacher education would not result in language being considered alongside other factors in the classroom. Rather, we need a more profound and deep discussion of how to change the references, or points of reflection, that shape our educational policies, including requirements for teacher certification. Simply put, if the current policy is inadequate in its implicit assumptions, where are better sources of influence to inform policy and, ultimately, classroom practice?

Changing the Referent Points: Students and Their Worlds

To reshape the state of linguistically and culturally responsive education, departments of education and teacher education programs cannot afford to look backward to existing requirements or even laterally to other states' requirements. As shown through the results of the survey of the states, the gaps and silences in knowledge of language are incommensurate with the contemporary needs of diverse students. Therefore, these policies must begin with different reference points to more accurately shape more generative possibilities for culturally relevant pedagogy.

First, policymakers, administrators, and educators should inform their practices and policies based on a systemic and in-depth consideration of who currently composes the student population in their schools. Simply reckoning with the number of cultures and languages found in today's classrooms should substantively shift what foundational knowledges, skills, and practices teachers need to work with these students. This type of inquiry, though, should not stop with demographic information about numbers of languages spoken by students. This information is readily available on most states' and districts' websites. Often cited in a spirit of multiculturalism, this quantitative number has not been enough to reshape educational policies. Knowing the numbers of languages spoken by today's students has not yet been enough to systematically alter what it means to be a competent teacher. Or, another possible assessment is that the amount of linguistic diversity has resulted in requirements such as courses in multicultural education but has not taken up, in detail, the knowledges necessary to truly engage with the pedagogical and curricular complexities of supporting learning for linguistically and culturally diverse students. A course in multicultural education, or worse, a course that pathologizes linguistic diversity with documented disabilities (Orellana & Gutierrez, 2006) does not begin to address the level of detail and specificity needed, for example, to support language learning within scientific discourse.

Rather, the inquiry about today's students must go much deeper to research the contexts in which today's students live, work, and use language. Policymakers need to know the kinds of language practices students use in and out of school, the situations in which these language practices occur, students' prior experiences with language learning in school, their attitudes toward language and academic English, and their abilities in home- and school-based codes and registers, to name a few areas of necessary research. Put simply, more empirical evidence of students' linguistic lives is needed to more accurately shape policies for students' needs. From Luis Moll's (Moll, Amanti, Neff & González, 1992) conceptualization of funds of knowledge to Kathy Au's (1998) culturally responsive work with native Hawaiian children, an anthropological view of young people would first inform adolescent literacy policies from arguably the most important stakeholders' perspective: the young person sitting in the classroom. Pedagogically, it is futile to plan without a specific learner's needs, abilities, and interests in mind. Policies that require local knowledge of participants work from the same premise. Without this type of material referential information, policies will continually be resigned to using imprecise knowledge, at best, and conjecture, at worst, to articulate requirements for teacher knowledge.

In addition to knowledge of students, policymakers also need to closely examine a second point of reference for their policies: the larger societal, cultural, economic, and political spheres into which students navigate their life pathways. Put simply, we need to know not only who our students are but also who they are likely to be in the future. What kinds of life pathways are they likely to follow? Through this question, I do not mean to suggest an individualistic career planning effort but rather an inquiry into the types of economic, cultural, and political realities that shape the skills and knowledges that our students need to be successful in their lives.

In current contexts of high-stakes assessment, classroom pedagogy and curricula are often influenced and explicitly tailored to prepare students for standardized assessments. Although this influence is an understandable and somewhat justifiable possible source of power on classroom practices, it is also short-sided. Students' needs do not end with a standardized assessment. School-sanctioned language practices, literacies, and their assessments have been widely criticized on two major grounds: lack of resonance with self-sanctioned literacies engaged by many young people (Chandler-Olcott & Mahar, 2003; Knobel, 2001; Moje et al., 2004) and lack of resonance with the dynamic, multimediated language uses and literacies required in an information age and globalized economy (Hargreaves, 2003; Luke, 2002; New London Group, 1996; Stevens & Bean, 2007). Therefore, policies that draw on traditionally school-sanctioned literacies and their accompanying measures may in fact be preparing students better for the 1950s (days of blackboards and chalk talk) than for the life pathways they are likely to encounter in a digitally mediated world (Gee, 2002). Particularly considered within today's globalized information age, students' linguistic and literacy needs far exceed what is required from print-based, multiple-choice items about school-based curricula. At least under contemporary schooling practices, educational policies that prepare teachers who then prepare students to succeed in school are using severely myopic lenses of what competencies will serve students best beyond the school contexts of blackboard, textbook, and essays.

A possible objection to the referent points of investigating our students and their current and possible future life pathways is that the information yielded will become unavoidably dated and need to be repeated. Without a doubt, inquiries into who our students are and what their needs will likely be provide relevant answers for only a defined population and amount of time. However, rather than seeing this as a reason not to engage in this type of inquiry, this inherent quality of a limited shelf life can be seen as asset. In fact, this is a productive limitation, as such research and inquiry should mark policy-making and educational practices generally. We should be consistently, recursively, and repeatedly investigating our students and the worlds in which they currently live and will live in the future. These are questions that will never be summarily answered, as the world will continue to shift. Schools and education as an institution must become more systematically accountable to the contexts in which they are found.

References

Au, K. (1998). Constructivist approaches, phonics and the literacy learning of students of diverse backgrounds. *National Reading Conference Yearbook, 47*, 1–21.

California Department of Education Press. (2005). *Educational Resource Catalog*. Sacramento, CA: CDE Press.

Chandler-Olcott, K., & Mahar, D. (2003). "Tech-Savviness" meets multiliteracies: Exploring adolescent girls' technology-mediated literacy practices. *Reading Research Quarterly, 38*(3), 356–385. doi: 10.1598/RRQ.38.3.3.

Edmondson, J. (2004). *Understanding and applying critical policy analysis: Reading educators advocating for change*. Newark, DE: International Reading Association.

Fillmore, L. W., & Snow, C. (2002). What teachers need to know about language. In C. T. Adger, C. Snow, & D. Christian (Eds.), *What teachers need to know about language* (pp. 7–54). McHenry, IL: Center for Applied Linguistics.

Gee, J. P. 2002. Literacies, identities and discourses. In M. J. Schleppegrell and M. C. Colombi (Eds.), *Developing advanced literacy in first and second languages* (pp. 157–176). Mahwah: N.J. Erlbaum. (159-176).

Hargreaves, A. (2003). *Teaching in the knowledge society: Education in the age of insecurity*. New York: Teachers College Press.

Knobel, M. (2001). "I'm not a pencil man": How one student challenges our notions of literacy "failure" in school. *Journal of Adolescent and Adult Literacy, 44*(5), 404–419.

Lee, O. (2005). Science education with English language learners: Synthesis and research agenda. *Review of Educational Research, 75*(4), 491–530.

Lemke, J. (1990). *Talking science: Language, learning and values*. Norwood, NJ: Ablex.

Luke, A. (2002). What happens to literacies old and new when they're turned into policy. *Adolescents and literacies in a digital world*. New York: Peter Lang.

Martin, J. R., & Veel, R. (Eds.). (1998). *Reading science: Critical and functional perspectives on discourses of science*. New York: Routledge.

Moje, E., Ciechanowski, K., Kramer, K., Ellis, L., Carrillo, R., & Collazo, T. (2004). Working toward third space in content area literacy: An examination of everyday funds of knowledge and discourse. *Reading Research Quarterly, 39*(1), 38–70. doi: 10.1598/RRQ.39.1.4.

Moll, L. C., Amanti, C., Neff, D., & González, N. (1992). Funds of knowledge for teaching: Using a qualitative approach to connect homes and classrooms. *Theory into Practice, 31*, (2), pp. 132–141.

New London Group (1996). A pedagogy of multiliteracies: Designing social futures. *Harvard Educational Review, 66*(1), 60–93.

Orellana, M. J., & Gutierrez, K. (2006). What's the problem? Constructing different genres for the study of english language learners. *Research in the Teaching of English, 41*(1), 118–123.

Readence, J. R., Bean, T. W., & Baldwin, R. S. (2006). *Content area literacy: An integrated approach*. Dubuque, IA: Kendall Hunt.

Romine, B. G., McKenna, M. C., & Robinson, R. D. (1996). Reading coursework requirements for middle and high school content area teachers: A U.S. survey. *Journal of Adolescent & Adult Literacy, 40*(3), 194–198.

Sleeter, C. E. (2001). Preparing teachers for culturally diverse schools: Research and the overwhelming presence of whiteness. *Journal of Teacher Education, 52*(2), 94–106.

Stevens, L. P., & Bean, T. W. (2007). *Critical literacy in K–12 classrooms: Theory, context, and praxis.* New York: Sage.

Stone, D. (1997). *Policy paradox: The art of political decision making.* New York: W.W. Norton & Company.

Unsworth, L. (1999). Developing critical understanding of the specialised language of school science and history texts: A functional grammar perspective. *Journal of Adolescent & Adult Literacy, 42*(7), 508–521.

Vacca, R. T., & Vacca, J. L. (1999). *Content Area Reading Literacy and Learning Across the Curriculum* (6th ed.). New York: Longman.

14

Language, Culture, Policy, and Standards in Teacher Preparation

Lessons from Research and Model Practices Addressing the Needs of CLD Children and Their Teachers

Alicia Ardila-Rey
American Association of Colleges for Teacher Education

The preparation of teachers for culturally and linguistically diverse (CLD) learners constitutes an increasing challenge for schools, colleges, and departments of education. The face and language of American schools is changing rapidly, even faster than projected by census statistics. Of every ten children in K–12 schools, four are children of color and two come from homes where languages other than English are spoken (U.S. Department of Education, National Center for Education Statistics, 2003, 2006). In addition, accountability measures established in the No Child Left Behind Act of 2001 (NCLB) call for English language learners (ELLs) to be assessed yearly. Decisions about schools', teachers', and students' futures are being made based on the results of such assessments. The NCLB also includes provisions regarding teaching quality that are challenging states to examine and reform their teacher certification processes and to ensure teachers have mastery of their content areas (Education Commission of the States, 2002). However, teachers are coming out of teacher preparation programs with minimal tools or no training to help them address the needs of CLD children. While standards for children's learning and performance expectations are being revised to adapt to the population changes, standards for teacher's preparation programs seem to remain unaffected in most cases.

This chapter explores how teacher preparation and accreditation standards address issues of PK–12 accountability for the academic achievement of CLD children. The following questions emerge:

- To what extent do standards for teacher preparation programs reflect the reality of the children those teachers will find once they are in the classroom?
- How do teacher preparation accrediting agencies address diversity issues in teacher candidate curricula? Is there enough specificity? Are there specific provisions for preparing teachers for CLD children and, more specifically, for ELLs?
- To what extent do standards for teacher preparation reflect or relate to standards for CLD children's learning put forward by the different discipline organizations or to standards and requirements for teacher's licensure developed by individual states?

This chapter looks at how teacher preparation accreditation agencies (such as the National Council for Accreditation of Teacher Education [NCATE], the Teacher Education Accreditation Council [TEAC], and the National Association for the Education of Young Children [NAEYC]) address issues of diversity and language in their standards and guidelines. Specifically, the chapter looks at research and practices regarding:

1. Specific linguistic and academic needs of ELLs that go beyond support for cultural diversity in schools
2. Specific standards for academic disciplines—How are needs of ELL children incorporated?
3. Federal legislation and teacher certification requirements in different states—How are diversity and language incorporated?
4. Accrediting institutions' standards for teacher preparation programs—How is diversity assessed both in program content and format? Is language incorporated? How does this intersect with linguistic needs or language acquisition needs of ELLs?
5. Existing model or good teaching practices that foster linguistic and academic achievement of ELL and CLD children—What can we borrow from these model practices in order to improve teacher preparation programs?

Recommendations for policy and improvement of standards are made at the end of this chapter, based on the research findings and model practices described in the previous chapters of this volume.

What are the Specific Linguistic and Academic Needs of ELLs that Go Beyond Support for Cultural Diversity in Schools?

The rapid increases in the CLD and ELL population in PK–12 schools throughout the United States, paired with policy changes made during the last decade, shifted the burden of preparing these children for academic success from the English as a second language (ESL) teacher, to essentially all teachers. In 2004, 50% of all PK–12 schools in the United States (including public and private schools) reported having ELL students (Strizek, Pittsonberger, Riordan, Lyter, & Orlofsky, 2006). In many areas of the country, CLD students, including ELLs, will soon constitute the majority of the PK–12 enrollment. In 2002, one-fourth of all students in California were ELL service recipients, and Texas reported one out of seven students receiving ELL services (U.S. Department of Education, 2003). The largest percentages of ELL students in 2002 were found in California, New Mexico, Alaska, Arizona, Texas, and Nevada (Kindler, 2002). However, this growth trend is also true in states in which linguistically diverse populations have not traditionally been present. For example, the Hispanic population in Oregon has doubled since 1990 to 8% of the total state population. In North Carolina, from 1990 to 2000, the Latino population grew by 394%, the largest percentage increase of any state in the country (U.S. Census Bureau, 2000). Based on the 2000 Census data, non-Hispanic whites accounted for 69% of the population that year, whereas Hispanics (who can be of any race) made up 13%, African Americans 12%, and Asian Americans 4%. In the next 50 years, the number of Hispanic and Asian Americans in the United States will triple, while the white non-Hispanic population will increase by only 7%, according to U.S. Census Bureau population projections released in 2004. In 2050, non-Hispanic whites will make up just 50% of the population, with Hispanics accounting for 24%, African Americans 15%, and Asian Americans 8% (U.S. Census Bureau, 2004).

Thus, based on these projections, any teacher in any state or locality will be likely to find a classroom with a high percentage of children whose first language is not Standard English and who have specific language-related academic needs that are different from the "mainstream" PK–12 population. All teachers, then, need to acquire and develop the appropriate knowledge, skills, and dispositions to ensure CLD children have equitable opportunities to succeed.

Who are these children and what are their specific educational needs? Are the knowledge and skills that teachers acquire in teacher preparation programs not appropriate and enough to understand these children's needs and work effectively with them? The CLD children teachers may encounter today in their classrooms include immigrant children with little or no English proficiency as well as American-born children whose home language and cultural backgrounds and understandings are different than those valued by the mainstream school culture (native children, children of immigrants, black children whose home language is African American Language [AAL], Deaf children). As research depicted in previous chapters in this volume shows (see Clayton, Barnhardt, & Brisk, chapter 2; Boutté, Chapter 3; Hoffmeister, chapter 4; and de Jong & Harper, chapter 6), children whose first or home language is different from the Standard English used and valued in schools need very different teaching approaches to achieve school success, and even the best-intentioned and highly prepared teachers are failing them. Teachers' own socialization in the dominant culture tied to cultural preconceptions, lack of knowledge about the language and culture of the CLD students in their classrooms, and lack of interactions with CLD communities may shape their perception of these children into stereotypical views that lend to low expectations for their future (see Macedo, chapter 1; Boutté, chapter 3; de Jong & Harper, chapter 6; Herrera, Murry, & Pérez, chapter 7). In order to get past these perceptions, teachers would need to understand that only in relation to the dominant culture (in this case, the school) are these cultural groups viewed as "not able." For example, as Boutté (chapter 3) notes, children who use AAL are viewed as less competent or not able to speak and write correct English. However, AAL has been identified as a complete language system, rule based and systematic, with roots in West African languages. On the other hand, teachers from minority backgrounds may themselves be perceived through similar deficit stereotypes by parents or administrators accustomed to the White teacher model (Macedo, chapter 1; Rochon, Tanabe, & Horstman-Riphahn, chapter 10).

CLD children, particularly ELLs, not only face the task of grasping the content of what is being taught in the classroom but must also face the enormous task of learning and mastering the language in which the content is being delivered and, in most cases, of grasping the nuances and understandings of a culture foreign to their own. This is true if the child speaks AAL, if she or he speaks one of the 400 or more languages spoken by the PK–12 U.S. population (Kindler, 2002), or if the child is Deaf. According to the National Council of Teachers of English (2006), ELL children's language-related needs include:

Acquisition of social language proficiency
Acquisition of academic language vocabulary
Skills to engage with texts and comprehend content.

To ensure children's academic success, as the various chapters in this book describe, the acquisition of English vocabulary and the ability to function socially in this second language do not suffice. According to Hoffmeister, "Success involves knowing and using two languages; learning and developing academically, socially, and linguistically; and becoming social beings" (chapter 4, p. 80). Even though Hoffmeister is referring here to Deaf children, this statement applies equally to any child whose home language is different than the school language.

Language and culture are inextricably linked with each other. Children in a process of second language acquisition are also going through a process of acculturation (Clayton et al., chapter 2). The outcome of one affects the other, and both have an impact on the child's school achievement. As children go through the schooling process, they are also developing cultural identity. A healthy cultural identity may facilitate the process of acculturation and language acquisition (see Clayton et al., chapter 2). A common theme in the previous chapters is the need for children to feel that their culture and language are acknowledged and valued. Children need to have adult language and culture models in the classroom (Hoffmeister, chapter 4) who act not only as role models but also as brokers between the school, the child, the family, and the community.

Research presented in chapters in this book dealing with Deaf children, AAL speakers, Native Americans, and other CLD populations show, in summary, that successful teachers of ELLs need to have:

- Knowledge about language, including:
  - Basic constructs of bilingualism
  - Process of language development and second language acquisition
  - Relationship between what a child knows in his or her home language and what he or she can learn in the new or second language.

- Knowledge about culture as it influences thinking, ways of doing things, ways to relate to the world.
- Knowledge about identity formation, including knowledge about acculturation processes and the dynamics of identity development.
- Knowledge of the social, political, and economical factors affecting their students as well as their families and communities. This includes understanding the demands that mainstream education (which reflects many of those social and political factors) places on CLD children and families (Clair & Adger, 1999)
- Understanding of the interactions between culture, language, and academic performance
- High expectations for all children.

In sum, teachers need to be provided with the knowledge and experiences necessary to help them set aside their own cultural preconceptions in order to be able to see the legitimacy of the others' cultural wealth. Teachers need to understand and value children's cultural knowledge (language and beliefs) and build on this previous knowledge to help them acquire the standard school language and be able to grasp curriculum content. Teachers need to understand and incorporate children's linguistic and cultural processes in their work, as a tool to provide ELL children with the space and respect to develop "cultural voice" (Macedo, chapter 1) and a healthy bicultural identity. Finally, as stated by Walqui-van Lier and Hernandez (2001, 2006) teachers need to develop a vision of ELL students as individuals who are capable and for whom limited academic skills or limited English proficiency do not represent inadequacies and are not incurable or permanent conditions.

Are the standards for academic disciplines and teacher preparation programs addressing the needs of CLD children and their teachers as detailed above?

Standards for Academic Disciplines

The standards movement in the 1990s, which arose in response to increasing demands for accountability, resulted in the development of all types of standards for K–12 and higher education (Carter, 2003). Yet, only recently have academic discipline organizations begun to take into consideration the needs of ELLs in either their standards or their guiding principles and position statements. Providing equitable learning opportunities and assuring achievement for all children are common topics in the revised standards for the teaching of reading, mathematics, and science. Recommendations offered by the professional associations include use of first language or bilingual techniques to deliver instruction, accommodations for assessment, use of mixed groupings for peer scaffolding, and avoidance of tracking. Below are examples of how several of these professional discipline organizations have addressed CLD-related issues in their standards.

Reading Standards

The International Reading Association (IRA) put forward a position statement on literacy instruction for second language learners. In this statement, the IRA asserts that multilingualism should be promoted as a positive value. The IRA's position supports the notion of beginning literacy instruction in the child's home language, when possible, and calls for respect for bilingualism and diverse cultural practices when instruction in the home language is not possible or if it would be conducive to ethnic segregation in public schools (IRA, 2001). The IRA also developed twelve standards for reading instruction, two of which specifically address respect for diversity and issues related to second language acquisition. The IRA's Standard 9 refers to the curricular goal for students to "develop an understanding of and respect for diversity in language use, patterns, and dialects across cultures, ethnic groups, geographic regions, and social roles" and Standard 10 refers to the use of home language to deliver instruction, indicating that "students whose first language is not English make use of their first language to develop competency in the English language arts and to develop understanding of content across the curriculum" (IRA, 1996). The IRA also developed standards for reading professionals, which are endorsed by the NCATE. These standards emphasize the need for teacher preparation programs to pay close attention to cultural and linguistic differences and prepare all candidates to teach in ways that capitalize on the children's cultural background and knowledge (IRA, 2004).

Alicia Ardila-Rey

Mathematics Standards

The National Council of Teachers of Mathematics (NCTM) includes an "Equity Principle" as the first one of its six "Principles for School Mathematics," which refer to critical issues in school programs and are meant to serve as guidelines for the planning and implementation of mathematics curricula and the professional development of teachers (NCTM, 2000). Other principles include curriculum, teaching, learning, assessment, and technology. The "Equity Principle" calls for high expectations for *all* children as well as strong support to help fulfill these expectations. The principle affirms that "all students, regardless of their personal characteristics, backgrounds, or physical challenges, must have opportunities to study—and support to learn—mathematics" (NCTM, 2000, chapter 2) This refers specifically to tracking as a practice that excludes children—particularly ELLs and children from lower-income, minority, or diverse backgrounds—from rich mathematics experiences. The NCTM advocates for high-quality mathematics instruction to become the norm rather than the exception and encourages alternate practices, such as mixed groupings and instruction that focuses on in-depth learning rather than on fast learning.

NCTM's "Equity Principle" emphasizes the need to accommodate for differences to help all students learn and focuses on the specific need to accommodate for the accurate assessment of ELL children:

> Some students may need further assistance to meet high mathematics expectations. Students who are not native speakers of English, for instance, may need special attention to allow them to participate fully in classroom discussions. Some of these students may also need assessment accommodations. If their understanding is assessed only in English, their mathematical proficiency may not be accurately evaluated. (NCTM, 2000, chapter 2)

This call for accommodation is also reflected in NCTM's "Assessment Principle," which recognizes the need for teachers to ensure that all students are given equal opportunities to demonstrate their learning, suggesting that teachers use communication-enhancing and bilingual techniques to support ELLs.

Science Standards

The National Science Education Standards, put forward by the National Academies of Science through its National Committee on

Science Education Standards and Assessment (1996), address issues of equity in its system, program, and teaching standards. Although the 1996 standards do not specifically address issues of language, the National Academies recognizes in its system standards the barriers to learning science for students from diverse and underrepresented groups and calls for equity principles to be incorporated into science education policies. The program standards call for all students, regardless of cultural or ethnic background, to have the opportunity to obtain high levels of scientific literacy. Programs based on these standards should ensure that activities are adapted to their students' diverse needs. The teaching standards request that teachers "recognize and respond to student diversity and encourage all students to participate fully in science learning" (National Committee on Science Education Standards and Assessment, National Research Council, 1996, p. 32). Even though issues of language were not specifically addressed in the 1996 standards, a more recent statement on assessment (National Research Council Center for Education, 2001) addresses the need to consider language differences in the assessment process and provides recommendations on equitable assessment practices for ELLs.

Federal and State Policies

Student Achievement

The implementation of NCLB has had a great impact on the daily activities of PK–12 schools throughout the country. NCLB includes accountability provisions that require students' progress to be measured annually ("adequate yearly progress," or AYP). Every school district in every state is responsible for ensuring that students meet state proficiency standards in reading and math by 2014. Schools are required to use disaggregated data to ensure that all groups of students are making adequate progress. Due to this emphasis on accountability for student achievement in NCLB, school instruction has been aligned with state standards and standardized tests. Analyses of the effects of these policies thus far show inconsistent results related to improving minority achievement and reducing achievement gaps, which are the main goals of this legislation. In July 2005, the federal government reported that 9-year-old Black and Hispanic students made greater progress than White students in reading and math on the National Assessment of Educational Progress. However, further analyses of these data has revealed improvements in achievement in middle grades but no positive changes in secondary education for CLD student populations (Education Trust, 2005). Additional analyses on states' performance have revealed that, although several states and districts showed success on these goals in initial assessment, the achievement gaps in many other states have not decreased or have even widened (Cronin, Kingsbury, McCall, & Bowe, 2005).

Title III of NCLB establishes specific policies for the language instruction of immigrant and limited English proficient (LEP) children. The purpose of these policies is to ensure that LEP children attain English proficiency and develop high levels of academic achievement. Federal regulations and the U.S. Department of Education have indicated flexibility in states' choice of instruction methods to achieve these NCLB goals. For example, a document by the Associate Deputy Secretary at the Office of English Language Acquisition, which administers Title III of NCLB, indicates that ESL instruction can be done through any type of research-based models such as bilingual education, dual-language immersion, and English-only instruction (Leos, 2006). However, several other factors, such as the name change of the Department of Education's Office on Bilingual Education to Office for English Language Acquisition, indicate a shift of focus from the use of both languages for instruction to a movement toward the elimination of bilingual education and a push for swift acquisition of English by all CLD students. Even the use of the term "limited English proficient" in place of "bilingual" reflects a deficit model that perceives LEP students as lacking skills and in need of remediation (Wright, 2005). Although the ultimate goal is to foster CLD students' achievement, these definitions seem to disregard the importance of the home language and cultural background of the student as essential aspects for achievement. NCLB emphasizes accountability and requires the testing of ELL and LEP children. However, in most states, ESL instruction is still done as a separate activity, disconnected from the mainstream classroom content while test scores of many LEP students are still being excluded from accountability numbers, creating a delusion of success that contributes to keeping ELL students behind (see Wright [2005] for an in-depth analyses of implications of NCLB for language minority students).

Teacher Quality

NCLB emphasizes the need for teacher quality as a vital factor for student achievement. NCLB's definition of what it means to be a highly qualified (HQ) teacher establishes that such teachers must hold at least a bachelor's degree from a 4-year institution, be fully certified or licensed by the state, and demonstrate competence in each core academic subject area in which they teach. The push for elimination of bilingual education, paired with the increasing numbers of linguistically diverse children in American PK–12 schools, would require for all teachers to be prepared to work effectively with CLD children within their regular classrooms. However, the federal definition of what it means to be a HQ teacher does not include any provisions on language or culture as requirements for this classification. Based on federal requirements, ELL teachers are not required to be classified as "highly qualified" and, in many states, ELL teachers do not need a certification in ESL or even a teaching certification credential as long as they are not teaching core content. A majority of states have adopted the federal definition and requirements for HQ teachers without any changes related to working with CLD or ELL populations. Only a handful of states have developed policies or standards for teacher preparation and credentialing that address issues related to diverse populations; even fewer have included provisions specific to the teaching of ELLs.

The few states that have defined policies on general teacher certification related to the linguistic needs of ELL or culturally diverse students are mostly those with traditionally large indigenous or immigrant populations, such as Alaska, California, Arizona, New York, and New Mexico, as well as other states where ELL populations are on the rise, such as Minnesota and Wisconsin. (See Stevens, chapter 13, for a detailed analysis of state requirements.)

No state so far has met the 2006 goal of having a HQ teacher in every classroom (Keller, 2006). What is more, studies of teacher quality in several midwestern and southeastern states show that teacher quality today is unevenly distributed, with low income and minority students attending schools where poorly prepared teachers are the norm (Peske & Haycock, 2006; Southeast Center for Teaching Quality, 2004).

How are teacher preparation programs, and particularly the agencies that accredit these programs, addressing the challenges that arise from current regulations and how are they addressing the teacher preparation needs defined above?

Accrediting Organizations

A number of national organizations have developed teacher standards for teacher preparation that outline what teachers of ELLs should know and be able to do. Among those organizations are the Center for Research on Education, Diversity, & Excellence, National Association for Bilingual Education, National Board for Professional Teaching Standards, and Teachers of English to Speakers of Other Languages. However, the organizations that in fact accredit teacher preparation programs have a much larger impact on the type and quality of curriculum and training experiences to which future teachers are exposed. Diversity as it relates to gender, exceptionalities, race, culture, and age has been addressed at different levels by different accrediting agencies. This section describes how higher-education accrediting agencies, such as NCATE, TEAC, and NAEYC (which accredits early childhood education programs in community colleges and 4-year institutions) address issues of linguistic diversity in their standards.

Established in 1954 as an independent accrediting body, NCATE accredits schools, colleges, and departments of education. NCATE's standards for teacher preparation programs were revised in 2000 to be performance-based in response to policymakers' concerns about standards and accountability. Institutions going through the accreditation process must provide evidence of competent performance of their teacher candidates. NCATE incorporates a standard that focuses specifically on the assessment of diversity, but issues of diversity are also addressed tangentially in its other standards as well. In the "Diversity Standard" (or standard 4), diversity is considered in terms of opportunities to interact with diverse groups (faculty, candidates, students) and be exposed to curriculum and experiences that allow candidates to "acquire and apply the knowledge, skills, and dispositions necessary to help all students learn" (NCATE, 2006a, p. 29) Before some revisions were suggested in the spring of 2006, issues of language diversity were rarely mentioned in the standards and, with minor exceptions, no provisions for addressing and assessing linguistic diversity issues in teacher preparation had been included.

A recent proposed revision included this topic in the wording of the "Diversity Standard" and assessment rubrics and added foreign languages and ESL to the list of specialized professional organizations with existing standards that teacher candidates are expected to meet. The revised language also specifies a requirement for institutions to submit candidate performance data and other program documents that respond to these professional standards for national or state review as part of the program review process (NCATE, 2006b).

Vavrus (2002) suggests, however, that the lack of specificity in many aspects of the existing standards language allows institutions to conceptualize issues of diversity in one-dimensional and noncritical manners. As several of the chapters in this book describe (e.g., de Jong & Harper, chapter 6; Abbate-Vaughn, chapter 8; Rochon et al., chapter 10) universities commonly comply with diversity requirements by including one or two courses on multicultural issues and by hiring one or two faculty of color. Abbate-Vaughn (2005) asserts that schools of education may resort to indiscriminately hiring faculty of color from diverse national origins to teach the "diversity" courses in their effort to comply with diversity standards. In doing so, institutions may not consider the real experiences, skills, and knowledge these people may or not have, as if their condition of minorities suffices to make them idoneous to teach such courses.

TEAC was recognized by the U.S. Department of Education as an accrediting agency in 2003 and obtained continued federal recognition in 2005. Unlike NCATE, TEAC accredits individual education programs—not schools, colleges, or departments of education as a whole. TEAC's goal for accreditation is to ensure that teacher education programs prepare "competent, caring, and qualified educators." Programs seeking TEAC accreditation are required to affirm this as the goal of their program, which must be shown by demonstrating compliance with TEAC's three "Quality Principles" and "Standards of Capacity for Program Quality." In general, references on diversity and multicultural issues found through TEAC's principles and standards are few and vague. In a few points, the multicultural/diversity topic has been elaborated further, but issues related to linguistic diversity are barely, if not at all, mentioned.

TEAC makes direct reference to diversity and multicultural issues, as well as some other indirect references in its Quality Principle 1: "Evidence of student learning and caring." This principle requires three general components to be addressed: evidence of candidate's subject matter knowledge, pedagogical knowledge, and teaching skills. Multicultural perspectives are included as one of three dimensions of the liberal arts and general education that permeate the teacher education curriculum and that should be common themes through these general components (the other dimensions are technology and learning to learn).

> Included in the liberal arts is the knowledge of other cultural perspectives, practices, and traditions. TEAC requires evidence that candidates for the degree understand the implications of confirmed scholarship on gender, race, individual differences, and ethnic and cultural perspectives for educational practice. For all persons, but especially for prospective teachers, the program must yield an accurate and sound understanding of the educational significance of race, gender, individual differences, and ethnic and cultural perspectives. (TEAC, 2005)

Other, rather vague, references to diversity are found in general throughout TEAC's quality principles. For example, in its pedagogical knowledge component, TEAC requires evidence that candidates are able to translate their knowledge of the subject matter into lessons that meet the needs of a "wide range" of students. It is then up to each institution to interpret what "educational significance" and "wide range" encompass. Do these include ethnic and cultural differences, developmental stages, learning styles, or linguistic backgrounds? Do these include the need for culturally appropriate practices? TEAC's standards as of this date do not provide clear guidelines to answer these questions.

NAEYC is the specialty professional association that recognizes early childhood education (ECE) teacher preparation programs at higher education institutions affiliated to NCATE. In 2005, NAEYC also began to accredit associate degree programs at community colleges. The NAEYC has developed separate sets of standards for initial and advanced licensure as well as for associate degree programs. In similar fashion to NCATE's standards, NAEYC's standards are performance based, focusing on what well-prepared ECE teachers need to know and be able to do. However, NAEYC expressly emphasizes commitment to diversity, inclusion, and collaboration with families and communities through all threes sets of standards as well as in a position statement on responding to linguistic and cultural diversity (NAEYC, 1995). Unlike NCATE and TEAC, NAEYC addresses issues specific to working with linguistically diverse populations in standard 2, "Building Family and Community Relationships" and in substandard 4a of its standard 4, "Teaching and Learning." For example, according with substandard 4a, "Connecting with Children and Families," a teacher candidate exceeds expectations if there is evidence of the candidate's sensitivity and skill in creating relationships with CLD children and families. Each institution must interpret how "sensitivity" is assessed and which skills are appropriate. The very focus of the standards on candidate performance may allow for individual institutions' loose interpretation of what it means to achieve the ability to work well with linguistically diverse children. As described by Vavrus (2002) in his discussion of NCATE, this may be conducive to a weakened interpretation of diverse or cultural issues. On the other hand, many institutions that prepare ECE teachers are accredited by state agencies and not by NAEYC and, as described above, most states do not have any existing provisions for the preparation and quality of teachers to work with linguistically diverse populations. As NAEYC states in the recommendations section of its standards document (Hyson, 2003), consistent policies at the federal and state levels are needed to promote connections and alignments among the different accrediting entities and teacher preparation programs.

Even well-intentioned standards and guidelines developed by accrediting institutions may fail to address the real dimensions of the growing CLD population needs if the programs that prepare teachers don't interpret these guidelines in appropriate ways. Programs described in previous chapters in this volume present examples of best practices that could inform future policy and standards for the preparation of teachers of CLD and ELL children.

What Can We Learn from Successful Practices?

Fortunately, as the previous chapters in this book so describe, increasing numbers of teacher preparation programs throughout the United States are involved in work that addresses the needs of CLD and ELL student populations. The examples in this book reflect successful and creative ways to help faculty and administrators develop programs that prepare teacher candidates and in-service teachers who understand the needs of CLD children and who have the knowledge, skills, and dispositions necessary to effectively teach these linguistically diverse children. Below is a summary of recommendations for infusion of language and culture issues into the preparation of preservice teachers and professional development of in-service teachers, faculty, and administrators, extracted from the practices described in the second section of this volume. Additional policy recommendations developed by participants in a Wingspread Conference that considered these same issues are included in the appendix.

Recommendations for the Preparation of Preservice Teachers

Recruit and retain more diverse teachers, particularly teachers from the local CLD communities in which the schools are located (see Au, Lefcourt, & Kawakami, chapter 9; Rochon et al., chapter 10). Doing so involves not only providing financial help or developing outreach programs but also providing mentoring and professional development as well as establishing lasting connections with the community (Au et al., chapter 9).

Prepare teachers that are able to respond to the specific needs of the communities in which they will serve. Some of the proven strategies toward this goal presented in this volume are:

- Providing prospective teachers with opportunities to immerse themselves in the communities in which they will work (Abbate-Vaughn, chapter 8; Au et al., chapter 9)
- Tying curriculum content with practical experiences with diverse children and communities (Abbate-Vaughn, Chapter 8; Au et al., chapter 9)
- Utilizing the cultural funds of children, their families, and the community to develop and introduce curricular content in ways that are more meaningful to the students (Au et al., chapter 9; Nelson-Barber & Lipka, chapter 5).
- Using reflective writing as a tool to help preservice and in-service teachers question their preconceptions and process their changing understandings of the diverse children and communities in which they are involved (Herrera et al., chapter 7; Abbate-Vaughn, chapter 8).

Recommendations for Professional Development of In-service Teachers

Create professional development opportunities for in-service teachers that focus on building critical capacities for accommodation readiness (Herrera et al., chapter 7). Building capacity for critical reflection provides a solid foundation for teachers to be able to spouse sound pedagogy and culturally responsive practices in their work with CLD children, families, and communities.

The Accommodation Readiness Spiral described by Herrera and colleagues (chapter 7) provides a theoretical model for the professional development of in-service teachers. This framework could be also used as a foundation for the development of teacher preparation and faculty development models that truly incorporate issues of language and cultural diversity.

Recommendations for Professional Development of University Faculty and Administrators

Two of the chapters in this book describe successful programs aimed at building capacity of teacher education faculty by familiarizing them with ways to incorporate issues of linguistic diversity in undergraduate and graduate teacher preparation courses (Brisk, chapter 11; Nevárez-La Torre, Sanford-DeShields, Soundy, Leonard, & Woyshner, chapter 12). Some of the effective practices toward this goal presented by these authors are:

- Developing semester-long seminars to provide faculty with knowledge about language and culture and ways to incorporate this knowledge in their courses
- Providing opportunities for faculty to share experiences and critically reflect on actual practices with CLD students and problem solve real situations they have encountered
- Bringing experts in the field as well as PK–12 community members to share research and experiences
- Taking into consideration a department's culture and faculty academic freedom when designing programs
- Including in these programs not only faculty but also graduate students who teach the undergraduate courses or who have expertise in this topic
- Involving administrators in seminars and discussions
- Providing materials and support to help faculty implement changes in their syllabi and administrators implement changes in their practices
- Institutionalizing such programs so that they are not dependent on individual faculty to be sustainable.

Conclusion

Educational organizations, as well as federal and state legislation, consider the need to pay attention to issues of language and culture. In most cases, however, the wording is vague and, for the most part, language is neglected. It behooves educators involved with preparing teachers and teachers themselves to acquire knowledge that is more specific about language and culture to guide their work with teacher candidates and their students. As Justice Douglas held in relation to the *Lau v. Nichols* court case (1974), "There is no equality of treatment merely by providing students with the same facilities, textbooks, teachers, and curriculum; for students who do not understand English are effectively foreclosed from any meaningful education" (p. 566). Thus, schools and teachers that use Standard English to educate their students need to also consider the recommendations stated in this volume to engage CLD students with the goal of equality of outcomes.

References

Abbate-Vaughn, J. (2005, February). *Assessing preservice teacher understanding of and long-term commitment to practices responsive to low-income, culturally and linguistically diverse (LCLD) students.* Paper presented at the 57th Annual Conference of the American Association of Colleges for Teacher Education (AACTE), Washington, DC.

Carter, N. P. (2003). Diversity and standards: Defining the issues. In N. P. Carter (Ed.), *Convergence or divergence: Alignment of standards, assessment and issues of diversity.* Washington, DC: American Association of Colleges for Teacher Education.

Clair, N., & Adger, C. T. (1999). *Professional development for teachers in culturally diverse schools* (Report No. EDO-FL-99-08). Washington, DC: ERIC Clearinghouse on Languages and Linguistics. (ERIC Document Reproduction Service No. ED435185.)

Cronin, J. G., Kingsbury, G., McCall, M. S., & Bowe, B. (2005). *The impact of the No Child Left Behind Act on student achievement and growth: 2005 edition.* Northwest Evaluation Association. Retrieved June 13, 2006, from http://www.nwea.org/assets/research/national/NCLBImpact_2005_Study.pdf

Education Commission of the States. (2002). *No state left behind: The challenges and opportunities of ESEA 2001. Special report.* Denver, CO: Author.

Education Trust. (2005, January). *Stalled in secondary: A look at student achievement since the No Child Left Behind Act*. Available from http://www2.edtrust.org/edtrust/Product+Catalog/special+reports

Hyson, M. (Ed.). (2003). *Preparing early childhood professionals: NAEYC standards for programs*. Washington, DC: National Association for the Education of Young Children.

International Reading Association. (1996). *Standards for the English language arts*. Available from http://www.reading.org/resources/issues/reports/learning_standards.html

International Reading Association. (2001). *Second language literacy instruction: A position statement of the International Reading Association* [Brochure]. Newark, DE: Author.

International Reading Association. (2004). *Standards for reading professionals—Revised 2003*. Available at http://www.reading.org/resources/issues/reports/professional_standards.html

Keller, B. (2006, May). No state meeting teacher provision of 'No Child' law. *Education Week, 25*(38), 1–16.

Kindler, A. (2002). *Survey of the states' limited English proficient students and available educational programs and services 2000–2001 summary report*. Washington, DC: National Clearinghouse for English Language Acquisition. Available from http://www.ncela.gwu.edu/policy/states/reports/seareports/0001/sea0001.pdf

Lau v. Nichols, 414 U.S. 563 (1974).

Leos, Kathleen. (2006, February). *Office of English Language Acquisition*. Power point presented the OELA/SMU Joint Policy Summit on English Language Learners in Texas, February 2006. Retrieved May 30, 2006, from http://www.smu.edu/teacher_education/esl/SMU.presentation1.ppt

National Association for the Education of Young Children. (1995). *Responding to linguistic and cultural diversity: Recommendations for effective early childhood education*. Washington, DC: Author.

National Committee on Science Education Standards and Assessment, National Research Council. (1996). *National science education standards*. Washington, DC: National Academy Press.

National Council for the Accreditation of Teacher Education. (2006a, March). *The NCATE unit standards: Proposed revisions*. Retrieved June June 13, 2006, 2006, from http://www.ncate.org/documents/Standards/May06_revision/NCATEUnitStds.doc

National Council for the Accreditation of Teacher Education. (2006b). *Professional standards for the accreditation of schools, colleges, and departments of education—2006 edition*. Washington, DC: Author.

National Council of Teachers of English. (2006). *NCTE position paper on the role of English teachers in educating English language learners (ELLs)*. Prepared by the NCTE ELL Task Force. Retrieved May 30, 2006, from http://www.ncte.org/about/over/positions/category/div/124545.htm

National Council of Teachers of Mathematics. (2000). *Principles & standards for school mathematics: An overview*. Retrieved May 30, 2006, from http://standards.nctm.org/document/chapter1/index.htm

National Research Council for Education. (2001). Classroom assessment and the National Science Education standards. J. M. Atkin, P. Black, & J. Coffey (Eds.). Center for Education, Division of Behavioral and Social Sciences and Education. Washington, DC: National Academy Press.

Peske, H. G., & Haycock, K. (2006). *Teaching inequality: How poor and minority students are shortchanged on teacher quality*. Washington DC: Education Trust. Retrieved June 14, 2006 from http://www2.edtrust.org/NR/rdonlyres/010DBD9F-CED8-4D2B-9E0D-91B446746ED3/0/TQReportJune2006.pdf xhttp://www2.edtrust.org/NR/rdonlyres/010DBD9F-CED8-4D2B-9E0D-91B446746ED3/0/TQReportJune2006.pdf

Southeast Center for Teaching Quality. (2004, August). *Unfulfilled promise: Ensuring high quality teachers for our nation's students*. Chapel Hill, NC: Author.

Strizek, G. A., Pittsonberger, J. L., Riordan, K. E., Lyter, D. M., & Orlofsky, G. F. (2006). *Characteristics of schools, districts, teachers, principals, and school libraries in the United States: 2003–04 schools and staffing survey* (NCES 2006-313, Rev.). U.S. Department of Education, National Center for Education Statistics. Washington, DC: U.S. Government Printing Office.

Teacher Education Accreditation Council. (2005). *Guide to accreditation*. Available from http://www.teac.org/literature/index.asp

U.S. Census Bureau. (2000). *United States Census 2000: Rankings and comparisons population and housing tables (PHC-T series)*. Retrieved June 13 2006, from http://www.census.gov/population/www/cen2000/tablist.html

U.S. Census Bureau. (2004, March). *U.S. interim projections by age, sex, race, and Hispanic origin*. Retrieved June 13, 2006, from http://www.census.gov/ipc/www/usinterimproj/

U.S. Department of Education, National Center for Education Statistics. (2003). *Overview of public elementary and secondary schools and districts: School year 2001–02* (NCES 2003-411). Washington, DC. Retrieved May 30, 2006, from http://nces.ed.gov/pubs2003/overview03/#8

U.S Department of Education, National Center for Education Statistics. (2006). *The condition of education 2006* (NCES 2006-071). Washington, DC: U.S. Government Printing Office.

Vavrus, M. (2002). *Transforming the multicultural education of teachers: Theory, research, and practice.* Multicultural Education Series, J. A. Banks (Ed.). New York: Teachers College Press.

Walqui-van Lier, A. (2006, April). *Developing accomplished instructional support specialists: Applying Shulman's model to ELL education.* Paper prepared for the 2006 meeting of the American Educational Research Association, San Francisco, CA.

Walqui-van Lier, A., & Hernandez, A. (2001). *A scaffold for change: Professional development for teachers of English learners.* San Diego, CA: San Diego County Office of Education.

Wright, W. E. (2005). *Evolution of federal policy and implications of No Child Left Behind for language minority students.* Tempe, AZ: Education Policy Studies Laboratory Arizona State University. Available from http://www.asu.edu/educ/epsl/LPRU/features/

Conclusion

This volume addresses a present challenge to American education: how best to prepare teachers to instruct the increasing numbers of students enrolled in schools whose language is something other than Standard English. The first part of the book describes these students and provides basic information on language and culture necessary to understand their educational needs. The second part illustrates successful teacher education programs, analyzing the ways, in particular, that they prepare teacher candidates to work with culturally and linguistically diverse (CLD) students and the differences in preparing teachers who come from the same and from different linguistic and cultural backgrounds from the students. The second part concludes with chapters that explore the preparation of teacher educators. The third part considers present federal and state policies as well as policies of educational organizations. A special contribution of this volume to preparation of teachers for diverse populations is the focus on language, often neglected in the discourse of teacher education.

CLD students represent a great variety of linguistic and cultural knowledge and experiences. Some speak a language other than English because they were born in another country. Others were born in the United States, but their families and communities use a different language. A large percentage of African American students speak African American language (AAL), described in Boutte's chapter as a legitimate language and not a deviation of English. Deaf students communicate face-to-face using American sign language (ASL) while they learn to read and write in English, their second language (see chapter 4).

Language and culture are delicate factors in educating children and developing healthy identities. The authors of this book agree that CLD students must develop functional Standard English language skills to succeed academically. But, unlike those who argue that those skills can best and most quickly be achieved by replacing their original language with Standard English, the authors of this book argue that CLD students should *add* Standard English to their repertoire. We begin with the assumption that language is situational, that the appropriateness of different languages or dialectics depends on the context in which they are used. For example, students working in a group to accomplish an educational task may use a common language other than English or their everyday variety of English but, when they present their findings, orally or in writing, to a general audience, they need to do so in academic English, not because English is superior but simply because Standard English is the language primarily used in formal academic contexts. We recognize that CLD students must develop Standard English fluency to be able to function not only in familiar settings of family, friends, and neighborhood but also in larger society.

The authors, in different ways, argue that teaching academic English successfully benefits from acknowledging students' particular linguistic and cultural backgrounds. There is some evidence that demonstrates that when students' backgrounds are not accepted, students will resist academic English as the language of an "oppressor." In addition, Nelson-Barber and Lipka illustrate in chapter 5 that the culture of students is a viable medium for successfully conveying academic knowledge.

Preparing teachers and teacher candidates to also address the needs of CLD students requires rethinking of teacher education curriculum and field experiences. Best practices are not enough, as de Jong and Harper aptly observe in chapter 6. Knowledge of bilingualism, second language acquisition, and the nature of academic English in the different content areas as well as the effects of culture on learning helps teachers develop strategies that foster language acquisition and content learning.

Some competencies needed by teachers differ depending on teachers' background. Because large number of teachers and teacher candidates do not share the social, linguistic, and cultural experiences of CLD students, they must develop deeper understanding and positive attitudes toward such students. Abbate-Vaughn (chapter 8) illustrates the gradual transformation of teacher candidates immersed in the community of CLD students while reading autobiographical works by CLD writers. These teacher candidates wrote various drafts of their reflections on the literature and their experiences with these children. Over time, this writing reflects their transformation. Herrera, Murry, and Pérez in chapter 7 propose a six-step process to produce advocates. The process needs to be different when the teacher candidate population comes from CLD communities because they also are confronting an institutional context with different linguistic and cultural norms. Rochon, Tanabe, and Horstman-Riphahn (chapter 10) illustrate the hardships of these teacher candidates and underscore the importance of their presence in schools and universities. Au, Lefcourt, and Kawakami, in chapter 9, describe a program to prepare early childhood and elementary teachers recruited from the local population in Hawaii. This program enjoys cooperation of a college, community agencies, and public schools. The chapter finds that five elements were vital to supporting the program: connecting with the community, recruiting candidates at the high-school level, understanding education as a process of social change, pairing preservice with mentor teachers, and building a leadership network.

Teacher education faculty and programs need to undergo their own knowledge development and transformation. Preparing teachers to provide quality education to CLD students cannot be the effort of isolated faculty in teacher education programs. Rather, the needs of CLD students must be reflected throughout the teacher education curriculum. Development of faculty expertise on issues of language and culture are essential in enriching the curriculum. Chapter 11 illustrates how a teacher education program transformed itself through seminars for faculty and informed syllabus modification, whereas the teacher education program discussed in chapter 12 achieved change through faculty reflection and research on their own teaching and beliefs.

Institutions receive scarce encouragement or guidelines from policy makers. The final two chapters of this volume describe limited efforts at the federal and state levels. Various organizations have some reference to the needs of CLD students but, for the most part these references are vague, leaving it up to institutions to put into practice vague mottos such as "to educate for diversity … [or] for all students."

Improving the quality of education for CLD students requires explicit teaching of language, incorporation of culture, and development of healthy identity. This book introduces the knowledge needed and gives examples of successful practices. We hope that its contents inspire teachers and teacher educators to revisit their present practices and consider how they can best accommodate the needs of CLD students and in the process improve education for all.

Appendix: Proceedings and Recommendations from the Wingspread Conference[1]

Racine, Wisconsin, September 2005

From September 19–21, 2005, the American Association of Colleges for Teacher Education (AACTE)* convened a group of representatives from major national educational associations and higher education institutions at the Wingspread Conference Center to discuss the need to prepare highly qualified teachers to better teach the increasing numbers of linguistically diverse children in PK–12 classrooms. Culturally and linguistically diverse (CLD) student populations often present unique challenges to their school communities. Given the trends in demographic changes in the United States, it is crucial that we identify and implement policies and practices that respond to the specific needs and characteristics of these CLD children and provide them with equal opportunities to achieve.

The conference addressed these pressing realities through dialogue on knowledge, practice, and current policy issues. Discussions were based on the research, practices, and policies described in the book being prepared by members of the AACTE Committee on Multicultural Education of 2003–2005. Participants reviewed definitions and requirements for "highly qualified" teachers in 35 states and formulated recommendations for development of language standards for teacher preparation and program accreditation. A statement redefining "high quality" teacher preparation to include the role of culture and language was also formulated as result of the conference discussions. This

---

* The conference was cosponsored by AACTE, the Johnson Foundation, the National Education Association, and Lumina Foundation.

357

statement and recommendations represents a consensus of participant individuals and institutions with the goal of impacting policies for the preparation of better teachers for all children.

Among the 35 conference participants were representatives from various major education associations and members of the AACTE board of directors. The diverse group of conferees included also college presidents, deans, researchers, and faculty members, as well as an elementary teacher from Boston Public Schools, a doctoral student, and an undergraduate Wingspread student fellow (see participant list below).

Background for the Discussions

Policy

Requirements on teacher quality established by Title II of the No Child Left Behind Act of 2001 (NCLB) have challenged states to examine and reform their teacher certification processes and ensure that teachers have mastery of their content areas (Education Commission of the States, 2002). Additionally, new accountability measures established in the NCLB call for English language learners (ELLs) to be assessed yearly regardless of language ability, which is an immense challenge for most states and districts. ELL children are expected to develop English proficiency within 3 years of enrollment and are expected to meet the same academic content and achievement standards that all children are expected to meet.

Demographics

Whereas 40% of children in K–12 schools in the United States today are from minority or diverse backgrounds and 20% come from homes where languages other than Standard English are spoken (National Center for Education Statistics [NCES] 2003), only about 14% of all teachers are from minority backgrounds and less than 12% have received training to teach ELLs (NCES, 2002).

Statement of the Problem

Teachers are coming out of teacher preparation programs with minimal tools or no training to help them address the needs of CLD children (Menken & Antunez, 2001; NCES, 2002). ELL and African American students who are not proficient in Standard English are disproportionately overrepresented in special education classes, in language-speech pathology services, and in school dropouts. Thus, CLD populations present unique challenges to the development of appropriate educational services in the communities in which they reside. It is imperative to formulate more culturally responsive educational policies and practices and prepare teachers who are ready to respond to the specific linguistic needs and characteristics of these children.

Summary of Discussions

Language in the classroom holds the key to CLD students' access to education; however, language and culture are not explicit on current definitions of the term "highly qualified teacher" (HQT), both at the state and national levels. Some state definitions single-out special education. Why not language? Should English as a second language (ESL) and special education be treated different?

What's Missing from Definitions of Highly Qualified Teachers?

Current HQT definitions at the federal level and most state levels include:

- Bachelor's degree
- Demonstrated competency in content
- Licensure for the assignment.

Not included in HQT definitions are:

- Professional dispositions toward teaching
- Knowledge, skills, and dispositions specific to language and cultural competencies
- Ability of teacher preparation programs to instill in students those particular knowledge, skills, and dispositions

- Knowledge of the local community
- Empathy
- CLD paraprofessionals
- ESL as core area
- Faculty professional development.

Why Is It So?

Obstacles to addressing language and culture in definitions of HQT can be found in the current policy context, in definitions of diversity, in policy holes, and in teacher preparation institutions and associations.

Obstacles in Current Policy Context
- Federal and state authorities are working against strong teacher preparation programs (e.g., NCLB defines HQT purely in relation to content knowledge; Texas does not require student teaching for certification).
- Colleges and schools of education are seen as creating obstacles to the preparation of teachers.
- Recommendations that address strengthening teacher preparation requirements regarding diversity are actively resisted at all levels.

Obstacles in Definitions of Diversity
- Expanded conceptions of diversity create confusion about priority areas in equity and social justice.
- Lack of priority in conceptions of diversity promotes "safe" diversity experiences.
- Absence of reference to language in definitions of diversity, skirts a crucial need to achieve success in school..

Obstacles in Policy Holes
- NCLB and some state laws and standards promote content knowledge and ignore all other essential aspects of teacher preparation (e.g., pedagogical knowledge, knowledge of the students and community).
- NCLB and some state laws ignore scientific findings and diminish the importance of first language development in ELL student achievement.
- Assessment of teacher proficiency in educating ELLs is problematic if not absent.

Obstacles in Teacher Preparation Institutions and Associations
- Diffusion of responsibility
- Failure to socialize conflict

Recommendations

Recognizing the previously mentioned obstacles, how should we develop recommendations for a solution?

Guiding Principles for a Solution

- Increasing the diversity of teachers will help solve many of the problems of student achievement among CLD students. This will require major efforts to recruit teachers (especially from within the local school community), retain them, and create increasing prestige for the teaching profession.
- Recruiting teachers who are members of local communities enables the development of effective standards.
- Preparing all teachers to effectively teach children from diverse cultural and linguistic backgrounds must be a prime goal of teacher preparation programs.

To ensure that *all* teachers are prepared for CLD students, changes must be effected in:

- Institutional policy
- Accreditation agencies (e.g., National Council for Accreditation of Teacher Education, Teacher Education Accreditation Council)
- National professional organizations or Specialized Professional Associations (SPAs)
- Federal definition and legislation of HQT
- State regulations for licensing.

Recommendations on Teacher Recruitment
- Provide more resources for recruiting CLD teacher candidates.
- Create incentives for entering and remaining in the teaching profession (e.g., loan forgiveness, differentiated career progression opportunities).
- Recruit teacher candidates from members of local communities.

Recommendations for Policy on Teacher Certification

- Reaffirm the three essential dimensions of teacher preparation: (1) knowledge of students—how they learn, their languages, communities, and families; (2) knowledge of subject matter (including language), and (3) knowledge of teaching and learning (pedagogy).
- Paramount in the development of a HQT should be the ability to connect what is being taught in classrooms to the needs and interests of the communities from which the students come.

Recommendations for Teacher Preparation Programs

- Reaffirm the commitment to field experience as a requirement for certification.
- Require the immersion of teacher candidates in the communities of the schools in which they will teach.
- Provide training and experience in assessment of student performance for CLD students.
- Require courses in language development and second language acquisition for all teacher candidates.
- Identify and prepare cooperating teachers who are sensitive to community interests and who can provide positive experiences for student teachers.
- Situate teacher preparation in local communities (e.g., site-based methods classes, professional development schools).

Recommendations for AACTE and Other National Associations and Organizations

- Share these issues with stakeholders (e.g., national education groups such as Learning First Alliance).
- Socialize the conflict or problem.
- Bring it to the table.
- Decide what we can agree to do.
- Formulate a policy statement.
- Seek public support through the media.

How to Do This?

1. Develop a website for CLD student populations.
2. Update and reissue the 2002 AACTE white paper on CLD teacher preparation.
3. Organize a regional conference or hearing sponsored by AACTE, Teachers of English as a Second Language (TESOL)/National Association for Bilingual Education (NABE), Association of Teacher Educators (ATE), and state legislators.

4. Develop a resource directory and network of people working on these issues.
5. Include in AACTE's national annual conference sessions on this issue.
6. Include in AACTE's national annual conference a conference strand on CLD students.
7. Address issues of language and culture at the ATE conference.
8. Continue discussions with TEAC on ways to address culture and language in its accreditation process.
9. Encourage and sponsor political training for faculty at JFK (Harvard) School of Government.
10. Create an advocacy group to develop an action plan to influence policy.

Recommendations for Accrediting Agencies   Teacher preparation for culturally and linguistically diverse students must be made explicit in all accreditation standards and candidates must demonstrate competency in teaching CLD student populations.

How to Do This?

- Revise accreditation standards (such as those of National Council for Accreditation of Teacher Education [NCATE], Teacher Education Accreditation Council [TEAC], and State Education Agency [SEA]) to explicitly address language and culture knowledge, skills, and dispositions.
- Develop a rubric for assessing language and culture knowledge, skills, and dispositions.
- Develop definitions of dispositions that address language and culture within accreditation guidelines.
- Award a unit that emphasizes CLD populations in accreditation (at AACTE annual meeting).

Specific Recommendations to Revise and Enforce NCATE's Training and Compliance of Standard 4. Currently:

- Even if element 3 (candidate diversity) is not met, standard 4 is met when element 1 (curriculum and experiences) is fulfilled.
- The standard does not enforce, check, or assess involvement with communities and families.

NCATE should:

- Revise wording in standard 4

- Revise target for standard 4, element 1
- Revise supporting explanation for standards 1, 5, and 3
- Insert language related to ELLs in standard 3.

Recommendations for Professional Associations

- Standards for professional associations (e.g., National Council of Teachers of Mathematics, Association for Childhood Education International, National Association for the Education of Young Children) should clearly address the preparation of teachers for CLD and ELL populations.
- Standards must overlay such that content standards clearly reflect teaching CLD student populations and CLD standards clearly reflect the teaching of content.
- Issues of CLD and ELL students should apply not only to preservice teacher preparation but also to practicing in-service teachers and faculty as well.

Recommendations for Revisions to Current Definitions of Highly Qualified Teachers

- In addition to content knowledge, teachers must have skills, knowledge, and demonstrated competencies on how culture and language functions in the classroom and how to apply this knowledge with a full range of children from various backgrounds.
- Language is part of the "content knowledge" teachers must have. ESL should be considered a core academic area.
- A HQT should be empathic about the role of language and culture in teaching and learning as demonstrated through practice, including but not limited to, field experiences, course work, and professional development.

Questions Going Forward

Are we assuming that teaching is the only key to making change and ensuring achievement? This issue must be framed as part of a broader social, political, economic, and cultural agenda focused on improving the academic achievement and broader social access of students, including those historically denied access. Furthering this goal requires answering the following questions.

How Do We Affect Policy?

The appropriate mechanisms need to be identified and the right people contacted. Further conversations should be carried out with such people as:
  a. Policy makers
  b. Great city schools
  c. Board of education members
  d. Superintendents
  e. State commissioners
  f. Education Commission of the States forum.

Participants

Jorgelina Abbate-Vaughn, University of Massachusetts, Boston
Leslie Agard-Jones, William Paterson University
Alicia Ardila-Rey, AACTE
Ray Barnhardt, University of Alaska–Fairbanks
David Beaulieu, Arizona State University
Thomas Blanford, National Education Association
Gloria Swindler Boutté, Benedict College
María Estela Brisk, Boston College
M. Christopher Brown II, AACTE
Courtney Clayton, Boston College
Ester de Jong, University of Florida, Gainesville
Mary E. Dilworth, National Board for Professional Teaching Standards
Segun Eubanks, National Education Association
Candance Harper, University of Florida, Gainesville
David Hecker, American Federation of Teachers
Socorro G. Herrera, Kansas State University
Robert Hoffmeister, Boston University
Clara Jennings, DePaul University
Sabrina Hope King, Bank Street College of Education
Gerardo Lopez, Indiana University
Elizabeth MacDonald, Boston Public Schools
Carol E. Malloy, University of North Carolina–Chapel Hill
P. Rudy Mattai, State University of New York–Buffalo
Sharon Nelson-Barber, WestEd
Vernon C. Polite, Eastern Michigan University
Sharon P. Robinson, AACTE
Ronald S. Rochon, State University of New York–Buffalo
Richard Ruiz, University of Arizona

Ana Maria Schuhmann, Kean University
Saron Tettegah, University of Illinois, Urbana–Champaign
Josefina V. Tinajero, University of Texas–El Paso
Boyce C. Williams, NCATE
Ronald Williams, Prince George's Community College
Sam Geraci, Wingspread Fellow, Benedictine University

Proposed Highly Qualified Teacher Definition

Wingspread Conference September 21, 2005

Rationale

In the existing definitions of HQT, attention to language is missing. We believe that HQTs must communicate the benefit of knowing and using more than one language, must have high expectations of children regardless of proficiency in English, and must know and respect linguistically and cultural diverse students and their families.

Defining Highly Qualified Teachers

- All HQTs who use English as the medium of instruction must be English language teachers as it relates to their content area (i.e., a teacher who teaches biology must also teach the language to do biology).
- All HQTs must have a set of guided experiences in schools and school communities with culturally and linguistically diverse students, families, and community partners.
- All HQTs must be able to demonstrate the ability to work with CLD students to develop language and literacy, to succeed academically, and to successfully function in school and their communities.
- All HQTs must be able to use culturally relevant teaching techniques and exhibit dispositions that reflect the above requirements.
- The preparation of a HQT would include coursework that speaks to language, culture, and community.
- All HQTs will have had coursework *and* experiences that prepare them for the above requirements.

References

Education Commission of the States. (2002). *No state left behind: The challenges and opportunities of ESEA 2001.* Denver: Author. Retrieved May 5, 2004, from *http://ecs.org/clearinghouse/32/37/3237.doc*

Menken, K., & Antunez, B. (2001). *An overview of the preparation and certification of teachers working with limited English proficient (LEP) students.* Washington, DC: National Clearinghouse for Bilingual Education. Retrieved May 6, 2004, from *http://www.ncela.gwu.edu/ pubs/reports/teacherprep/teacherprep.pdf*,

National Center for Education Statistics. (2002). *1999–2000 schools and staffing survey: Overview of the data for public, private, public charter, and Bureau of Indian Affairs elementary and secondary schools.* Washington, DC: U.S. Department of Education, Office of Educational Research and Improvement.

National Center for Education Statistics. (2003). *Overview of public elementary and secondary schools and districts: Year 2001–02.* Retrieved May 5, 2004, from *http://nces.ed.gov/pubs2003/overview03/#8*

Endnote

1. Alicia Ardila-Rey, from AACTE, is the primary author of this report, which compiles contributions from the conference participants listed at the end of the document.

About the Authors

María Estela Brisk, Editor

Dr. María Estela Brisk is a professor of education at the Lynch School of Education, Boston College. She received her Ph.D. in linguistics and bilingual education at the University of New Mexico in 1972. Her research and teacher-training interests include bilingual education, bilingual language and literacy acquisition, methods of teaching literacy, and preparation of mainstream teachers to work with bilingual learners. Dr. Brisk has served as a consultant in legal matters pertaining to bilingual education and has worked closely with regional and local groups and school systems in developing their bilingual programs as well as with mainstream programs that serve bilingual learners. Dr. Brisk was the 1991 Boston University recipient of the Metcalf Cup and Metcalf Prize for excellence in teaching. She is the author of the books:

- *Bilingual Education: From Compensatory to Quality Schooling*
- *Literacy and Bilingualism: A Handbook for ALL Teachers*
- *Situational Context of Education: A Window into the World of Bilingual Learners*
- with P. Menyuk, *Language Development and Education: Children with Varying Language Experiences.*

Professor Brisk, native of Argentina, is a fluent speaker of Spanish.

Jorgelina Abbate-Vaughn

Dr. Jorgelina Abbate-Vaughn is an assistant professor of teacher education at the University of Massachusetts Boston. She earned her Ph.D. in curriculum and instruction and teacher education at Boston College in 2002. Her research, which has been published in a number of national and international peer-reviewed journals in both English and Spanish, focuses primarily on urban teacher education, teacher beliefs, diversity, and literacy. Dr. Abbate-Vaughn is a former urban practitioner, having taught at the elementary, middle, and secondary levels to bilingual and mainstream student populations.

Socorro G. Herrera

Dr. Socorro Herrera currently serves as a professor of elementary education at Kansas State University and is Director of the Collaborative Intercultural and Multilingual Advocacy (CIMA) Center. Certified in elementary education, bilingual education, and school counseling, Dr. Herrera's recent publications have appeared in the *Bilingual Research Journal* and the *Journal of Latinos and Education*. Her recent research and teaching in education have emphasized emergent literacy, reading strategies, the differential learning needs of second-language learners, and mutual accommodation for language learning students. Dr. Herrera has authored and coauthored textbooks relating to early literacy development, as well as reading instruction and assessment for English language learner (ELL) students. Socorro was recently honored as a *Distinguished Alumnus* by Eastern New Mexico State University.

Tamara H. Horstman-Riphahn

Tamara H. Horstman-Riphahn is serving as executive assistant to the Dean of the School of Education at Buffalo State College State University of New York. She holds a master's degree in education-professional development from the University of Wisconsin–La Crosse and completed a research project that examined the impact of the first teachers of Hmong descent on Wisconsin PK–12 schools. Ms. Horstman-Riphahn's research seeks equitable educational access and support, the strengthening and renewal of communities, and culturally, historically, and linguistically respectful instruction.

Kevin G. Murry

Dr. Kevin G. Murry is currently an associate professor of secondary education at Kansas State University (KSU) and is the director of Research and Development for the CIMA Center. His work in research and development has focused on English as a second language (ESL)/dual language programming in secondary public schools and teachers' accommodation readiness for ELL and transnational students. Dr. Murry and the CIMA Center were recently recognized as the *Outstanding Unit* among colleges at KSU. Dr. Murry's recent research has emphasized differentiated assessment strategies for culturally and linguistically diverse students, the professional development of highly qualified teachers for ELL students, the linguistic and cross-cultural dynamics of ESL instruction, and school restructuring for linguistic diversity. Kevin is the author of two recent textbooks on ESL methods and ESL assessment. His recent publications have appeared in the *Journal of Continuing Higher Education*, *AACTE Briefs*, and the *Bilingual Research Journal*.

Sharon Nelson-Barber

Dr. Sharon Nelson-Barber is a sociolinguist and directs the Culture and Language in Education Research program at WestEd. Her work explores ways in which teachers can more effectively teach the full spectrum of students in today's classrooms and centers in particular on the teaching knowledge and abilities of educators in nontraditional settings spanning indigenous settings in the lower 48 states, Alaska, and the Northern Pacific islands of Micronesia. She also teaches at Stanford University's Center for Comparative Studies in Race and Ethnicity. She combines expertise in qualitative research and culturally competent assessment and evaluation with years of experience providing equity assistance to schools, organizations, and service agencies serving diverse communities, focusing in particular on cultural issues in the teaching and learning of mathematics and science. Dr. Nelson-Barber has published extensively, is active in major organizations and meetings in anthropology and education, and serves on a number of national advisory boards.

Della R. Pérez

Dr. Della R. Pérez currently serves as an assistant professor at Kansas State University and is the associate director of Undergraduate Programming for the CIMA Center. Her research focus and teaching in education have emphasized literacy development for the ELL, differentiated high-quality sheltered instruction for second-language learners, and emphasized language acquisition and development for diverse language populations. Dr. Pérez has coauthored articles and presented nationally and internationally on effective strategies to promote literacy development and instructional programming for ELLs. Her most recent publication is entitled *The 5 Components of Reading Development: A Classroom Teacher's Guide to Scaffolding Reading Instruction for ELL Students.*

Ronald S. Rochon

Ronald S. Rochon is dean of the School of Education and associate vice president for Teacher Education at Buffalo State College State University of New York. He holds a Ph.D. from the University of Illinois at Urbana-Champaign in educational policy studies and his research centers on the recruitment, retention, and successful matriculation of culturally, linguistically, and racially diverse students across university campuses. Dr. Rochon works to strengthen the relationships between academic institutions and the community as well as to develop strategies to enhance the implementation of culturally relevant, respectful, and responsive curricula serving children within our nation's public schools. Over the past 7 years he has collaborated with Hmong communities in the Midwest and cofounded and directed the Research Center for Cultural Diversity and Community Renewal, a program focused on enhancing educational opportunities and services for traditionally underserved student populations.

Clifton S. Tanabe

Clifton S. Tanabe is an assistant professor at the University of Hawaii at Manoa. He holds a Ph.D. in educational policy studies and a law degree, both from the University of Wisconsin–Madison. His research interests include a focus on educational philosophy, policy, and law as they relate to the issues of justice and equality. His most recent work has been on affirmative action in higher education admissions. In addition, Dr. Tanabe has worked extensively with the Hmong community in Western Wisconsin and has served as director of the Research Center for Cultural Diversity and Community Renewal, which houses several programs dedicated to improving access to culturally relevant schooling.

Alicia Ardila-Rey

Alicia Ardila-Rey is associate director for Professional Issues and Partnerships at the American Association of Colleges for Teacher Education (AACTE). She has been involved in the development of AACTE's policy initiatives for early childhood teacher preparation, and for the recruitment and preparation of teachers for culturally and linguistically diverse students. She is currently conducting work on teacher dispositions, assessment, and accreditation of teacher preparation programs. Alicia also directs the Holmes Scholars™ Program for minority doctoral students in education.

Supplementing her extensive experience as teacher, administrator, and researcher, she has conducted and published research on early literacy, preschool teachers' beliefs, as well as on young children's moral reasoning and conflict resolution. A preschool teacher in her native Colombia, Dr. Ardila-Rey served as a child development specialist consultant for Child Resource Centers and Even Start programs in Maryland, where she designed, implemented, and evaluated educational and recreational programs for low-income Hispanic immigrant children and families. Dr. Ardila-Rey, a Fulbright Scholar from Cartagena, Colombia, earned both her Ph.D. and M.Ed. in human development from the University of Maryland, where she was recognized with the "Outstanding New Professional in Education" award. She has a B.A. in early childhood education from the *Universidad de San Buenaventura,* in Bogotá, Colombia and an associate's degree in the same field from the *Colegio Mayor de Bolivar* in Cartagena, Colombia.

Kathryn H. Au

Kathryn H. Au, Chief Executive Officer of SchoolRise, is an internationally recognized literacy researcher and the first person to hold an endowed chair in education at the University of Hawaii. Kathy's research interest is the school literacy learning of students of diverse cultural and linguistic backgrounds. She is best known for her studies of culturally responsive teaching, and her current research is on school change to improve literacy achievement. She has published about 80 articles and chapters, as well as two edited volumes and three textbooks, including *Multicultural Issues and Literacy Achievement* (Erlbaum, 2006). Kathy has been elected president of the National Reading Conference, vice president of the American Educational Research Association, and to the board of directors of the International Reading Association (IRA). She has been recognized as a Distinguished Scholar by the AERA Standing Committee on the Role and Status of Minorities in Educational Research, was named a fellow of the National Conference on Research in Language and Literacy, and has been elected to the Reading Hall of Fame. She received the first National Scholar Award presented by the National Association for Asian and Pacific American Education, the Oscar Causey Award for outstanding contributions to reading research presented by the National Reading Conference, and the Native Hawaiian Education Award presented by Kamehameha Schools.

Ray Barnhardt

Ray Barnhardt is a professor of cross-cultural studies at the University of Alaska–Fairbanks, where he has been involved in teaching and research related to Native education issues since 1970. He has served as co-director of the Alaska Rural Systemic Initiative for the past 10 years. Over the past 35 years, he has also served as the director of the Cross-Cultural Education Development (X-CED) Program, the Small High Schools Project, the Center for Cross-Cultural Studies, and the Alaska Native Knowledge Network. His research interests include Indigenous knowledge systems, Native teacher education, distance/distributed/higher education, small school curriculum, and institutional adaptations to rural and cross-cultural settings.

Gloria Swindler Boutte

Gloria Swindler Boutte is the author of *Multicultural Education: Raising Consciousness and Resounding Voices: School Experiences of People from Diverse Ethnic Backgrounds*. She has published numerous journal articles in the area of cultural diversity and early childhood education. Additionally, she has presented nationally and internationally on curriculum, instruction, and diversity issues. She is currently a full professor at Benedict College and is the principal investigator for the statewide Center of Excellence for the Education and Equity of African American Students (CEEEAAS). She has also taught at the South Carolina State University, the University of South Carolina, and at the University of North Carolina at Greensboro.

Courtney Clayton

Courtney Clayton is a doctoral candidate in Curriculum and Instruction at the Lynch School of Education at Boston College. She also teaches in a bilingual program at the International School of Boston. Her interests include bilingual education, literacy development of bilingual students, literacy curriculum, and teacher preparation for bilingual learners. She is the recipient of a dissertation fellowship in the Lynch School of Education for her research on exemplary teachers of English language learners for 2006–2007. She is also recipient of a Teacher as Researcher grant from the International Reading Association for 2006–2007.

Ester J. de Jong

Ester J. de Jong is an assistant professor in Bilingual Education/ESOL at the College of Education, University of Florida, Gainesville. After obtaining her Master's degree in the Netherlands, she received her doctorate degree in Literacy and Culture Studies with a specialization in Bilingual Education from Boston University in 1996. She moved to the University of Florida in 2001 after several years as an assistant director of Bilingual Education in the Framingham Public Schools, Massachusetts. Her research interests include bilingual education with a particular focus on two-way immersion programs, educational language policy, and teacher preparation for standard curriculum K–12 teachers working with bilingual students. With Charles Glenn, she collaborated on the book *Educating Immigrant Children: Schools and Language Minorities in Twelve Nations.*

Candace A. Harper

Candace A. Harper is an assistant professor in the College of Education and coordinator of the ESOL/Bilingual Education Program at the University of Florida. Her research and teacher education interests center on the development of second language literacy, the expertise of specialist language teachers, and the preparation of general educators to work effectively with English language learners. She has consulted with school systems throughout Florida and in Texas to help develop and implement curriculum and instruction for inservice teacher preparation. Dr. Harper has lived and worked as an English language educator in the United States, Australia, Bosnia, and France. She is the outgoing chair of the TESOL Standards Committee and an author of the TESOL/NCATE Standards for P–12 Teacher Education Programs. She has published in the TESOL Quarterly, the *Journal of Teacher Education,* and the *Journal of Adolescent and Adult Literacy,* and she recently co-authored a teacher resource book on cross-age literacy tutoring

Robert J. Hoffmeister

Robert J. Hoffmeister is currently the co-director of the Programs in Deaf Studies at Boston University and the director of the Center for the Study of Communication and the Deaf. He co-founded the Programs in Deaf Studies at Boston University in 1981. The Programs in Deaf Studies consist of the first undergraduate program in Deaf Studies, which is a liberal arts examination of the DEAF-WORLD, the graduate program in education of the Deaf, and the graduate program in ASL/Deaf Studies. He is a faculty member in the graduate programs in Literacy, Language and Culture and in Applied Linguistics. He received his Ph.D. from the University of Minnesota in psycholinguistics and education, and he holds a Masters degree in the education of the Deaf from the University of

Arizona and an undergraduate degree from the University of Connecticut. He has taught in residential, self contained, and mainstream programs and was an administrator of a large metropolitan program for the Deaf. Currently, he is working on four projects. He is researching the relationship between ASL and its influence on Deaf children's English reading skills and academic success, and the learning of ASL as a 2nd language in hearing persons. In addition to his research he is directing a Title 1 project aimed at the improvement of literacy skills and academic performance in Deaf children with the Scranton State School for the Deaf, and developing an ASL/English. He has worked in collaboration on a recent study investigating the role of language in Deaf children's thinking with Peter & Jill deVilliers of Smith College and Brenda Schick of the University of Colorado. From his research work he has been instrumental in the development of an ASL assessment for Deaf children. His publications cover work in language acquisition, the influence of ASL on the development of English, second language influences, effects of attitudes on parents and on the success of the Deaf child, and on hearing children of Deaf parents. He has published articles on ASL and education of the Deaf and co-authored a text with Harlan Lane and Ben Bahan entitled "A Journey into the DEAF-WORLD." His research and publications are focused on the improvement of language skills in Deaf children.

Yvonne Kaulukane Lefcourt

Yvonne Kaulukane Lefcourt is a recent graduate of the Ph.D. Program in Education at the University of Illinois at Urbana-Champaign and a Gates Millennium Scholar Alumna. Her research interests include teacher education and indigenous research and education with an emphasis on issues of equity in education; the implementation of an effective curriculum for diverse classrooms; and the recruitment and retention of Native Hawaiians to higher education. She is currently a teacher at Enchanted Lake School on the island of O'ahu, Hawai'i. Her previous publications have focused on *Cultural Identity and Culturally Responsive Instruction from the Perspective of Native Hawaiian Teachers* and *Re-conceptualizing Culture Literacy and Schooling for Native Hawaiian Pre-Service Teachers*.

Jaqueline Leonard

Jacqueline Leonard received her Ph.D. from the University of Maryland at College Park, Department of Curriculum and Instruction in 1997. She is an associate professor of Mathematics Education at Temple University. Her awards include the Patricia Roberts Harris Fellowship (University of Maryland) and the Outstanding New Scholar Award (University of Maryland). Her research focuses on the importance of context in learning mathematics, specifically, linking math to multicultural children's literature, science, and multimedia.

Jerry Lipka

Jerry Lipka has been working in the field of education for almost four decades. For the majority of this time he has been working in Alaska as a teacher educator and educational researcher, particularly with Yup'ik Eskimo teachers, Yup'ik elders, and school districts. In collaboration with Yup'ik elders, mathematicians, and educators he has been developing culturally based math curriculum. This has resulted in the publication of the *Math in a Cultural Context* series (supplemental math guides). Simultaneously, his group has done extensive classroom-based research on the efficacy of these modules, which consistently have produced statistically significant results. He has published extensively on this work.

Alice J. Kawakami

Alice J. Kawakami is a tenured associate professor of Education in the College of Education, University of Hawaii–Manoa and director of the Hawaii Institute for Educational Partnerships (HIEP). She received her Ph.D. in educational psychology there in 1989. Her research interests focus on the inclusion of indigenous perspectives in the teacher education, curriculum development and evaluation. She teaches social studies methods and curriculum and instruction to elementary pre-service teachers and coordinates field placements for the Ka Lama VI cohort. She has worked with Pacific education in many capacities including that of a part-time remedial reading teacher in urban schools of the Hawaii Department of Education, a research-demonstration laboratory school teacher, teacher development specialist, teacher researcher, and coordinator of in-service training for the Kamehameha Early Education Program (KEEP). She served as director of Research and Evaluation at the Pacific Regional Educational Laboratory and convener of the Pacific-wide Research and Development Cadre. While at the University of Hawaii–Hilo, she chaired the Education Department and was co-investigator of a three-year $675,000 NASA grant—New Opportunities through Minority Initiatives in Space Science (NOMISS). In 2005, she received the Native Hawaiian Education Award from the Kamehameha Schools with Dr. Kathryn Au and Ms. Sherlyn Goo, co-founders of the Institute for Native Pacific Culture and Education (INPEACE).

Donaldo Macedo

Donaldo Macedo is a full professor of English and a distinguished professor of Liberal Arts and Education at the University of Massachusetts Boston. He is the Graduate Program Director of the Applied Linguistics Masters of Arts Program at the University of Massachusetts Boston. He has published extensively in the areas of Creole languages, linguistics, critical literacy, bilingualism and multicultural education. His publications include: *Literacy: Reading the Word and the World* (with Paulo Freire, 1987), *Literacies of Power: What Americans Are Not Allowed to Know* (1994), *Dancing With Bigotry* (with Lilia Bartolome, 1999), *Critical Education in the New Information Age* (with Paulo Freire, Henry Giroux and Paul Willis, 1999), *Chomsky on Miseducation* (with Noam Chomsky, 2000). His work has been translated into several languages.

Aida A. Nevárez-La Torre

Dr. Aida A. Nevárez-La Torre is an associate professor in the TESOL Program at Fordham University where she also coordinates the Bilingual Education Program. She completed a doctorate in Reading from Harvard Graduate School of Education. Her research interests include Linguistic Diversity in Teacher Education, Practitioner Research, and Literacy Development in English language Learners. She has published her work in scholarly journals such as Bilingual Research Journal, Urban Review, and Education and Urban Society.

Lisa Patel Stevens

Lisa Patel Stevens is an assistant professor of literacy, language and culture at the Lynch School of Education, Boston College. She received her Ph.D. in curriculum and instruction from the University of Nevada, Las Vegas, in 2001. Her research and teaching interests focus on the ways in which people use language and literacy practices to make sense of themselves and enact their subjectivities. In particular, she uses critical ethnography and poststructural theories to examine the interactions of linguistically and culturally diverse teens in various spaces. She is the co-editor of *ReConstructing the 'adolescent:' Sign, symbol and body*, and is the co-author of *Critical literacy: Context, research and practice in the K–12 classroom.*

Jayminn S. Sanford-DeShields

Jayminn S. Sanford-DeShields is associate professor of education in the Department of Curriculum, Instruction and Technology in Education at Temple university, where she teaches required courses in the undergraduate and graduate teacher certification programs, and the program planning and evaluation courses required of doctoral students. Dr. Sanford-DeShields' teaching focuses on developing critical teaching strategies, refining pedagogical skills, and developing and evaluating programs, which address the educational needs of underserviced populations. She has expertise in urban schools and communities, teaching and learning, and collaborative school reform. Dr. Sanford-DeShields serves on several boards, and provides program evaluation services as a consultant with several urban-based educational and social service programs here and abroad. Dr. Sanford-DeShields earned her Ed.D. at the Graduate School of Education at Harvard University.

Catherine Soundy

Cathleen S. Soundy is an associate professor of early childhood elementary education at Temple University, Philadelphia, PA. She received her Ed.D. in early childhood and elementary education at Rutgers, The State University of New Jersey. Dr. Soundy teaches early childhood courses and conducts research on early literacy development and visual literacy.

Christine Woyshner

Christine Woyshner is an associate professor of education at Temple University's College of Education where she is an affiliated faculty member in Urban Education and Women's Studies. Dr. Woyshner also teaches in the University of Pennsylvania's Educational Leadership Executive Doctoral Program. She received her doctorate at Harvard University in 1999. A recipient of the Lindback Award for Distinguished Teaching at Temple (2005), Dr. Woyshner's research focuses on gender in the history of education. Her work has appeared in *Teachers College Record, The History of Education Quarterly,* and *Theory and Research in Social Education.* Dr. Woyshner is the co-editor of *Minding Women: Reshaping the Educational Realm* (Harvard Education Publishing Group, 1998) and *Social Education in the Twentieth Century: Curriculum and Context for Citizenship* (Peter Lang, 2003). She is currently writing a history of the PTA and civic engagement.

Index

A

AACTE (American Association of Colleges for Teacher Education), xvi
advocacy groups and, 363
ATE and, 362–63
CLD teacher preparation and, 362–63
Commissions on Multicultural Education and, xv, 357
equity issues and, 202n.2
highly qualified teachers and, 357–58, *see also* Highly qualified teachers
language diversity in teacher preparation and, xv, 357
multiculturalism and, 202n.2
NABE, 362
national education groups and, 362–63
political training for JFK School of Government, 363
TEAC and, 363
TESOL and, 362
Wingspread Conference and, 357–63
AAL (African American Language) (Ebonics), xx, 23
abandonment of, 54
African American students and, *see* African American students and ALL
African Americans and, 23, 48–49, 64–66
African diaspora and, 56
Black culture and, 59
as a bridge for Standard English proficiency, 60–61, 63–64
contrastive analysis and, 63–64, 65, 66
cultural invasion and, 59
definition of, 47

dominant ideology of oppression and, 48–49, 59
features of, 55–56, 57–60
Gullah as an, 56
instructional practices and, 47, 63–64, 334
linguistic parallels with other languages, 60–61
linguistic validity of, 48–49, 53, 56, 60
literature on, 47–48
negative attitude toward, 23, 47, 50–51, 53, 57, 64–65, 334
new terminology in, 57
as oral language, 63–64
phonology of, 56, 61
pragmatics and, 59–60
as a resistance strategy, 54, 57
sociopolitical issues of, 50–51
speakers of, 47–49, 51, 52–53, 59, 62, 66
Standard English and, 47–49, 50–51, 62–63
syntax of, 57–59, 61
teacher preparation programs and, 47–48, 65–66
tonal semantics and, 59–60
validation of, 62, 64, 66
West African languages and, 48, 55–56, *see also* Ebonics
Abbate-Vaughn, Jorgelina, xxi, 343, 354, 370
Academic English
ASL and, 86–88
learning through print, 86–87
Academic language
CLD students and, 154, 165, 334–35, 359, 361
Deaf children and, 85–88, 334
learning English through print, 86–87
proficiency, 85
Academic performance

B